Praise for

THE EMERALD MILE

~

"*The Emerald Mile* is the rarest of creations—a magical convergence of words and paper, wood and water, rock and sky, human character and cosmic caprice. Can an adventure story be as beautiful as it is heart-stopping and exciting? This one is, and Fedarko's book is as inspiring as a dory itself, flying down a wild river. I have no doubt it will become an instant classic, a timeless chronicle of what can still be legitimately called the American spirit."

—Bob Shacochis, author of *Swimming in the Volcano*
and *Easy in the Islands*

"Kevin Fedarko's new brilliant work . . . is the story about wilderness and the American mind, albeit an American mind juiced on Class V adrenaline. . . . Perhaps because we sympathize so strongly with the characters of *The Emerald Mile*—thanks in no small part to Fedarko's flowing prose—you'll feel yourself lurching along with them on wooden boats, in ocher-hued canyons, beneath cobalt skies, into the frenzied thrashings of the Colorado River as the very landscape of the West attempts to choke it."

—*Mountain* magazine

"*The Emerald Mile* re-creates an incredible voyage through the flood-swollen Grand Canyon in such heart-pounding detail that you need to pause every few pages to catch your breath. . . . [Fedarko] writes so vividly that your favorite reading chair becomes a spray-soaked perch on a bucking boat hit hard by a river running high and fast."

—*The Dallas Morning News*

"It would not be overblown to say *The Emerald Mile* deserves a spot on the bookshelf alongside such enduring classics as *Cadillac Desert*, *Desert Solitaire*, and *Encounters with the Archdruid*. It's that good."

—*The Durango Telegraph*

"At its heart an engrossing meditation on the eternal struggle between man and nature."

—*Pittsburgh Post-Gazette*

"From the bottom of our planet's most awesome landscape, Kevin Fedarko has found and rescued a great American tall tale that just happens to be true. As a boatman, Fedarko knows this world intimately. As a writer, he'll make you understand it, savor it, and ultimately love it as you never have before. Here is an instant classic of adventure literature—a story shot through with bravura but also touched by the rarest kind of grandeur."

—Hampton Sides, editor at large at *Outside* magazine
and author of *Blood and Thunder* and *Ghost Soldiers*

"Powerful and poetic passages put readers inside the adventurers' boats, even if they have only ever imagined the Grand Canyon or seen it in pictures. . . . Each piece of the story is assembled as lyrically as the epoch-spanning walls of canyon itself. . . . An epic-sized true-life adventure tale that appeals to both the heart and the head."

—*Kirkus Reviews*

"His poetic and descriptive writing should only brighten his accolades and helps his nonfiction book read like a fast-paced fiction adventure. . . . It isn't necessary to be a history buff or white-water expert to enjoy this story. . . . With meticulous research, notes, and epilogue, Fedarko tells a satisfying story that is quite an entertaining ride."

—*Deseret News*

"Fedarko's effortlessly engaging narrative . . . is a labor of passion from an adventurous journalist who still calls the Grand Canyon home."

—*Boulder Weekly*

"Kevin Fedarko's magnificent book covers a lot of ground—and water. . . . So it is a great boon of Fedarko's book that he tells the story of the dam, and of the engineers and technicians who built it . . . with as much respect and homage as he gives to the dorymen."

—*The Cleveland Plain Dealer*

"Grua's wild ride on the Colorado, how it mirrored his mercurial personality, is just one part of Fedarko's story; however, the ride, which runs through seven states, and the canyon, rich in both geological and political history, prove to be the real protagonists."

—Publishers Weekly

"Think Into Thin Air or The Perfect Storm. Fedarko spent years as an editor at Outside magazine, working with some of the best writers in the world; with The Emerald Mile, he has joined them as a thoughtful, thorough researcher and superb storyteller. . . . Fedarko's tale ostensibly focuses on the three rivermen who rode the maelstrom in a fragile wooden dory and emerged alive and with a speed record, but it's also the story of the canyon itself, as well as the river and the dam and the men and women, scientists and scoundrels who have made their lives there."

—The Oklahoman

"Take a raging river in full flood, a crumbling dam, three scofflaw river runners trying to set a speed record through the Grand Canyon, and you have the makings of one of the best Colorado River books ever. This spellbinding true story leaps from the inner workings of Glen Canyon Dam and the psyches of river guides to boat-eating whirlpools and a wooden river dory named the Emerald Mile. Kevin Fedarko's prodigious research and breathtaking narrative transcend the Southwest. It's a roaring adventure with wave after wave of spills and thrills. Let's hope Fedarko owns the movie rights."

—Bill Broyles, Southwest Books of the Year

"Journalist and part-time river guide Kevin Fedarko has produced a work of jaw-dropping scope and page-turning action in this account of a speed record of rowing the length of the Grand Canyon that remains unmatched. . . . Fedarko overlays and interweaves two compelling narratives: that of the river runners and that of the managers of the mammoth Glen Canyon Dam, which was in serious risk of overtopping and collapse. An unforgettable read, rendered in vivid, sometimes majestic, prose."

—Christine Wald-Hopkins, Southwest Books of the Year

The Epic Story of the Fastest Ride in History

Through the Heart of the Grand Canyon

THE EMERALD MILE

KEVIN FEDARKO

SCRIBNER

New York London Toronto Sydney New Delhi

SCRIBNER
A Division of Simon & Schuster, Inc.
1230 Avenue of the Americas
New York, NY 10020

First Scribner trade paperback July 2014

SCRIBNER and design are registered trademarks of The Gale Group, Inc.,
used under license by Simon & Schuster, Inc., the publisher of this work.

For information about special discounts for bulk purchases, please contact Simon &
Schuster Special Sales at 1-866-506-1949 or business@simonandschuster.com.

The Simon & Schuster Speakers Bureau can bring authors to your live event. For more
information or to book an event contact the Simon & Schuster Speakers Bureau at
1-866-248-3049 or visit our website at www.simonspeakers.com.

Manufactured in the United States of America

Book design by Ellen R. Sasahara
Cover design by David Ter-Avanesyan
Cover image based on a photo by Rudi Petschek

15   17   19   20   18   16   14

Library of Congress Control Number: 2012474432

ISBN 978-1-4391-5985-9
ISBN 978-1-4391-5986-6 (pbk)
ISBN 978-1-4767-3529-0 (ebook)

For my parents,
Robert and Rita

If there is magic on this planet,
it is contained in water.

—LOREN EISELEY

CONTENTS

~

THE EMERALD MILE

~ THE COLORADO RIVER AND THE GRAND CANYON ~

NEVADA

UTAH

Green River

The Confluence

Colorado River

Lake Powell

Lee's Ferry
GLEN CANYON DAM
Page

**GRAND CANYON
NATIONAL PARK**

Desert View

N

Las Vegas

Lake Mead
HOOVER DAM

Grand Canyon Village

Little Colorado River

ARIZONA

Flagstaff

Needles

WYOMING

CALIFORNIA

Colorado River

NEVADA

UTAH

Green River

COLORADO

Area of detail

0 Miles   50

0 Kilometers   50

Colorado River

NEW
MEXICO

CALIFORNIA

ARIZONA

UNITED STATES
MEXICO

Pacific Ocean

Sea of Cortés

MEXICO

Sea of Cortés

© 2013 Jeffrey L. Ward

LAUNCH

~

June 25, 1983

O N any given evening in summer, but most notably in late June, there comes a moment just after the sun has disappeared behind the rimrock, and just before the darkness has tumbled down the walls, when the bottom of the Grand Canyon gives itself over to a moment of muted grace that feels something like an act of atonement for the sins of the world. This is the fleeting interregnum between the blast-furnace heat of the day and the star-draped immensity of the night, and when it arrives, the bedrock bathes in a special kind of light, the pink-and-orange blush of a freshly opened nectarine. This is also the canyon's loveliest hour, when there is nothing sweeter, nothing more calming to the soul, than standing along the shallows at the edge of the Colorado River and breathing in the wonder of that place. The ramparts rising nakedly for more than a vertical mile above. The locomotive-size slabs that have peeled away from the terraced cliffs and shattered to pieces far below. And most bewitching of all, the muscular, sluicing, glimmer-gilded surface of the great river itself.

But June 25, 1983, was not any given evening. Not by a long shot. And with twilight now fading, the face of the water turned menacing and unknowable as the biggest flood in a generation throttled downstream into the night.

An hour or so later, the moon appeared, ascending with stately deliberation until it was suspended in all its fullness inside the thin ribbon of sky between the rims. There it hung, fat and heavy, casting the upper faces of the cliffs in a silver and faintly malignant glaze.

Deep within the canyon's corridor, the defile between the escarpments was too narrow to accept most of this illumination, and so the bottommost bands of rock, the ancient strata of Zoroaster granite and Vishnu schist that lined the edge of the river, were lost in shadow. But far upstream at a place called Lee's Ferry, where a breach in the cliffs marks the spot where all river journeys through the canyon begin, the walls widened and the river was able to open itself to the sky. Here, the moonbeams streamed down the hunched shoulders of Shinarump shale and spilled across the water, etching each wave, every ripple and eddy, in a spectral radiance.

Out there in the millrace, the rush of water was broad and powerful, and as the current pushed past, it did so with an eerie silence. But if you cocked your body at just the right angle, you could detect a faint thrum, a kind of basal tremor. The frequency of that vibration was impossible for the ear to pick up, but it registered unmistakably on the hairs of the forearms, the wall of the chest, and deep in the belly. This was the muffled resonance of a runaway river, the sub-audible bell-tone of water surging with ungovernable force into the throat of the canyon.

Just beyond the riverbank, a road led away from the water, snaking off in the distance toward Highway 89, the only thruway in this remote outpost of northern Arizona. The surface of that road was strewn with loose gravel, and about an hour before midnight, it crunched softly with the approach of a vehicle whose driver was proceeding guardedly.

Behind the headlights loomed the boxy silhouette of a small delivery truck, a contraption whose appearance, in this place and at this hour, was perplexing because it seemed to herald the sort of business that never unfolds at the ferry—an after-hours FedEx pickup, perhaps, or the arrival of a stack of tomorrow's newspapers. The mystery was resolved only after the driver wheeled across the parking lot at the edge of the water and it became clear that the truck was towing a metal trailer. Cradled on the bed of that trailer was a small wooden dory.

The boat's profile was distinctive—an upturned prow that terminated in a sharp point, and a hull whose bottom was curved like the blade of a scimitar. Lashed to her decks were two sets of ten-foot oars hewn from straight-grained Pennsylvania ash, and tucked into the footwell at the center of the boat lay a cable connecting a car battery to a pair of powerful searchlamps, the kind of devices that jacklighters use when hunting deer in the dark. There was just enough light to make out her colors—a beryl-green hull and bright red gunwales. And if you looked closely, you could discern the black-and-gold lettering emblazoned along the right side of her bow that spelled her name: *Emerald Mile.*

~

As the truck completed the arc of its turn, three figures leaped out and began racing toward the river while the driver, who had now cast off all signs of hesitation, backed the trailer smartly alongside a line of rubber rafts that were moored at the shore.

On the decks of those rafts lay a squadron of half a dozen slumbering river guides, who had arrived at the ferry's boat ramp several hours earlier, only to be told by the National Park Service ranger that the Colorado was closed due to the flood. As the guides awoke to this burst of activity, they scratched their heads in confusion. Then, intuiting what was about to unfold, they roused themselves from their sleeping bags and hustled over to lend a hand by loosening the straps that anchored the dory to the trailer and heaving her into the water.

She hit with a sharp slap and shot almost a quarter of the way across the eddy before coming to a stop, bobbing gently like a champagne cork. Meanwhile, the mysterious trio splashed through the shallows and hauled themselves on board.

The first of those figures presented an image that seemed to cut in two directions at once. In some ways, his appearance perfectly embodied the demeanor of the unbound river. His hair was wild and out of control, while his limbs moved with a fluid grace as he scrambled across the decking and positioned himself at the oar station in the center of the boat. But in other respects, he appeared to have no connection at all with the water he was about to ride. His breathing was even and measured, and the expression on his face was composed as he threaded the oars into their locks, curled his fingers around the handles, and waited calmly for his two companions to stow the spotlights and the battery, then settle themselves into their seats in the bow and the stern.

When everything was ready, all three men turned toward the shore, where their driver was now staring at his wristwatch while completing a silent countdown.

When the second hand on his watch reached exactly 11:00 p.m., the driver cried, *"Go!"*—and with a sharp intake of breath, the wild-haired boatman thrust his torso forward with his arms outstretched, a move that sent the shafts of his oars planing sternward. At the top of this stroke, he snapped both wrists at the same time, a maneuver that squared up the oar blades just as they entered the water. Then he pulled back with his entire body while driving the balls of his feet directly into the front end of the footwell.

His first stroke sent them skimming across the eddy, and the second speared them into the main current. There, the boatman paused for a half second to permit the stern to swing downstream. As the dory completed this clockwise turn, the river seized the hull and hurled them toward the swiftly rising walls of rock that marked the gateway to the Grand Canyon.

And just like that, they were gone.

~

Well, almost gone.

In the final moments before the boat vanished, another vehicle pulled into the parking lot at the ferry and a second set of headlights swept the edge of the river. Inside that vehicle sat a family that had driven all the way from New Mexico in the hope of embarking on a rafting vacation, only to learn from the ranger that all launches were forbidden—disappointing news, given the hassles they had gone through to secure a highly coveted noncommercial permit to run the canyon. After motoring back to Highway 89 for a late supper at a roadside diner, they were now returning to their tent and arrived just in time to catch sight of the mysterious boat as she cast off and disappeared—an incident that they planned on reporting to the ranger first thing in the morning. In the meantime, they were left to ponder what had just taken place.

What in the world were those clowns up to, they wondered, launching into the teeth of a flood on the near side of midnight with the assistance of a gaggle of guides who knew perfectly well that the Colorado was closed? Were they out of their minds?

In a way, yes, they truly were—although the men aboard that boat were also engaged in an urgent mission. A gesture of poetry and defiance quite unlike anything the canyon had ever seen. A quest that was inspired and driven by the obsessions of the fanatical boatman who was now gunning his dory toward the maelstrom that awaited them downstream.

Kenton Grua was a veteran of the river world as well as one of its most vivid and eccentric characters, a dreamer whose passions for the canyon ran deeper than almost anyone else's, and whose prowess as a dory captain was unmatched by all but a handful of boatmen. The voyage upon which he and his companions had just embarked, however, would call upon all of his skills and more.

Between Lee's Ferry and the Grand Wash Cliffs, the sandstone portals at the edge of the Mojave Desert that marked the western terminus of the canyon, lay almost three hundred miles of river, the worst of which were studded with the most storied white water in all of North America. Threading that gauntlet in a rowboat was an odyssey that typically lasted at least two weeks and could take as long as twenty-three days. Yet Grua's illegal pre-midnight launch on the crest of this flood tide was designed to smash that timetable to pieces.

If he and his accomplices could steer through the darkness and keep their bow square to the biggest waves; if they could somehow avoid capsizing or drowning or being broken apart on the rocks; if they could stay awake and maintain their pace by spelling each other at the oars while dodging the platoon of irate rangers who would soon be alerted to their unauthorized presence on the river—if they could carry out all of those tasks without a single hitch, it was possible that the swollen Colorado might serve as a kind of hydraulic slingshot that would pitch them all the way from the ferry to the cliffs so swiftly that the duration of the trip would be calibrated not in weeks, or even days, but in *hours*.

At which point, if everything unfolded according to plan, the little green dory with the bright red gunwales would be catapulted into legend as the fastest boat ever propelled—by oar, by motor, or by the grace of God—through the heart of the Grand Canyon.

LEVIATHAN

~

ROUGHLY thirty thousand yards upstream from the *Emerald Mile*'s point of launch on the evening of June 25, a distance of some fifteen miles, a rampart ascended into the night that bore no resemblance to the canyon and whose surface was burnished by a radiance that had no connection to the moon. Instead of running naturally along the edges of the Colorado, this wall stood directly athwart the river's current, thrusting more than seven hundred feet into the air from its foundation in the bedrock deep beneath the surface. The shape of that wall was a complex parabolic arch whose camber and curves had no organic analogue, and its texture was equally synthetic. Unlike the corridors of the canyon, whose facades are broken by the endlessly striating cracks and blemishes of living rock, the face of this barricade was smooth and flawless.

Something blunt and clean and undeniably impressive resided in the alabaster perfection of all that concrete. Nearly ten million tons of the stuff had been slung across the breadth of the river by an army of engineers and laborers who had started assembling its frame in 1960, pouring and shaping with such care and precision that, three years later, when they were finally through, it looked as if a highly skilled machinist had tooled the edges of a giant clamshell and dropped it neatly between the embrasure of stone. Aesthetics aside, however, the overwhelming impression that this monolith left on the mind, the element that overwhelmed the senses and blocked out everything else, was its sheer size.

The wall was more than twice the height of the Statue of Liberty and its length exceeded that of the *Seawise Giant*, the longest supertanker ever built. The dimensions were so implausible that, upon seeing this colossus for the first time, one was tempted to conclude that it could have been conceived only under conditions where the normal laws of gravity and physics did not apply. And this notion, that perhaps the structure did not belong fully to this world, was buttressed by an odd event now unfolding across its face.

At 11:00 p.m. on one of the hottest nights of the year, the entire wall appeared to have been overtaken by a snowstorm. Only when the eyes had adjusted to the scale did this agitated cloud reveal itself as a nation of disoriented moths, tens of thousands of them fluttering like confetti around a line of sodium-vapor floodlights, each of which was sending a pilaster of blue-tinted light upward, like the columns on a Greek temple, toward the parapet of the Glen Canyon Dam.

∾

Those arc lights were mounted along the flat roof of a windowless structure that was anchored at the very bottom of the dam, a building whose profile boasted none of the grace and symmetry of the great white wall behind it. Nine stories high and shaped like an enormous shoe box kicked onto its side, Glen's hydroelectric power plant was devoid of a single curve or bend that might have enabled it to harmonize with the face of the dam.

Located on the far west side of the plant, eight stories above the surface of the river, was a chamber roughly thirty feet wide and fifty feet deep known as the Control Room. Staffed by a team of ten technicians who worked on three eight-hour shifts that rotated at 8:00 a.m., 4:00 p.m., and midnight, the room housed as many as five employees during the day. At night, however, there were usually no more than two: an assistant who roved around to inspect the many gauges and valves within the power plant as well as the extensive network of tunnels that ran through the interior of the dam itself; and an operator required to stay put behind a large steel desk equipped with three telephones and a two-way radio.

The US Bureau of Reclamation, the arm of the federal government that had built the dam and was responsible for its operation, has long been particular about disclosing the names of its Control Room personnel, a security precaution that applies to all National Critical Infrastructure facilities deemed vulnerable to attack. Accordingly, the bureau has redacted from its logbooks the employee who was on duty on the night of June 25, and so we do not know his name. But the manager in charge of the Control Room during this period was Dick White. And according to White, if the normal pattern of behavior was being observed for the graveyard shift, his operator was sitting in a government-issued chair designed for air-traffic controllers, with his ankles crossed and his feet propped on the surface of the steel desk.

From this vantage, White's man was positioned at Glen's nerve center and serving as the cerebral cortex for the entire facility. Arranged before him was a bank of panels studded with so many lights and switches and dials that it looked as if he were monitoring the public transit system of a large city. Thanks to that instrumentation, he had his finger on the pulse of not just the dam itself but also the power plant and the transmission lines snaking out of the canyon. Every aspect of the chamber in which he sat—its cool colors, its neat lines, the unwinking vigilance of the lights and the protective symmetry of the encircling walls—upheld the principle of control: the affirmation that here in this place, at this hour, human beings were indisputably in charge of a renegade river that had once been the scourge of the Southwest.

For each member of the Control Room team, the gadgetry on those panels was as familiar as the knobs on his stereo at home. But according to White, every time you sat down at that desk, it was impossible not to feel a flitter of exhilaration and unease that flowed from the awareness of being in the driver's seat of one of the largest machines on earth. A piece of technology so enormous that it made other things that are often invoked as reference points for jumbo-size industrial design—the bridge of an aircraft carrier, the cockpit of a C-130 cargo jet, the command module of an Apollo rocket—seem puny by comparison.

But another factor was at work there too. Because, in addition to the dam's size, you also understood that out there in the darkness on the opposite side of that wall loomed one of the longest reservoirs on the planet, a body of water that extended 186 miles up the ancient bed of the Colorado and touched 1,960 miles of shore—longer than the Pacific coastline from Seattle to San Diego—and whose ponderous volume, somewhere in excess of nine billion gallons, was incessantly pressing against the upstream flanks of the dam.

That was an awful lot of water to be holding back. Water whose insistence on moving downhill harbored more power than one could imagine. As White well knew, the fury that water was capable of unleashing could be profoundly unsettling, especially if you dwelled on the idea too deeply.

But this was also what made the dam truly awesome.

~

There was no such thing as twilight inside the Control Room of the Glen Canyon Dam—no velvet hour when the floor and the walls were bathed in a peach-colored glow and the operator was able to heave a sigh of tranquillity. But on any given evening, whether it was the height of the summer solstice or the dead of winter, there was something almost as gratifying, perhaps even more so. Because whoever was sitting at the desk in front of the control panels at that moment got to play God.

The ritual usually kicked off just before 6:00 p.m., when a call arrived from the Western Area Power Administration dispatcher, a man sitting 350 miles to the northeast in Montrose, Colorado. This signaled the start of the evening surge, the moment when most of the twenty million people in an area stretching from eastern New Mexico to Southern California were preparing to return home from work, turn on their lights, preheat their ovens, and sit down to watch the evening news. The dispatcher in Montrose was responsible for ensuring that the load on the power grid would meet this spiking demand, and he anticipated the evening rush by ordering White's man to start calling up electricity.

The operator responded by pushing a black button that activated a high-pressure lube pump that shot high-viscosity oil into the thrust bearings inside one of the dam's eight generators. If you were standing on the floor of the power plant, this would register as a low whine. Five seconds later, the wicket gates would open at the base of one of Glen's penstocks—giant steel tubes that ran through the wall of the dam and whose intakes were positioned more than three hundred feet above the power plant on the reservoir side of the wall. At this point, the sound of the pump motor would give way to a roar of water.

The drop was enormous, and at the base of the dam, the column of water inside was bent into a horizontal stream, channeled into the power plant, and blasted against a set of runner blades attached to one of the plant's 155,500-horsepower turbines. The rush rose another notch as the blades threw torque into the battle-tank-size turbine, which spun faster and faster until it was whirling at two and a half revolutions per second.

Extending vertically from the top of the turbine was a shaft connected to a generator that housed a two-thousand-ton rotor whose perimeter was lined with forty-eight steel poles that functioned as electromagnets. When the rotor was fully engaged, this spinning steel forest created a magnetic flux sufficient to generate 125,000 kilowatts, enough electricity to power roughly one hundred thousand homes and businesses.

The current coursed from the top of the generator to a bank of transformers, which punched the electricity into a set of nine transmission cables that ran up to the switching yard on the rim. From there, the lines marched off across the desert toward the cities of the Southwest—to Phoenix and Tucson and dozens of smaller towns scattered around the Four Corners region, where, hundreds of miles away, the energy that had been locked inside the river was now released to civilization: zapping frozen microwave dinners, broadcasting Peter Jennings's image on the television, lighting up the forty-foot-tall neon cowboy sign on Fremont Street in Las Vegas.

Nothing about any of this was secret or unusual. Indeed, the process was so routine that most people had little appreciation that, perhaps more than anything else, this was the generative spark that separated the modern world from the Dark Ages. But for the man at the steel desk, there was nothing casual about cranking that dynamo into motion, hearing the roar, and watching the gauges and dials registering the amperage as the current shot from the bottom of the gorge and sped off to those distant cities and towns. Inside Glen's penstocks and turbines and generators, the river was literally being reborn as something else—water quickening into electricity. The performance had a kind of magic, and for every member of the Control Room team, the charge was to be savored.

Except that, on this particular night, the charge had been replaced by something else—an echo of the same chaos that was about to descend on Kenton Grua and his crew deep inside the Grand Canyon. Because on June 25, White and his colleagues were twenty-three days into a crisis that had no precedent in the history of hydroelectric dams. And by now, every single one of those men had forgotten what normal was.

~

The emergency they were confronting had been set in motion almost a year earlier and some eight thousand miles to the west of the Arizona desert, on the far edge of the Pacific Ocean. There, in October of the previous year, a massive El Niño event had triggered a series of barometric anomalies that had given birth to the largest spring runoff within the Colorado River basin in twenty-five years. The last time anyone had witnessed a runoff of comparable size, the dam had not even been built yet—which helped to explain why the network of agencies responsible for controlling the largest river in the Southwest had been caught flat-footed.

The details of how things had gone off the rails were still obscure, and the full picture of what had taken place would not emerge for months. But the upshot was that by early June, Glen was already holding back the runoff from 108,000 square miles, a region the size of Poland, and every additional acre-foot of floodwater that poured into the upper end of Lake Powell, the reservoir behind the dam, was arriving faster than it could be drained through the dam.

Fortunately, Glen was equipped with an emergency bypass designed for just such an event. On each side of the dam, a massive spillway tunnel had been bored through 675 feet of Navajo sandstone and lined with thirty-six inches of concrete. In theory, those twin monsters were capable of inhaling a combined flow of more than 200,000 cfs,* neatly channeling that water around the dam before dumping it back into the river. This should have been enough to absorb whatever the Colorado might care to throw at Glen. There was just one hitch. The tunnels had never been put through a full-on test drive, and in early June, something had gone terribly wrong.

Deep inside the spillways, a series of vicious shock waves had scoured away the concrete lining and exposed the soft sandstone walls to the full force of the river. As a result, water arcing out the mouths of both tunnels was laden with debris that included chunks of concrete, pieces of rebar, and boulders the size of refrigerators. In effect, the Colorado had begun to dismantle the spillways by tearing their guts to pieces.

Throughout the month of June, the goal of every person who worked at the dam was to funnel as much of the water in the reservoir as possible downstream into the canyon. To that end, they had been running the power plant nonstop for weeks, maxing out the turbines and the generators and dumping the extra electricity onto the grid at bargain rates. They were also redlining the river outlets, a set of four steel tubes running through the eastern portion of the dam, which bypassed the power plant and blasted water directly into the Colorado at 120 miles per hour. They were even harnessing the stricken spillways, sending as much water as they dared through the tunnels and keeping their fingers crossed. The scene was spectacular and chilling. You could hear the thunder of the discharge from the parapet, and if you walked out toward the hollow-jet valves on the east side of the power plant, you could actually feel the vibrations through the soles of your shoes.

And yet, none of that was enough.

As the runoff continued racing down from the tops of the southern Rockies, across the Colorado piedmont, through the badlands of Utah and into the upper tentacles of Lake Powell in one vast rush, the surface of the reservoir inched upward with each passing hour. Fifteen feet short of the parapet, the water would overwhelm the steel gates that guarded the spillways, then plummet back into the crippled tunnels and resume its excavation of the sandstone. At the very least, this would inflict dreadful damage on the gates and the tunnels while robbing the engineers of any ability to control the water they were releasing downstream. In effect, they would lose dominion over the river. Yet that was only the *third*-worst-case scenario.

---

*Floods are measured in cubic feet per second, also known as cfs, a dynamic calibration of both volume and force that is obtained by multiplying the average speed of the current by the river's cross section.

If luck was running against them, the hydraulic blast that had already ravaged the tunnels' interiors might cut laterally through the sandstone walls and create a breach just downstream from the foot of the dam. Even then, the damage could probably be contained, albeit at tremendous cost to the Reclamation's coffers and reputation. The last possibility, however, was nothing short of apocalyptic.

If things truly went to hell, the river could, in theory, establish a connection between the damaged spillways and the bottom of the reservoir behind the dam, triggering an "uncontrolled release." This would send the contents of Lake Powell down the length of the Grand Canyon, across Lake Mead, and over the lip of Hoover Dam. From there, the surge would bulldoze across western Arizona, where it would inundate the towns of Laughlin, Needles, Parker, and Yuma, along with almost every dam and river diversion structure along the lower Colorado. As a final grace note, much of that water would probably wind up taking out the infrastructure to California's Imperial Valley, one of the richest agricultural breadbaskets in the country, before dispersing into the Sea of Cortés.

During the first week of June, the engineers had dismissed the terminal scenario as absurd. But by the end of the month, no one at Reclamation could say with certainty what the river would or would not do. Hence, the Control Room team's primary concerns on the night of June 25 were the serious and far-reaching consequences of what was happening at the dam itself. Although they were aware that the torrent they were sending downstream had jacked the Colorado to a level that hadn't been seen in a quarter century, they had no inkling of the commotion this was causing deep inside the Grand Canyon.

At that very moment, more than two hundred boats and nearly thirteen hundred people who had left from Lee's Ferry prior to the river's closure were scattered up and down the 277-mile corridor within the canyon. The engineers had no idea that several of those boats had been destroyed, or that dozens of people had been dumped into the current, or that helicopters had been sent in to rescue the survivors, some of whom had been washed as far as ten miles downstream in fifty-degree water. And, understandably, the managers of the dam didn't have the faintest clue that an hour before midnight, a trio of boatmen had staged an illegal launch of a little wooden dory out of Lee's Ferry and were now racing straight toward the worst of the carnage.

~

Although the dam operators' myopia was neither malicious nor willful, their ignorance underscored one of the strangest and most confusing aspects of the drama about to unfold. For although the reservoir and the canyon were bound together by geology, by government oversight, and most important by the thread of the Colorado itself, they were actually two separate worlds. Indeed, Glen's hulking edifice represented one of the starkest divisions on the American landscape, a borderline that seemed to delineate the frontier between two different republics. And to say that the citizens of those rival domains did not always see eye to eye was a bit of an understatement, because each represented the antithesis of the other's deepest values.

To the engineers and the technicians who belonged to the world of the dam, Glen was no dead monolith but, rather, a living and breathing thing, a creature that pulsed with energy and dynamism. Perhaps even more important, the dam was also a triumphant capstone of human ingenuity, the culmination of a civil-engineering lineage that had seen its first florescence in the irrigation canals of ancient Mesopotamia and China, then shot like a bold arrow through the Middle Ages, the Renaissance, and the Industrial Revolution to reach its zenith here in the sun-scorched wastelands of the American Southwest. Glen embodied the glittering inspiration and the tenacious drive of the American century—a spirit that in other contexts had been responsible for harnessing the atom and putting men on the moon. As impressive as those other accomplishments may have been, nothing excelled the nobility of transforming one of the harshest deserts on earth into a vibrant garden. In the minds of its engineers and its managers, Glen affirmed everything that was right about America.

To Kenton Grua and the river folk who inhabited the world of the canyon, however, the dam was an offense against nature. Thanks to Glen and a host of similar Reclamation projects along the Colorado, one of the greatest rivers in the West had been reduced to little more than a giant plumbing system, a network of pipes and faucets and catchment tubs whose chief purpose lay in the dubious goal of bringing golf courses to Phoenix, swimming pools to Tucson, and air-conditioned shopping malls to Vegas. A magnificent waterway had been sacrificed on the altar of a technology that enabled people to prosper without limits, without balance, without any connection to the environment in which they lived—and in the process, fostered the delusion that the desert had been conquered. But in the eyes of the river folk, even that wasn't the real cost.

To the boatmen and the guides, the untamed Colorado embodied a current of values that ran far deeper than the celebration of economic progress. Chief among them being the idea that nothing offers a more compelling distillation of nature's beauty than a free-flowing river. In their eyes, Glen was a testament not to everything that was right with America but everything that was wrong with it. And it was here that the illicit adventure upon which the *Emerald Mile* had just embarked raised the possibility of something more provocative than simply setting a speed record.

On its surface, staging a clandestine race through the Grand Canyon was little more than a bold act of mischief. But to conduct such a race atop a runaway flood tide, and to do so at a moment when a hated hydroelectric dam was in peril—those things elevated the endeavor, at least in Grua's mind, to something more than just a stunt. To him, it offered a once-in-a-lifetime chance to participate, in the most visceral way imaginable, with the ancestral majesty of the Colorado. An act that was insane and reckless, to be sure, but that also stood as an expression of defiance against not only the ideals for which the dam stood but the arrogance of having built the thing in the first place.

Had Glen's engineers and technicians known of the speed run, they would have surely felt themselves justified in dismissing this notion as idiotic, thereby reinforcing the extent to which these two dominions, the world of the river and the world of the dam, were so fundamentally opposed. In fact, it was probably fair to say that no one on either side of this divide shared anything at all in common. But on the evening of June 25, members of both camps were inextricably united by at least one truth.

In its own way, each group was confronting the unsettling fact that on this night, at this hour, despite all the engineering and the technology, despite the colossus of the dam itself, the Colorado and the canyon that contained it were as wild, as ungovernable, and as mysterious as on the day they were first discovered.

By far the most sublime
of all earthly spectacles . . .
the sublimest thing on Earth.

—CLARENCE DUTTON

PART I

The World Beneath the Rims

The Grand Canyon at the Toroweap Overlook, by William Henry Holmes, 1882.

1

First Contact

It is a lovely and terrible wilderness, such a wilderness as Christ and the prophets went out into; harshly and beautifully colored, broken and worn until its bones are exposed . . . and in hidden corners and pockets under its cliffs the sudden poetry of springs.

—WALLACE STEGNER

IN the winter of 1540, just nineteen years after Hernán Cortés had marched into the heart of Mexico and looted the riches of the Aztecs, a young Spanish nobleman named Francisco Vásquez de Coronado was given supreme command of the largest expedition of conquest in the brief but magnificently profitable history of the New World. When Coronado's company mustered in the central square of the town of Compostela on a Sunday morning in late February, the column behind him included 230 horsemen recruited from the nobility of New Spain, sixty-two heavily armed foot soldiers, and five friars. Although the leaders of this glittering assembly were all Spaniards, the ranks were also enlivened by a smattering of other nationalities—five Portuguese, two Italians, a Frenchman, a Scot, and a bugler from Germany, plus more than a thousand Tlaxcalan Indians, whose primary duties involved tending to the fifteen hundred horses, mules, and cattle that shuffled inside the vast cloud of dust that rose in their wake. One witness in Compostela described them as "the most brilliant company ever collected in the Indies to go in search of new lands."

Coronado's military escort was led by Melchior Díaz, an intrepid horseman and scout who was destined within a few months to become the first European to cross the mouth of the Colorado River where it entered the Gulf of California—and who was fated, just a short time thereafter, to suffer a cruel and freakish death. (While attempting on horseback to run his lance through a dog that was attacking his sheep, he skewered his groin and bladder on the back of his own weapon.)

The vision that had drawn these men out of Mexico was Cíbola, a complex of seven cities that was rumored to lie far to the north and whose treasures were said to defy belief. If the stories that had been peddled to Coronado were true, the walls of Cíbola's palaces were encrusted with emeralds, the doors were studded with sapphires, and the handles of those doors were wrought from the purest turquoise. The rulers of Cíbola were said to sup on golden plates and quench their thirst from golden goblets, and on warm nights they lay beneath trees whose branches were festooned with tiny bells of hammered silver. But most tantalizing of all were the palace storerooms. Richer than the vaults of the Incas or the Aztecs, they were rumored to be stuffed with gold and silver, emeralds and pearls, and fine cotton shawls to a depth of nine feet.

Aside from their horses, the most valuable assets of Coronado's company were their arms, which were unlike anything seen before in that part of the world. In addition to the usual assortment of swords and maces and pikes and halberds, their weaponry included nineteen crossbows, seventeen harquebuses, and a handful of small brass cannons on wheels. Along with these implements of warfare, every soldier in Coronado's column carried a mental image of himself seizing some portion of Cíbola's fabled treasure for his own. Even a tiny piece of that hoard would be the making of a man's fortune, the thing that would change the direction of his life no less dramatically than the *acequias*—the irrigation canals that had been brought from Arabia to Spain by the Moors—can alter the shape and flow of a river by pouring it onto a man's fields.

That prospect was sufficient to pull Coronado's men through the arid plains of Sonora and across the border into what is now Arizona, past the silver-studded hills surrounding the future town of Tombstone, then up onto the highlands of the Mogollon Rim, through what would later become the Apache National Forest. By the middle of that first summer, however, the fantasy that spurred them had begun to break apart on the hardened surface of the baked desert that lines the western edge of New Mexico. It was there, less than fifty miles southwest of the present-day city of Gallup, that the explorers stumbled upon Háwikuh, a pueblo of the Zuñis, whose adobe abutments Coronado immediately prepared to storm in the belief that he was about to pillage the first of Cíbola's great cities.

Despite finding themselves hopelessly outmatched by the Spaniards' horses and guns, the Zuñis launched a ferocious counterattack with clubs and arrows that brought them almost to the hooves of the Spanish mounts, where they were able to knock the supreme commander senseless with a well-aimed rock. When he regained consciousness, Coronado was given the news that God had granted them a glorious victory in this battle, the first formal military encounter between Europeans and natives within the future territory of the United States. He was also informed that the Zuñi storehouses held no precious metals or gemstones. Háwikuh's stockpile of wealth, most of which was kept in simple clay pots, consisted primarily of dried corn and pinto beans.

This moment marked the start of an unpleasant awakening in which Coronado was forced to grapple with the disheartening possibility that Cíbola might be nothing more than a beautiful illusion, a chimera of the desert. Before succumbing to this truth, however, he persisted in watering the fading flowers of hope by ordering several small reconnaissance parties to break off from the main column and conduct exploratory forays on the chance that one of them might stumble upon something of value.

One of these teams, a squadron of twelve men led by an intrepid young captain named Don García López de Cárdenas, was dispatched from Háwikuh and ordered to ride deep into what are now the Navajo and Hopi reservations to chase down rumors of a "great river" that was said to lie somewhere off to the northwest and which might connect with the same river whose mouth the luckless Melchior Díaz had earlier crossed.

As September spilled into October, Cárdenas and his companions made their way to the Hopi village of Tusayan, then headed through a forest of piñon and juniper trees until, to their surprise, the ground abruptly gave way, and they found themselves gazing across what appeared to be an inland ocean of air. Here they confronted a vision that future visitors to this remarkable corner of the world would one day deem more wondrous than the mythical riches of Cíbola.

~

Perhaps it's worth pausing for a moment to acknowledge, from the standpoint of Europe's exploration and conquest of the New World, just how early in the morning it still was. In the autumn of 1540, there was not a single European settlement—not one—along any coastline or anywhere within the interior of what would eventually become the United States. It would be sixty-seven years before the first group of English settlers began battling starvation at Jamestown, and another thirteen years after that before the Pilgrims sighted the cliffs of Cape Cod from the decks of the *Mayflower*. George Washington would not be born for almost two more centuries, and the better part of a third would slip past before Lewis and Clark even started their great journey up the Missouri River system. Yet there stood Cárdenas and his men, on the brink of a prodigious chasm that was destined to emerge as perhaps the most iconic landscape feature of a nation that did not yet exist. Of all the natural wonders in America—the waterfalls of Yosemite, the geysers of Yellowstone, the great trees of Northern California—this was the very first to be discovered, although *discovery* was hardly the right word.

By the time Cárdenas arrived, much of the terrain inside that abyss had not only been traversed and explored but also inhabited, first by three successive waves of Ancestral Puebloans, the forerunners of the modern Hopi, then later by the Hualapai, the Paiute, the Havasupai, and half a dozen other tribes. The ruins of entire villages were down there, where the granaries had been stocked with corn and canals had channeled water across fields for hundreds of years until, sometime during the twelfth century, the bottom of the canyon was mysteriously abandoned. There were secrets and legends too—places where shamans had worshipped, where young men had conducted vision quests, and where the spirits of the dead were said to cross over into the afterlife. Nevertheless, Cárdenas's arrival marked a crucial point in the history of this landscape.

At that moment, the continent from which these explorers hailed was at a peculiar crossroads, with one foot testing the waters of the Renaissance and the other still firmly planted in the Middle Ages. The printing press, one of several technologies that would do the most to shape and transform the future, had barely begun shouldering aside the impossibly laborious business of copying illustrated manuscripts by hand. Johannes Kepler, Sir Francis Bacon, and Galileo had not yet been born. Mercator projection maps had not yet been invented; complex numbers were still awaiting discovery. The words *geography* and *geology* had not even been added to the English language. And yet, the first tremors of the seismic shifts that would rock the face of the world were already being felt.

From a three-story tower within the walls of the city of Frauenburg, the great Polish astronomer Nicolaus Copernicus was preparing to publish *On the Revolutions of the Celestial Spheres*, his treatise positing the radical notion that Earth was not the center of the universe, which would herald the arrival of the scientific revolution. In Rome, Bologna, and Venice, the Italian polymath Leonardo da Vinci had teased out the conceptual principles behind single-span bridges, comparative anatomy, plate tectonics, aeronautics, and the science of fluid mechanics. And oddly, although Spain was still a stronghold of religious orthodoxy—and thus fiercely resistant to these new ideas—the country that had given birth to Coronado and Cárdenas stood at the fore-front of these developments in one crucial respect, because no country had a greater command of water. It was on the Iberian Peninsula that the Romans had done some of their most impressive work on arched dams. Here was where the Muslims had laid down the foundations of reservoir-driven irrigation, and where Christian engineers were now refining the concept of hydraulic power. In short, Spain was the seedbed of the technologies that would eventually con-verge to harness one of the most unbridled but potentially useful forces in all of nature, a wild river.

Thus the era of Cárdenas's arrival at the edge of the canyon offered the first promise of a world that was not only ruled but also controlled by man. And now, here where the piñons and the junipers gave way to the buff-colored cap-rock, that vision was colliding against one of the most implacable expressions of nature's indifference to grand schemes—a landscape whose essence sug-gested that such a conceit was perhaps no less arrogant, and no less rife with the potential for unintended consequences, than a horseman's thinking that it was a simple matter to run his lance through a dog that was pestering his sheep.

~

Years later when Pedro de Castañeda, one of the chroniclers of the Coronado expedition, set down the story of this first encounter, he offered not a single detail of Cárdenas's reaction as he and his men peered into the abyss for the first time. But if those men had anything at all in common with the tens of millions of visitors who would later follow in their footsteps, it's a reasonable guess that not one of them said a word—that they simply stood, rooted in silence, their breath snatched away by the vision that had been laid at their feet.

Although no one now knows precisely where this incident took place, it's almost certain that it occurred along a section of the South Rim that is known today as Desert View. This promontory offers one of the most dramatic of all vantage points into the canyon—a place where it completes a great arc, bend-ing from the east to the north in a sweep whose view is so arresting that the Fred Harvey Company would later erect a tall stone watchtower for public enjoyment.

Somewhere close to this spot, Cárdenas and his men found themselves looking out at a formation called the Palisades of the Desert, a dramatic set of banded cliff faces that form the canyon's southeastern rampart. From the base of the Palisades, a series of benches and precipices descends like a crudely hewn set of stairs toward a glittering ribbon of silver and green that winds through the bottom far below. On the opposite side of that stream, a matching set of cliffs and ledges ascends to the North Rim. And yawning between those two rims stretches a void as wide and deep as a landlocked sea, an impression strengthened not only by the shimmering blueness of the air itself but also by the armada of clouds that scud past at eye level, casting shadows beneath their bellies that ripple and dance amid the shattered stones that lie shipwrecked below.

Gazing down toward that thin trickle of water winding sinuously between the buttes and mesas rising from the center of the gorge, Cárdenas scoffed at the claims of his Hopi guides, who assured him that this was no mere stream, but a mighty desert river whose width measured half a league across—several hundred yards. Certain they were exaggerating, the Spanish captain dismissed their pronouncements as absurd, judged its true breadth to be no more than eight feet, and ordered his party to begin moving west along the rim in search of a promising place to descend to this creek.

Three days later, they arrived at a break in the escarpment where Cárdenas directed Captain Pablos de Melgosa and two of the nimblest foot soldiers to scramble down to have a look. Many hours later, they returned with news that this giant arroyo was far more treacherous than the view from the top had led them to believe. In fact, Melgosa reported, they had penetrated only a fraction of the way down before further descent became impossible—although they had gone far enough to confirm that the Hopi had not overstated the size of the river. But what sobered the reconnaissance party even more were the monstrous dimensions of the interior—a landscape so huge that even its minor features had made them feel hopelessly diminished. To illustrate the point, Melgosa pointed to a single stone column. From the rim, it appeared to be roughly the height of a man, did it not? But no. In fact, it had proved taller than the great tower of Seville, the belfry that rose 344 feet from the Catedral de Santa María de la Sede, the largest cathedral in the world and, tellingly, a crowning point of reference for a Spaniard of that era. They must have felt that they had lost their bearings entirely.

In both a literal and a symbolic sense, this was entirely true. Without a single familiar object to impart some sense of scale—a man sitting beneath the shade of a tree; an ox pulling a plow through a field—it was impossible for the Spaniards to gauge the immensity of this declivity. They had no conception that they were staring into an abyss whose volume exceeded a thousand cubic miles, a distance and depth that dwarfed anything they or any other European had ever encountered. They had no notion that, for much of its length, the top and the bottom of this canyon were separated by more than a vertical mile of rock, which meant that if it had somehow been possible to lift up every peak in the Pyrenees and drop them neatly into that expanse, each mountain would easily fit inside the bottom and not a single summit would peer above the rim.

They also had no way of fathoming that, from its eastern reaches to its western terminus, the abyss ran for 277 miles, arguably the longest canyon on earth. Nor did they comprehend that the span between the South Rim and the North Rim averaged roughly ten miles, or that the canyon's six hundred bays and tributary arroyos could push that width back to fifteen, twenty, even thirty miles. Finally, they were unable to grasp or appreciate that the river of which the Hopi spoke served as the premier drainage channel for the entire Southwest, a waterway that gathered together all the runoff of a region larger than Spain and Portugal combined.

Their inability to frame themselves in relation to this stupendous tableau, however, was not simply spatial but also extended into a fourth dimension, the realm of time. And here, they were truly out of their depth. They had no idea, for example, that the very rock beneath their feet, a honey-colored limestone known as the Kaibab, was older than the oldest things they knew of. Older than the basilica that was built upon the slope of Vatican Hill in Rome or the shrine in Jerusalem where the Prophet Muhammad had initiated his ascent to heaven. Older than the temples of ancient Greece or the walled cities of Sumeria— older than any city in the world, in fact, or even the land itself. So old that the Kaibab actually predated not only the continent on which they stood but also the ocean they had spent nearly three months sailing across to get there, as well as all the rest of the continents and all of the oceans between them. And as astonishing as all of that may have seemed, what would have brought them to their knees in awe was that this topmost layer of rock wasn't really very old at all in comparison with the age of what was lost in the tremulous shadows below.

They could see that the walls of the canyon formed a crumbling staircase, but they had no way of knowing that each riser on those stairs was composed of rocks that had been deposited *before* the step above and *after* the step below—a vertical concatenation of time that had been laid down in horizontal strata.* This meant, among other things, that if Cárdenas and his men had elected at that moment to force a descent, they would have confronted not only a formidable physical challenge but also a temporal one. In effect, the canyon served as a kind of self-propelled time machine, a terrestrial chronometer in which each step they took would have hurled them into a deeper and more distant precinct of the past.

Their progression into this well of time would not have been uniform. Depending on where they were, they might have passed through fifteen mil-

---

*This is not a revolutionary idea to us, but it would have been to Cárdenas and his men. Another 129 years would pass before Nicholas Steno, the son of a Copenhagen goldsmith, framed this notion in the Principle of Superposition, one of the defining concepts of the emerging science of geology.

lion years in a single stride, while the next dozen paces may only have taken them through a few millennia. But regardless, every step of their journey would have catapulted them backward through entire ages and epochs as they dropped deeper and deeper into a world whose buttresses had been laid down long before anything human had ever taken place. And as they penetrated each stratum—through the hardened deltas of dead rivers, the floors of vanished oceans, the petrified dunes of antediluvian deserts—they could have calibrated their progress by noting each successive benchmark in the fossil record that they passed.

Past the conifers, the reptiles, and the amphibians. Past the first seed plants, the first beetles, the first sharks. Past the spiders, the scorpions, and the centipedes, then past the first creatures ever to have left the ocean and ventured forth upon the land. Not long after that, they would pass the point where the first terrestrial plants—the mosses and worts and ferns—had begun to colonize the land. By this point, they'd be inside a realm that had been framed when the land was so empty and barren that all of its rivers ran over bare rock, unadorned by so much as a single green leaf.

When you get down that deep, the rock record has big gaps, so without even realizing it, the Spaniards would have found themselves skipping over some important opening movements in the pageant of biology: the first armor-plated fishes, the first vertebrates, the first coral reefs. At around this point, too, things would begin to grow quiet as orders and classes and, eventually, entire phyla in the taxonomic regnum of life successively winked out.

First to go would be the gastropods, followed swiftly by the sponges and the echinoderms. And by the time Cárdenas and his men had reached the layer of smooth, tan-colored sandstone now known as the Tapeats, the sea lilies and the brachiopods would also be gone, followed soon thereafter by trilobites—the horseshoe-crab-shaped creatures that had peered through the shallows of lost Paleozoic oceans with eyes made of calcite, the earliest vision systems on earth and a lyrical merger of biology and geology, a living form of rock.

Somewhere below the last of the trilobites, Cárdenas's company would have stepped across a final threshold and entered into the stillest and most silent epoch of all—the time of everything that preceded visible, multicelled life. This was a world that had been populated by whorled chains of the earliest cyanobacteria, anaerobic creatures whose chemistry had coalesced shortly after the crust of the planet had begun to cool and life's initial moments of respiration unfolded amid an atmosphere devoid of a single molecule of oxygen.

Eventually, they would have been able to go no farther. By this point, they'd be standing at the edge of the river itself, a kingdom walled off by elegant foliations of Vishnu schist, rock that had been compressed and deformed by heat and pressure so intense that the minerals inside the stone had recrystallized and metamorphosed into something surreal and otherworldly. This was stone whose bloodlines extended further back than the human mind could possibly conceive—seventeen million centuries into the past, nearly half the life span of the planet and one-tenth the age of the universe itself. A stone so dense and so black that a man felt, upon seeing it for the first time, that its polished surface must surely mark some kind of nadir. Certainly no other rock on the surface of the earth seemed to glitter so darkly with the dawn light of creation.

Had Cárdenas and his men succeeded in completing this odyssey, they would have found themselves suspended so far down inside the nocturnes of deep time that their connection to everything that was familiar and comforting would have dropped away like a severed umbilical cord. This domain was older and deeper, by far, than anything they could even pretend to imagine—a dimension of time and space where God himself seemed to be a deluded and laughable idea and, in the same instant, more radiant than a flame.

～

Electing to forgo the descent, Cárdenas and his men continued their sojourn along the South Rim, slowly making their way west. During the better part of the following week, they were afforded ample time to absorb the scene before them in all of its glory. There was color everywhere, and as each day unfolded, the leaning light of late autumn would have put the countenance of the canyon through a range of complex and alluring changes.

The show began early each morning, as the company prepared to resume its journey. Just before dawn, the plateaus stretching beyond the rims took on a pale pink luster, while the upper band of cliffs appeared to be floating on a lake of darkness that slowly compressed as the light poured over the edges and squeezed night out of the abyss. Later in the afternoon, as the light turned flat, the chasm was engorged with a harsh glare that strained eyes and made temples throb. Then, at sunset, the upper strata were once again hammered into a molten gold that gradually cooled to lavender during the twilit minutes before the long shadows returned, the completion of a magnificent burning that spanned the entire visual spectrum, all the named and unnamed hues of candescence.

If they were moved by such wonders, their response was never recorded, and in any case, aesthetics were irrelevant to the object of their quest. For Cárdenas was chasing after a harder grade of wealth, and the canyon seemed to contain none of it. There were no precious metals or gems to plunder in the name of his king, no farmlands or estates to seize, no inhabitants to enslave and convert. The impossibly distant river offered no great artery of transportation, and if the

Hopi were to be believed, the only mineral worth excavating was salt. As for the gilded cities of Cíbola, they were nowhere to be seen.

And so, at the end of the week, Cárdenas did the only thing that made sense from his perspective. He pointed his squadron in the direction from which they had come and led them back toward the main body of the expedition—which went on to spend the next two years in a search that took them across the Texas Panhandle, through Oklahoma, and deep into the plains of central Kansas. It was the longest and most arduous march conducted by any group of conquistadores in the sixteenth century, and when they finally returned to Mexico in disgrace in the spring of 1542, they brought back, in the pages of their letters and reports, accounts of many singular encounters, including the first prairie dogs, the first jackrabbits, the first meetings with the tribes of the Great Plains, and the first buffalo. But they had failed to find anything that they deemed to be of value.

"The villages of that province remained peaceful," the expedition's chronicler wrote of the country surrounding the great canyon, "since they were never visited again, nor any attempt made to find other peoples in that direction." It was as if the defining element of the entire continent—the greatest testament on earth to the passage of time and to the power of water—had been rendered invisible.

More than three hundred years would pass before the most important of Coronado's successors returned, less than an eyeblink when measured by the scale of Grand Canyon time. But even so, the arrival of those first Spaniards marked a fundamental turning point, a rotation of the great wheel. Because it was the children of Cárdenas, not the Native Americans, who would eventually come back to codify the canyon's boundaries and catalog its wonders, to map out its grid lines with transits and a surveyor's chain, and to lay down the foundations that would eventually enable them to harness the power of the river itself.

2

The Grand Old Man

*I do not know much about gods; but I think that the river
Is a strong brown god—sullen, untamed and intractable . . .
Keeping his seasons, and rages, destroyer, reminder
Of what men choose to forget.*

—T. S. ELIOT

JUST before two o'clock on a blustery Monday afternoon in May of 1869, a
westbound Union Pacific train was clattering past a strip of ragged, tent-
roofed shacks that clung like a piece of gristle to the pale gray badlands
of southwestern Wyoming. Directly ahead, a trestle spanned a broad, shallow
river whose olive-colored current was restless and kinetic, alive with the sluicing runoff of late spring. As the locomotive approached the lip of the bridge,
the engineer throttled his speed back to five miles an hour, a shift that would
have been manifest inside the walnut-paneled Pullman Palace saloon carriage,
several cars behind the tender, by a faint tinkling of the chandelier and a subtle
jolt to the small organ resting atop the richly brocaded Brussels carpeting. If, at
this moment, any of the first-class passengers on the left side of the saloon car
had been curious enough to push aside the heavily looped curtains framing the
windows, they might have found themselves staring down on a diminutive navy
of rowboats preparing to cast off on one of the most remarkable chapters in the
history of American exploration.

Those boats were manned by a squadron of bleary-eyed, rumple-haired men who had spent much of the previous forty-eight hours attempting to drain the entire liquor supply of Green River Station, a town whose population of several dozen roustabouts and blackleg gamblers had gathered along the shore to spit tobacco juice and call out farewells. The boatmen were not in the best of shape. Their faces were unshaven, their clothes were disheveled, and they subjected the spectators to "much blowing off of gas and the fumes of bad whiskey." But despite these handicaps, they had somehow managed to complete the final steps in loading up their impressive array of gear and provisions.

Inside the watertight compartments of the boats were enough bacon, flour, dried apples, sugar, and coffee beans to sustain a party of ten men for almost an entire year. An ample cache of ammunition accompanied a small arsenal of rifles and shotguns, plus the set of steel traps that they hoped would enable them to supplement their larder with fresh venison and beavertail soup. There was also a kit for surveying and mapmaking, including sextants, compasses, and four barometers—each featuring a thin tube of glass filled with a column of mercury and carefully packed in a protective layer of fresh straw. These would be used for determining their altitude as the river carried them on the better portion of its long journey from the Rocky Mountains to the Sea of Cortés.

By the time the train was rattling past on the trestle overhead, the stowing of this entire duffel—all seven thousand pounds of it—was finally complete, much to the satisfaction of a figure whose appearance gave little indication that he was destined for both greatness and notoriety. At thirty-five years old, Major John Wesley Powell stood barely five and a half feet tall, weighed less than 125 pounds, and scowled sternly at the world from behind the hedgerow of a beard that appeared to have been assembled from a box of steel wool—traits that made him look, in the words of one of his less deferential biographers, like "a stick of beef jerky adorned with whiskers." His most notable feature, however, was that his right forearm, from the elbow down, was missing—a critical impediment, one might assume, for a man who was proposing to lead a flotilla of oar boats down one of the world's most dangerous and least understood rivers.

In truth, the missing forearm was merely one item in a long list of liabilities and shortcomings, none of which seemed to have had any effect whatsoever on the Major's confidence. Unperturbed by the perils he was courting by launching downstream in the company of a ragged band of inebriates aboard an unwieldy set of heavily laden boats, he issued the order to embark, and off they went.

As the boatmen put their backs into the oars and sent the bows of their boats shouldering into the current, it is impossible to know whether Powell or any member of his crew glanced up at the trestle and pondered how the labored chug of a steam engine passing over this highway of water represented the intersection of two epic subnarratives within the larger story of America, one of those semaphores in history that signaled the passing of one age and the arrival of another.

Just two weeks earlier, and less than two hundred miles to the west, at a place called Promontory Summit, a California-based politician and industrialist named Leland Stanford had picked up a maul and hammered home a golden spike that completed the final link in the nation's transcontinental railroad. Within a few years, coal-burning locomotives would be hurtling passengers and freight between the east coast and San Francisco—a journey that once took as long as six months in a Conestoga—in as little as eighty-three hours, consigning the wagon trails to obsolescence while flinging open the door to cross-continental commerce and trade on a scale that had never before been seen.

The telegraph was already in operation, and the telephone was just around the corner, to be followed swiftly by the electronic stock ticker and the incandescent lightbulb. These and a thousand other changes were transforming the country from a pastoral agrarian republic into an industrialized powerhouse that would soon lead the world in mechanized production, agricultural output, capital formation, and real income. In just a dozen years, the frontier would be declared officially closed by the US Census Bureau and the historian Frederick Jackson Turner would compose a landmark essay on the significance of its passing. New York City was already planning its first subway lines. San Francisco, until just a few years earlier little more than a vast collection of tents sheltering mud-spattered miners and squatters, now boasted ostentatious Victorian mansions, one of the busiest ports in the world, and a population that was climbing toward 150,000. And like those burgeoning cities, the nation itself was feverish with expansion. In five months, Congress would take formal possession of Alaska, which had been purchased two years earlier from Russia, and augment the nation's territory by more than 20 percent. Before the turn of the century, Hawaii would be annexed, Puerto Rico invaded, and the Midway Islands declared a US possession.

And yet, despite the unstoppable growth, the ballooning wealth, the breathtaking speed with which the United States was expanding and ripening, parts of the country were ferociously resisting the pull of the modern age. All along the northern and southern Plains, the fiercest and most defiant Indian tribes were battling against the advancing waves of Anglo-European settlement using Stone Age technology, and in some cases they were actually winning. In seven years, the Lakota and the Northern Cheyenne would inflict a brutal defeat on George Custer's Seventh Cavalry along the Little Bighorn River in eastern

Montana. A thousand miles to the south, the Comanche—a tribe that had risen to prominence for their unrivaled mastery of horses descended in part from the herd that was brought north during the Coronado expedition—had not only succeeded in stopping cold the advancement of white civilization on the prairies of central Texas, but had in some places actually managed to drive it *back*, forcing the line of settlement to retreat more than a hundred miles to the east. It was almost as if America was a kind of double nation composed of two parts: one surging forward relentlessly, even heedlessly, toward the rapidly looming approach of the twentieth century; the other digging in its heels and doing its utmost to remain anchored to the past. And nothing symbolized that resistance more eloquently than that an entire quadrant of the country's backyard, a region bigger than all of Germany and roughly the size of France, remained as remote and obscure to its own citizens and government as the South Pole or the dark side of the moon.

~

That region was called the Plateau Province, and almost nothing was known about its secrets, except that it received scant rainfall, possessed a surreal and almost otherworldly beauty, and was awesomely unreceptive to human beings. Stretching north toward Salt Lake City, south toward Phoenix, east toward Albuquerque, and west toward Las Vegas, its territory overlaid significant parts of what is now Utah, Arizona, Colorado, and New Mexico—an expanse of 130,000 square miles that contained some of the most impassable terrain on the continent. The other thing that was known about the place was that somewhere through the middle of it ran the Colorado River—although, in the 329 years that had passed since Cárdenas had stumbled upon the great chasm that lay near its heart, almost no one had been back to explore that artery.

A handful of expeditions had succeeded in circumnavigating much of the canyon's periphery, but had barely ventured inside it. In 1776, a pair of Spanish friars had traversed a portion of the Plateau and forded the Colorado just east of the Grand Canyon at a point known thereafter as the Crossing of the Fathers. That same year, another Franciscan priest had poked along the South Rim of the canyon and worked his way into the hidden sanctuary of the Havasupai Indians in the western part of the canyon. This venture was followed by another two generations of silence until the 1820s and 1830s, when a handful of trappers ventured into the canyon country in search of beaver, but left little in the way of written records.

The only hard data available on any portion of this terrain came from the US Army's one organized expedition, which had been confined to the lower reaches of the Colorado, a relatively flat stretch of water that extended north from the river's delta at the Sea of Cortés. In 1857, a young lieutenant with the army's Corps of Topographical Engineers named Joseph Christmas Ives was ordered to examine the navigable portion of the river by taking a steamboat as far upstream as he could travel. After chugging nearly three hundred miles from Fort Yuma in an ironclad paddle wheeler with a crew of twenty-four men in the direction of present-day Las Vegas, his odyssey was brought to an abrupt halt when the little steamship slammed into a submerged rock in a crash so violent that the men near the bow were thrown overboard and the engineer was flung halfway into the firebox.

Ives then struck out overland, heading east through the Grand Wash Cliffs and making his way onto the plateau that forms the South Rim of the Grand Canyon. After conducting two brief surveys down a pair of tributary canyons, he declared his exploration complete and returned home to announce, in his published report, that the region was so bereft that "the deer, antelope, the birds, even the smaller reptiles, all of which frequent the adjacent territory, have deserted this uninhabitable district." He then offered one of the most infamous pronouncements that has ever been made about the Grand Canyon:

> Ours has been the first, and will doubtless be the last, party of whites to visit this profitless locality. It seems intended by nature that the Colorado River, along the greater portion of its lonely and majestic way, shall be forever unvisited and undisturbed. . . . Excepting when the melting snows send their annual torrents through the avenues to the Colorado, conveying with them sound and motion, these dismal abysses, and the arid table-lands that enclose them, are left as they have been for ages, in unbroken solitude and silence.

That was all anyone really knew about this giant expanse in the middle of the Southwest, which constituted the last truly uncharted territory in the country. The most authoritative map of the United States featured a single, provocative word emblazoned in the middle of its four-foot expanse: "unexplored."

The implications of that word struck the patriotic boosters of Manifest Destiny as intolerable. "Is any other nation so ignorant of itself?" railed Samuel Bowles, editor of the *Springfield Republican*, whose views were shared by many. The mission of uncovering this "great mocking mystery of our geography," Bowles declared, was a task "more interesting and important than any other which lies before our men of science. The wonder is that they have neglected it for so long."

In fact, there was little wonder. Lieutenant Ives may have been wrong about the destiny of the canyon, but his assessment of its isolation and inaccessibility was accurate. In a landscape that was incised by countless arroyos that branched off from the main stem of the canyon, any form of overland travel was virtually impossible. The distance a raven could cover in a few minutes might take a week or more for a man to traverse on foot or on horseback. In the absence of wings, the only conceivable way to explore the place was by boat, and until the spring of 1869, no one was mad enough to give this a try.

But now, here beneath an obscure railway trestle in a remote corner of the Wyoming Territory, as unlikely a figure as one could ever imagine—a one-armed Civil War veteran—was proposing to barnstorm his way into the center of this blank spot by rowing down the upper reaches of the Colorado to the point where published knowledge dried up, and from there to venture forth into what he rather poetically called "the Great Unknown."

~

John Wesley Powell was the eldest son of an immigrant Methodist circuit preacher and grew up on a frontier farm in Walworth County, Wisconsin, sixty miles south of the place where the distinguished naturalist John Muir was raised in almost identical circumstances. Like Muir, Powell had a deep interest in botany, geography, and geology. As teenagers, both men indulged their fascination with science and nature by capping off fifteen-hour days of backbreaking farm labor with bouts of nighttime reading in order to teach themselves the rudiments of natural history. And, like Muir, Powell seized the first chance he got to break loose from his family and set out on a series of long, solitary, rambling excursions that deepened his love of the land. But the two men differed in one key respect. While Muir eventually found his spiritual calling amid the craggy peaks and wind-raked mountaintops of the High Sierra, Powell's passions revolved around rivers and boats.

In the spring of 1856, at the age of twenty-two, he took a skiff down the navigable length of the Mississippi from the Falls of St. Anthony in Minneapolis all the way to New Orleans, an odyssey that the historian Donald Worster would later speculate may well have taken him past a steamship on which a young river pilot named Samuel Clemens was learning the rudiments of reading water. The following spring, Powell took a train to Pittsburgh and floated the Ohio to St. Louis, tracing the classic natural-history route into the West that had been followed by Lewis and Clark, Thomas Nuttall, and a dozen other of the West's first scientists. Then, in 1857, Powell rowed down the Illinois River to its mouth, and from there up the Des Moines. On the way, he put together a collection of mollusk fossils, a diverse class of ancient marine invertebrates, that would later win several prizes from the Illinois State Agricultural Society.

His rowing and mollusk-gathering days, along with the modest career in academia for which he seemed destined, ended abruptly in the spring of 1861, when he enlisted in the Union Army and went off to war. By April, he was a second lieutenant and serving on Ulysses S. Grant's staff as a captain of artillery and an expert on fortifications. A year later, on the first afternoon of the Battle of Shiloh in southwestern Tennessee, as he raised his right hand to signal his gunners to stand clear of the recoil of one of the half-ton cannons that he commanded, a Confederate minié ball entered his wrist and plowed toward the elbow, shattering his entire forearm. The following morning, in a makeshift military hospital set up in the town hall of Savannah, Tennessee, the arm was sawn off two inches below the elbow and tossed onto the pile of amputated limbs outside the building.

He returned to command the men of Battery F in nine more battles during the next three years, eventually rising to the rank of major before resigning in January of 1865. Within two years of mustering out, he was appointed professor of geology and natural history at the Illinois State University at Normal. Around the same time, he was also named curator of the Illinois State Natural History Society. Both positions served as a springboard for trips to Colorado during the summers of 1867 and 1868 to gather museum specimens—and there he came up with the scheme of resolving the mysteries of the canyon country by launching a fleet of small wooden boats down the most pugnacious and defiant river in the entire West.

～

The river that transected, knit together, and defined the last unexplored region in the United States had not one source but two. The first, the Green, was originally known to members of the Shoshone tribe, and later to the mountain men of the American fur-trade era, as the Seedskadee. Born amid the black and ice-studded tarns of Wyoming's Wind River Range, just south of what is now Yellowstone National Park, the Green serenely gathered up the waters of a succession of small creeks cascading down from a tiny corner of the Gros Ventre Range and meandered southward through a wide, shallow valley carpeted in sagebrush and lined with cottonwood trees, where, from roughly 1825 to 1840, several hundred trappers staged a rendezvous each summer to sell their peltries and replenish their supplies of salt, gunpowder, lead, and whiskey.

At the southern end of this valley, the Green bent to the southeast and continued boring across the alkaline plains of western Wyoming until it reached the trestle bridge of the Union Pacific at Green River Station, where Powell and his bedraggled boatmen were launching their expedition. Fifty or more miles south, somewhere near the border separating the territories of Utah and

Wyoming, the river ran smack up against the Uintas, the only major mountain range in the United States that runs from east to west, speared through a fault in the cliffs of flaming-red quartzite and shale that marked the portal to a massive gorge, and disappeared.

Meanwhile the Green's sister stream, known in Powell's day by the now half-forgotten name of the Grand, was making a roundabout journey from its own point of origin in an idyllic Colorado meadow located in the heart of what would later become Rocky Mountain National Park. Tumbling out of a range called the Never Summers, the Grand cut a diagonal slant down the western slope of the Continental Divide, following a west-trending route that would eventually accommodate a long stretch of Interstate 70. Along the way, it collected the runoff from half a dozen or more tributaries, all of them cold, white-water streams cascading from the tops of the Rockies: the Fraser, the Blue, the Eagle, the Roaring Fork, the Fryingpan, and the Crystal.

At the center of a crescent-shaped valley that would later become the farming town of Grand Junction, the Grand picked up the Gunnison River, then crossed into Utah, wheeled left, and began drilling south through the same badlands into which the Green had disappeared—an impenetrable landscape of bald mesas, wrinkled cliffs, and isolated pockets of mountains whose snowy peaks looked like icebergs marooned in an ocean of impossibly blue air. Somewhere out in that maze of wind-raked stone, the two rivers, which by now had covered a combined distance of nearly twelve hundred miles, arrived at a secret place deep inside what is now Canyonlands National Park, a spot known as the Confluence, and merged to form the Colorado.

More than five hundred miles downstream from the Confluence, the Colorado emerged from the Grand Canyon and was joined by the Virgin, a tributary whose waters arrived just east of where Lieutenant Ives's steamboat had come to a crashing halt. Almost everything that lay between those two distant points was a complete mystery. In fact, explorers had reached and forded this stretch of the Colorado at only a handful of places, and since the time of Cárdenas, no one had undertaken a systematic effort to navigate or chart the course of the river. On the Corps of Topographical Engineers 1855 map of the Southwest, the most definitive piece of cartography of the day, a dotted line of almost lyrical uncertainty traced across the empty space to represent the engineers' best guess as to where the water ran. But the actual details of most of that journey—whether the Colorado doubled back on itself, whether it cascaded over waterfalls the size of Niagara, or bored through underground tunnels—was anybody's guess. Herein lay yet another unique attribute of the challenge that Powell had laid before himself.

When white explorers advanced into the American wilderness for the first time, they were almost never pioneering a new route. Men like Lewis and Clark, Jedediah Smith, and John Charles Frémont were, with rare exceptions, following the immemorially ancient trails used by Native Americans for trade, hunting, and war. Not so with Powell. Although parts of the Grand Canyon were known intimately, many sections had never been touched. The shoreline of the river itself was so riven by impassable cliffs that the first traverse on foot would not take place until 1976. In Powell's day, Indians and mountain men alike traded in the widespread belief that no one who ventured upon the Colorado would emerge from the canyon alive. The river's isolation and secrecy, however, were only part of what made it superlative. There was also its vertical drop.

The Colorado's watershed encompasses a series of high-desert plateaus that stretch across the most austere and hostile quarter of the West, an area encompassing one-twelfth the landmass of the continental United States, whose breadth and average height are surpassed only by the highlands of Tibet. Each winter, storms lumbering across the Great Basin build up a thick snowpack along the crest of the mountains that line the perimeter of this plateau—an immense, sickle-shaped curve of peaks whose summits exceed fourteen thousand feet. As the snowmelt cascades off those summits during the spring and spills toward the Sea of Cortés, the water drops more than two and a half miles. That amounts to eight vertical feet per horizontal mile, an angle that is thirty-two times steeper than that of the Mississippi. The grade is unequaled by any major waterway in the contiguous United States and very few long stretches of river beyond the Himalayas. (The Nile, in contrast, falls only six thousand feet in its entire four-thousand-mile trek to the Mediterranean.)

Also unlike the Nile, whose discharge is generated primarily by rain, the engine that drives almost all of this activity is snow. This means that the bulk of the Colorado's discharge tends to come down in one headlong rush. Throughout the autumn and the winter, the river might trickle through the canyonlands of southern Utah at a mere three thousand cubic feet per second. With the melt-out in late May and early June, however, the river's flow can undergo spectacular bursts of change. In the space of a week, the level can easily surge to 30,000 cfs, and a few days after that it can once again rocket up, surpassing 100,000 cfs. Few rivers on earth can match such manic swings from benign trickle to insane torrent. But the story doesn't end there, because these savage transitions are exacerbated by yet another unusual phenomenon, one that is a direct outgrowth of the region's unusual climate and terrain.

On most sections of the Colorado Plateau, rainfall is sparse and infrequent. Many areas receive less than six inches a year, roughly equivalent to what falls on Africa's Kalahari Desert. It is not unusual, however, for almost the entire annual quota to fall during a single storm or two—brief but exceptionally violent and highly localized cloudbursts that hammer into the dry dirt like a power washer. With so little vegetation to hold that dirt in place, the loose soil is swept into the canyons in muddy torrents, creating flash floods that transfer colossal loads of sediment directly into the river, turning it the color of chocolate. Rolling with a muscular, heavy viscosity that makes it seem more solid than liquid, the river annually removes nearly sixty dump trucks of sediment for each square mile within its watershed, dismantling the landscape grain by grain, pebble by pebble, and freighting the entire mass toward the Sea of Cortés.

As a result, the Colorado is one of the siltiest rivers in the world. It's probably safe to say that no other river anywhere can match the compulsive intensity with which it cuts away the topography and bulldozes those materials downstream. Prior to 1963, the year that the Glen Canyon Dam was finished, the Colorado transported an average of nearly half a million tons of sand and silt through the Grand Canyon every twenty-four hours. (Its record, set in 1927, was more than twenty-seven million tons of sand and silt in *a single day*.) The Nile and the Mississippi are both renowned for their alluvial deltas, but the Colorado's silt-to-water ratio leaves them in the dust. A single cubic foot of the semisolid Colorado is seventeen times more silt-laden than the so-called muddy Mississippi, a river that carries twenty-four times more volume and drains an area five times the size of the Colorado's basin. And for every acre-foot of water—defined as a unit of water equal to one acre covered one foot deep—the Colorado freights eleven *tons* of silt. One way of putting this into perspective is to consider that France and the United States together excavated 357 million tons of dirt while digging the Panama Canal, during roughly fifteen years of total labor. In Powell's day, the ancestral Colorado was capable of hauling the same amount of soil, by weight, in less than a fortnight.

The virgin Colorado was so saturated with silt that, during certain times of the year, only about 48 percent of the cocoa-colored slurry sluicing past Lee's Ferry was actually composed of water. Among the handful of settlers who first lived within the canyon country during the nineteenth century, it was said that the river was "too thick to drink and too thin to plow." Others joked that on windy days dust could be seen blowing off the water's surface. This was no laughing matter, however, to the Mormon sheepherders who attempted to ford their flocks at Lee's Ferry and stood helplessly as the animals sank beneath the surface, pinned down by the weight of the sediment trapped in their wool.

This unusual combination of gradient, volatility, and sediment distinguishes the Colorado as the most tempestuous river on the continent—savage and unpredictable, often dangerous, and almost psychotic in its surges. No river in

Europe, no river in South America, no river in Russia, compares to it. Pakistan's Indus and the Tsangpo in Tibet exceed its drop. The Nile and the Mississippi deliver a larger gross tonnage of silt. A number of rivers in Canada match or exceed the savagery of its rapids. But none of them combine these elements like the Colorado. And those qualities, put together, account for its greatest claim to fame. No other river on earth has ever cut canyons to rival those of the Colorado.

All of this meant that Powell was about to take on an almost impossibly daunting set of challenges in the spring of 1869. In the thousand miles that lay between the head of the Green in Wyoming and the Grand Wash Cliffs, the river and its tributaries had excavated seventeen major canyons. When the expedition launched in the shadow of the railway trestle at Green River Station, a dozen of those canyons had not even been named, and three of them featured bigger white water than anyone in North America had ever boated—a gauntlet of almost five hundred separate rapids.

The Major and his companions had no knowledge of any of these obstacles. Nevertheless, they intended to tackle them all.

3

Into the Great Unknown

Wherever we look there is but a wilderness of rocks; deep gorges, where the rivers are lost below cliffs and towers and pinnacles; and then a thousand strangely carved forms in every direction; and beyond them, mountains blending with clouds.

—JOHN WESLEY POWELL

FOR such a momentous undertaking, the crew of nine that Powell had corralled together was a remarkably ragged bunch, a band of mavericks, fugitives, and Civil War veterans, most of whom had been drawn to the expedition in the hope of finding adventure or a quick way to get rich. Bill Dunn was a classic mountain man: a ferociously competent hunter who dressed in a filthy pair of buckskin pants and wore his hair so long it fell the length of his back. Billy Hawkins was rumored to have committed some sort of mysterious crime in Missouri and was now running from the law while earning his keep as a trapper. John Sumner, who would emerge as the acknowledged leader of the group in Powell's absence, was a combative, sharp-tongued scout who enjoyed bragging about how he had once thwarted a war party of Utes by planting himself on a keg of gunpowder with a cocked revolver and offering to blow them all to hell. And George Bradley was a hazel-eyed sergeant from New England who had been raised in the Maine cod fishery and was later wounded at Fredericksburg. Fearless in a crisis and tough as a badger, Bradley was the only member of the crew, aside from Powell, who knew anything about boats.

The others included Oramel Howland, an ex-Vermonter who had transplanted himself to the West and preferred gunning for elk and bear to practicing his established trade as a printer and editor. At thirty-six, he was the oldest member of the group. Oramel's younger half-brother, Seneca, was a quiet and pensive young man with deep-set gray eyes who had fought at Gettysburg. Andy Hall, the youngest member of the expedition, was the cheerful eighteen-year-old son of Scottish immigrants who worked as a bull whacker, a teamster who drove oxen. And Frank Goodman was a florid-faced Englishman who was rattling around the West in search of gold or excitement—and so keen to find either that he offered to pay Powell for the privilege of signing on.

Rounding out the company was the Major's younger brother, Walter, who had spent ten months at Camp Sorghum, a notorious prisoner-of-war camp in South Carolina, where inmates were confined in an open-air stockade, with almost no food, amid their own excrement. Walter had emerged from this ordeal a bitter wreck of a man whose impenetrable depressions could be broken only through volcanic outbursts of rage or by singing war ballads. (He had a baritone that an angel would envy.)

These men knew almost nothing about the details of their route except that it would bring them within walking distance of only a single settlement, a trading post on the Uinta Indian Reservation in northeastern Utah. Beyond that point, they would be irrevocably committed, with no chance of turning back. Inside the deepest canyons, it was taken as a given that entire stretches of river would offer no way of climbing out—and if they did somehow reach the rims, they would probably confront hundreds of miles of open desert. As daunting as all that was, what loomed most disturbingly in the back of everyone's mind was a question that arose from one of the few hard facts available to them.

Their point of departure sat at 6,115 feet above sea level, and the elevation at the mouth of the Virgin River, about thirty miles east of present-day Las Vegas, was at roughly 800 feet, so they knew that the river would be descending slightly more than one vertical mile. The question was how that drop was apportioned, and whether any of it might involve waterfalls. Wyoming's Yellowstone River featured two enormous cascades, the second of which, at three hundred feet, was almost twice as high as Niagara. If Powell and his men encountered a drop of even a fraction of that height in a section where the canyon walls were too sheer to beach their boats and the current was too swift to resist, the entire party could easily be swept to its death.

Exacerbating all of these issues was the fact that none of them had ever run a rapid or knew the first thing about white water. Perhaps the most graphic evidence of their ignorance about the kind of savagery that a river such as the Colorado could unleash was that only one member of the entire crew, the man who was missing an arm, was equipped with a life jacket. The other compelling testament to how little they knew about what they were getting into was their four boats.

Custom-made in Chicago to Powell's specifications, they were Whitehalls, a sleek design that had originated in New York City around 1820 and was so efficient in the water that the boats were favored by the gangs of thieves who plundered the ships in the city's harbor, as well as by the police who pursued them. They were also spectacularly unsuited to a wild desert river. The *Maid of the Canyon*, the *Kitty Clyde's Sister*, and the *No Name* were twenty-one feet long with double stems and sternposts, and they were heavily planked with oak for added strength. Each weighed close to half a ton and would carry an additional two thousand pounds in cargo. In consequence, they were backbreaking on a portage. But the Whitehalls' biggest liability lay in their rounded bottoms and their keels, features that made them all but impossible to pivot, a key ability on a river where maneuverability was essential.

The fourth craft, which was shorter and lighter but scarcely more maneuverable than its sisters, was named in honor of Powell's wife. The *Emma Dean* would serve as the pilot boat and lead the way, with Powell issuing orders to the trio of "freight boats" in his wake by waving signal flags with his one good arm.

～

When the crew spun out into the swift and glossy current on May 24, the heavy loads forced the freight boats to ride so low in the water that the oarsmen kept running up against sandbars. That night, they decided to pull five hundred pounds of bacon from the storage compartments and dump all of it overboard, a move that would later haunt them.

Over the next fortnight, one mishap followed another. Just after lunch on June 8, while attempting to wallow through a rapid the men later coined Disaster Falls, the *No Name* struck a boulder hard enough to throw out her three-man crew, then blundered broadside into another rock, broke in half, and sank. In addition to the loss of the boat, the wreck cost them a third of their rations.

During the following week, they managed to drive the remaining three boats into rocks hard enough to cause all of them to leak. Then, late on the afternoon of June 17, Billy Hawkins, the cook, built his fire too close to some dead willows and sparked a blaze that swiftly turned their entire camp into a conflagration, forcing them to grab whatever they could and make a mad dash for the water. As the men tumbled into the boats, they were literally aflame, frantically attempting to douse their beards while tearing away their burning clothing. Meanwhile, Hawkins leaped into his boat, his arms filled with the mess kit, lost his footing on the gunwale, and tossed almost every piece of cookware—plates, cups, knives, and forks—directly into the river.

As they struggled with these disasters, the river established what would become a familiar pattern. It wheeled sinuously through broad valleys and unpopulated parklands until it ran up against a range of mountains, then cut through the barricade to form a canyon. Inside these declivities, the walls would rise, the world would narrow, and the current would contort into rapids that could last for miles. Eventually, the ramparts would fall back, and as the river flowed into another valley, the land would open up again, affording another dramatic view of banded buttes in the foreground and, shimmering in the distance, the snowcapped subranges of Wyoming, Colorado, and Utah. As they made their way downstream, they christened every major feature the crew encountered—the buttes, the promontories, the side streams—like Adam naming the animals.

The days swiftly became weeks, and as spring gave way to summer, the portages grew ever more frequent, one following upon the back of the next, sometimes by as little as a hundred yards. The labor was brutal and exhausting and the men worked like stevedores, unloading thousands of pounds of cargo and hauling everything downstream by hand, then shuffling back upstream to carry the boats or to lower them along the shore with ropes. But they were making progress. By the middle of June, they had reached an idyllic stretch of calm water in southeastern Utah that they named Echo Park, and just a few miles downstream from this point, they conducted a twenty-mile hike to the last outpost of civilization, the trading post on the Uinta reservation. There, Goodman, the adventure-seeking Englishman, announced that he had endured enough and resigned. Then it was back to the river and through Desolation, Gray, Labyrinth, and Stillwater Canyons until, at 4:45 p.m. on the afternoon of July 16, they looked to the left and saw that the Green was about to be joined by another river with an equally strong current, which they immediately identified as the Grand.

They had reached the Confluence and were, finally, riding the back of the old man himself, the Colorado proper.

By now their skin was cracked and sunburned, their hands were blistered and chafed, and their bodies had been battered by being dragged over the rocks when they lined the Whitehalls through the rapids. Miraculously, no one had suffered a debilitating injury such as a torn ligament or a broken leg. But they were in poor shape, and the boats were faring even worse. The hulls required constant patching, while any oars that were lost or shattered meant that new ones had to be laboriously sawed from driftwood. As for their commissary, much of the flour was now congealed with river water, the apples and the coffee beans were coated in silt, and the bacon was slowly turning green. Thanks to the loss of the *No Name* and the damage inflicted by the fire, none of the crew had an entire suit of clothes left, and several were all but naked. "I had a pair of buckskin breeches [and] they were so wet all the time that they kept stretching and stretching," Hawkins wrote in his journal. "I kept cutting off the lower ends till I had nothing left but the waist band."

Under such strain, tempers frayed and arguments flared, and by late July, as they were nearing the end of Utah's Cataract Canyon, the crew were approaching mutiny. Much of their frustration was directed at Powell, who was so cautious about white water that he rarely risked running a rapid when it was possible to order yet another hated portage. While the men set about unloading the boats for the third or fourth time that day, the Major would wander off to "geologize"—collecting rocks, taking barometric readings, and compiling notes on the weather, the terrain, and the stars. None of that would have been a problem with a different type of leader, but Powell was prickly, aloof, and in practical matters, often rather incompetent. His flair for choosing the worst possible place to camp was especially galling. "If I had a dog that would lie where my bed is made tonight, I would kill him and burn his collar and swear I never owned him," George Bradley seethed in the pages of his diary. Later he added, "If we succeed, it will be *dumb luck*, not good judgment that will do it."

And so, amid increasing psychological disarray—divided by anger, racked by anxiety, undermined by a distrust of their leader that seemed to deepen with each passing mile—the crew crossed another key threshold on August 5 when, at the downstream end of a placid and beautiful canyon they had named Glen, they reached an open pocket where the cliffs came down to river level. The spot, which would later be known as Lee's Ferry, marked the entrance to the landmark that was not only the very first great feature in the territory of the United States to have been discovered but, perhaps fittingly, the very last to be explored.

～

From the moment they entered the Grand Canyon, the walls rose higher, the space between them narrowed, and the scale of everything shifted. By the end of that first day, several new layers of limestone and sandstone had pushed out of the shoreline next to the river and shouldered the rimrock a quarter of a mile into the sky. As each stratum stepped back from the next in a stairlike progression, the entire ensemble began to take on the contours of a giant wedding cake of rock. By the third day, the walls displayed a horizontally banded palette of some half a dozen colors that ranged from tawny gold to deep maroon and, later, a rose-petal pastel that seemed to smolder with an inner fire, as if it bore the reflected glare of a furnace deep inside the earth. As the boats penetrated farther into this labyrinth, the cliffs were sculpted into dimensions that were both breathtaking and sublime.

Unfortunately, the little band of boatmen had neither the time nor the inclination to appreciate most of this display. Tributary gorges were now spearing in from both the left and the right, and at the mouth of each tributary, a fan-shaped deposit of rocky debris bottlenecked the river, creating sharp hydraulics whose size and viciousness surpassed all but the biggest white water they had so far encountered. They quickly learned to tune their ears to the deep-throated, express-engine roar that signaled the approach of yet another rapid. Echoed and intensified by the rising walls, the thunder of the water quickened their pulses and deafened their ears. Their voices were all but lost as they shouted warnings and directions to one another.

The deeper they went, the more remote and lost they felt until, on August 10, they arrived at a muddy stream known as the Little Colorado, which entered from the left. Here, at this isolated confluence surrounded by slabs and pillars that would dwarf all the cathedrals of Europe, Powell inserted his most famous passage into the report that he later published:

> We are three quarters of a mile in the depths of the earth, and the great river shrinks into insignificance, as it dashes its angry waves against the walls and cliffs, that rise to the world above; they are but puny ripples, and we but pigmies, running up and down the sands, or lost among the boulders. We have an unknown distance yet to run; an unknown river yet to explore. What falls there are, we know not; what rocks beset the channel, we know not; what walls rise over the river, we know not.

Powell wasn't overstating their ignorance. At this point, they had no clear idea how far they had come or how much canyon lay ahead of them. They did not know how many turns the river would make, how many rapids there might be, or whether their supplies would sustain them through the time it would take to negotiate these obstacles. And they had no way of knowing that their most serious challenges lay ahead.

Just downstream from the Little Colorado, the river cut into a layer of metamorphic rock, the Vishnu schist, whose polished black surface framed what would later come to be called the Granite Gorge, a place that was dark and gloomy and so deep that the rims were no longer visible. Here, where the river narrowed to one-third its width, the water increased in both depth and power. The schist's ferocious resistance to erosion gave rise to rapids unlike any they had yet seen—a gauntlet of truly colossal hellbenders. They lined or portaged whenever possible, but often the walls were so sheer that they were forced to work their way along the sides of the rapids by clawing at the sides of the canyon with their fingers. When the fingerholds gave out, they had to run rapids far beyond their skill. "The boats are entirely unmanageable," Powell later wrote. "No order in their running can be preserved; now one, now another, is ahead, each crew laboring for its own preservation."

By now, the battered Whitehalls demanded constant attention and ceaseless repair to stay afloat. Each day, the boats had to be recaulked with pine pitch, which the men collected by climbing the walls to the tree line. But the chief concern was their commissary. They had been forced to discard the last of their bacon—too spoiled even for famished men to choke down—and now they were subsisting on a diet of biscuits, soggy apples, and coffee. They had less than three weeks of rations left, and thanks to the hapless Billy Hawkins, their larder was about to get even less appealing.

On August 15, Hawkins broke one of his oars and nearly capsized, resoaking the supplies they had just dried out and forcing them to pull over for repairs and redrying. While they searched for a suitable piece of driftwood from which to saw a new oar, one of the boats swung around in the current, and its anchor line swept the baking soda, which Hawkins had left sitting on a rock, into the river. For the rest of the trip their nightly meal would consist of unleavened biscuits made from "rotten flour mixed with Colorado river water."

To add to their problems, the summer monsoons arrived—the time when cloudbursts empty into the canyon with shocking violence. As the rain sheeted down the canyon walls, the water coalesced to form hundreds of brownish-red waterfalls that exploded over the ledges and slurried into the river, dropping trainloads of gravel and rendering the river so gritty that they were forced to quench their thirst by lapping like dogs at puddles in the rocks.

With the barometers out of commission, their location and their proximity to the end of the canyon had now become a matter of guesswork, and the river disoriented them further by constantly changing course, looping back on itself in a series of twisted bowknots. From the Little Colorado, it jogged south before swinging west, then northeast and doglegged south again. "If it keeps on this way," Bradley scribbled in his journal, "we shall be back where we started from."

Their days were reduced to the torturous sessions of lining and portaging, punctuated by terrifying, watery battles that must have felt something like war. At night, the rain ensured that they had little relief. Crouched beneath their rotted canvas among the rocks, two or three men to a blanket, they twitched and jerked with dreams of white water and famished men's visions of food.

"Starvation stared us in the face," Jack Sumner later wrote. "I felt like Job: it would be a good scheme to curse God and die."

By now, all pretense that this was a scientific expedition had been dropped. Their survival hinged on which would arrive first: the end of their food supply or the end of the canyon. After taking stock of their remaining flour and apples, Powell summed up their predicament with a single phrase:

"It has come to be a race for a dinner."

~

On August 27, exactly 239 miles into the canyon and two days into their last sack of flour, they reached one of the worst rapids they had yet seen—a double set of falls created by a pair of tributary canyons that entered the Colorado on opposite sides of the river, squeezing the current into a fifty-yard-wide maelstrom that Sumner described as a "perfect hell of foam." After hours of scouting, Powell declared that he could see no way through and concluded that their only option was to lower the boats through the upstream waterfall with ropes, then risk a run through the second falls—an announcement that was greeted with silence.

That night, while the rest of the crew pondered this plan, Oramel Howland approached the Major and asked him to walk up the side canyon so that they could speak in private. He explained that after discussing matters with his brother Seneca and Bill Dunn, the three men had concluded that it was madness to go on. Instead, Howland proposed that the entire expedition abandon the river, climb out the side canyon to the north, and attempt to reach the Mormon settlements that lay somewhere along the Virgin River. If Powell refused, then the Howland brothers and Dunn intended to leave and take their chances alone.

After Oramel had bedded down for the night, Powell spent the next several hours pacing back and forth along the riverbank. Then he began waking the other members of the crew to solicit their views. While none were pleased by their situation, they all said that they preferred to stay with the boats and the river. When morning arrived, everyone gathered together and begged the three dissenters to reconsider. Dunn and Oramel Howland refused, and although Seneca was prepared to relent, he decided that his duty lay in sticking with his brother.

The parting was solemn. In the absence of a full crew to man each of the boats, one would have to be left behind. The contents of the *Emma Dean* were transferred to the Whitehalls, and the little pilot craft was tied to shore, where it would be abandoned along with the barometers, a portion of the ammunition, and virtually the entire collection of rocks and fossils that Powell had painstakingly amassed over the past nine hundred miles. Dunn and the Howlands were presented with two rifles and a shotgun, plus a pan of biscuits that Hawkins had prepared. Powell handed Oramel Howland a letter addressed to his wife, and Sumner gave him a watch to mail to his sister. Then, with pained farewells, the two groups said good-bye.

With Dunn and the Howland brothers watching from the cliff, Bradley wrote, the *Maid of the Canyon* and the *Kitty Clyde's Sister* "dashed out into the boiling tide with all the courage we could muster." The boats scraped against several rocks, plunged over the ledge, and were nearly swamped by the crashing waves. But in no more than a few seconds, they were safely through and bobbing in the tail waves. Delighted by their success, the six men pulled to shore and fired their guns into the air to encourage their friends to clamber along the cliffs and rejoin them. They waited for two hours, to no avail. "The last thing we saw of them," Sumner later wrote, "they were standing on the reef, motioning us to go on, which we finally did."

The river still wasn't finished with them. Six miles downstream they confronted an even worse rapid. Somehow they made it through, with Bradley performing his most heroic feat yet when the tether on the *Kitty Clyde's Sister* broke free and he fought her through by himself.

The following day was a Sunday, and Bradley, who had previously objected to Powell's refusal to observe the Sabbath, noted that it was good they didn't stop. "This is the first Sunday that I have felt justified running," he wrote. "It has now become a race for life."

A few miles downstream, however, the river bent to the northwest and by nightfall the granite had receded into the earth for the last time. By noon of the following day, just over twenty-four hours after Dunn and the Howlands had parted company, they passed through the gates of the Grand Wash Cliffs and found themselves staring across the shallow hills studded with Joshua trees and creosote bushes where the canyon gives way to the Mojave Desert.

~

On August 30, three white men and an Indian were drawing in a fishing net along the north bank of the river where the Virgin flows into the Colorado, a spot just twenty miles upstream from where the little ironclad steamship commanded by Lieutenant Joseph Christmas Ives had collided against a rock sixteen years earlier during his aborted attempt to explore the river from the opposite direction. The whites, who were Mormons, were under special orders from Brigham Young in Salt Lake City to monitor the current for any wreckage that might drift downstream from the Powell expedition, which had been reported lost several weeks earlier.

Sometime around midafternoon, the fishermen spotted a pair of battered and badly leaking boats drifting in their direction, crewed by a company of half a dozen men. In the first of those boats, one of the crew members was standing up and staring at them through a spyglass while a second man seemed to be pulling a piece of cloth from a storage compartment and attaching it to the bow.

As the boats drew near, the fishermen on the riverbank were astonished by what they saw. All six boatmen were unshaven, sunburned, and hollow-eyed. Most of them had no hat, several were in their bare feet, and none possessed more than a few scraps of clothing that hung from their exposed skin in ragged strips. They were also terribly thin—their bodies so emaciated that it was clear they were teetering on the threshold of starvation. But perhaps the most note-worthy detail—which offered a testament not only to the adversities they had endured but also to the purpose behind those trials—was the piece of fabric dangling from the bowpost of the lead boat.

It was the Stars and Stripes.

When the fishermen asked the boatmen if they needed something to eat, they said yes. All they had left was a day-and-a-half supply of flour and eighty pounds of coffee beans.

~

Two days later, Powell bade farewell to his men, four of whom had elected to continue rowing downriver toward the Sea of Cortés, and turned north with his brother for Salt Lake City. As they made their way up the edge of the Great Basin, they received word that Dunn and the Howland brothers were dead, apparently murdered by a party of Shivwits Indians after the three white men had raped a squaw who had been gathering seeds—a tale that seemed prepos-terous, to say the least. Many years later, evidence would emerge to support a more plausible theory that the men had been taken into custody by Mormon fanatics and executed as federal agents. Neither tale would ever be proved.

Despite this tragedy, the reception back East was jubilant. As Powell went off on the lecture circuit, trumpeting his accomplishments from one city to the next, he became a national hero, acclaim that he was able to parlay into a $10,000 appropriation from Congress so he could set out and do the whole trip all over again—which he did in May of 1871, producing the maps and the topographic data that had not been possible on the first venture. Several years after that, he conflated the events that had taken place on both expeditions into his official report, entitled *Exploration of the Colorado River of the West and Its Tributaries.* Despite some rather wild inaccuracies that would later sow confu-sion and provoke fierce arguments among historians, Powell's account stands as an expressive work of classic adventure-travel literature.

To this day, Powell's trips are celebrated by many as one of the greatest achievements in the history of American exploration, even as Powell is denounced by others for his distortions and exaggerations. But no one can dispute the essence of what was achieved. On May 24, 1869, ten men and four wooden boats plunged down an unknown river through the heart of the last blank spot on the map of the United States. Ninety-nine days later, and just shy of a thousand miles downriver, six men and two boats emerged. They had run through 414 rapids and portaged or lined another hundred. In the process, they enabled America to take full possession of this last, hidden landscape feature, while simultaneously laying the foundation by which that same landscape would eventually turn the tables and take possession of Americans who would fall under its spell.

But all of that lay, as it were, far downstream. For the moment, it is enough to acknowledge that although Don García López de Cárdenas may have been the first European to lay eyes on the Grand Canyon from above, he had failed to take the measure of its depth and power. In part, that was because the mind of a sixteenth-century conquistador was incapable of calibrating its wonders, but mainly it was because Cárdenas had never touched the thing that had created the canyon and imbued it with its vitality. That task had been left to Powell, and his odyssey, not that of Cárdenas, would come to define the place.

The Major went on to do great things. His river explorations eventually springboarded him into a distinguished career in government that included heading up the US Geological Survey, which was charged with mapping and surveying the West, while simultaneously leading the Bureau of Ethnology, which he founded. When he died in 1902, at the age of sixty-eight in his summer home in Maine, his obituary in the *Washington Post* ranked him with Columbus, Magellan, and Lewis and Clark.

Powell's presence is woven into the fabric of the canyon and haunts the river in ways that are impossible to ignore even today. His exploits are recounted and debated around each campfire, and a copy of his report rides on almost every trip. On the maps that are used by the boatmen and guides, more than a hundred buttes, rapids, and plateaus bear the names that he and his men assigned to these features. He cut the line. He set the narrative. Everything that would subsequently unfold on the river—including the *Emerald Mile*'s deranged quest in June of 1983—would flow from the themes that were inscribed by the one-armed major and his fleet of little wooden boats in the summer of 1869.

PART II
America's Pyramids

I have climbed the Great Wall of China and crawled through the Pyramid of Cheops in Egypt. But these are dead monuments. Dams have to be the greatest structures made by man. They are not only gigantic, they also pulse with life.

—HENRY FALVEY, US Bureau of Reclamation

Hoover Dam, the colossus that tamed the Colorado.

4

The Kingdom of Water

*The more a man can achieve, the more he may be certain that the
devil will inhabit a part of his creation.*

—NORMAN MAILER

P OWELL'S first trip down the river had an important postscript, a half-
forgotten coda representing the last leg of the odyssey whose details
were largely ignored amid the publicity and accolades. Within a few
days of the Powell brothers' departure for the East, George Bradley and Billy
Hawkins anchored the *Maid of the Canyon* and left the river to strike out overland
for California. But Andy Hall, the sweet-tempered Scottish bull whacker, and
Jack Sumner, the combative frontiersman with the long black hair, kept on going
in the *Kitty Clyde's Sister*. The Colorado wasn't yet finished, and neither were they.

Upon emerging from its penultimate canyon at the Grand Wash Cliffs,
the river uncoils and begins gliding south along the western edge of Arizona
toward its final destination on the far side of the Mexican border, where the
Sonoran Desert touches the top of the Sea of Cortés. The antipodal segment of
this journey, a stretch of about 400 miles, takes the Colorado through some of
the hottest, driest, and most desolate terrain in North America, an area where
the ash-colored wastes on the east and west sides of the river were once dotted
for miles with shattered wagons and sand-encrusted skeletons of mules that
had belonged to miners bound for the California gold rush.

Through the angled light of late September, the two men permitted the current to carry them past the stark, bone-dry mesas and beneath the jagged escarpments of isolated desert mountain ranges such as the Blacks, the Spirits, and the Deads. Drifting through shadows laid down by thick stands of willow, they penetrated into the northern end of the Sonoran Desert, where, more than 1,750 miles from its source in the icy mountain tarns of Wyoming, the river formed a giant, restless, ever-changing delta—a flat and sweltering region, twice the size of Rhode Island, that was so intricately interlaced with marshes and sloughs that its contours could neither be mapped nor surveyed because the land itself refused to stay in one place.

Properly speaking, this maze of ephemeral creeks and shifting atolls belonged neither to Mexico nor to the United States because, in essence, it was a nation unto itself, a watery republic populated by a prolific confederation of wild creatures that fed upon its riches. The water teemed with schools of crayfish and shrimp. The rushes and sedges sheltered deer and bighorn sheep and small wild hogs, all of them hunted by coyote and cougar and even jaguar. Most impressive were the boundless flocks of waterfowl—endless skeins of egrets and cormorants, bitterns and herons, ducks and pelicans migrating along the Pacific Flyway.

Somewhere out there in that estuarine Eden at the tail end of September, the stern of the *Kitty Clyde's Sister* touched salt water, and Hall and Sumner became the first men in recorded history to row from Wyoming to the Sea of Cortés. This landmark achievement truly brought their journey to a close. But if the two men were moved by what they encountered down there in the lowest reaches of the river, or by their own act of completion, their diaries and letters failed to capture those feelings.

Sumner, in particular, was unimpressed and downright grouchy. He described the low valleys on either side of the river as "burned to a cinder" and dismissed the delta as "nothing to brag of." The whole place left him wallowing in a listless depression. "I find myself penniless and disgusted with the whole thing, sitting under a Mesquite bush in the sand," he wrote in his journal at the end of it all. "I never want to see it again."

He had no idea that, within just a few years, the sun-scorched wasteland located just north of the delta would become a focal point of energy and ambition that would reverberate up the entire length of the river, transforming not only the Colorado, but also the great canyon whose passage they had unlocked, in ways that neither Sumner, Hall, nor even Powell himself would have conceived of in their wildest dreams.

The section of the lower river where the landscape had been "burned to a cinder" belonged to one of the strangest parts of the entire Colorado—a place that, in its own way, was as alien and exotic as the Grand Canyon. Here, deep in southern Arizona and just above the Mexican border, the terrain flattened, the current slowed, and the vast loads of sediment suspended within the river began to drop through the water and settle along the riverbed. As this material built up in sheetlike layers, one upon the other, the streambed began to elevate, inch by inch and foot by foot, until the channel became so clogged that the current would periodically break free from the confinement of its banks and go tearing off across the desert in some new direction like a headless brown serpent.

This bizarre trick of river geomorphology repeated at irregular intervals, usually once every few decades, and over the centuries the Colorado had developed the habit of returning to some half a dozen alternative channels. One of these channels embarked on one of the most perverse detours anywhere on earth—a wandering circuit that, like the route of a lost band of thirst-addled gold seekers, dipped into Mexico, then careened back into the United States at the California border before making a beeline for a bowl-shaped depression at the foot of a bone-dry set of ridges known as the Chocolate Mountains, about forty miles southeast of present-day Palm Springs.

This treeless inferno was known as the California Desert, and its lowest point, which lay below sea level and endured heat rivaling that of Death Valley, was called the Salton Sink. Here the fugitive river would form a vast, evanescent lake that was known to the native Cocopah Indians—the only people who had lived in the area long enough to recognize this as a recurring pattern—as the Palm of the Hand of God, and that the whites would eventually call the Salton Sea. For years at a time, the Colorado would pour into this dead-end lake until the two main detour washes, later known as the New and the Alamo Channels, accumulated enough silt to force the prodigal river to return once again to its old bed and resume its route back through the delta to the Gulf of California. Meanwhile, the Salton Sea would slowly evaporate until a new laminate of fine sediment, particles that had been excavated from within the Grand Canyon, lay baking and exposed under the relentless desert sun.

Neither Hall nor Sumner was aware of the existence of the Salton Sink. But it caught the eye of men who followed in their wake, and what drew their attention was the dirt. The entire valley was almost pure topsoil, packed with a rich conglomerate of minerals and other nutrients that had been finely abraded, thoroughly mixed, and drenched in sunshine for 360 days a year. The only drawback was the lack of rain in the Sink, which amounted to roughly 2.4 inches a year, less than half of what the Gobi Desert typically receives. But just a few miles away lay the greatest river in the Southwest. If someone could devise a way to funnel the water onto that rich matrix of soil, the California Desert would find itself transformed into an agricultural terrarium that would be the envy of the nation.

~

The man who finally managed to put all of this together, a driven engineer from Michigan named Charles Rockwood, had a jaw set like a bulldog's and hands so huge that it was said he could crush an apple in one palm. After helping to survey railway routes through the Rockies and across the Columbia River basin, Rockwood made his way to the Southwest around the turn of the twentieth century and focused his considerable energies on the task of turning the Colorado into an irrigation spigot and aiming it at the Salton Sink. The plan that he and his associates devised was audacious, elegant, and laden with the potential for disastrous mishap.

By cutting a diversion channel into one of the river's ancient detour routes, they reasoned—correctly—that they could employ this dry arroyo system as a conduit to transport a portion of the river's flow to the flat, silt-enriched soils just south of the Salton Sea. There, a series of canals and irrigation ditches would distribute the water onto the fields of settlers who, upon learning of this new paradise—billed as America's last great farming frontier—would stampede to get in on the ground floor.

Rockwood didn't waste any time. By the spring of 1901, he and his team had cut an opening in the west bank of the Colorado and prepared their diversion channel. They opened the headgates in May, then stood back and watched with satisfaction as a significant portion of the river started pouring into a network of freshly prepared canals. As word got out, settlers followed the water and poured into the valley too. Within a year, the population had jumped from exactly zero whites and Europeans to more than five thousand. Three years later, there were seven towns, nearly eight hundred miles of irrigation canals, and 120,000 acres under cultivation. All that was needed was a new name for the place. So they started calling it the Imperial Valley.

Conditions were primitive—families lived in canvas tents or huts knocked together from rough lumber—and the heat was unspeakable, almost 125 degrees in the shade. But how the crops thrived! Cantaloupes and tomatoes, lettuce and broccoli, cauliflower and cotton, grapes and shoulder-high wheat and barley—all of it flourished, maturing weeks ahead of the harvest in other parts of the country and thus commanding premium market prices when it was shipped east by the Southern Pacific Railroad. Although no one thought to point it out, the residents of Memphis and St. Louis and New Orleans might have been intrigued to learn that, when these consignments of produce arrived at their tables and they bit into the winter vegetables and fruit of the Imperial Valley, they were literally eating the Grand Canyon.

The entire venture was a smashing success, and the exuberance it unleashed was captured by the slogan adopted by the valley's first newspaper. "Water Is King," the *Imperial Press* proclaimed in a tagline across the top of its front page. "Here Is Its Kingdom." The people who read those words had no idea how unerringly true this was. But the Colorado was about to teach them, in the harshest and most graphic terms one could care to imagine, the folly and hubris of trying to tame it.

~

The first in what would prove to be a series of back-to-back flash floods hit the Imperial Valley and its surrounding region in the spring of 1905, when a massive surge made off with a control gate in one of the diversion channels just south of the Mexican border and opened a six-foot-wide breach. No one knew it at the time, but this marked the moment when the Colorado was once again about to skip out of its main channel and go off on another mad breakaway run to recharge the dead-end sea in the heart of the desert.

With a newly reborn and rapidly expanding Salton Sea rising by seven inches a day at the lowest point of the Imperial Valley, Rockwood led the first three attempts to plug the breach. His initial effort to cut off the river in March of 1905, with a sixty-foot dam made of wooden pilings, brush, and sandbags, was a failure. A flood surge swept it aside as if it were made of dried leaves. Weeks later, a second dam, longer than the first, was carried away by yet another flood tide. By June, the gap had widened to 160 feet, and the water flowing toward the gulf had slowed to a trickle as most of the river hurtled toward the Sink. Rockwell's third and final try, a six-hundred-foot barrier that took several weeks to assemble and cost $60,000, was wiped out by an overnight flash flood on the thirtieth of November.

Defeated and out of money, Rockwood had no choice but to turn the job over to the Southern Pacific, which had invested heavily in the valley and could not afford to see its interests destroyed. Responsibility then fell to Harry T. Cory, one of the railroad's most competent construction engineers, who had started his career at the age of twenty-six as a full professor of engineering at the University of Missouri. His job was to stop the Colorado, using any means necessary.

By this point, however, powerful and poorly understood forces were arrayed against Cory. As the breach expanded to a quarter of a mile, end to end, virtually the entire Colorado was now diverting north through the desert and roaring into the Salton Sea, which had already spread to cover four hundred square miles and was leaving farms and homes submerged in an inexorably rising tide of sediment-saturated water as thick and dark as a pot of gumbo. Even more alarming than the sheer size of this reservoir, however, was the "cutback," a strange and rarely witnessed phenomenon in which a river equalizes the gradient of its streambed by creating a waterfall that actually migrates upstream.

The mobile cascade, which started at the point where the water was pouring into the sparkling inland sea, was more than twenty feet high and spent most of that spring clawing its way south toward the main channel of the Colorado at about a mile a day, cutting deeper and deeper until the drop of the waterfall grew to eighty feet. To anyone standing along the banks, the river appeared to be eating its own entrails at the pace of a slow walk. As this rather grotesque and frightening process—which essentially created a brand-new canyon—marched upstream, the current gouged into the banks on either side, widening the channel to half a mile. For the settlers of the valley, it seemed as if the river had gone berserk. All along the banks of the channel, enormous chunks of soil were now cracking, giving way, and plummeting into the boiling current like walruses returning to the sea.

When the cutback reached the border town of Mexicali, whose buildings had expanded to the channel's edge, the brown serpent slowly began devouring the streets. Residents watched in disbelief as the walls of one adobe house after another trembled, teetered, and collapsed into the river, where they dissolved like lumps of sugar. On June 30, 1906, a brick hotel, the railroad station, and a dozen other buildings in the main business district all crumpled and slid into the current, sending geysers of water shooting forty feet into the air.

Knowing that it would take a colossal effort to bring the runaway river under control, Cory asked his boss, the head of the Southern Pacific, how much money he was authorized to spend.

"Damn the expense," came the reply. "Just stop that river!"

～

Orders in hand, Cory started battling the Colorado in toe-to-toe combat using every weapon he could think of. He stationed pile drivers on opposite ends of the breach and ordered his men to begin pounding a vertical row of ninety-foot logs into the riverbed to create a picket line across the now-submerged bank of the river. As the wall of pilings extended toward midstream, a pair of steamboats lumbered up and down the channel with loads of freshly cut arrowweed and willow bush, which a gang of laborers hired from the Cocopahs and half a dozen other indigenous tribes—the only men willing to work for standard wages in the crushing heat—wove into brush "mattresses" in front of the pilings. When this was done, a pair of railway trestles was constructed on top of the line of pilings.

Meanwhile, Cory was putting together a fleet of special freight trains using three hundred flatbed dump cars, known as battleships, which he had requisitioned from the Union Pacific. When the trains were assembled, he ordered them to begin hauling huge granite boulders from quarries as far away as Los Angeles. As the trains arrived at the work site, they clattered onto the trestle and lined the battleships up directly over the breach. Then men with crowbars began upending the boulders into the current. The dumping proceeded until a makeshift dam began to rise above the brown surface of the river.

Over the next few months, Cory and his crews built a series of several rock dams, each larger and more expensive than the last, then stood back and watched as a succession of floods methodically obliterated their work. After every defeat, he regrouped and redoubled his efforts, flinging more men, more money, and more material at the river. By the end of the year, his crew had grown to fifteen hundred laborers, recruited from all over the Southwest at top wages. He exhausted every rock quarry within four hundred miles and consumed every available piling in Southern California, forcing him to request that trains hauling lumber and piling from New Orleans be given special right-of-way.

Six work trains were now lumbering across the trestles night and day. A battleship was being dumped every five minutes. Boulders that were too big to be rolled off quickly were dynamited inside the battleships and their pieces kicked into the current. Finally, on February 10, the largest dam was completed and, unlike the six that had preceded it, resisted the efforts of the river to wash it away. After an all-out campaign that had cost in excess of $3 million, the breach was finally plugged and the Colorado was forced to resume its course through the delta to the Sea of Cortés.

The flood was unlike anything that had been seen in the Southwest. When it was over, the northern portion of the valley was underwater. The Salton Sea, which stretched for more than five hundred square miles and was seventy-eight feet deep in the middle, was now the largest lake in California (a distinction it still holds, although it has shrunk by almost half). Most of the rest of the valley was marred by ruined fields, deep arroyos, washed-out railroad tracks, and partially destroyed towns. Four-fifths of Mexicali had simply disappeared.

~

To those who participated in the events of 1906 in the Imperial Valley, perhaps the only thing more astonishing than the havoc wrought by the flood was that the river had managed to unleash all that chaos by exploiting a gap in the riverbank no wider than the door of a barn. That single detail underscored perhaps the most salient feature of the Colorado, the kernel of truth that transcended everything else, which was that it was totally out of control. The river that had carved the Grand Canyon was basically an outlaw, a renegade that moved according to its own rules. Which imbued it, in the eyes of everyone, with a unique status.

True, the Colorado was decisively outranked and outgunned when it came to the mundane metrics by which rivers are conventionally measured—length and flow, volume and power, navigability and biological richness. By those yardsticks, the Colorado surely took a backseat to the Mississippi, the Columbia, the Missouri, the Hudson, and a dozen other waterways, each of which occupied a more important niche within the country's economy and had woven itself more deeply—and with far more poetry—into the nation's mythology. But when it came down to headstrong exuberance, the refusal to permit itself to be corralled into any scheme other than its own, and a willful insistence on asserting its autonomy, the Colorado was in a class by itself: the most *American* river on the continent. The canyons it had carved, the rapids it framed, the silt it carried, and the annual saturnalia of flooding in which it indulged rendered it the scourge of the Southwest.

Thanks to those attributes, the Colorado simultaneously thwarted and held the key to the development not only of the Imperial Valley, but also of the entire region. Which meant that it was only a matter of time before the country whose spirit the river embodied with such savage eloquence would turn to the task of breaking it. A job, as it happened, that a brand-new agency was keen to handle—a branch of the federal government, established under the Department of the Interior, whose mission would include opening vast areas of the West to agriculture through the construction of massive water projects. And like everything else that happened on the Colorado, this organization was directly, albeit somewhat distantly, connected to the one-armed Civil War Major.

In June of 1902, three months before Powell died at his summer home in Maine, Congress had created the Reclamation Service, and among the engineers who were transferred to this fledgling agency to help it get off the ground was Powell's nephew, Arthur Powell Davis. Not surprisingly, he had been immersed in the lore of his uncle's river since early childhood.

When Davis first started out, the Reclamation Service was small potatoes among the federal bureaus, concentrating mainly on building irrigation canals. But Davis, who was appointed Reclamation's chief engineer in 1903 and became the head of the organization in 1914, was determined to change all that—and the Colorado was the means by which he intended to realize his ambition.

As his star rose within the service, Davis began to advocate for something considerably more far-reaching than a project that would merely buffer floods and aid irrigation in the Imperial Valley. He championed hydropower—using falling water to crank dynamos and produce clean, reliable kilowatts that could be wholesaled to factories and towns. The process had already been pioneered in 1882 at a diminutive plant in the tiny town of Appleton, Wisconsin, and was later scaled up at Niagara Falls during the early 1890s. Now, Davis proposed hydropower as the rationale behind a series of dams on the Colorado that would not merely control the river and prevent flooding, but actually *harness* the river's energy and sell it.

It would take another decade for the political forces to properly align themselves, including dividing up the water rights among the seven states through which the river flowed and surveying it from top to bottom. But when everything came together during the final weeks of 1928, the groundwork had been laid for what probably qualifies as the greatest dam ever built.

~

To subdue a river such as the Colorado—not simply to whip it into submission for a season or two, but to break and yoke the thing by taming its rampages, vanquishing its moods, and converting its kinetics into energy that serves human beings—such a task is not only a colossal technical undertaking but, perhaps even more significant, a monumental act of audacity. The challenge requires more than merely superb competency and monstrous ambition; it also demands a level of hubris that was unimaginable to the world of Cárdenas, an undertaking that lay far beyond even the boldest dreams of the Renaissance and the ages of exploration and discovery that followed. It required the kind of ruthless, steely certainty that humans only began to touch for the first time, perhaps, in the late nineteenth and early twentieth centuries. This was the age of iron and steel—not only in terms of materials but also in the way the world was understood: a place whose laws were rigid and immutable, but also now capable of yielding to the even stronger forces of man's intellect and will.

The site where Davis proposed to build the structure that would aim to subdue the Colorado was located in a place so perfect, so ideally suited in every possible way, that it left dam experts half-convinced that God must have had a degree in civil engineering. At the point where the southern shard of Nevada stabs into the side of Arizona, many miles upstream from the diversion channels that lead to the Imperial Valley and roughly eighty miles downstream from the Grand Wash Cliffs, lay the last real gorge on the Colorado, a place called Black Canyon, where Lieutenant Joseph Ives had reached the "end of navigation."

The walls of Black Canyon were almost vertical and rose nearly fifteen hundred feet from the surface of the river, paltry by the standards of the great canyon that lay just upstream, but more than sufficient for the task at hand. The gap between those walls was relatively narrow—less than four hundred yards—and the bedrock that supported them lay less than forty feet beneath the bottom of the river. But the best feature of all was the stone itself. It sat directly upon a mixture of micaceous schists and pre-Cambrian granites that formed the core of the craton, the backbone of the tectonic plate that was the foundation for most of the contiguous United States. It was as immutable as the continent itself.

No one had ever before tried to stop a river this powerful, and the first challenge was to blast four massive tunnels through the sides of the canyon walls—which took eighteen months—and then force the river into them using the same trick that Harry Cory had employed during his fight to save the Imperial Valley twenty-six years earlier, except that dump trucks took the place of railway battleships. On the evening of November 12, 1932, a fleet of one hundred heavy trucks began jettisoning their loads at a rate of one every fifteen seconds. Fifteen hours later, the Colorado sluggishly turned into the smooth maws of the tunnels and began to snake around the section of bedrock where the dam could now be raised.

For the next two years, an army of five thousand men swarmed the bottom and sides of Black Canyon, toiling in temperatures that reached as high as 130 degrees in the summer. While high-scalers armed with crowbars and jackhammers dangled from ropes prying fresh rock from the canyon walls, laborers at the bottom of the chasm excavated the river channel until they reached the bedrock that would anchor the dam.* Then they started pouring concrete, which

---

*High-scalers hold a special place in the history of American dams. They were regarded as almost mythic figures within the construction community, and newsreels captured their daring moves as they swung in giant, sweeping arcs across the faces of the cliffs, using ropes slung from the canyon rims, dislodging loose pieces of rock with jackhammers, and placing sticks of dynamite. They received the highest wages of anyone on the payroll, compensation for the dangers to which their duties exposed them. They also tended to die in spectacular ways—usually by plunging hundreds of feet to the canyon floor. In Black Canyon, ninety-eight of them perished in this manner—sacrifices that are memorialized in the bronze statue of a high-scaler that now stands near the dam's concession facility, the High Scaler Café.

arrived in giant steel buckets that were lowered into the chasm on suspension cables. The pouring continued virtually nonstop: sixteen tons per minute, 220 cubic yards an hour, twenty-four hours a day, for twenty-one months, until a titanic wedge whose base was the thickness of two football fields had risen up between the sides of the canyon. Finally, on February 1, 1935, the edifice was complete, and a set of massive steel gates was lowered over the entrances to the diversion tunnels so that the river, blocked from its downstream course, began lapping at the bottom of the newly completed Hoover Dam.

Overstating the significance of Hoover is almost impossible, so thoroughly did the dam surpass—in the scale of its components, in the novelty of its construction, in the sheer audacity of its design—everything that had come before. It soared 726 feet and five inches above the bed of the river, double the height of any other dam on earth. Its spillways, intake towers, generators, and powerhouse were the largest of their kind. Lake Mead, the body of water behind the dam, would take years to fill and would become the largest man-made reservoir in the world, stretching 115 miles upriver and capable of holding more than twenty-six million acre-feet, enough water to flood the entire state of Connecticut to the eaves of a one-story house. As Michael Hiltzik points out in *Colossus*, one of the finest books on the dam, the weight of that impounded water would deform the surface of the earth along the reservoir and trigger a series of earthquakes that would topple chimneys and buckle roadbeds between Boulder City and Las Vegas well into the 1960s.

Those statistics were remarkable. But no less astonishing was the lack of any antecedent, model, or foundational paradigm for building such a thing as Hoover. Instead of tweaking or improving upon what came before, Reclamation's engineers, who represented some of the sharpest technological minds in the country, were forced to surmount obstacles by making wholesale leaps into the unknown. They ventured into unexplored subdistricts of complex geometry, and they pioneered daring new techniques such as trial-load analysis and crown-cantilever adjustments. Those forays were aided by the explosion in the disciplines of civil engineering, hydraulics, and fluid mechanics during the latter part of the nineteenth century and the early part of the twentieth. But resolving the problems on the ground, as opposed to on paper, also required a willingness to adopt bold and highly unorthodox ideas. The entire project was one giant experiment.

Perhaps the best example involved the challenges posed by the fact that concrete gives off chemical heat as it cures and hardens. This had previously limited the size of such structures because, if they were made from a continuous pour, they would fracture. So instead of building a seamless slab, the engineers designed the dam as a matrix of blocks, each roughly the size of a house, interlocked like Legos. In between those blocks, they ran a network of pipes carrying chilled water. Having thus turned the dam into a giant concrete refrigerator, in effect, they essentially cut the cooling time from 125 years to three. As with everything else at Hoover, this was accomplished without anyone's truly knowing that it would actually work.

Three generations later, viewed from the standpoint of the digital age, a structure such as Hoover can appear to suffer from a kind of vulgarity of size— a thing so enormous and monolithic as to seem preindustrial, almost primitive. Like fascist architecture, that soaring wall of concrete, for all its Art Deco adornments, can strike the postmodern eye as embarrassingly elephantine and childishly simplistic. Yet one only need page through the dam's elegant blueprints to realize that this is a machine that, in its own way, is as sophisticated as a Boeing 747—a marvel of engineering, of mathematics, of human thinking, of vision, and, yes, of art. For all these reasons, Hoover is regarded by many civil engineers as one of America's most impressive achievements. It may not be much of an overstatement to say that, along with splitting the atom and sending the *Voyager* spacecraft beyond the solar system, Hoover is the most remarkable thing this country has ever pulled off.

Unlike those other achievements, however, Hoover arose in the midst of an era of nationwide fear and collective self-doubt, the darkest period of the Great Depression, when factories were idle, corporations were going bankrupt, and millions of ordinary Americans had begun to doubt the future. The manner in which the dam rose up, like a cathedral of technology from the depths of Black Canyon during a moment when everything else was falling to pieces, did more than buoy the hopes of millions of the nation's citizens. The dam also seemed to offer demonstrable, concrete proof that the key to human progress lay with scientific savoir faire and technological know-how.

Perhaps no one captured this optimism better than J. B. Priestley, a prolific English novelist who traveled extensively throughout the Southwest during the 1930s (and who would later have some rather illuminating things to say about the Grand Canyon). "This is a first glimpse of what chemistry and mathematics and engineering and large-scale organization can accomplish," Priestley declared in an article in *Harper's Magazine*. "You might be tempted to call it a work of art; as if something that began with civil engineering ended somewhat in the neighborhood of Beethoven's Ninth Symphony."

～

Among its many other hallmarks, Hoover represented a watershed moment in the relationship between Americans and their landscape, especially their rivers. Inspired by the achievement at Black Canyon, the Bureau of Reclamation and its sister agency, the US Army Corps of Engineers, didn't wait for Hoover to be finished before setting off on an ambitious crusade to erect dams across every major US river, from the Rio Grande, the Snake, the Missouri, and the Arkansas to the Sacramento, the Hudson, the Mississippi, the Tennessee, and the Ohio. The aim of that crusade—embodied in the bureau's motto: "Our Rivers: Total Use for Greater Wealth"—was to harness and exploit virtually every drop of free-flowing water in the country.

If that sounds a bit far-fetched, one need only consider the superlatives that attached themselves to the dam-building projects on which the federal government embarked during this era. By 1936, five of the largest structures on the planet, all of them dams, were simultaneously under construction along the rivers of the western United States: Hoover on the Colorado, Shasta on the Sacramento, Bonneville and Grand Coulee on the Columbia, and Fort Peck on the Missouri. Moreover, each of these projects was surpassed in size and scope by its successor. As colossal as Hoover was, Shasta was quite a bit bigger, and both were dwarfed by Grand Coulee, whose mass outstripped that of Hoover and Shasta put together—the first man-made structure to exceed the volume of the Great Pyramid of Cheops.

When Hoover was finished, it was the greatest single source of electricity in the world. But several months later, when Grand Coulee went online, its power plant was capable of generating half as much electricity as the rest of the entire *country*. By the 1940s, Coulee's generators were powering factories that produced thousands of warplanes bound for the aircraft carriers that would turn the war in the Pacific in America's favor while simultaneously powering the top-secret Hanford installation in eastern Washington that produced the plutonium-239 that fueled the atomic bomb.

For the next thirty years, tens of thousands of dams—a few of them large and magnificent, but the vast majority unapologetically functional and devoid of any symphonic romance—were erected from one end of the country to the other. By 1980, when the National Park Service finally completed an inventory of all the rivers in the contiguous United States, more than seventy-five thousand dams had been erected on the country's three-thousand-plus waterways—roughly one dam for every forty-eight hours that had passed since the summer of 1540, when Cárdenas had first stumbled upon the Grand Canyon. As the author Bruce Barcott has pointed out in his provocative treatise on a dam in Belize, *The Last Flight of the Scarlet Macaw*, every major river in the United States had been dammed except for one, the Yellowstone. There were twenty-nine dams on the Mississippi, thirty-six on the Columbia, forty-two on the Tennessee.

In the end, however, nothing compares to what we did to the Colorado.

~

From the moment the gates to Hoover's diversion tunnels were slammed shut in the winter of 1935 and water began rising along the upstream face of the dam, the days of the lower Colorado's uncontrolled rages were numbered. There would be no more mad dashes into the Salton Sink, no more jumping whimsically from one channel to the next across the desert. Nor would the power of the river—the energy contained inside its gradient—be permitted to go to waste. It would now be converted to electricity that would help drive the vast industrial expansion that was about to take place in the shipyards, aircraft factories, and light-metal refineries of Southern California.

But if this marked the end of the Colorado's unbounded freedom, as far as the government's water engineers were concerned, it was only the first in a series of problems that had to be solved. The completion of Hoover was a monumental achievement, but it brought only the lower section of the Colorado under control. The work of harnessing the rest of the river had just begun.

In March of 1946, the Interior Department published a massive report that contained a blueprint for the development of the entire Colorado. It was the fruit of decades of painstaking survey work, geologic mapmaking, sheer-strength analysis of rock samples, plus a dozen other forms of sniffing, testing, and prodding. Nicknamed the Blue Book, the tome contained 293 pages, weighed more than four pounds, and put forth a mission statement that was neatly encapsulated by the tagline on the title page: "A Natural Menace Becomes a Natural Resource." Inside, what was perhaps most revealing was the manner in which it was written. In language exhibiting both a stridency and a frankness that no government document would display today, the Colorado was portrayed as a criminal and a deadbeat that was running amok and obstructing the creation of wealth.

To correct these abuses, the Blue Book outlined 134 potential projects, one in virtually every major canyon and farming valley along the length of the river. The sheer numbers of dams, reservoirs, hydro plants, and irrigation projects slated for the river and its tributaries dwarfed anything planned for any other waterway of comparable size. The bureau was clear that not all of these schemes could be developed—doing so would exceed the Colorado's flow by 25 percent and send the river into "deficit." Instead, the purpose of the document was to provide its intended audience—the politicians who represented the interests of the mountain and desert states through which the Colorado coursed—with a menu of options, a kind of buffet table from which they could put together a plate of goodies for the constituents of every district the river touched. "Only a nation of free people have the vision to know that it can be done and that it must be done," the report declared. "Tomorrow the Colorado River will be utilized to the very last drop."

That last sentence was no mere catchphrase. Over the next two decades, thanks to a series of massive congressional appropriations bills, Reclamation would construct nineteen large dams and reservoirs along the Colorado and its tributaries between the Rockies and the Mexican border. This epic sequence of projects would complete the river's transformation from the wild and savage beast explored by Powell almost a century earlier into something that resembled a municipal waterworks system. It would make the Colorado the first major river in the world to come under almost total human control. Every cubic foot of its water was gauged and metered and accounted for. The timing and volume of each discharge through every set of penstocks and turbines was carefully calibrated to optimize the supply of electricity and maximize power revenue. Nothing happened on the river that had not been carefully planned, reviewed, and approved—and for good reason, because the Colorado was now the lifeblood of the entire Southwest, a resource on which a dozen cities and more than thirty million people were completely and totally dependent.

By the 1970s, no river in the Western Hemisphere was more rigorously controlled, more stringently regulated, or more ruthlessly overused than the Colorado. No river in the world was the subject of fiercer litigation and dispute. And none was exploited so thoroughly that, according to calculations run by hydrologists at the bureau, every drop was used and reused seventeen times before reaching the sea—a claim that achieved a rather surreal dimension of impressiveness (or absurdity, depending on one's point of view) since, in all but the wettest years, the final remnants of the river dried up in the desert south of the border before a single drop ever reached the Sea of Cortés.

In the exertion of human control over one of the wildest and most ungovernable forces in nature, no river had more seminal importance than the Colorado. As the author Marc Reisner explains in *Cadillac Desert*, his groundbreaking study of water policy in the West, civil engineers not only built the first great dam here but also learned the lessons that would enable them to control the greatest rivers in North America while giving others the tools to harness massive rivers all over the world, from the Volga, the Niger, and the Indus to the Zambezi, the Paraná, and the Yangtze. During the 1970s and 1980s, this dam-building boom spread to virtually every major river on the planet. By the year 2000, the amount of water that was stored behind the giant dams on earth was between three and six times more than existed in all the world's rivers—a redistribution of the planet's supply of freshwater significant enough, according to the water expert Peter Gleick, to account for "a small but measurable change in the wobble of the earth as it spins."

Yet this is only half the story of the Colorado's significance. Because although the era of the great dams was inaugurated and later reached a kind of engineering apotheosis on this river, the Colorado is also where the flood tide finally smashed up against something that refused to yield and ultimately broke the wave.

What no one realized at the time was that the demise of the greatest era of dam-building in human civilization had actually been seeded into the blueprint that was drawn up for the Colorado—and the stage upon which both acts would play out was nothing less than the Grand Canyon itself. What had begun at the bottom of the canyon with a stupendous dam that symbolized a future without limits was fated to conclude at the opposite end of the same chasm with yet another dam—one that would eventually come to stand, in the minds of many, as a kind of anti-symbol to everything that Hoover represented: a titanic monument to human overreach.

The fight to preserve the cathedral of stone between those points was what turned the wheel. The people who waged that war would establish a direct line between the end of the dam-building era in the late 1960s, a full century after Powell's voyage, and the great runoff of 1983, when a reckoning finally descended upon the canyon, and the river conclusively demonstrated that man wasn't in charge to the extent he believed. And at the very center of that story— the narrative that brought the age of great dams to a close—stood a barnstorming World War II pilot and a devotee of the dance that unfolds between wooden boats and white water.

His name was Martin Litton.

Flooding the Cathedral

Something will have gone out of us as a people if we ever let the remaining wilderness be destroyed. . . . We need wilderness preserved—as much of it as is still left, and as many kinds—because it was the challenge against which our character as a people was formed.

—Wallace Stegner

WHEN Martin Litton was born in February 1917, Pancho Villa was being pursued on horseback through northern Mexico, and the last grizzly bear in California would not be shot for another five years. That same month, the very first jazz record had just been produced, and patent offices were reviewing applications for a new-fangled clothing fastener with interlocking teeth known as the zipper. In keeping with the spirit of the times, the bucolic little town of Gardena, which lay on the outskirts of the soon-to-be expanding city of Los Angeles, seemed poised on an ambivalent threshold between a past that had yet to fully recede and a future that had not quite arrived.

Litton's father, a migrant from Tennessee who had moved West just after the turn of the century seeking work on the farms of the Imperial Valley, was now setting himself up as a veterinarian who specialized in doctoring farm animals but also found lucrative work treating the chimpanzees and lions that were serving as extras in a new series of *Tarzan* films. He purchased a small house on a slight rise overlooking the Santa Fe railroad tracks, and almost every night in the summer, he and his wife would gather their four children in the backyard to sit on apple crates and watch the sunset. This innocuous thing, staring into the darkening sky awaiting the arrival of night, left a powerful impression on their oldest boy, who marveled not only at the choreography of light but also that such beauty was freely available to anyone who took the trouble to step outdoors and plant his backside on an apple crate.

The principle of nature's accessibility and openness extended to embrace most of California, whose splendors rendered it one of the fairest places on the planet. In the 1920s, much of the state's primal glory was still intact—and oddly enough, the impulse that drove Litton to go out and explore those wonders originated with John Wesley Powell, whom he first encountered at school, in his typing class. When Litton was instructed to transcribe several pages of the Major's report, he found himself pecking out sentences that, many decades later, he would effortlessly recite at the drop of a hat:

> *We are now ready to start on our way down the great unknown. . . .*
> *. . . The great river shrinks into insignificance as it dashes its angry waves against the walls and cliffs that rise to the world above. . . .*
> *. . . We have but a month's rations remaining. . . .*
> *. . . The sugar has all melted and gone on its way down the river.*

Those images fired Litton's imagination and sent him out on a series of exploratory ventures to places such as the Pinnacles, a set of dramatic spires east of the Salinas Valley that would later become a national monument, and the Kern Plateau, a landscape that would one day form the heart of the Golden Trout Wilderness. When he and a friend rented a mule for seventy-five cents a day and headed off to climb Mount Whitney, they were gone for nearly two weeks. He returned from those adventures not only imbued with an abiding love of wilderness but also equipped with powerful arms and a massive chest that would enable him to join the eight-man varsity crew squadron at UCLA. There he rowed stroke until 1941, when he and the rest of his generation found themselves swept into the whirlwind of the Second World War.

He enrolled in the Army Air Corps shortly before Pearl Harbor with hopes of becoming a fighter pilot, an ambition that was swiftly derailed when his vision tests revealed that he was color-blind. Booted out of flight school, he refused to accept the results and concocted a bold scheme to get himself assigned to the only other outfit where he might still be permitted to fly.

The spearhead to virtually every major Allied airborne operation in Europe involved the US Glider Corps, a fleet of crude, motorless gliders that were crammed full of troops and equipment, everything from jeeps and small tanks to ammunition and medical supplies. Known as flying coffins, these fragile transport machines were strung behind an armada of tow planes, and their pilots were forced to make a low and fast descent directly into the combat zones. The gliders, which were fashioned from steel tubing and covered with strips of canvas, had no weaponry and no armor plating to protect against enemy fire—and the men who flew these machines were equally devoid of frills. Unable to take evasive action, they were consigned instead to playing the role of clay pigeons as they drifted through a withering hail of antiaircraft and 20mm machine-gun fire. Those who survived this ordeal then confronted the challenge of making their way through the German lines, back to the coast, and across the Channel to England, where they would be handed another mission and made to go through the exercise all over again.

The pilots, who were either selected or volunteered for these barnstorming assignments, were highly unusual—"the most uninhibited individualists in the army," in the words of one historian. Deciding that he fit the Glider Corps to a tee, Litton and a friend conspired to sneak into the hospital at his air base and steal a copy of the test booklet for the color-blindness exam. After petitioning to retake the test, he passed, was granted a special waiver, and before long was merrily practicing Cuban Eights, Immelmann turns, and the rest of the aerial combat maneuvers that were part of a glider pilot's repertoire.

He arrived in England in May of 1944, and a month later found himself delivering troopers into northern France during the invasion of Normandy. Three months after that, when the Allies put together an airborne mission known as Market Garden to free the port of Antwerp and set the British up to smash a hole through German defenses in the Netherlands, he led a formation of gliders into Holland, then made his way back to the Channel from sixty-five miles behind enemy lines, for which he was awarded an Air Medal.

Later that winter, he volunteered, along with roughly a hundred other pilots, to fly ammunition, gasoline, medical supplies, and a team of nurses and combat surgeons into Belgium to relieve members of the 101st Airborne Division, which had borne the brunt of a German counterattack in the heavily forested Ardennes and was now completely surrounded in the village of Bastogne. To enable the defenders of Bastogne to hold out until General George S. Patton's tanks could break through the German encirclement, the Allied high command flung several waves of gliders through a curtain of massed antiaircraft and small-arms fire on the day before Christmas.

Casualties were extremely high, almost 35 percent in the first wave. Although Litton was not in that vanguard, his formation suffered heavy losses—the sky seemed to be filled with flaming transport planes as he made his approach, and he watched several tugs in front of him get blown to pieces. Nevertheless, he managed to land and deliver his supplies within the Bastogne perimeter. When Patton's tanks broke through a few hours later, the 101st justifiably received front-page coverage from London to San Francisco, but the newspapers were largely silent about the glider pilots. To this day, their achievement remains one of the more obscure and unheralded feats of the war.

~

Upon returning home, Litton took a position as a "roadman" in the circulation department of the *Los Angeles Times*, which required him to travel all over the state, managing sales accounts with the paper's dealers. The job enabled him to return to many of the places he had visited as a boy, and what he saw left him dismayed by what was being done to California's scenic wonders as the nation entered a period of postwar expansion and prosperity. All around the state, it seemed, remaining pockets of wilderness were under siege. In Tuolumne County, he saw that an entire forest of majestic sugar pines was being logged. From the Sierra foothills to the northern coast, he noticed new roads and highways being pushed into the last stretches of virgin sequoia and redwood trees. To Litton, it was evident that Californians were destroying their birthright without understanding the value of what they had been given or how, like the medieval cities of Germany that had been firebombed during the war, the original splendor could never be restored once it was gone.

Incensed, he purchased a typewriter and began banging out articles for the *Times* on a long list of subjects that upset him. He criticized a plan to flood the Tehipite Valley, an enclave of unprotected land in the Sierras almost completely surrounded by Kings Canyon National Park. He put together an exposé about how overcrowded Yosemite had become. Another piece took Californians to task for flinging trash all over the state's highways—a story that provoked snickers in the newsroom and earned him the nickname Mr. Litterbug.

None of this may sound especially radical now, but at the time, almost no one was talking about such things. Conservation had yet to develop as a powerful political force, and the word *environmentalism* had not even been coined. But what made Litton's ideas even stranger—and so at odds with prevailing sentiment—was the depth of his rage. Without quite realizing it, he was emerging as a ferocious and rather prescient expositor of a white-hot, no-surrender brand of environmental purism: the unyielding, unapologetic (and, his critics would later charge, unreasonable) defense of wilderness. "People often tell me not to be extreme," he would repeatedly declare. " 'Be reasonable!' they say. But I've never felt it did any good to be reasonable about anything in conservation, because what you give away will never come back—ever. When it comes to saving wilderness, we cannot be extreme *enough*."

In short, he had no compunction about being nasty, and he didn't particularly care whom he might offend. No part of California was too small or too obscure to arouse his ire, and as his anger amplified, so too did the scope of his interests. The event that did more than anything else to trigger this expansion occurred in 1953, when his attention was pulled far beyond the borders of California to a remote corner of northeastern Utah. What was taking place there was about to connect Litton to the river of John Wesley Powell, eventually drawing him into the Grand Canyon itself.

～

Shortly after emerging from the Canyon of Lodore, near the northeastern corner of Utah, the Green River enters a charmed little pocket where flooded meadows and thick groves of cottonwood and box elders are framed by smooth ramparts of white sandstone. In June 1869, this place had offered a much-needed respite to Powell and his battered crew after the hapless Billy Hawkins had set fire to their camp and pitched most of their mess kit into the river. Because the surrounding area, which was known as Echo Park, had been declared a national monument in 1938, the place was almost as pristine in Litton's day as it had been in Powell's. Unfortunately, however, Dinosaur National Monument lacked adequate funding for proper surveillance (the budget was so tiny that the handful of rangers didn't even have money to purchase a raft to conduct river patrols). As a result, no one had taken much notice when a team from the Bureau of Reclamation showed up just before World War II with transits, drills, and maps, looking for dam sites that could be included in the Blue Book, the bureau's catalog of prospective hydro projects along the Colorado and its major tributaries.

After three years of survey work and geologic testing, the members of the team were pleased to report that they had located not one site, but two. The reservoirs of these dams would flood the heart of the monument to depths as great as five hundred feet, and it was of no concern to the Bureau of Reclamation or its allies in Congress that the law required this area to be preserved in a manner that would leave it "unimpaired for the enjoyment of future generations." In 1949, when Reclamation formally unveiled a massive water-development package calling for the construction of six major dams and twelve irrigation projects in the upper Colorado River basin, the most prominent part of the package included the pair of dams in the center of Dinosaur.

At the time, Litton knew almost nothing about the Colorado—its peculiar blend of violence and grace, or the otherworldly beauty that lay beneath the rims of the canyons that the river had carved. But having spent three years fighting the Nazis in Europe, he was viscerally offended by the possibility that a lawfully protected wilderness area could be trampled at will by politicians and developers. So he began plastering stories all over the pages of the *L.A. Times*, accusing Reclamation of "a dictatorial plan for a gigantic boondoggle." Among the readers who took note of those diatribes was an amateur butterfly collector and former rock-climbing bum from Berkeley named David Brower, who had just been appointed executive director of a conservation group known as the Sierra Club.

When Brower telephoned Litton to ask if he might be interested in joining the Sierra Club, Litton was amused. As far as he could see, the club was little more than a group of weekend hikers who were primarily interested in socializing and planning picnics. But at Brower's urging Litton enrolled and started attending gatherings, where he distinguished himself by lighting up cigars and disdainfully blowing smoke at those sitting around the table. He was disputatious and irreverent, and his presence was often resented. But gradually he and Brower formed an odd partnership.

In Litton, Brower found someone who possessed detailed knowledge about the wild places of California that needed protection, especially where the greatest stands of redwoods and sequoias and the most pristine pockets of coastline were located. Brower also valued Litton for his toughness, his refusal to compromise with corporate or government interests, and his willingness to needle Brower about the perils of compromise in matters of conservation. In turn, Litton saw that Brower commanded skills that he himself lacked—in organization, in leadership, in diplomacy. Litton also thought he saw a man who was beginning to show a willingness to take on powerful forces, an impression that was confirmed when Brower decided to take up the defense of Echo Park, a place he had never been, on a river he knew virtually nothing about, as a personal crusade.

As it turned out, that crusade would change the trajectory of Litton's life and reshape the destiny of the Grand Canyon.

~

To battle against the Echo Park dams, the Sierra Club and a coalition of some seventeen other conservation groups pooled their resources and launched a publicity drive designed to build public opposition. The decisive part of the fight took place in Washington, DC, at a venue that was normally the last place one would expect to find high drama: an offshoot of the House of Representatives' Committee on Interior and Insular Affairs known as the Subcommittee on Irrigation and Reclamation. This was where the nuts and bolts of the project would be hammered out and debated, and a portion of the testimony would be duly allotted for the opposition, a group that Utah senator Arthur Watkins dubbed "the abominable nature-lovers."

Though Brower was a rookie lobbyist, having never before appeared in front of a congressional committee, he aggressively attacked the data that Reclamation had used to justify the Echo Park dams, arguing that there were several preferable alternative spots to build dams whose reservoirs would not invade Dinosaur. In particular, he pointed to a site on the Colorado River some 450 miles downstream from Echo Park, where the same volume of water could be stored with significantly less loss to evaporation. In driving this point home, Brower used a blackboard and a piece of chalk to demonstrate that the government's engineers had committed a fundamental math error by neglecting to subtract the Echo Park reservoirs' evaporative loss from that of the downstream alternative. He concluded his presentation by declaring that it would be folly for members of the subcommittee to rely on the claims of an organization whose employees "cannot add, subtract, multiply, and divide."

It is difficult to overstate just how extraordinary this kind of criticism was. Since the 1930s, Reclamation's administrators and engineers had been lauded as heroes who had helped the country weather the Great Depression and win the war that followed. But when Brower's assertions were proved more or less valid, they punctured the myth of Reclamation's infallibility in matters of hydrology and the science of dams. The testimony had a devastating effect—especially when combined with the negative publicity generated by the conservationists' media campaign—and by the autumn of 1955, several of the dams' leading proponents were starting to reconsider their support for the Dinosaur dams.

Among those who took particular note of the mounting negative publicity was Wayne Aspinall, a congressman from Colorado who wielded enormous power over the development of the country's natural resources. When 4,731 letters flooded the subcommittee following the hearings, only 53 of which expressed anything remotely approaching support for the Dinosaur dams, Aspinall concluded that an all-out fight to defend those dams might result in the entire package going down in flames. Deciding to compromise—an art at which Aspinall excelled—he brokered a deal with Brower and his cohorts. In exchange for the conservationists' assurance that they would not object to any other projects in the package, the Dinosaur dams were struck from the plan.

For Brower and his colleagues, this victory marked a seminal moment in the politics of conservation. For the first time ever, a powerful coalition of federal bureaucrats and their allies had been bested by a band of "punks," as one cabinet official had derisively dubbed the conservationists. But while all of this seemed to offer ample cause for celebration, the victory had come at a steep price.

At the center of the compromise to which Brower agreed was a dam that was slated to be built on the Colorado River some fifteen miles upstream from the Grand Canyon. This would be far larger than either of the two proposed structures inside Dinosaur—indeed, it would be the biggest and most important feature of the package, second on the Colorado only to Hoover itself. Even though Litton and a handful of others had urged Brower to reject Aspinall's compromise, Brower's reasoning was not without merit. The dam's reservoir would inundate a little-known river corridor called Glen Canyon, which was not part of any park or monument. Whatever wonders that obscure canyon might contain, it had never received federal protection of any kind—and that, after everything was said and done, was what the Dinosaur fight had been about.

Nevertheless, by agreeing to the compromise, Brower had, in effect, traded away something he had never seen on the assumption that it could not possibly match the value of what he was trying to save. This, as he was about to discover, was a terrible mistake.

~

The Glen Canyon Dam was authorized almost immediately, and its construction kicked off in the fall of 1956 with an unusual piece of theater. During the second week of October, a pair of high-scalers were lowered on ropes from the rim of the canyon almost down to the level of the river. Dangling from bosun's chairs, the men wedged a pigtailed string of dynamite into a crack that ran behind a house-size rock positioned directly above the place where the first of two diversion tunnels would be drilled. When the explosives were set in place, they were tied to a long line of primer cord that was run back up the face of the cliff and connected to a plunger on the rim.

At precisely 11:30 on the morning of October 15, President Eisenhower tapped a telegraph key from his desk in the Oval Office, sending an electronic signal from Washington, DC, to Arizona, where the message was relayed first by radio, then by a flagman, to Arthur Watkins, the Utah senator who had made the remark about "the abominable nature-lovers" two years earlier. When Watkins rammed the plunger down, a massive explosion shook the bottom of the canyon. Boulders arced into the air, followed by a cloud of dust and grit that rose toward the rim. Within minutes, crews were drilling into the cliff at the portal to the diversion tunnel, which would route the river around the dam site during construction.

The massive dam that began to rise from the dry section of riverbed at the bottom of the canyon the following spring was in many ways a mirror of and a companion piece to Hoover—but it was not a revolutionary structure. Unlike Hoover, Glen's technology was already well established. Even its status as the third-highest dam in the world would last only a few months, until the Swiss finished a pair of even higher dams. Nevertheless, Glen possessed enormous symbolic significance because it signaled a remarkable act of transformation for the feature that lay at its feet, the Grand Canyon.

The canyon of Cárdenas, a place that was defined by its capacity to dwarf human endeavor, to instill humility in those who gazed into its depths and found themselves staring eternity in the face, would now be hog-tied between two of the largest and most impressive machines that had ever been built by human beings. They would frame it like a matched set of immense concrete bookends, and the water that coursed through the canyon's heart would be controlled by a spigot and a set of tap handles above, while the discharge was collected by an immense bathtub below. The river of John Wesley Powell might still feel wild and dangerous and free, but every ripple and wave of that river would now be metered and gauged and rationed by bureaucrats and engineers.

At this point, however, Brower was far less concerned about the symbolic neutering of the canyon below the dam than about the real loss of the canyon *above* it. Because in the summer of 1962, while construction was still taking place but the river had not yet been dammed, Brower had set out on a series of river trips that granted him his first look at the mysterious place that had been traded away for Echo Park.

He was shocked by what he found.

～

If the Grand Canyon is geology's Götterdämmerung, a thunderous "Twilight of the Gods" composed in stone, then Glen was a tectonic version of the *Moonlight Sonata*—a canyon that was neither imperious nor magisterial, but lyrically finessed, elegantly sculpted, and ethereal. Unlike the Grand, Glen was defined neither by the violence of its white water nor by the grandiosity of its rock formations, but instead by gentleness and tranquillity. Here, the river and its tributaries had carved a trellis of intimate side canyons, many of them so narrow that they were bathed in shadow-cooled twilight at noon. Deep inside this sinuous and hidden world were countless springs and vaulted grottoes, where thin cascades of clear water dropped into pools surrounded by maidenhair fern. This exquisite labyrinth was what Powell had discovered as his boats drifted languorously through Glen's curves and goosenecks during the final days of July 1869, just prior to their grueling "race for a dinner" through the Grand Canyon. And those same qualities—the honey-colored light, the polished walls, the vivid green cottonwood leaves fluttering softly in the morning air—seduced and saddened Brower when he floated through this haunted landscape during its twilight months in the golden summer of 1962.

As he recognized with a growing sense of remorse, Glen was much like Echo Park, only better in every way. The splendor of what had been sacrificed far surpassed the charms of what had been saved upstream. Within Glen's side canyons alone, Brower would later declare, the place boasted "the equivalent of several Dinosaur National Monuments."

By the end of 1962, even as a team of workers prepared to start the process of filling Glen's reservoir, Brower had resolved to make a last-ditch effort to stop the process that he had unwittingly sanctioned by petitioning the one person who had the power to apply the brakes. On the morning of January 21, 1963, he flew to Washington to see Interior Secretary Stewart Udall, the man whose job it was to reconcile and balance the competing interests of the National Park Service and the Bureau of Reclamation.

Upon arriving at Interior's headquarters on C Street, Brower was informed that Udall had a packed schedule and would be unable to meet with him personally. However, the secretary was about to conduct an important press conference in which he and the commissioner of the Bureau of Reclamation would make an important announcement regarding the Colorado River. If Brower wished, he was told, he was welcome to attend. And it was in this manner that he came to learn that the government was planning to flood yet another canyon and national park, perhaps the greatest of them all.

~

That morning Udall unveiled a plan intended to complete and, in some ways, surpass the vision for the Colorado River that Reclamation's engineers had been shaping and refining since the days of Arthur Powell Davis, more than sixty years earlier. Having already erected the cornerstone of their great scheme at Hoover, and having recently completed a whole smorgasbord of dams, power plants, and irrigation projects along the upper Colorado, the bureau had all but one remaining section of the river under its control.

Among dozens of marvelous things, the plan that Udall outlined would create a whole *new* set of dams, tunnels, and canals in Northern California that would deliver water south, to the residents of Los Angeles and the farmers of the San Joaquin Valley, replacing water that was currently being supplied to those areas from the Colorado. In turn, that Colorado water would be shunted east, through yet another system of pumps and canals, to the rapidly growing cities of Phoenix and Tucson. The only catch was that delivering this water would require enormous amounts of energy. But this, Udall explained, was the most elegant part of the whole scheme, because that energy would come from electricity generated by the deepest canyons and the steepest gradient on the

Colorado, thanks to a pair of giant new dams that would be built directly in the heart of the Grand Canyon.

These two additional dams would not only produce enough electricity to pump water to Phoenix and Tucson but would create a surplus that could be sold to private utilities, thereby generating income that would eventually reimburse the government for its investment in the entire system. The project would essentially pay for itself, which is why the Grand Canyon dams—known as Bridge Canyon Dam and Marble Canyon Dam—were dubbed "cash registers."

As Udall sketched out these details, he could see Brower scowling in the back of the room. He knew that the conservationist was angry, but what he did not know was that this announcement was an epiphany for the executive director of the Sierra Club—a moment that neatly bridged the chasm that yawned between the hopes with which Brower had come to Udall's office that morning and his sense of betrayal at what the secretary was revealing. The lesson that Brower decided he had been taught by Glen Canyon, something that Litton had repeatedly stressed, was that compromise was a vile and dangerous thing, an arrangement that destroyed a man's principles while rendering him powerless.

If further proof of that conceit was needed, it was unfolding at that very moment at the head of the Grand Canyon, where the job of closing off Glen's diversion tunnels was already in full swing. Earlier that morning, a crew of laborers had finished chipping winter ice out of the vertical tracks on a pair of guillotine-shaped gates that were poised above the entrance to the tunnels. When they sent the steel gates slicing into the frigid, sugary-brown current coursing into the tunnels, the water purled and eddied as the river, robbed of any other path, made its way over an earthen barrier and slowly began to claw its way up the ten-million-ton edifice of the newly finished dam. The sound of a living river had been replaced by the silence of a reservoir.

It would take almost twenty years for that reservoir to fill to capacity. But Lake Powell, named in honor of the one-armed Civil War major who had braved the once-unstoppable river, had been born.

In that moment, perhaps the only thing that surpassed Brower's sense of contrition was his resolve. Having had the perils of compromise drummed into him so painfully, he would take the lesson to heart. Now there would be another battle—one far bigger and with far greater stakes than had already been fought over Dinosaur. That struggle would be waged without negotiation or horse-trading, and the principle that would remain inviolable—subject neither to debate nor qualification—was that the Grand Canyon, the foremost of America's natural wonders, should be left alone.

Before Brower could embark on his campaign, however, he faced the intensely irritating task of having to persuade his colleagues at the Sierra Club to give him the green light. This would not be easy. The club's old guard, the men who had helped nurture and sustain the organization through the first half of the twentieth century and now sat on the board of directors, valued decorum and dialogue. Many of those directors were on good terms with the government officials and bureaucrats who controlled the nation's wild spaces, and they placed a premium on behaving honorably and refraining from personal attacks. The club's purpose, as they saw it, was not to stand in the way of development but to argue, in a friendly and reasonable manner, for compromises that would enable progress to unfold while preserving places that were special.

One of the most powerful proponents of this approach was Bestor Robinson, a prominent lawyer from Oakland who had extensive business and social connections at almost every level of government. Robinson specialized in crafting evenhanded deals that were advantageous to everyone, and he was convinced that it was unwise to declare war against Stewart Udall and the entire Interior Department. The rational course, therefore, was to negotiate.

Brower knew that if he wanted to defeat the entire Grand Canyon dams project, he was first going to have to defeat Robinson at the club's annual board meeting, which was scheduled to take place in May 1963. The outcome of that debate would determine whether Brower would be given license to deploy the club's considerable resources in an all-out fight against both dams. And for assistance, Brower decided to turn to one of the few people who could be even more stubborn and irascible than he was.

In some ways, this was a dangerous gambit. The board was well aware that Martin Litton embodied some of the very worst qualities of the Colorado River. He was willful and tempestuous, ungovernable and, at times, downright mean. A force of nature that recognized no one's authority and tended to go tearing off in bizarre directions. Brower, however, understood that when Litton's energy was properly channeled, the weight of his influence could be enormous. He was also aware that Litton held an important trump card—because, unlike anyone else in the Sierra Club, he not only knew the Grand Canyon firsthand but had also developed a philosophy about the place that hinged on the allure of wooden boats.

~

During the fifteen years following his first encounter with John Wesley Powell's journals in his high school typing class, Litton had made contact with the rim of the canyon on only three occasions. He saw the place briefly for the first time on a road trip in 1938, then got a slightly longer look a few years later when he and his wife, Esther, had spent the first night of their honeymoon at El Tovar, the main hotel on the South Rim. Following those two visits, Litton had also made a trip to Toroweap, a remote overlook on the North Rim, to write a story for the *L.A. Times*. But it wasn't until 1955, the year that the Echo Park conflict was resolved, that he was given his first opportunity to actually run the river at the bottom of the canyon.

He and Esther signed on with a boatman named P. T. Reilly, who had assembled a fleet of small rowboats. Two had been hand-built by Reilly, while the third, an odd duck called the *Gem*, was a hybridized version of a white-water boat that had evolved on a river almost nine hundred miles to the north, in Oregon—a type of craft with which Litton would later develop a lasting connection. From the moment they pushed off, Litton found himself bewitched by the unique world of water and stone. Every mile or so, the walls opened and gave way to yet another side canyon filled with secret springs and waterfalls. The air was alive with pink-and-lavender dragonflies that paused, twitchingly, on the shafts of their suspended oars. In the mornings, the trilling notes of the canyon wren, the sweetest song of the river, dribbled down the walls. As they worked the boats beneath laced canopies of maidenhair fern that clung to the rock where the springs jutted out, they paused in secret, nameless grottoes where they marveled at the shades of the water and the textures of the surrounding cliffs. Like tiny particles of sediment, the impressions of this world worked their way into the bedrock of Litton's sensibility: the color of the river when it was rinsed in morning light, the little tendrils of perfume that ascended from a brittlebush flower just before the rain arrived, the quiet music a boat hull made when moored inside an eddy at night.

In many ways, this was very much *not* the canyon of John Wesley Powell. There were dangers and complications, to be sure, but Litton's predominant impression was that this was not a place where nature was an implacable enemy to be battled, but instead something to be enjoyed and savored. Moreover, the beauty of the river world and the sense of wonder it evoked set up a powerful contrast with the prevailing message of the rocks. The place seemed to transmit a shattering reminder of the insignificance and irrelevancy of human affairs when set against the twin pools of deep time and geologic indifference. At the same time, Litton found himself undergoing a rebirth of the kind of delight that only children truly possess. The juxtaposition left him enlightened and enriched—a feeling he later summarized as a "major order of experience."

He was so impressed that he returned the very next summer and did the whole thing all over again, which only deepened the connection. He would probably have kept coming back had he not found himself beset by the pressures of making a living (by now he had left the *Times* and taken a demanding job as the travel editor at *Sunset* magazine). But then something unusual happened, because, in the summer of 1961, he found himself in Oregon, covering the McKenzie River White Water Boat Parade for *Sunset*—and there he encountered his first true white-water dory.

The dories on the McKenzie, which were locally known as drift boats, were reminiscent of the *Gem*, the unusual little craft that had taken part in Litton's first run through the canyon. Unlike the *Gem*, however, these boats were the real thing: double-ended cockleshells with open decks and a sharp upward rake on their pointed bows and sterns. They had been specially engineered for the fast, shallow, highly technical white water of the McKenzie, and Litton was smitten by their beauty. But he also saw something intriguing: the possibility that, with some modification, they might stand up to the giant hydraulics of the Colorado.

Upon returning to California, he telephoned Reilly and suggested that they each purchase one of these boats and take them on a test-drive through the canyon. When Reilly agreed, Litton placed an order with a boatwright named Keith Steele, who lived in the little town of Leaburg, Oregon. The following June, Litton and Reilly hauled the boats down to Lee's Ferry and shoved them into the Colorado.

When the trip was over, Reilly pronounced his dory the finest thing he'd ever rowed. Litton, however, went even further. Something about those boats—their elegance and symmetry and balance—seemed to dovetail exquisitely with the canyon itself. In Litton's mind, the dories and the river fit together in a way that was difficult to articulate but impossible to ignore, perhaps because each seemed to frame and perfect the other. The river imbued the boats with context and purpose, while calling forth their dexterity and grace. In turn, the dories provided a visual metaphor that distilled the essence of the canyon: its seductiveness, its vulnerability, its aura of timelessness and classicism. The connection was no less real for being subtle, and it was sufficiently compelling that, as far as Litton was concerned, each was somehow incomplete without the other.

By now, Litton's response to the entire canyon—what he saw in the place, what he valued, what he knew of the truths that were embedded in its heart—had become inextricably entwined with the boats. And thanks to the manner in which the dories had crystallized those sensibilities, he found himself in a singular position when Brower telephoned him in the spring of 1963 and explained that the Sierra Club's directors were preparing to grapple with the Grand Canyon dams question. Not only did Litton understand the river more intimately than anyone else in the organization, but he was also able to speak about the place with unique authority and persuasiveness. So when Brower asked if Litton would consider giving a presentation on why the club should fight against the dams with everything it had, he immediately said yes.

~

The meeting convened at 10:14 a.m. on May 4, 1963, in the main conference room at the Jack London Hotel in downtown Oakland. Robinson opened the debate, and the case he presented was compelling.

He pointed out, correctly, that the new dams would not actually "flood" the entire canyon by filling it up to the rims; they would merely inundate several hundred feet of an abyss that was more than a mile deep. In fact, neither reservoir would be visible from any of the hotels or the popular lookout points where most tourists gathered. The club's smartest move, Robinson argued, was agreeing not to oppose the dams in exchange for extracting some concessions in how recreation would be handled on the reservoirs. His proposal was that the club insist—adamantly—that a set of elevators be built to enable anglers on the South Rim to access the blue-ribbon trout fisheries that would thrive in the cold, clear water pouring from the tailraces at the bases of the two dams.

Brower had warned Litton that this might happen, but Robinson's proposal nevertheless sent him into a fit of rage. Before the meeting, he had gathered together some Magic Markers and drawn a map of the canyon on the side of a grocery box. Clutching his cardboard sketch, he rose from his chair, climbed onto the dais, and began to quote from a speech that Theodore Roosevelt had delivered from the South Rim on May 6, 1903:

> In the Grand Canyon, Arizona has a natural wonder which is in kind absolutely unparalleled throughout the rest of the world. I want to ask you to keep this great wonder of nature as it now is. I hope you will not have a building of any kind, not a summer cottage, a hotel or anything else, to mar the wonderful grandeur, the sublimity, the great loneliness and beauty of the canyon. Leave it as it is. You cannot improve on it. The ages have been at work on it, and man can only mar it.

Then Litton started laying into Robinson's arguments. Unfortunately, no one bothered to transcribe his words. But the gist of the stem-winder he uncorked is well remembered to this day.

He began by declaring that it didn't make a hoot of difference that the canyon might not look any different from the top if the dams were put in. The river was the essence of the place, its heart—the thing that had not only carved and shaped the rock but also sustained the unique and fragile ecosystem at the bottom. If the river were dammed, the spirit of that place would vanish, and what replaced it would be a poor substitute: a pair of stagnant reservoirs whose surfaces would endlessly and noisily be crisscrossed by powerboats and houseboats and water-skiers.

What this amounted to, Litton continued, was the annulment of a space whose value resided not in the fact that it was accessible, but rather in that it was isolated and untrammeled. Indeed, access to the masses was the very thing that would destroy what made the place so precious by canceling out those elements that the canyon now possessed in abundance—the silence, the solitude, and the fact that it was so implacably cut off from the rest of the world. Those qualities were as fragile as a little wooden boat, and as Roosevelt's words clearly implied, the willingness to nurture and protect such treasures amounted to a national test of character, as well as a covenant with future generations of Americans. A test that the Interior Department and the Bureau of Reclamation had demonstrably failed. Inside the canyon, Litton thundered, Interior and Reclamation are *interlopers*, and we don't have to surrender to their scheme because the place doesn't belong to them. It's *our* canyon. It's *our* national park.

As for the idea that the government was too big and powerful to confront head-on, Litton's contempt was scathing. Of course it will be an uphill battle, he said. Of course our resources are limited and our numbers are few. But in God's name, how can anyone in this room look themselves in the mirror if we don't resolve to go after this with everything we've got?

Historians often minimize or discount the impact that any one individual can have on human destiny—and for good reason. Given the broad tides in the affairs of men, and the complexity of the forces that shape and change history, it is almost always a mistake to ascribe too much significance to the actions of a single person. But even the most jaded observer can concede that, every now and then, a man or woman steps up to the plate and takes a mighty swing that clears the bases and fundamentally changes the game. In the Jack London Hotel that morning, this is what Litton achieved.

After an hour and a half of debate, it was moved that the club should oppose any further dams and diversions in the canyon. The motion carried.

Many years later, when asked how he had primed Litton for his presentation, Brower chuckled. "Martin doesn't have to prime for a speech," he replied. "Martin poured it on—what a ridiculous thing this would be to do—and the audience applauded, and Bestor subsided, and we voted 'no.'"

Later that afternoon, when the meeting had wrapped up, Litton was sitting out in the hotel's lobby having a drink with a friend when Robinson approached their table.

"Well now, just because we don't agree on everything doesn't mean we're not friends," Robinson said, extending his hand agreeably to Litton.

"Oh?" Litton retorted. "I wouldn't say that."

~

Later that summer, Litton submitted a strongly worded essay to the *Bulletin*, the Sierra Club's magazine, urging the organization's twenty-two thousand members to write directly to their political representatives to voice their opposition to the dams. This kicked off a media campaign that would continue through the fall and winter of 1963. Meanwhile, at Brower's urging, Litton commissioned another dory from Oregon, gathered his tiny fleet, and set off the following spring for the Grand Canyon with a writer and a pair of photographers on a special river mission.

As they left Lee's Ferry on April 26, they passed by a line of bright red fire hydrants that had just been installed for the marina that would service the boaters and water-skiers who would flock to the reservoir once Marble Canyon Dam, the first of the two new structures, was built. Thirty-nine miles downstream, they passed by a set of scaffolds that climbed several hundred feet up the cliffs on both sides of the canyon. Here, a series of test tunnels had been drilled to determine the quality of the rock where the dam would be anchored. Much farther downstream, the river took the boats beneath a steel cable that marked the spot where similar test bores had been drilled at the second site, for Bridge Canyon Dam. At each of these landmarks, and everywhere in between, the photographers shot rolls of film while the writer, a journalist named François Leydet, took careful notes.

When they reached the Grand Wash Cliffs, they had enough material to fill a coffee-table tome highlighting every feature inside the canyon that would be obliterated by the dams. It took six months to compile, with Brower writing the foreword and Litton doing most of the editing and contributing photos of his own. They called the book *Time and the River Flowing*, and it conveyed the same message that Litton had expressed in front of the board of directors eighteen months earlier. The Sierra Club fired off a copy to members of Congress and every news outlet they could think of.

That was only one arrow in Brower's quiver. While Litton pressed on with the media effort by helping to develop a traveling photo exhibit and a movie about the canyon, other members of Brower's task force set about pressing news organizations to cover the controversy. By the following winter and spring, articles opposed to dams had begun to appear in *Life*, *Newsweek*, and *Outdoor Life*, precipitating an avalanche of mail to members of Congress, Stewart Udall's office, and President Lyndon Johnson.

Bowing to mounting pressure, an exasperated Wayne Aspinall scheduled a renewal of hearings before the Interior Committee, which gave Brower his next opening. In a reprise of the Dinosaur strategy, he recruited experts who could expose the government's misuse of its own facts and brought those people to Washington. His trump card was a trio of young graduates from MIT—an economist, a nuclear engineer, and a mathematician named Jeff Ingram, who demonstrated how the payback plan that the bureau had devised for the new hydropower facilities was built around a numerical house of cards. Using the bureau's own figures, Ingram proved that the construction of Bridge and Marble Canyon Dams—whose hydropower sales were supposed to pay for the network of new canals and river-diversion schemes in central Arizona—would actually *reduce* the amount of revenue that would accrue to the government until the year 2021.

While testimony unfolded, Brower launched a third offensive. On the morning of June 9, 1966, he ran a set of expensive and highly inflammatory full-page advertisements in the *New York Times*, the *Washington Post*, the *San Francisco Chronicle*, and the *Los Angeles Times*. "Now Only You Can Save Grand Canyon from Being Flooded . . . For Profit," the headlines screamed in oversize type. Emphasizing that the canyon belonged to all Americans, the text of the ad closed with an admonition that echoed what Litton had told the board of the Sierra Club: "There is only one simple incredible issue here. This time, it's the Grand Canyon they want to flood. *The Grand Canyon*."

～

One of the people who took note of those ads with particular displeasure was a congenial lawyer and banker from Tucson named Morris Udall, who had taken over his older brother Stewart's seat in the House of Representatives when Stewart was appointed Interior secretary. Morris was so outraged by what he read in the paper that morning—which he regarded as a wildly irresponsible misrepresentation of the truth—that he stood up on the floor of the House and denounced Brower's entire ploy as "phony, irresponsible, utterly and completely false."

The following afternoon at 4:00 p.m., a messenger from the San Francisco district office of the IRS delivered a letter to the headquarters of the Sierra Club stating that it was now under investigation for violating IRS regulations concerning lobbying. In the opinion of the IRS, the letter stated, the club was engaged in substantial efforts to influence legislation, a direct violation of federal tax law, and its donors should be made aware that their contributions might no longer qualify as tax deductions. In short, the government had stripped the Sierra Club's tax-exempt status as a nonprofit organization.

To this day, no one knows who initiated this investigation—Brower alleged that it was Morris Udall, who vehemently denied the charge, and his brother, Stewart, later suggested that someone in the White House was responsible. But whoever set the train in motion launched a graphic demonstration of the law of unintended consequences. Brower counterpunched by handing out copies of the letter to every reporter he knew. As word spread, it unleashed an absolute firestorm. If people were upset by the idea of the dams, they were positively apoplectic over the IRS's attempting to strong-arm a group of conservationists who were trying to do nothing more than save the Grand Canyon. This triggered outrage, even in places where conservation was regarded with skepticism or disdain. The *Wall Street Journal* denounced the IRS's move as "an extraordinary departure from its snail's pace tradition." The *New York Times* went a step further, calling it "an assault on the right of private citizens to protest effectively against wrong-headed public policies."

The most thunderous reaction of all, however, came from ordinary people. Congressional offices were immediately flooded with telegrams and phone calls from enraged citizens, and a few days later, the letters started pouring in. The secretary of the interior's office alone received more than twenty thousand. Morris Udall described it as a "deluge."

"I never saw anything like it," Dan Dreyfus, an official at the Bureau of Reclamation, later told the journalist Marc Reisner. "Letters were arriving in dump trucks. Ninety-five percent of them said we'd better keep our mitts off the Grand Canyon."

By late summer, *My Weekly Reader*, the newspaper for elementary-school children, had taken a vehement stand against the dams. "You're in deep shit when you catch it from them," remarked Dreyfus, ruefully recalling the incident. "Mailbags were coming in by the hundreds, stuffed with letters from schoolkids."

It took another eighteen months for the endgame to play out, during which Morris Udall explored a possible deal that would involve eliminating one of the dams if the Sierra Club would agree to withdraw its opposition to the other—a proposal to which Brower responded by declaring, "One bullet to the heart is just as deadly as two."

By the autumn of 1968, a final version of the bill—minus the hydroelectric dams in the Grand Canyon—was approved by both houses of Congress. When President Johnson signed the bill into law, the Sierra Club—captained by Brower and goaded by Litton, among many others—completed the transformation it had begun twelve years earlier in Echo Park from a group of alpine picnickers into the first truly powerful conservation lobby in America. Brower was heralded by *Life* as "his country's number-one working conservationist," and the environmental movement had scored one of its greatest victories, a platform upon which more sweeping successes, such as the Clean Air Act, the Clean Water Act, and the National Environmental Policy Act, would eventually be built. While many disagreed with the manner in which this victory had been achieved, no one could deny that the battle over the Grand Canyon dams marked the coming of age of American wilderness conservation.

Something else was true too. By the time the fight was finally over, most Americans believed deeply in the principle that the Grand Canyon should not be messed with—not now, not ever, not for any reason. People from places as diverse as New Jersey and Alabama and North Dakota—people who might never set foot in the Southwest, much less see the canyon with their own eyes—now viewed it as a kind of national cathedral of geology and light: a wonder of nature that, foremost of all the country's treasures, was sacrosanct.

Although many conservationists had participated in the effort to bring this about, the lion's share of the credit rightfully redounded to Brower—even though Brower himself was never entirely comfortable with this distinction. Whenever someone pointed out that he was the star of this play, its virtuoso performer, he would emphasize that the campaign had been waged by hundreds of people, men and women who would go on to make deep and lasting contributions to the way that Americans think about landscape, nature, and human responsibility to the world we all share.

Among this group, Litton was by no means the most important. In many ways, his role was fairly minor. But in one crucial respect, he was absolutely vital—and many years later, Brower went to some effort to point this out:

"Some people get the kudos and others, out of inequity, don't," he declared. "Martin Litton is due most of those addressed to me in error: more years than I will ever admit, he has been my conservation conscience."

~

If he wanted, Litton could easily have continued to follow Brower, who was forced out of the Sierra Club, but went on to found two new conservation groups. Instead, the irascible old glider pilot decided to follow an entirely different heading, a tack inspired by one of the men he admired most, and whose spirit he increasingly seemed to embody.

Seduced by his fleet of wooden boats, Litton disappeared down the Colorado in the footsteps of John Wesley Powell, where his story was about to intersect with that of a dory called the *Emerald Mile*.

PART III

The Sweet Lines of Desire

If rightly made, a boat would be a sort of amphibious animal, a creature of two elements, related by one half its structure to some swift and shapely fish, and by the other to some strong-winged and graceful bird.

—HENRY DAVID THOREAU

Martin Litton's fleet of dories, moored at Bright Angel beach in the heart of the Grand Canyon.

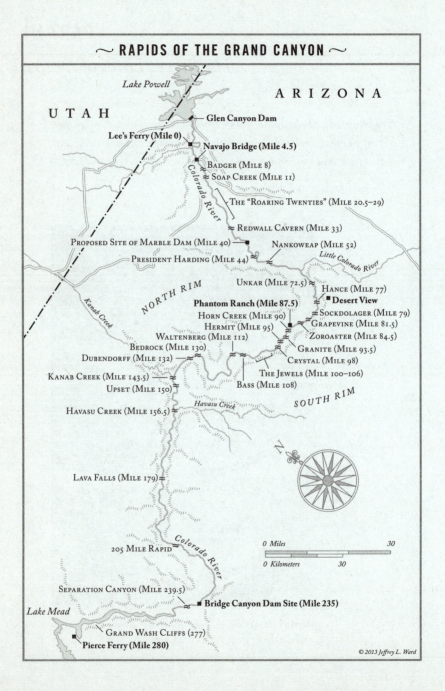

~ RAPIDS OF THE GRAND CANYON ~

UTAH

ARIZONA

Lake Powell

Glen Canyon Dam

Lee's Ferry (Mile 0)

Navajo Bridge (Mile 4.5)

≈ Badger (Mile 8)
≈ Soap Creek (Mile 11)

The "Roaring Twenties" (Mile 20.5–29)

≈ Redwall Cavern (Mile 33)

Proposed Site of Marble Dam (Mile 40)

Nankoweap (Mile 52)

President Harding (Mile 44)≈

Little Colorado River

Colorado River

NORTH RIM

Unkar (Mile 72.5)≈

Hance (Mile 77)

Phantom Ranch (Mile 87.5)

Desert View

Horn Creek (Mile 90)

≈ Sockdolager (Mile 79)

Hermit (Mile 95)

Grapevine (Mile 81.5)

Waltenberg (Mile 112)

Zoroaster (Mile 84.5)

Kanab Creek

Bedrock (Mile 130)

Granite (Mile 93.5)

Dubendorff (Mile 132)

Crystal (Mile 98)

Kanab Creek (Mile 143.5)≈

The Jewels (Mile 100–106)

Upset (Mile 150)≈

Bass (Mile 108)

Havasu Creek (Mile 156.5)≈

Havasu Creek

SOUTH RIM

N

Lava Falls (Mile 179)≈

0 Miles   30

0 Kilometers   30

Colorado River

205 Mile Rapid

Separation Canyon (Mile 239.5)

Bridge Canyon Dam Site (Mile 235)

Lake Mead

Grand Wash Cliffs (277)

Pierce Ferry (Mile 280)

© 2013 Jeffrey L. Ward

6

Dories

The glory of the dories is their lightness and maneuverability; the way they go dancing over the waves, the way you can turn them like the knob on an outhouse door.
If you sacrifice that . . . you've lost the whole goddamned ball of wax.

—P. T. REILLY

AMONG its many other consequences, the Grand Canyon dam fight wound up kicking the river-running industry into high gear. Drawn by the controversy, a number of celebrities and prominent politicians began booking excursions on the Colorado during the mid-1960s to see the place firsthand. Perhaps the most famous of these was Robert F. Kennedy, who took his entire family down the canyon, along with a group of friends that included the mountaineer Jim Whittaker, a member of the first American team to summit Mount Everest; the humorist Art Buchwald; and the singer Andy Williams. The publicity surrounding this and other trips proved to be a direct stimulant to river travel. By the time President Johnson signed the legislation that closed the door on the dams, a Grand Canyon white-water trip had emerged as the classic American wilderness experience, a pilgrimage at the top of the bucket list for anyone who loved the country's natural wonders.

Responding to this accelerating demand, new commercial outfitters began springing up almost overnight. Within a few years, twenty-two companies had obtained guiding permits from the National Park Service, and every one of those outfitters was experimenting with some form of rubberized raft, many with outboard motors attached to the back. Each company had its own theory about the best way to put together these contraptions—the size, the rigging, the style of frame—and the results were as varied as the layers of rock in the canyon walls. Some suspended their engines from wood frames that extended off the back of army-surplus bridge pontoons, oval-shaped tubes that had enabled George Patton's armored tank divisions to race over the rivers of France and Germany in their drive toward Berlin. These were known as tail-draggers. Others preferred tying three or four pontoons together lengthwise, which were called J-rigs or snouts, depending on how they were lashed, and could fit up to thirty people. Another popular option was a smaller, sixteen-foot raft equipped with a single set of oars that was capable of carrying five passengers, plus several hundred pounds of supplies. Each outfitter was convinced that his setup was the best, and perhaps the only thing everyone could agree on was that the era of the small, hard-hulled boat was over. Rubber was the future, wood a thing of the past.

Martin Litton stepped into this scene during the summer of 1969, shortly after deciding that he was fed up with writing stories on family-travel vacations for *Sunset* magazine. Having quit in a huff and then realizing, somewhat belatedly, that he now had to find another way to make a living, he concluded that the logical move—at least for now, he told his wife—was to use his trio of wooden dories to build his own commercial guiding company in the canyon. Characteristically, he made his entrance with a splash.

That summer marked the centennial of Powell's pioneering voyage, and Litton decided to commemorate it by re-creating the bulk of the Major's trip, launching above Dinosaur National Monument and running all the way to the Grand Wash Cliffs. The dories were temporarily renamed after Powell's boats, and at every stop, Litton disappeared into the bushes to paste a set of fake whiskers to his face and don a nineteenth-century black frock and hat. Tucking his right arm under the coat and pinning the empty sleeve to the lapel, he made his way down the river in stages, shuttling the boats around the dams and reservoirs, giving speeches, and happily hamming it up for the newspaper photographers and reporters who flocked to cover the spectacle. After leapfrogging down the Green and the upper Colorado, he spent most of August in the Grand Canyon. When the entourage reached the Grand Wash Cliffs on August 30, the date that Powell and his starving crew had completed their journey, Grand Canyon Dories was officially launched.

To say that Litton's boats offered a less than ideal platform for a commercial river company during this new era of white-water travel was something of an understatement. His dories were incapable of carrying more than four passengers, which put them at a disadvantage with the large, motorized rafts that could ferry five or six times as many people down the canyon at more than twice the speed. Even more problematic, Litton's boats had a tendency to break if they got anywhere near a rock, often requiring extensive and time-consuming repairs. But something about their history and their shape had seduced him, and to fully appreciate the depth of his infatuation, one needed to know a little about where those boats came from and how they had evolved.

~

When he'd first encountered the dories in Oregon seven years earlier, Litton had learned that their story was murky and the subject of some rather contentious debate. One version argued that they were part of a tradition that reached back to medieval Europe, where they were invented by Portuguese fishermen, then adapted by maritime communities throughout Britain and Scandinavia. Others argued that they had been developed in America by a Massachusetts boatwright named Simeon Lowell in the late 1700s, and were later adopted by New England cod fishermen for use in the North Atlantic, especially off the Grand Banks. The rivermen of the McKenzie rejected all of that history, however, and defiantly insisted that they had invented the things themselves, right there in Oregon, tailoring the boats to the unique conditions of their home waters to the point where, in the 1920s and 1930s, they became the favorite fishing vessel of celebrities such as Clark Gable, Babe Ruth, Winston Churchill, and Ginger Rogers. And perhaps that was the case—although it's much more likely that all three versions of the story contained a kernel of truth. As with many designs of practical value, variations of the craft may well have arisen spontaneously in different places, with each group of inventors borrowing ideas and deriving inspiration from elsewhere. What no one could dispute, however, was that something about the boats was rather magical.

Thanks to their toughness and durability, the dories of New England were famously capable of absorbing a ferocious beating. Cheap, unpretentious, and dependable, they were the Missouri mules and the Ford pickup trucks of their day. The McKenzies, by contrast, were fragile and demanded great dexterity to avoid being smashed to pieces. But regardless of where they came from, they all shared the same mysterious property, which was that their profile was deeply pleasing to the human eye. For reasons that no one could quite put his or her finger on, the little boats evoked passion and loyalty among everyone who built, rowed, or simply looked at them.

Despite differing theories about why these craft added up to more than the sum of their parts, an unspoken consensus held that the dories' charm was rooted in the blending of three elements: simplicity, balance, and ruthless reductionism. These qualities fused into an austere beauty not unlike the effect that the Shaker cabinetmakers strove to achieve—and maybe too the Shinto-temple builders of Japan. Like the very best products of human craftsman-ship—indeed, like all small objects that have been fashioned with great care from humble materials—the boats were charged with the power of honesty, composure, and time. They embodied a peculiar kind of perfection that gave pleasure to anyone who admired that narrow strip of ground where utility and art converge—an allure that was captured best by John Gardner, a naval archi-tect from Massachusetts, who was the foremost historian of this craft. "There must be something about dories that intrigues people," Gardner wrote. "The sweet lines of some of them all but took my breath when I saw them for the first time, out of the water in all their naked elegance. I reveled in their good looks and desired them as much for their beauty as for their use."

This notion offers perhaps the finest encapsulation of why Litton was deter-mined to stick with his wooden boats, despite their impracticalities. At the end of that first summer, Grand Canyon Dories was—and would remain—the only commercial outfitter to guide the Colorado exclusively in dories.

~

Somewhat to Litton's and everyone else's surprise, the dories were an imme-diate hit with the passengers, and as word leaked out, more and more people began telephoning his house in California to ask about booking a trip for the following summer. They were partly drawn by the connections to the past—the notion that while every other outfitter was embracing new technology and design, Litton's outfit harkened back to the earliest river runners. But an equal measure of the attraction stemmed from aesthetics. While rubber rafts were considerably more resilient and far easier to manage, they could be downright ugly. Fat, bulbous, and squishy, they lacked the dories' elegance and grace, quali-ties that were further enhanced by Litton's decision to paint each of the boats in the same colors—red, white, and turquoise—which supported the primary hues of the canyon, and they fit in beautifully. He also inaugurated a tradition of naming every craft after a natural wonder that, in his view, had heedlessly been ruined by the hand of man—"to remind us of places we've destroyed with-out any necessity," he would bark to anyone who inquired, "so that maybe we'll think twice before we do it again."

Litton's original dory, the *Portola*, was thus renamed the *Diablo Canyon* in honor of a pristine stretch of California coastline where the Sierra Club had lost a bitter battle in 1968 to prevent the construction of a nuclear power plant atop an earthquake fault. P. T. Reilly's old boat, the *Suzie Too*, was like-wise rechristened. Her new name, the *Music Temple*, commemorated one of the many gemlike features inside Glen Canyon that now lay submerged beneath the waters of Lake Powell. They were followed by the *Hetch Hetchy* (Yosemite's sister valley, drowned by a dam in 1913), the *Diamondhead* (the volcanic crater in Waikiki whose interior serves as a US military reserve), and the *Malibu Canyon*, a hidden pocket in the Santa Monica Mountains that had been Litton's favorite spot in the world before it was marred by a commuter highway.

The other outfitters had no idea what to make of all this. A man stubborn or foolish enough to reject improvements in order to wallow in the past was clearly out of his mind. But as the phone continued to ring, Litton found that each winter he had to expand the size of his fleet by making repeated dashes up to Oregon to order additional batches of boats. By now he had broken with his original boatbuilder, who was unable to keep up with production demands, and shifted over to a gifted boatwright named Jerry Briggs, who lived in the little town of Grants Pass along the banks of the Rogue River. With each new order, Litton and Briggs strove to improve their design, parsing which features didn't seem to be working and often brainstorming their way through the solutions by scratching makeshift blueprints in the sand next to Briggs's driveway with sticks. They tweaked the rocker back and forth. They made adjustments to the length and the beam. They tinkered with the height of the bow and the angle of the flare, juggling elements back and forth until finally, in the summer of 1971, Briggs nailed it.

The boat he wheeled out of his shop was sixteen and a half feet long from bowpost to stern, with side panels fashioned from quarter-inch, marine-grade plywood and braces made of aromatic Port Orford cedar. Briggs had reduced the flare on the sides, and crucially, he had dampened the rocker amidships so that the middle of the bottom of the boat was virtually flat, and only the bow and the stern had an upward rake. He also straightened the chine, the corner along the length of the hull where the sides and the bottom come together, and he adjusted the freeboard amidships, so that the oar handles rested at the perfect ergonomic position—halfway between the boatman's belly and his chest—for pulling a stroke.

The changes were subtle, but their effect was noticeable the moment the boat was placed on the river. The chine now acted as a kind of keel, helping to keep the hull parallel to the direction of the river current. This enabled her to track, building the momentum she needed to catapult over the biggest hydraulics, while the upward kick on her stern and bow enabled her to pivot on a hot dime. The prow was high enough to split all but the largest standing waves, while the watertight decking easily shed the hundreds of gallons of water that came rushing over the sides. Most important, she achieved a balance of geometry—a blending of ballast, beam, and the angle of her oars—that simply felt right.

Thanks to that equilibrium, she was capable of catching every nuance of the current and responding instantly to changing conditions inside a rapid. Unlike the rafts and the motor rigs or the generations of wooden boats that had preceded her, she didn't plow piggishly through the waves, but instead seemed to dance over them. As she planed across the surface of the river, breaking the water into a series of interlocked, V-shaped ripples, she achieved a bewitching visual alchemy, almost if she were suspended partly on the surface of the river and—through some ineffable trick of her rocker, her rake, and her radiance—partly on the air itself. She was unlike anything else that had ever been seen on the Colorado.

~

After her maiden run that July, Litton informed Briggs that their days of scratching with sticks in the dirt were over. What he wanted now were copies, fashioned to the boat's exact specs. Briggs would spend the next few years cranking out more than two dozen reproductions that mirrored her lines. This meant that the 1971 boat served as the matriarch of Litton's little armada, the de facto flagship of the fleet.

As his roster of dories grew, Litton bestowed upon each new boat the name of yet another vanished wonder. The *Music Temple* was swiftly joined by half a dozen sisters christened after equally lovely features from the lost world of Glen Canyon: the *Hidden Passage*, the *Tapestry Wall*, the *Dark Canyon*, the *Ticaboo*, and the *Mille Crag Bend*. The *Flaming Gorge* bore the name of one of the first canyons that Powell had confronted on the upper Colorado, now drowned beneath a giant dam. The *Vale of Rhondda* was a green valley in Wales destroyed by a coal-mining operation; the *Skagit* was a river in British Columbia stilled by a series of dams; the *Celilo Falls* commemorated the cascades on the Columbia River that were submerged by the Dallas Dam. And for the special boat that spawned all the rest, the one whose lines had served as the blueprint for everything that followed, Litton selected perhaps the most beautiful name of all. It was a gesture of remembrance in honor of a dense and towering stand of continuous old-growth redwoods tucked deep in the coastal forests of Northern California—an entire mountainside mantled in some of the tallest virgin trees in the world, until a chunk of it was clear-cut during the early 1960s by a logging company that was hoping to disqualify the grove from inclusion in a national park.

"Truly something to cry about," Litton had declared at the time. And so she became the *Emerald Mile*.

As each new boat completed the trip down from Oregon, it was wheeled into Litton's boathouse in the tiny town of Hurricane, Utah, located just north of the Arizona state line along the North Rim country of the Grand Canyon, and painted with a different configuration of the distinctive company colors. Every boat was thus unique but also part of a matrix that was imbued with cohesion and meaning.

In the years to come, a handful of other boatwrights from Oregon, Montana, and Idaho would attempt their own designs. But none would ever quite capture the sleekness of those first twenty-seven dories that emerged from Briggs's shop next to the Rogue River. Bobbing through the canyon with their haunted names emblazoned on their bows, clad in their gay palette of colors, they resembled a collection of floating Easter eggs that provoked delight from everyone who spotted them. Nothing else on the water looked quite so gorgeous or compelling. And it was this, more than anything else, that enabled Litton to assemble his unique crew of boatmen, a band of river guides who would, with time, gradually mature into something as distinctive as the boats they rowed.

$\sim$

Like most outfitters of the day, Litton recruited his early guides from an eclectic mix of young men in their late teens or early twenties. Several came from among the drifters, dropouts, and misfits of Northern California, many of whom worked as ski instructors during the winter and lived in tepees or tents or the backs of their pickups during the summer. Others were jaded hippies, betrayed by the broken promises of the counterculture, uncertain of anything other than that they didn't fit into mainstream America. But most were simply confused young men who found themselves caught in that limbo following high school or college when they had not yet gotten a fix on the trajectory that their lives would take.

Almost all of them were convinced they did not yet have a home, a place where they truly belonged, and although not a single one knew the first thing about white water or could tell the difference between a gunwale and a chine, they found themselves bewitched by the beauty of Litton's boats and the hidden world at the bottom of the canyon. For all of these reasons, and because they were, to a man, young and free and looking for adventure, each was willing, indeed eager, to fling himself down the river armed with little more than his toothbrush, his tennis shoes, and, for the worst rapids, a hockey helmet.

Those things drew them in initially. But with time, other elements began to emerge, powerful forces that none of them could have anticipated and that would later cement them together around a body of ideas and principles that ran deeper than mere adventure. This was partly because Litton was unlike anyone else they had ever met, perhaps the first leader many of them had encountered who truly seemed worth following—although this charisma was initially masked because Litton often displayed the demeanor of a cantankerous bear emerging from a troubled hibernation. Within his belligerent blue eyes, his gruffness, and the stream of profanities that seemed to fly off him like sparks from a grinding wheel, they found an intimidating taskmaster and leader. He could also be wildly mercurial, marveling at the colors of a Claret-cup cactus blossom in one moment, then in the next losing his temper over what a ridiculous knot someone had used to tie up his boat. But as one summer bled into another, they began to understand that both the man himself and the company he was building possessed an unusual spirit that seemed to set Grand Canyon Dories apart from every other outfitter on the river. His boats were certainly central to this emerging ethos. But they were only a part of the picture.

This quality was not easily pinned down, in part because, although Litton was a fighter, he was never an evangelist. He had little interest in telling people what they should think or how they should behave, preferring instead to state what *he* thought and then permitting his listeners to draw their own conclusions. As a result, he issued no philosophical statements about what his company stood for or how his boatmen should conduct themselves. But with time, they began to realize that Litton was offering his clients much more than the wilderness equivalent of a trip to Disney World.

One clue was his oratory. Regardless of where they might find themselves in the canyon, Litton seemed to treat every rock and bush as an excuse to launch into an impromptu conservation lecture, extolling the surrounding wonders while fulminating against the forces of greed, commercialism, and ignorance that conspired to neutralize nature's power. In someone less eloquent or lacking his rough but endearing charm, this kind of behavior would have been boorish and impossible to tolerate. But the passengers who signed up for those early trips couldn't get enough of it. They stared, rapt, when he ordered the boats to pull over at the Marble Canyon Dam site and pointed to the sides of the cliffs where the core samples had been drilled from the rock, then drank in his words as he uncorked a speech filled with graphic descriptions of what the reservoirs would have done to the bottom of the canyon. At night, they gathered around and pelted him with questions about David Brower, the Sierra Club, and the Eden that had been drowned upstream by the Glen Canyon Dam.

In addressing those queries, Litton also gave himself license to range freely over interests of his that had nothing to do with the canyon or the Colorado. At any given moment, he was immersed in half a dozen conservation campaigns involving parts of the country that lay far beyond the river. There was an effort to expand several parks and monuments in Northern California that protected the remaining stands of redwoods and sequoias. There was a crazy scheme to set up a refuge for a surviving population of California condors and feed them with dogs and cats that had been euthanized in Santa Barbara's animal shelters. There was his ongoing boycott of products manufactured in Japan to protest that nation's whaling industry. (According to one of his boatmen, after rashly offering a free river vacation for anyone who could find a single Japanese item on any of his dory trips, Litton was forced to spend an entire day going through the gear and grinding off *Made in Japan* from every piece of cookware in the kitchen.) In talking about these matters, he peppered his passengers with his opinions, entertained them with his invective, and invited them to warm their hands at the fires of his rage. And what his guides began to notice was that many of the people who completed those trips seemed to emerge from the bottom of the canyon with deepened convictions about the importance of fighting to protect not only the river itself, but all wild places that were threatened by development.

The guides also noticed that Litton offered few luxuries and charged his passengers almost nothing. In an era when the price of a one-week motorized run through the canyon was less than $500, he was charging roughly the same for a no-frills trip that could last up to twenty-three days. When the cost of his supplies and his payroll had been subtracted, his profit was almost nonexistent. Yet, on top of the already low prices, he also insisted on giving away many trips for free. Politicians, pundits, photographers, writers, and anyone else in a position to influence legislation or public opinion on matters concerning the environment were brought down the canyon at no charge. The reasons behind this, the guides eventually realized, had nothing to do with altruism. During the fight to block the Grand Canyon dams, Litton had become convinced that the best way, the *only* way, to protect the country's remaining scenic treasures was to enable a wide range of citizens—schoolteachers, janitors, housewives, hairdressers, factory workers—to see these places firsthand and to experience their wonders for themselves. Only then could they fathom the magnitude of what was at stake. In Litton's eyes, the rock-bottom prices for ordinary folks and the giveaways to people such as Diane Sawyer, James Taylor, Bruce Babbitt, Richard Holbrooke, and Bill Moyers were investments that might reap valuable dividends if people could simply be induced to step into his boats and be exposed to what the river, the canyon, and Litton himself had to say.

In noticing these things, Litton's guides also couldn't help but notice the glaring and undeniable truth that their boss was an abominable entrepreneur who didn't have the faintest clue about how to run a business. His fiscal largesse ate away at the company's bottom line to the point where GCD was soon stumbling from one season to the next on the threshold of bankruptcy. Even worse, perhaps, Litton's efforts to stem the flow of red ink were often rather crude. While other companies were providing expensive amenities such as tents, sleeping cots, and steak dinners on the grill, his commissary consisted mostly of canned goods—baked beans, stewed tomatoes, fruit cocktail—and instead of handing out tents, he gave everyone a tarp and told them to decide how to rig it. He also tried to trim costs by buying up consignments of day-old bread and cases of cheap beer near his home in Palo Alto and then flying them to Hurricane in his single-engine Cessna 195, a vintage tail-dragger with a radial engine and a propeller that had once exploded in the middle of a take-off. Whatever pennies he might have saved on the food were consumed in the cost of aviation fuel required for the flight, but this never seemed to dawn on Litton (perhaps because the only thing he loved more than boating was flying). Upon landing at the little airport in Hurricane and delivering the supplies to the boathouse, he would start rummaging through the trash cans, pulling out used paintbrushes and seizing upon half-empty tubes of glue, demanding to know why these perfectly good items were being thrown away.

This combination of big-picture profligacy and nit-picking parsimony might have been amusing to the boatmen if his most effective cost-saving measure, by far, had not been to pay his guides the lowest wages in the entire industry. While boatmen at motor companies were earning as much as $60 a day, Litton's biggest earners pulled down no more than $25 for each day they were on the river—and on top of this they were expected to devote additional days to repairing whatever damage they inflicted on their boats without any pay whatsoever. One might assume that under such conditions his employees would have trickled out the door along with the lost revenue. Oddly, however, their sense of loyalty seemed to grow only stronger with time.

In river hydrology, a phenomenon known as headwater capture touches, at least metaphorically, on what may have been taking place inside the heads of these men. Headwater capture is based on the notion that a river is an erosive machine that is perpetually transporting rocks, pebbles, and fine sediments downstream, continuously cutting back from its point of origin like a kind of liquid buzz saw. As this work unfolds—as more and more material is taken up and carried away—the headwaters recede until the river eventually cuts its way through to a basin occupied by an entirely different river. At this point, whichever river is flowing at a higher elevation will change course and begin flowing into its captor. This process informs a compelling theory that attempts to explain how the Grand Canyon was originally carved—the idea being that the canyon was incised by not one ancestral Colorado but by two separate rivers, the more powerful of which seized the other and turned it from its original course. Headwater capture is also an imperfect but useful concept for understanding what happened to Litton's guides: men whose lives were flowing in one direction, then hijacked and irrevocably changed.

Partly, this rerouting stemmed from the pull exerted on them by the beauty of the dories, an attraction strengthened by Litton's practice of assigning each member of the crew his own boat, which would be his alone to row and care for. But the most potent element in the equation was the subversive sense of purpose the boatmen derived from belonging to a company that offered the longest, slowest, cheapest expeditions in the canyon as a way of building a constituency of ordinary-citizen activists who would fight to protect the environment. Following Litton's lead, his guides gradually began to see themselves not as part-time summer employees but as role models and teachers. This imbued them with a sense of purpose—one might even call it a mission—for why they were there and what they were doing, responsibilities that went considerably beyond the challenges of mastering a set of delicate and unforgiving boats.

The issue of mastery, however, was destined to remain an unsolved problem that would make extraordinary demands on Litton's fledgling crew throughout those early years. And here, too, they found that Grand Canyon Dories occupied a unique and sometimes unenviable niche within the river hierarchy, one that would put them through a miserable series of trials until they had honed their skills to become some of the finest oarsmen the canyon had ever known.

7

The Golden Age of Guiding

*Believe me, my young friend, there is nothing—absolutely nothing—
half so much worth doing as simply messing about in boats.*

—KENNETH GRAHAME, *The Wind in the Willows*

DURING the *Emerald Mile*'s heyday, the years between 1971 and
1975, no one had the faintest clue how to run the complex current
that ran through the bottom of the Grand Canyon smoothly and
safely, time after time, in small wooden boats filled with commercial clients.
Litton's crew quickly realized that the dories had two glaring liabilities. First,
they were so delicate that even a tentative scrape against a rock was enough to
administer nasty dings and scratches, while a direct hit enabled the canyon to
drive its fist straight through their hulls. Second, they were exceptionally finicky. The slightest miscalculation would dump them upside down.

The boats also had the potential to do things that no other craft could, which
meant they could be absolutely thrilling to drive. But they could only achieve
that kind of performance at the hands of an oarsman who understood the
nuances of white water and knew exactly how to thread the eye of the needle. In
the earlier years, not a single doryman, including Litton himself, came close to
meeting those standards. As a result, most of those initial dory trips resembled
exploratory free-for-alls whose carnage invited comparison with that of the
days of John Wesley Powell. "Try and imagine a group of boatmen who had
no idea what the hell is around the next bend," recalls John Blaustein, one of

Litton's first guides, who had never touched an oar before his first trip in 1970. "Christ, it was like a war zone down there."

During the first few seasons there were zero instructions and just one general rule, which was that everybody had to follow the boss, the only person in the company who possessed at least a vague notion of how the rapids worked. Litton, however, had an incorrigible habit of taking his eye off the ball, as he was often likely to be in the midst of yet another instructional lecture or anecdote, rather than paying attention to the river. Thus he'd be caught completely unaware—pointing out some feature of the canyon, building to the punch line of a long story, or concentrating on lighting up a cigar—while merrily drifting downstream with his back to an upcoming rapid. When one of the passengers gently inquired about the jet-engine roar emanating from around the bend just ahead, he would spring to action, ordering life jackets to be fastened, drinks put away, hatch lids slammed down and battened, all the while looking for a dry space to stow his cigar. In the midst of this frenzy, he would stand up to take stock of where they were, then turn to face the line of boats behind him and issue instructions about the name of the rapid and what needed to be done:

All right, everybody, this next rapid is called Forester, so we're going to swing left at the tongue. . . .

Hang on—this doesn't look like Forester. . . .

Oh, Jesus, it's Waltenberg! Pull right! *For God's sake PULL RIGHT!*

As each oarsman struggled to relay this message back to the next boat and prayed he didn't screw things up too badly, Litton braced for the onslaught. What unfolded next was often spectacular.

One afternoon at a rapid known as Bedrock, the *Bright Angel* was sucked into an immense chunk of granite that splits the river in two, and its entire side panel was raked off. (A portion of the hull had to be rebuilt the following morning, using pieces of driftwood before the crew could complete the trip.) On another occasion, the *Lava Cliff* smashed up against a rock in the middle of the river and submerged, forcing her guide and passengers to abandon ship. Forty-eight hours later when the river subsided, a Park Service helicopter lowered a river ranger onto the wreckage to attach a cable, the other end of which was run through a winch onshore in the hope of pulling the carcass loose. As the boat swung downstream, the cable snapped and the dory vanished for good, never to be seen again.

Litton's attitude toward these disasters was philosophical, perhaps because he realized that nothing that might happen on the river could compare with the ordeal of crash-landing gliders into the Netherlands or Bastogne. In the summer of 1970, Blaustein (whose nickname was JB) rammed the poor *Hetch*

Hetchy into yet another midriver rock at a place called Unkar, where the river cuts along the base of a five-hundred-foot sandstone cliff. He struck with enough force to split the hull from oarlock to oarlock.

"It was a terrible mess," he recalls glumly. "I basically broke the boat in half."

Litton, however, was unbothered. "Don't feel too awful, JB, the dories have been damaged this badly before," he said. "Just never all at once."

After each of these disasters, the crew was forced to pull the boats onto a sandy beach and attempt to repair the worst of the devastation using whatever materials presented themselves: duct tape, steel wool, marine putty, loose pieces of lumber that had washed ashore. When the boats were finally able to float, the dorymen would drift down to Lake Mead, hobble back to their Utah warehouse, and rebuild the fleet for the next trip. Then they'd go out and break everything all over again.

The learning curve was steep and painful. Gradually, however, Litton and his team began to unlock some of the mysteries of the river's hydraulics. The key to it all, they eventually realized, lay in the arcane art of reading white water.

~

Along the 277 miles that separate Lee's Ferry from Lake Mead, the Colorado falls nearly two thousand vertical feet, but half of this drop takes place inside roughly 160 discrete pockets of white water whose linear distance, when added together, amounts to less than 10 percent of the canyon's length. This configuration, which is referred to as a pool-and-drop phenomenon, means that the river is composed of long, languorous stretches of tranquillity punctuated by intervals of unholy chaos. Those pockets of chaos are strewn along the entire length, but they tend to run in clusters. While a handful are located in the upper and lower parts of the canyon, the majority are clumped in an area known as the Upper Granite Gorge. Here, where the cliffs are almost vertical and the Vishnu schist is exposed, the river corridor narrows and the hydraulics can turn exceptionally violent. Within the gorge, the consequences of an accident grow geometrically.

One of the things a novice boatman realizes upon meeting white water for the first time is that the waves in a river are not at all like those in the ocean. The most salient difference is that in the ocean the water remains in a fixed position and the waves move in lateral pulses, almost always rhythmically, often predictably, and generally in more or less the same direction. On a river, precisely the opposite set of mechanics unfolds: the water moves downstream, while the primary hydraulic features of a rapid—eddies, whirlpools, and waves of all shapes and sizes—essentially remain fixed. Among many other consequences, this means that while ocean waves tend to be far larger than their riparian counterparts, a stretch of white water on a fast-flowing river can achieve an explosive-ness that is rarely encountered on the open sea. Another difference is that the obstacles on a river that must either be avoided or surmounted—rocks, tree limbs, complex bends, and irregular features of the shoreline that jut into the current—are often impossible to discern until one is virtually on top of them. And because the current is continuously hurtling downstream without a break or pause, even small errors are compounded with breathtaking speed by the instant and terrible force that the river can bring to bear on a boat in trouble. The challenge is perhaps best envisioned by trying to imagine being caught in the middle of an avalanche as it roars down the side of a mountain.

Among the many problematic features lurking within the interior of a rapid, perhaps the most treacherous is known as a hydraulic jump, or, in river runner's parlance, a keeper hole. This is a crater that forms on the surface of the river as water races across the top of a submerged ledge or boulder. Large keeper holes can achieve formidable dimensions—sometimes up to thirty feet deep and fif-teen feet wide—and they are often paired with an enormous stationary wave, or "haystack," on their downstream edge that breaks back upon itself, and is thus constantly flushing anything buoyant—a raft, a wooden oar, a person wearing a life jacket—back into the hole in an endlessly recirculating swirl. It is a dif-ficult thing to imagine without having seen it firsthand, but perhaps the most lucid expositor of this hydrodynamic phenomenon is the science writer David Quammen, who is also an expert kayaker. As Quammen explains it, a keeper hole is essentially "a whirlpool laid on its side with its axis of rotation perpen-dicular to the main current—a cylinder of moving water that rotates continu-ously, like one of those giant spinning brushes at an automatic car wash." For a rough approximation of how it feels to become entrapped in one, Quammen invites his readers to take a pass through the car wash while riding a bicycle.*

Although keeper holes often form the deadliest part of a rapid, a host of other features must also be navigated, including boils, laterals, cauldrons, eddy fences, rooster tails, and always, of course, boulders—some exposed but many others, often the deadliest, concealed just beneath the surface. All the river-running advice in the world cannot adequately prepare a person for his first encounter with truly gigantic white water: the ferocity of the noise and turbu-lence, the mosaic of whorls, the fugues of competing currents that follow sepa-

---

*The interior of a hydraulic jump within a major rapid inside the Grand Canyon is subjected to some shocking forces, and the ordeal of being trapped in one of these underwater tornadoes is called "getting maytagged." As a further illustration of how dangerous they can be, consider that sometimes the only option for a person trapped inside a keeper hole is to dive toward the bottom of the river in the hope of becoming caught in the downstream current, thereby funneling *under* the breaking wave.

rate and unpredictable paths—colliding, snapping like the tail end of a whip, or diving straight to the bottom of the river, where they can scour out holes up to ninety feet deep inside the Grand Canyon. To a casual observer, the combined picture is one of total insanity, a raging mess of tangled lines, studded with rocks and drenched with spray that flies in every direction.

Each rapid, however, possesses an architecture of its own, and an adept boatman is often able to scan and trace the layout as clearly as an electrician can interpret a circuit drawing—a talent that was captured best, perhaps, by Mark Twain, who was a skilled riverboat pilot long before he became a famous writer. "The face of the water, in time, became a wonderful book—a book that was a dead language to the uneducated passenger, but which told its mind to me without reserve, delivering its most cherished secrets as clearly as if it uttered them with a voice," Twain wrote in *Life on the Mississippi*. "And it was not a book to be read once and thrown aside, for it had a new story to tell every day."

For Twain, a river was a series of fluid riddles that could be unlocked and solved. And this was the task to which Litton and his crew would have to apply themselves if they were to have any hope of threading through the chain-linked sequence of maelstroms at the bottom of the canyon.

~

By the 1990s, all of the monster rapids had been exhaustively surveyed, mapped, and ranked according to a rather complicated scale, unique to the Grand Canyon, composed of Arabic numerals ranging from 1 to 10 and spread across four different levels of water with pluses and minuses to connote gradations. In the early days, however, the maps were crude and the rankings had not yet been refined. But everybody agreed that roughly thirty rapids were more than capable of smashing your boat, ending your career, or killing you.

Badger, Soap Creek, House Rock, Unkar, and Dubendorff could all get you into serious trouble at low water. A couple of the Roaring Twenties, a series of ten back-to-back rapids between Mile 20 and Mile 29, could be especially nasty at high water (although one or two of them turned ugly at low water too). The same was true of another chain farther downstream, whose links were named after semiprecious stones—Agate, Sapphire, Turquoise, Ruby, Emerald, and Serpentine—and were thus collectively referred to as the Jewels. Grapevine, Zoroaster, Specter, and Granite Park were mostly benign, but each concealed a feature or two—a rock, a standing wave, a reversal—that could easily knock you into next week. A bright handful, such as Sockdolager, Hermit, and Upset, were mostly pure fun, but they would flip you in a second if you failed to maintain your angle. Hance, Granite, and Horn Creek were complex and mercurial, while others—almost always Bedrock and invariably Lava Falls—were just plain vicious. Beyond the rapids themselves, the river also concealed a host of other obstacles, wicked spots whose names offered a sufficiently graphic warning of what they would do to you if you let them. The Fangs. Helicopter Eddy. The Green Guillotine. Forever Eddy. The Devil's Spittoon.

No two of these challenges were alike, and when Litton's crew came to realize that the linchpin of good boatmanship lay in fluency at reading water, they all became devoted scholars of the current. The bulk of these studies took place when they anchored their boats at the top of a nasty stretch of the river, climbed to a vantage on the cliffs that afforded a comprehensive view, and sat down on the rocks to dissect the rapid with their eyeballs. At irregular intervals, one of them would stand up, pad back to their anchorage point, gather up an armload of driftwood, and start tossing it into the current. As the sticks hurtled downstream, the veil that concealed the matrix of white water was pulled back and the crew was able to take apart the features piece by piece, mapping them out in their minds. This they would do for hours, watching and waiting as each of them framed a plan. Then they would select another vantage that offered a slightly different angle and go through the whole exercise all over again. Finally, they would talk things over exhaustively, and when the talking was done, silence would set in as each boatman retreated into a private space to memorize his run, codifying and rehearsing the sequence of moves he would make so that he would have something to hang on to when the chaos hit. When each man was satisfied, it was time to return to the boats and give the theories a try.

So they proceeded in this staccato fashion. Running, stopping to scout, then running a mile, or maybe ten, and stopping for another scout. Day after day, week after week, until they had floated through the Grand Wash Cliffs and arrived at Pierce Ferry, their takeout point on the eastern end of Lake Mead. Then they pulled the dories from the water, hauled them back to Hurricane for repairs, and made the long drive up to Lee's Ferry to greet another group of clients and start the same journey all over again. Down the length of the summer, past the equinox and deep into autumn, they wove their way through the labyrinth, pausing only for a hiatus in winter before once again rejoining the flow of the Colorado when the snows started to melt the following spring.

In tracing this route, they formed a community unlike any other, a brotherhood of boatmen bound by their love of the canyon, their infatuation with the dories, and above all, the witchery of white water. And somewhere in the midst of this circuit, the river came to lose the bilateral dimensions of a linear highway and was instead transformed into something that more closely resembled an enchanted circle, an endless loop—not unlike the hydraulic jumps whose secrets they strove to unlock—that revolved back upon itself in a continuous swirl of wonder and madness.

~

To a doryman who applied himself to learning to read white water in this manner, each rapid, from the smallest riffle to the biggest hellbender, gradually came to develop a face, a personality, and a range of moods—and the key to unlocking those rapids' riddles lay in finding one's line. On any given day, for any given set of conditions, which could vary in accordance with the speed and level of the water, the strength and direction of the wind, the angle of the light, and a host of subtler variables, a path almost always led through the chaos, a ribbon of relatively smooth downstream current that would enable you to thread the gauntlet. Often, this line was extremely narrow, no more than a couple of feet. But if you could tease out its arc and then assemble the proper sequence of moves—skirting a rock here, kissing an eddy there—it was sometimes possible to skate through the entire mess as cleanly as a Cooper's hawk cleaves the leafy canopy of a forest. It required a high degree of precision to pull that off consistently, however. And the challenge was further exacerbated in an unsettling but also thrilling way because the medium was fluid, always in flux, and therefore the line did not hold. Some days it would shift, occasionally it would dead-end, and every now and then the damn thing would disappear altogether.

This meant that one's command of white water was slippery and elusive, could come and go without warning. Sometimes the river itself changed: a rapid that seemed benign and forgiving on one trip would turn dark and ugly a month later. Other times, the shift took place inside one's head. It was not unusual to nail a difficult stretch of white water for a season or two, snapping off one flawless run after another, and then, for some unfathomable reason, find that you had lost your mastery. Then you would be consigned to flipping repeatedly or smashing against the rocks time and again until things shifted back into place and your mojo returned.

One insight the dorymen drew from this was that only a frog's hair of difference separated a successful run from a complete cock-up, a space that was defined by a few inches of current or a quarter stroke of an oar. Which side of that gap you were on depended heavily on your skills and your competency, and the connection you had cultivated with your boat and the river. But it depended even more on something you had absolutely no control over. When it came to rapids and wooden dories, an awful lot of luck was involved. The river was a beast that could be neither controlled nor tamed, only run with.

And to be allowed to run with the beast, you had to accept and embrace and ultimately find a way of celebrating its inscrutable, ungovernable, glorious wildness.

That didn't, however, dissuade the dorymen from trying to figure out the key to the code. Their days and weeks unfolded, good or bad, in accordance with their skill at discerning those ephemeral lines, and so they discussed them endlessly. Hunched over their coffee in the mornings, gathered around the kitchen at night after the passengers had gone to bed, they compared notes, traded theories, attended to one another's sermons. They choreographed wavy pieces of performance art in the air with their hands, and they scratched out elaborate diagrams in the wet sand with the tips of their fingers. Many of them also kept careful notes, filling up their maps and logbooks with checklists, reminders, admonitions, and curses. Immersed within the canyon's hidden republic of white water, they struggled so obsessively to unravel its mysteries that it sometimes seemed as if nothing else mattered. At night, the rapids flowed through their dreams.

As their knowledge deepened, growing more detailed and intimate with each passing season, their verbal shorthand changed until they found themselves speaking a kind of secret language, all but unknowable to the passengers and the rookies, whose vocabulary was peppered with expressions that made no sense to people who could see only chaos when they gazed into the current. The dorymen knew that on the left side of Hance was a partially submerged sleeper, a boulder they called Whale Rock, which acted as a kind of hydraulic magnet, almost as if it had its own tractor beam that would pull you onto it and leave you marooned in the middle of the river. They reminded one another that Hermit boasted twelve separate haystacks, the biggest and loveliest of which was the fifth—but you had to hit it "dead-nuts square" or it would flip you end over end. They talked about how the right side of Sockdolager featured a pair of staggered crunchers that seemed impossible to split, but if you punched the first wave slightly off-center with the left side of your bow, its crest would knock you to the right and set you up perfectly for the second. At Upset, they understood that the key to skirting the giant hog trough at the bottom was to get on the inside ridge of the left lateral, then tell yourself that, even though it seemed as if the hand of God Himself was about to spear you into the left wall, the invisible ribbon of current would whisk you straight through the maelstrom and deliver you—soaked, safe, and happy—into the tail waves.

Because their lives spun around an axis of entropy, rituals and superstitions arose, and with these things came something that bordered on mysticism. They called the wind Mr. W because they believed that naming him out loud would call him down to play havoc with their runs. They carried special charms—heart-shaped stones, girlfriends' bracelets, clay amulets baked in midnight campfires—and rubbed their surfaces for good luck. They reminded one another constantly that each encounter carried the potential for both disaster and ecstasy. Some rapids could hurt you, some could drown you, and some could render you impotent with rage. There were rapids rich in gradation and texture, and rapids that were existentially wretched in the simplicity of their violence. There were rapids that you feared and rapids that you hated and rapids that you would be a fool to take for granted, even under the most benign conditions imaginable. But on those days of wonder, when the tumblers in the lock were oiled and turning flawlessly, any one of those rapids could also transport you into a dimension of pure, unadulterated joy that had no analogue in any other part of your life.

The taste of that joy was absolutely intoxicating, a kind of drug, and perhaps the most potent part of the charge lay in the irrevocability of the moment when you untied your boat, and you and your partners peeled out into the current above a rapid in a tight and graceful little arc like a formation of miniature fighter jets. For a minute or two, you would find yourself drifting on a flat and glassy cushion of serenity as the current slowly gathered its speed and heft beneath the bottom of your boat and you drifted toward this thing that waited, invisible, just beyond the horizon. It was silent during those minutes, the only sounds being the creak of your oars in their locks and the dipping of the blades as you made a few microadjustments in the hope of putting your hull squarely on the one tiny patch of current that would insert you through the keyhole in the cosmos. Then in the final seconds, you would start to hear the dull, thunderous roar, and you could see the little fistfuls of spray being flung high into the air.

This, perhaps, was the most riveting moment of all, because by now all of your decisions had been made—you had done your homework and sought a point of balance between instinct and analysis, listening to the data flowing from both your brain and your gut, and now you were well and truly committed. This thing you were running down had no brakes, no rewind, no possibility of a do-over. You would ride the surge of your adrenaline and surf the watery crescendo that was about to explode before you, and you would accept the consequences, good or bad, along with whatever gifts or punishments the river was prepared to dish out. There were lessons there, insights a man could put in his pocket and take out later, long after he was out of the canyon, tiny compass points to steer by during those seasons when the river that was your life turned turbulent and ugly. You could learn things about yourself that you would never learn in civil society. And if you were lucky, you might navigate to a place that would enable you to glimpse, however obliquely, a bit of who you truly were.

There was nothing else quite like it, the way this river could braid terror and rapture so tightly together. And although it wasn't always possible for Litton's crew to fear and love the rapids in the same instant, sometimes those feelings toggled back and forth with such fury that they generated a charge not unlike the voltaic current that was running through the power cables at the base of the Glen Canyon Dam. Once you had felt that energy coursing through your synapses, you simply had to return to it again and again, chasing the elusive electric butterfly into the vortex.

In this way, white water became the dorymen's elixir and their narcotic. Because they literally lived on the river—riding its back by day, bobbing asleep in their boats upon the eddies at night—they became part of the water itself. It ran down their veins and bored into the chambers of their heart. It framed their world, it greased their engines, it shaped the subtext of the dialogue they conducted with themselves, with one another, with the gods they worshipped. And out of all of this emerged a connection that bound the dorymen to the water, the rocks, and the boats they rowed more intimately than any of the generations of river runners that had preceded them. As far as they were concerned, anyone in a motor rig or a rubber raft had only run his or her fingers along the surface of those truths. Even John Wesley Powell himself, they were half convinced, had barely touched the magic.

~

The other companies didn't necessarily see it this way. Massive rubber rafts had their own quirks and challenges, and when you threw motors into the mix—their habit of pulling tricks such as breaking down in the middle of a rapid—things could become complicated indeed. All of which meant that rival outfitters often took a rather dim view of the dories—not necessarily of the boats, which they coveted, but of the boatmen and what they thought of themselves. To many of these outfitters, Litton and his crew seemed little more than a gang of snooty purists who subscribed to the delusion that they were better than everybody else, an impression that was convincingly underscored by Litton's insistence on referring to the rubber rafts as "baloney boats" and his penchant for warning his passengers that, in addition to being ugly, the boats were dirty and unsafe. "God, no!" he would declare whenever one of his clients asked if he had ever ridden on a motor rig. "Lord knows what can happen aboard those contraptions—not to mention the diseases you're liable to contract."

Unfortunately, this gave rise to some intense rancor and ill will, which in turn created lasting divisions within the guiding community, pushing the river-running industry in the direction of a loose confederacy of tribes whose members considered everyone else a bunch of knuckleheads who had no business being on the river. However, on one thing everyone was united.

During this period, a remarkable geomorphic event took place deep inside the canyon that changed the face of the river. They all agreed that it was more or less the biggest thing that had happened to the bottom of the canyon in the 426 years since Cárdenas had stumbled onto the place. Among other consequences, it created, in the space of a single winter's night, the meanest and ugliest stretch of white water that anyone had ever seen.

8

Crystal Genesis

In the rock record, the tranquillity of time is not well represented. Instead, you have catastrophes. In the Southwest, they live from one catastrophe to another, from one flash flood to the next. The evolution of the world does not happen a grain at a time. It happens in the hundred-year storm, the hundred-year flood. Those things do it all.

—JOHN McPHEE, *Annals of the Former World*

ONCE every thirty-three years, the comet Tempel-Tuttle returns to the inner solar system, casting off a dense stream of frozen gas particles that generates one of the loveliest and most prolific displays of shooting stars in the heavens. The Leonid meteor shower is often spectacular, but the storm of 1966 was truly singular—especially in the western United States, where, on the night of November 17, the stars rained down at an uncountable rate, etching the sky with a tracery of silver so dense and so luminous that witnesses later said they felt as if the planet were hurtling into a celestial blizzard, like a car driving through a snowstorm. On the highways of Nevada and the interstates of eastern California, drivers pulled to the side of the road, got out of their vehicles, and stared upward, transfixed. In small towns from New Mexico's Tularosa Basin to the Texas Panhandle, parents plucked sleeping children from their beds, padded into their backyards, and slowly turned in circles. For three hours, people stood spellbound by a silent explosion that yielded more than forty falling stars a second. Many witnesses later said it was the most remarkable natural phenomenon they had witnessed in their entire lives. Yet, just two weeks later, an equally bizarre storm took place in the highland deserts just north of the Grand Canyon—something far more violent and, in its own way, even stranger than a meteor shower.

Unlike with the Leonids, however, not a single human being was there to see it.

During the winter months, the country along the canyon's North Rim, more than six thousand feet above the river, is essentially deserted. Once the first snowfall has closed off the forty-seven-mile road that connects the park's entrance station to the rim, all vehicular traffic comes to a halt and the place is cut off from the outside world. During this lockdown, the alpine meadows and the dense glades of aspen trees are suspended in stasis. The only full-time resident is the winter caretaker at the Grand Canyon Lodge, which sits at the top of the North Kaibab Trail, leading down to Phantom Ranch. The lodge has almost no visitors, and almost none of them bother to venture into the backcountry, where dozens of side canyons and pocket drainages notch into the rim like the bays and inlets along the coastline of British Columbia. From late October through mid-April these areas, which may not see a single human being until spring, are some of the most isolated places in the entire Southwest—which is why no one was there when, shortly after 1:00 a.m. on the night of December 3, it started raining on the North Rim.

This was hardly an unusual event. Winter storms are common from November through March all across the highlands of northern Arizona. But this rainfall was different. At the park's entrance station, which sits at eighty-eight hundred feet, the rain fell steadily for twenty hours on Saturday, paused briefly, then started back up and didn't stop until 4:00 a.m. on Wednesday. Much of this deluge splattered atop approximately six inches of snow, which swiftly melted and joined the runoff, adding to the magnitude of what unfolded over the next three days. But the sheer intensity of the rain was what was most remarkable. Within a small pocket of roughly a dozen square miles, a series of storm cells dumped fourteen inches in just thirty-six hours. Precipitation that heavy is commensurate with the kind of rainfall that the jungles of Panama receive at the height of the rainy season. In the desert uplands of the Kaibab Plateau, such precipitation is breathtakingly extravagant—nearly twice as much as the area normally receives during an entire year.

Unlike the tropics, the desert has little soil and scant vegetation to cushion and absorb this kind of impact. Instead, the rain simply lollops off the bedrock and forms rivulets that race indiscriminately through the beds of the dry arroyos. (Hence the name for these storms: gully washers.) As smaller gullies enter from the sides, the speed and mass of the runoff builds and intensifies with each passing minute. This can have blunt consequences—especially along the North Rim, where the south-tilting slopes of the Kaibab direct the entire discharge toward the limestone caprock that defines the edge of the rim and dump virtually all of this water directly into the canyon.

~

At the lip of the rim, the ground drops through a sequence of cliffs and slopes whose angles vary according to the stability of the rock in each layer. The harder rocks—the limestones and some of the sandstones—which are relatively stable and resistant to erosion, tend to form vertical cliff faces. By contrast, the mud-stones and the shales are crumbly and weak and are thus more vulnerable to the pull of water and gravity, which results in steeply angled slopes. This progression from hard rock to crumbly shale, from cliff face to slope, accounts for the distinctive terracelike appearance of the canyon's walls. Under the right conditions—the appropriate combination of slope angle and intensity of rainfall—entire sections of this colossal staircase can catastrophically fail.

One of the weakest links in the entire chain of rock, the brittle, maroon-colored Hermit shale, sits directly beneath the cliffs of Kaibab limestone and Coconino sandstone that form the rim of the canyon. When subjected to the fire-hose effect of high-intensity, storm-induced runoff, these slopes become so saturated they simply give way, slumping into the flood and contributing to the formation of a highly viscous sedimentary slurry.

This slurry has some intriguing properties. Only about 40 percent of its volume is actually composed of water; the rest is made up of unconsolidated silt, fine sand, and a heterogeneous blend of chert and limestone fragments. But there is also a third ingredient, the thing that gives the slurry its rather freakish potential for violence.

As the author Craig Childs explains in *The Secret Knowledge of Water*, marine mudstones and shales often contain clays and minerals that can act as crude lubricants when they are combined with relatively small concentrations of water. The Hermit shale, for example, has heavy concentrations of the minerals illite (a component of soap and lip gloss) and kaolinite (which is used in the manufacture of glossy paper). The result is a glutinous, oily-looking goulash that has the consistency of cake dough or, perhaps more accurately, wet cement. Like cement, it is dense and rather grabby, and as the liquid avalanche roars downhill, it begins snatching up rocks and boulders, which are rapidly entrained into the mix. At this point, materials that are normally solid and fixed undergo a startling change into something fluid.

This type of flash flood is known inside the Grand Canyon as a debris flow, and because most of the 529 tributary drainages within the canyon that are capable of yielding debris flows are remote and inaccessible, few of these incidents have been witnessed firsthand. One of the most vivid accounts we have was provided by Robert Brewster Stanton, a gifted engineer who took part in a disastrous expedition to conduct a river-level railway survey along the bottom of the canyon during the summer of 1889.

On the morning of July 18, having watched helplessly as three of their comrades were drowned in the Colorado, Stanton and his exhausted party of surveyors were attempting to make their escape to the rim by clawing their way up a steep tributary when a heavy thunderstorm broke directly above them. Stanton described what happened next:

As the rain increased, I heard some rock tumbling down behind us, and, looking up, I saw one of the grandest and most exciting scenes of the crumbling and falling of what we so falsely call the everlasting hills. As the water began to pour over from the plateau above, it seemed as if the whole upper edge of the Canyon had begun to move. Little streams, rapidly growing into torrents, came over the hard top stratum from every crevice and fell on the softer slopes below. In a moment they changed into streams of mud, and, as they came farther down, again changed into streams of water, mud and rock, undermining huge loose blocks of the harder strata, and starting them they plunged ahead. In a few moments, it seemed as though the slopes ... were moving down upon us, first with a rumbling noise, then an awful roar. As the larger blocks of rock plunged ahead of the streams, they crashed against other blocks, lodged on the slopes, and, bursting with an explosion like dynamite, broke into pieces, while the fragments flew into the air in every direction, hundreds of feet above our heads, and as the whole conglomerate mass of water, mud, and flying rocks came down the slopes nearer to where we were, it looked as if nothing could prevent us from being buried in an avalanche of rock and mud. It was a scene of the wildest fury of elements!

Fortunately, Stanton and his men were able to dodge this cascade and it passed them by. "After a few minutes," he wrote, "the rain soon ceased and the whole canyon resumed its deathlike stillness except for the noise of the little stream of muddy water running in the creek bed at our feet."

Others have not been so lucky. Seventy-five years later, in August of 1963, Roger Clubb was hiking with his eight-year-old son, Roger Jr., along the Bright Angel Trail on the opposite side of the canyon from Stanton's near miss. They had stopped for lunch under the cottonwood trees at Indian Gardens, an oasis next to Garden Creek located about halfway between the South Rim and the river, when they were caught in a brief downpour. After the rain abated, Clubb was leading his son back toward the South Rim when he heard a deep rumble, looked up the trail, and spotted a ten-foot-high wall of water and mud surging downhill through the Garden Creek drainage.

Clubb had several seconds to scramble out of the way by clambering up the slope next to the trail. But when he turned to warn his son, he realized that Roger Jr. had lagged behind and was now a few dozen yards downstream, plodding along directly in the path of the debris flow. Instead of climbing to safety, Clubb turned and began sprinting through the streambed in the hope of snatching up his boy before the flow hit.

What happened next is described by Michael Ghiglieri and Tom Myers in *Over the Edge: Death in Grand Canyon*, a comprehensive analysis of more than six hundred fatalities that have taken place inside the canyon during the past 150 years. According to several hikers who witnessed Clubb's desperate race, he never stood a chance, despite the fact that "he was running as wildly as any human being could." The slurry of mud and rocks engulfed the father first, then the boy. Both disappeared instantly. Searchers later found Clubb's body about four hundred yards downstream and nearly buried by debris, but it took another five days to find Roger Jr. He was wedged beneath a deposit of mud and rocks less than a hundred yards from where his father lay.

~

These two events—Stanton's narrow escape and Roger Clubb's mad dash to save his son—bracket a critical period in the understanding of what was taking place during the storm of 1966. In Stanton's day, this kind of landslide didn't even have a name, perhaps because the event was so at odds with the way everyone thought geology worked.

In the early part of the nineteenth century, there were two schools of thought on the mechanism of geomorphic change: "catastrophists," who argued that the earth was shaped by abrupt, cataclysmic events like Noah's flood; and "uniformitarians," who believed that geological changes unfolded at a glacial pace over immense spans of time. For centuries, the catastrophists had enjoyed the upper hand, in part because religious scholars in Europe declared that the earth was less than seven thousand years old.* During the scientific advances of the eighteenth century, however, researchers of all stripes began stumbling upon compelling evidence that the age of the planet was measured not in thousands

---

*In 1650, the Church of Ireland's archbishop, James Ussher, completed a careful study of the Bible and announced that the earth had been created at midday on October 23, 4004 BC.

of years but rather in hundreds of millions, perhaps even billions of years. By the end of the nineteenth century, the gradualists had not only won this long-running debate, they had prevailed so decisively that the pendulum was pushed too far in the other direction.

Up through the first half of the twentieth century, most tourists who contemplated the walls of the Grand Canyon assumed that this landscape was shaped slowly and gradually over tens of millions of years. This is true, but only in the broadest sense—which is to say, by stretching the process out on the scale of deep time. In the 1950s and 1960s, however, the geologic credo was further refined and scientists began to appreciate that the steady march of geomorphic change is punctuated by catastrophic bursts: brief moments of exceptionally brutal violence in which things happen very quickly indeed. In the canyon, these bursts take the form of debris flows.

In just a few minutes, a debris flow can achieve speeds that only the most extreme flash flood can match, and it is capable of moving objects that none but the largest floods could ever dislodge. Geologists who have studied debris flows in mountain ranges and canyon systems all over the world are now convinced that they constitute one of the signature events of the Grand Canyon. They are, in a sense, the canyon's architects and civil engineers. The river may have carved the main corridor of the gorge, but the debris flows have expanded its width, scribed its profile, and molded the castellated formations that fill the canyon's interior.

In addition, debris flows are responsible for one other thing. Among the 160 white-water rapids laced like beads on a necklace between Lee's Ferry and Lake Mead, almost every one of them owes its existence to the kind of event that was triggered during the storm that took place in the first week of December 1966.

~

Sometime between Saturday night and Wednesday morning, nearly a hundred separate debris flows were touched off inside eleven creeks and drainages all along the North Rim. Some of these avalanches were fluid and fast; others were gelatinous and slow. Most lost their momentum quickly and petered to a halt less than half a mile from where they started. But at least nine of them went considerably farther, and two managed to punch all the way from the rim to the river at the bottom of the canyon.

The larger of this pair began at the head of a drainage located about a dozen miles southwest of the park's entrance station, along a remote and little-used section of the North Rim known as Dragon Creek. Here, the ground drops off steeply, falling more than a thousand feet in a series of stairsteps that conclude at the base of the Hindu Amphitheater, a hanging subcanyon cut into the north wall directly to the west of the Bright Angel Creek drainage. The amphitheater consists of two main drainage streams—Crystal Creek and Dragon Creek—that are separated by a towering, razor-backed ridge known as the Dragon. Lacking eyewitness reports, a group of six scientists with the US Geological Survey have analyzed debris within this area and pieced together a reasonably detailed scenario of what took place.

Once over the rim, the water cascaded into a number of side canyons and tributary gorges, each channel funneling its discharge into a larger gully, forming a network of rivulets that mirrored the way the twigs of a tree are connected to its trunk. As the deluge intensified, the flow expanded until the heads of both creeks were pounding into the softer layers of shale directly below the rim. As these slopes gave way, tons of loose soil, greased with an infusion of micaceous minerals, formed a roiling brown tide that raced through Dragon Creek, picking up additional loads of debris and mud as tributaries poured in from both sides. As this half-solid, half-fluid torrent intensified, it started biting off clumps of sediment and snatching up boulders with each twist and turn. Soon the sides of the channels were giving way, dumping even larger clumps of dirt and even heavier boulders into the mix.

By now, the cascade looked like chocolate-colored cement, and as it tore downhill, this slithering mass began to come alive in a manner that was both surreal and grotesque. The surface was agitated and boiling, like the lava flow from a volcano, but on fast-forward. It also developed some impressive hydraulic features, albeit nothing like what one might encounter on a normal river. When the torrent rounded a bend, for example, it generated so much centrifugal force that the surface actually tilted so that the height of the flow on the outside bend was twelve feet higher than on the inside bend, resembling the banked turn of a high-speed racetrack. Meanwhile, sections of cliffs were unbolting from the sides of the subcanyon, peeling away and shattering to pieces like icebergs calving off the terminal end of a glacier.

Deep inside the Hindu Amphitheater, Dragon Creek intersects with a smaller tributary named Milk Creek. About a mile and a half upstream from this confluence point, the roaring debris flow did something unusual.

Just above the juncture between the two creeks lay the ruins of a mescal pit, a shallow depression lined with stones used by prehistoric Pueblo Indians, who inhabited the canyon prior to 1150, to roast the hearts of the agave plants that they harvested in these tributaries. The Puebloans were well aware of the danger posed by flash floods and debris flows, and they took pains to build their mescal pits in protected places—in this case, several dozen vertical feet above the streambed on the right side of Dragon Creek. This pit had been left undisturbed since the Puebloans had abandoned the canyon. The debris flow obliterated it.

By now, the body of this raging brown serpent was snapping back and forth between the walls, lashing at the terraces on either side and flinging spatters of mud dozens of feet into the air. As it thundered through Dragon Creek toward yet another confluence with Crystal Creek, it was now sixty feet wide, forty-four feet deep, and flowing at somewhere between 9,200 and 14,000 cfs—almost thirty dump-truck loads of material rushing past each second. This was close to the average annual rate of the Colorado itself. In effect, a cataract of liquidized mud and rock comparable to the size of the Colorado was now hurtling down Crystal Creek on a collision course with the main-stem river.

~

When the debris flow burst from the mouth of the Crystal Creek drainage at the bottom of the canyon, it was probably traveling faster than a human being could run, but not in a smooth, continuous rush. Instead, it pulsed and throbbed in a series of ebbs and surges that resembled the peristaltic heaves that take place inside the gut.* The sound it made was unearthly—a roar that can best be likened to the noise a diesel locomotive pulling a train of coal cars might make if it derailed and plunged over a bridge.

All of that would have appeared bizarre. But the feature that would have been most surreal, had anyone been there to witness it, was what was riding on the surface of the creature that crashed from the mouth of Crystal Canyon. Suspended on its dark and oily back were boulders the size of refrigerators and small automobiles. The largest of these objects was fourteen feet in diameter, and in apparent defiance of any law of physics, they all bobbed like corks, exhibiting a buoyancy and lightness totally at odds with their weight, with the heaviest of them being nearly fifty tons.

The moment this avalanche emerged from the narrow confines of the Crystal Creek drainage, the edges spread out laterally and began to decelerate. Even so, the central mass of debris easily plowed straight over the boulder-studded delta at the mouth of the drainage and slammed into the Colorado at Mile 98 with tremendous force. The impact was explosive, generating enormous waves and sending spray high into the air while literally bulldozing the current toward the south wall of the canyon, thereby creating a sharp bottleneck. One moment,

---

*There are two theories about what may cause this: fresh loads of sediment contributed when a tributary hits the main stream, or boulders that jam up to create temporary dams. Probably both theories are true.

the river was 280 feet wide, nearly the length of a football field. Seconds later, it was constricted to a channel of about 55 feet, the width of a street in New York City.

This was hardly the first time something like this had happened. On average, a drainage such as Crystal Creek produces a debris flow once or twice a century. Nevertheless, the event was singular in several respects. It was the first major debris flow to be extensively documented in the scientific literature on hydrology and geomorphology. It created the largest geomorphic channel change in the recorded history of the canyon. But perhaps the most sobering element was that mescal pit.

"The prehistoric Indians must have experienced flash floods," concluded the first paper that was published on the event, "but the flood of December 1966 probably was greater than any since the general abandonment of eastern Grand Canyon by the Pueblo Indians about A.D. 1150." If this assertion is true—and it is worth noting that it has since been contested by at least one scientist—it was the biggest thing that happened inside that drainage since the twelfth century.

Finally, the debris flow of December 1966 also wound up creating a rapid that would eventually reign as the deadliest stretch of white water in the Grand Canyon—although several months would pass before anyone discovered it.

~

On February 24, 1967, Ken Sleight, the president of the Western River Guides Association, sent out an emergency letter to every guide and outfitter in his organization. In the letter, Sleight explained that a ranger named Frank Betts had learned that the December storms along the North Rim had wrought tremendous changes to the Colorado River at Crystal Creek. According to a group of US Geological Survey scientists who were conducting research in the area, the debris flow at Mile 98 was so massive that the government's topographic maps would need to be revised. Betts had also spoken to the helicopter pilot who had shuttled the researchers into the canyon. "He has flown the river many times over the past two years and knows a good rapid when he sees one," wrote Betts. "He says Crystal rapids is now the most vicious he has seen."

A month later, Sleight sent out another letter to his members. In March, a company called Cross Tours and Expeditions had undertaken its first river trip of the year, and John Cross, Jr., the son of the company's owner, had just submitted the first direct report on Mile 98. Prior to this trip, Cross had spoken to the same helicopter pilot who had talked to Betts in February, and the pilot had told Cross that he did not think the rapid was navigable. Cross disagreed, but the pilot's warning was sobering, so Cross was braced for something big. When he reached Mile 97, a stretch of the river where the current had previously flowed at a moderate clip, he found himself motoring across a mile-long pool of calm, smooth-as-glass water that felt less like a river and more like a lake. As he made his way across the pool, Cross could hear the roar of something major over the sound of his motor.

Just ahead, an ugly fan-shaped delta of debris, still bespattered with a thick coating of mud, had forced the river against the south wall of the canyon. Several yards upstream of this constriction, the center of the current formed a narrow tongue of dense green water, hard and luminous as a shard of emerald. The water in that shaft was unbelievably fast and steep, and it hurtled directly into a vicious array of enormous standing waves backed by tremendous holes. Complicating matters further were rocks up to seven feet in diameter that had been strewn throughout the rapid, including a huge, jagged sleeper—a boulder positioned just beneath the surface of the water—at the narrowest part of the bottleneck.

The hole created by that sleeper, which would soon be known simply as the Big Hole, would become infamous in the years to come, and the water on its downstream side shot through a hundred yards of eight-to-ten-foot haystacks. These obstacles were formidable enough, but even worse, directly downstream from the jagged boulder the current was split by a large pile of exposed rocks that had been deposited midstream. While half the river continued to run through the series of huge holes next to cliffs on the left side, the rest of the current made a ninety-degree turn to the right before swinging downstream on the opposite side of the boulder pile.

As Cross correctly perceived, this new rapid offered a boatman two unpleasant alternatives—either a "wild ride" down the left that would send one directly through the holes or a risky cut to the safer channel on the right that would require enormous power to execute, and where the price of a mistake would be steep. "It is my opinion," Cross wrote to Sleight, "that a boat trying to break out of the current and get around the right side would probably hit the boulders at the center."

Cross opted for the roller-coaster ride on the left and made it through without a hitch. But the ferocity of the rapid left him sobered. The flood and the debris fan had narrowed the river to one-quarter its former width, doubled the drop, and increased the speed by a factor impossible to quantify. "Any way you look at it, Crystal has become one of the worst rapids in the Canyon," Cross scribbled on a drawing of this new hellbender enclosed with his report. "I would rate Crystal at a 10. It looks like it might be worse at lower water."

~

In the past, whenever a debris flow had created a new rapid like this, the river got to work on the bottleneck. Within a few years, a major spring flood would send enough water roaring through the canyon to sweep away the obstacles, rearrange the rock, and expand the breach. In this manner, the river has managed, over time, to erode its rapids with remarkable uniformity.

Unlike the other rapids on the river, however, Crystal would never have the opportunity to "mature" through seasonal flooding. Only three years prior to the 1966 debris flow, the headgates to the Glen Canyon Dam had been slammed shut, and annual spring floods were a thing of the past. The measured discharges now passing through the dam would make minor adjustments to the rocks, nudging them here and shifting them there, widening the channel slightly. But the giant boulders that had created the rapid's topographic and hydraulic contours would remain firmly in place. The river no longer had the muscle to move them aside.

Literally overnight, Crystal had been transmogrified into one of the most dreadful stretches of white-water rapids in the West. Every young boatman gunning for a career as a river guide would now have to figure out how to unlock its secrets and navigate its dangers. And none of those boatmen would have a tougher time mastering those nuances than the band of oarsmen—Kenton Grua among them—that rowed Martin Litton's little wooden dories.

9

The Death of the Emerald Mile

> *And the river was there*
> *—fascinating—deadly—*
> *like a snake.*
>
> —JOSEPH CONRAD

D URING the summers that immediately followed the 1966 debris
flow, the entire Grand Canyon guiding corps flung itself into
the task of mapping Crystal's floor plan and piecing together the
sequence of maneuvers that would enable them to thread through its jumbled
mayhem. The challenge, they discovered, was to surmount not just one or two
discrete obstacles, but to untangle a long, half-mile series of problems braided
into a wicked hydraulic knot. It was not enough merely to avoid the Big Hole at
the top, although that was certainly everyone's biggest concern. Directly to the
left of that hole lurked a turbulent vortex that came to be known as the Slate
Creek Eddy, whose boils were so powerful that, once inside it, one had virtually
no chance of breaking back into the main current without first flipping upside
down. And that was just the top of the rapid.

About two hundred yards downstream from that eddy, the current slammed
into a vertical wall of Vishnu schist. If your boat was raked along the side of
that cliff, you would be treated to the horrific sound of a disintegrating propeller, or a neoprene tube being ripped open, or the shaft of an oar exploding into
splinters. Among other complications, that kind of damage would rob you of

124

any chance to reach the only safe place to pull over—a tiny indentation on the *opposite* side of the river that was tucked all the way down at the tail end of the rapid and known as Thank God Eddy. Any boat that failed to make that haven would find itself hurtled straight into a small but vicious stretch of white water that featured a ninety-degree left-hand bend and a massive midstream boulder dubbed Nixon Rock because it was extremely difficult to "get to the right of it."

Those were all formidable obstructions. But perhaps the nastiest aspect of Crystal was the Rock Garden, the island of half-submerged boulders that had been dumped directly into the center of the river about halfway through the rapid. The upstream end of that island featured a Buick-size chunk of sandstone known as Big Red, which boasted a unique geologic distinction. Of the trillions of rocks of all shapes and sizes that had fallen off the cliffs and crashed into the Colorado over the centuries, none was responsible for more carnage or despair than Big Red. It was probably the most hated rock in the entire canyon.

In essence, Big Red acted as a kind of oversize mousetrap that sought to bait and ensnare any boatman who was so busy congratulating himself on having skated past the obstacles at the top of the rapid—the Big Hole, the Slate Creek Eddy, the cliff on the left—that he forgot to pay attention to what was coming next. At this moment the current would catapult him straight into Big Red and smear his boat to the side of the rock like shrink-wrap. This vicious entrapment could truly ruin your day—but that was only if you were lucky enough to collide with Big Red at high water, when waiting a few hours for the river to subside might relieve the pressure and enable you to pry the boat free. For the luckless guide who got in trouble at low water, his nightmare was just getting started.

As the water rose, the river would claw its way up the sides of Big Red and the force of the current would dramatically increase. As the stricken boat slowly disappeared beneath the surface, the river would rummage through the gear that had diligently been tied down earlier that morning, tearing everything to pieces like a bear inside a station wagon. Every half hour or so, the water would strip away the lashings on yet another key item—somebody's tent, a cooler stuffed with fresh vegetables, a watertight box housing the trip's only radio and an unread love letter from the boatman's girlfriend. The river would hoist each item to the surface and hold it there briefly, just beyond the reach of the hapless guide, as if taking stock of its value. Then it would contemptuously hurl the thing downstream, where it would sink and disappear.

This spectacle kept the boatman and his passengers occupied until someone on shore figured out a way to get out to the Rock Garden without becoming caught in the same predicament. If it was too late in the day to complete this operation before sunset, the stranded party might find itself forced to spend the night out there in the middle of the Colorado. As darkness set in, the noise of the waves and the spray coming off the rising surface of the water could make the place feel like an atoll in the North Sea.

The following morning, the passengers would be gathered up and distributed among the rest of the boats, and the boatman responsible for this disaster would settle into his new duties as somebody's swamper, or assistant, for the rest of the trip. Meanwhile, the Park Service would set in motion a plan to clean up what was left of the abandoned boat, which was now officially considered litter. A day or two later, a swift-water rescue team would show up with a set of pulleys and winches, and if Big Red *still* didn't want to hand the boat back in one piece, the crew would go to work with their cutting tools. When they were finished, the pieces of slashed rubber and mangled aluminum would be placed in a net, slung out of the canyon beneath the belly of a chopper, and trucked off to a landfill on the South Rim.

Finally, a month or two later, the guide who had lost his boat might find himself called into the boss's office and asked if he had any interest in taking a look at the bill the company had just received from the Park Service. If this was the boatman's first major screwup, he'd stand there and listen as the boss launched into a long harangue about the duplicitous treachery of Crystal and the critical importance of never, *ever*, taking your eye off Big Red. If this was the boatman's second or third encounter with that miserable chunk of sandstone, the boss would probably inform him that it was time to go look for work at another outfitter.

~

Crystal spent the next several years merrily clobbering every kind of boat at every conceivable level of water. But unlike another major hellbender about eighty miles downstream that was also giving everybody fits, Crystal had riddles with answers. Untangling its lines and solving its many problems required ugly trial and error, but by the early seventies, almost every outfitter in the canyon had managed to more or less figure out what needed to be done. The one glaring exception to this trend was Litton's platoon of dorymen.

For anyone in a tiny wooden boat, Crystal seemed utterly insoluble. When the water was low, there was no surefire way to avoid the rocks. When the river ran high, the giant haystacks flipped the boats over like hot tortillas on a griddle. The dorymen were still trying to find an answer to these challenges when Litton found himself standing on the scouting terrace at Mile 98 on a blistering June afternoon in the summer of 1970 with a group of five dories and a baggage raft. Scratching his head, he considered the backbreaking prospect of a portage—the only guaranteed method of preventing Crystal from chewing through the boats and ejecting them like the spent cartridges on a machine gun—and decided he wanted no part of it. "We're not going to carry these boats around," he declared, "even if I have to row this thing myself."

The first dory he took through was sucked straight into the Big Hole, dragged upside down along the side of the Rock Garden, and spit through the tail waves while Litton trailed behind in the water, clinging to the stern line, which he managed to fling around a rock at the very bottom of Thank God Eddy. He anchored the shattered boat in the shallows, hiked up the right shoreline, seized hold of the second craft, and put her through a similar sequence of shocking crashes that sheared off her hatch lids and shattered her oars. This time he wound up on the left bank, which meant that after tying up the boat he now had to jump back into the water and swim across the river. Fifteen minutes later he emerged, soaking wet and out of breath, staggered past his crew, and clambered aboard the third boat with a young guide named Ned Andrews, who said he wanted to help—an impulse that left Litton wondering about Andrews's sanity. The results were the same.

After this third pounding, Litton was steeling himself to head back upstream to deal with the fourth boat when a guide named Ron Hayes, who couldn't bear to watch Litton being sent through Crystal's wash cycle a fourth time, took off with two passengers. When Hayes crested the rapid's main wave, his dory stood vertically on end, and Hayes was sent careening backward, out of the cockpit and toward the stern. The two passengers in the bow saved him from being dumped into the river by grabbing his ankles and hauling him back into his oar station. The shift in weight propelled them over the top, and Hayes slammed his oars back into their locks just in time to steer them clear of the Rock Garden.

That left only two guides, Curt Chang and John Blaustein, standing at the top of the rapid next to the *Music Temple*, along with a baggage boatman named Charlie Stern.

"So, do you want to hike down, or do you want to ride through with me?" Chang asked Blaustein.

"What are the chances of another flip?" Blaustein shrugged as he climbed aboard the *Music Temple*.

Chang pulled into the current, followed closely by Stern in the baggage raft. Both boats promptly turned upside down, and Stern was washed all the way to Tuna Rapid, almost a mile downstream, before he finally made it to shore. Hayes's boat was the only one that made it through intact on what would henceforth be referred to as "that miserable dog-day at Crystal."

The damage was so extensive that the dorymen were forced to spend the next two days patching the boats back together using every spare piece of plywood in their repair kits and several lengths of driftwood that they cadged from the shoreline. On the second morning of repair work, Litton was patching a hole using a scrap of plywood and a batch of homemade glue he'd somehow concocted with a box of Bisquick, the instant baking mix. To speed up the drying, he decided to place a hot frying pan on the chine and wound up compounding their problems by setting the dory on fire.

So it went. By the end of that summer, every doryman in the company was convinced that Crystal was an implacable adversary with whom they were at war. That fall, Litton grumbled that it might not be a bad idea for the Park Service to send in a demolition team with a couple of boxes of dynamite and blast a fish ladder down the right side of the rapid so the boats could be gently lowered through.

"We really could do without it," he would bark whenever the subject of Crystal came up. "I don't think it's a necessary rapid."

~

Ironically, though, Crystal *was* a necessary rapid. Because it was this stretch of white water more than any other that was responsible for transforming the dorymen from a band of beleaguered yahoos into a squadron of crack oarsmen who came to regard rowing wooden boats through the canyon as a form of art, an enterprise imbued—at least in their own minds—with all the drama and emotional intensity of a Beethoven symphony or a dance by Balanchine.

Litton had by now assembled a corps of about twenty guides, a dozen of whom were regulars, and each of them loved everything about their job except for the execrable pay and that the boss still insisted on policing the garbage cans. They were now divided into two main crews, each of which had a permanent leader who called all the shots about how far they ran each day, where they camped at night, and the order in which they tackled the rapids. The first team was led by Regan Dale, who had signed on with a motor company in the spring of 1971, then two years later took a pay cut to go work for Litton when he realized that rowing a dory was what he wanted to do for the rest of his life. The second crew was led by Wally Rist, a high school teacher from St. Louis who lived in Phoenix and was something of a whiz at math.

Under Crystal's harsh tutorials, both of these trip leaders—or TLs, as they were called on the river—achieved levels of finesse and competency that Litton himself couldn't be bothered to cultivate. Dale, a laconic skipper who never said a word more than he needed to, would build a reputation as a chilly minimalist whose brevity with language was eloquently mirrored in his rowing style. He came to understand current so well—where it was heading (often tricky and sometimes invisible), where it actually *wanted* to go (not always the same thing), and where he himself needed to be (a separate trajectory that could waft imperiously above the first two calculations)—that he was reputed to take the fewest number of oar strokes of any boatman on the river.

Rist, on the other hand, would become perhaps the premier scholar of dam fluctuations—the daily ebb and flow of Glen's discharges that were dictated by the electricity demands in places such as Phoenix and Las Vegas—which played havoc with the river by boosting the flow from 3,000 to 30,000 cfs, then ratcheting it back down again in the space of twelve hours. As an added complication, those discharges proceeded downstream at speeds that could vary between four and six miles per hour. The deeper you were in the canyon, the harder it became to calculate how long the ebbs and the surges would take to reach you. This turned the river corridor into a bizarre version of a marine ecosystem whose tides varied according to how many miles downstream from the dam you were. Rist set out to master these nuances, and he succeeded magnificently.

Applying themselves to their respective specialties, Dale and Rist became absurdly good at what they did, and they added value to their achievements by passing knowledge and skills along to their subordinates. During the scouts, they permitted everyone to take in the contours of whatever rapid they were surveying, then conducted impromptu lectures that usually began with one of them declaring, *Okay, all you new guys, listen up.* After an exhaustive review of the hydraulics feature and a graphic description of what would happen if each doryman failed to read the current correctly, these tutorials would conclude with an announcement of the running order: who would lead, who would chase the leader, who would run sweep, and who would be placed in the safety slots in the middle. Under this instruction, the crews gradually began to get a handle on their runs—memorizing the lines, codifying the marker rocks that would prevent them from getting lost in the chaos, rehearsing the sequence of moves that would see them through. As their understanding deepened, they noticed a commensurate improvement in performance. Their skills sharpened, the mistakes they committed became less frequent, the quality of their oarsmanship grew ever more refined.

Around this point, everyone realized that the holiest grail they could pursue would be for one of them to pull off an entire run—not merely skating through Crystal but threading through the entire canyon from top to bottom—without suffering a single crash, flip, or ding. There is some confusion about who first achieved this feat, but when the moment finally arrived, it was deemed so miraculous that it was commemorated by the scrawling of the words *Golden Trip!* on the inside cover of the boatman's right cross-hatch in Magic Marker. Within a few seasons, the best of the dorymen were nailing one or two of these runs every summer. By the midseventies, the hatch lids of almost every boat in the fleet were filled with golden-trip markers.

With Dale and Rist running the show, and the rest of Litton's guide corps gradually getting the hang of the river, the boss no longer felt he needed to lead every trip himself. Instead, he kept tabs on things with his airplane. He'd load up the passenger seats of his Cessna with blocks of ice and cases of Schaefer beer, and then in a maneuver borrowed from his World War II days, he'd barnstorm through the canyon at 140 miles an hour, buzzing the tops of the tamarisk trees and looking for his camps. "We'd hear his approach and it'd be like—*here he comes, everybody run!*" recalls Andre Potochnik, a veteran of this era. "Pedal-to-the-metal Martin. He'd swoop in, strafe us with supplies, then roar off to Washington to lobby for the redwoods or whatever other wilderness issue he was fighting at the time."

Although this meant that Litton was no longer as much of a direct presence inside the canyon, some things didn't change, especially when it came to his view of the baloney boats. He continued to disparage them at every opportunity—and thanks to his behavior, most of the motor and raft companies continued to regard the dorymen as insufferable elitists. But now a new twist began to emerge, one that changed the dynamic in an unexpected manner. Whenever Litton returned to the canyon to participate in a river trip, guides who worked for other outfitters were pulling alongside him in the eddies, or strolling over to his camp at night, and beseeching him for a job. "They'd come up to me with these big cow-eyes and ask if there was any chance they could get on with us," he would later recall. "I can't imagine why, but I guess they admired what we were doing." Perhaps that was part of their motivation. But the driving force behind those entreaties was that scarcely a boatman in the canyon didn't dream of one day strapping himself into the driver's seat of a dory.

By the middle of the 1970s, Litton's crew perceived themselves to be perched like catbirds on the pinnacle of the unique and hidden world of white water at the bottom of the canyon. Even those who were convinced that the dorymen were a detestable pack of prima donnas almost always felt a stab of jealousy. The dorymen had their own valets—an entourage of earnest baggage boatmen who attended to the niggling details of setting up camp each night and then breaking it down the following morning, paying their dues in the hopes of one day piloting a dory of their own. The dorymen also had their own cooks—all women, each harboring a fantasy that one day Litton might be persuaded to set aside his chauvinism and allow her to row.* In short, the dorymen had forged themselves into one of the most rarefied fraternities in all of the out-doors: a society of tanned swashbucklers who were paid to live and work aboard the world's sweetest fleet of rowboats in the heart of America's most famous national park. And although they were by no means universally loved by their rivals, they were the envy of the canyon.

Unfortunately, however, the boat that was largely responsible for creating this state of affairs wasn't faring nearly so well. In fact, she was about to be taken to the threshold of complete destruction.

~

On the morning that the *Emerald Mile* had first been launched into the river at Lee's Ferry for her maiden run in the summer of 1971, one of the boatmen had turned to Litton and asked how long he expected her to last. "Oh, if we get ten trips out of her, I'd be happy," Litton casually replied. Five years later, she had surpassed those expectations many times over, racking up so many voy-ages through the canyon that her odometer—if she'd had one—would have registered more miles than almost any other dory. She had also borne a greater share of hardships. Trip after trip, season after season, the rocks and the riffles, the surging eddies and the punishing haystacks, the sun and the rain and the thousand-pound loads had all taken their toll, and by now the river had exacted a steep price from her frame and her hull. Having weathered five seasons of uninterrupted abuse, she was no longer the queen of the fleet.

As the oldest and most battered boat in Litton's roster, she also suffered from the indignity of having been claimed by no one, which deprived her of the care and the attention that was lavished on her sisters and daughters. She was thus a logical choice when an extra boat was needed in Idaho, where Litton was expanding his guiding operations on the Snake and the Salmon—highly technical rivers that lacked the enormous hydraulics of the Colorado but were studded with the kinds of rocks that could peel open the bottom of a dory like a can opener. There, in the little river town of Lewiston, she met her next care-taker: an athletic young drifter with shoulder-length brown hair named Steve Reynolds, known to his friends as Wren, who was destined to play a leading role in the legend of the *Emerald Mile*.

Wren hailed from a logging burg 175 miles north of San Francisco, a tiny place called Cummings, which boasted 127 residents, a redwood tree with a

---

*In the years to come, a number of these women would demolish Litton's prejudices by matching or surpassing the best among their male counterparts, eventually emerging as some of the finest guides in the canyon.

tunnel carved in its trunk that you could drive a car through, and a little twelve-unit motel by the side of Highway 101 that his parents owned. After spending much of his boyhood hunting deer and fishing for trout in the forests behind his home, he had drifted east searching for work in the ski resorts around Lake Tahoe, then eventually hitchhiked his way into Lewiston, where Litton's Idaho operations were based. After spending a summer season learning the ropes in the cockpit of a baggage raft, he was promoted to a full guide slot and permitted to take the oars of the battered little dory that had just arrived from the Grand Canyon, a decision whose wisdom was immediately questioned when Wren headed down the Snake and rammed her directly into a submerged rock in the middle of Wild Sheep, the first rapid in Hells Canyon.

The damage was bad—by the time the rapid finished clobbering the *Emerald Mile*, she had lost her gunwales and oarlocks, along with a few pieces of her bowpost and stern. When they finally got her back to the boathouse, Wren was given a pep talk familiar to many novice dorymen, a little homily stressing that a wreck such as this was simply an unpleasant rite of passage and that he had all the makings of a fine oarsman. At the end of the speech, he was informed of Litton's you-break-it-you-fix-it policy.

When the rest of the Idaho crew realized that Wren knew absolutely nothing about repairing a wooden boat, the entire boathouse pitched in to help, and a month or two later the stricken dory looked ready to take another run at Wild Sheep. However, a phone call arrived from the boss ordering the Idaho operations manager to get the *Emerald Mile* loaded onto a trailer and sent south, where she was needed for yet another tour of duty in the Grand Canyon. Wren was livid. Having spent weeks restoring her to life, he had begun to think of the dory as his. He watched as she was wheeled out of the boatyard and disappeared down the highway with the assumption that he would never see her again.

Back in Hurricane, the *Emerald Mile* was promptly demoted to "guest boat," the dory reserved for guides who worked on rivers in other parts of the country and were making their first trip through the canyon. Late in the summer of 1977, she was handed over to one of Wren's colleagues from Idaho, a wiry guide with dark, curly hair named Steve Dalton, whom everyone called Stevie Sperm because he was too energetic to sit in one place for long. The trip was led by Regan Dale, and for the first two weeks, Dalton did a yeoman's job of piloting her safely through the gauntlet until, late in the afternoon of July 23, the crew arrived at a sinister column of black lava that soared sixty feet from the middle of the river, the core of an extinct volcano that is known as Vulcan's Anvil and that marks the entrance to the only rapid in the canyon more ferocious than Crystal. There, the *Emerald Mile*'s steadily diminishing stream of luck finally trickled to a halt.

~

One hundred and seventy-nine miles downstream from Lee's Ferry, directly below the Toroweap Overlook, the greatest river in the West runs up against a picket line of submerged boulders, roars over the edge, and detonates. This is Lava Falls, a quarter-mile stretch of white water that is considered by many to be the biggest navigable rapid in North America. Here the river drops almost fifteen vertical feet, creating a marbled chaos of water and rock that has destroyed more boats and shattered the composure of more guides than any other rapid in the canyon.

Lava's hydraulics are so vicious that in 1869 John Wesley Powell ordered his entire fleet to be lowered along the shore with ropes, and the first confirmed run wasn't made for another twenty-seven years. Even today there is no guarantee that a boat will make it through Lava safely, and when things go wrong, the results can be shocking to watch. Motor rigs are folded in half like tacos. Boatmen are blown from their seats. Broken oar shafts cartwheel through the air as the welds on aluminum frames snap like dry twigs and passengers are forced to dog-paddle for their lives.

What makes Lava Falls so insidious is that there's not a single good line, a fact that is painfully evident the moment you climb up the cliff of scorched basalt on the right bank of the river that serves as the scouting point. The entire left side of the river is studded with enormous rocks and pour-overs that cannot be negotiated in a hard-hulled boat at any water level below 13,000 cfs. In the center of the river, the current plummets into a recirculating keeper hole, while the right side of the river features a line of black rocks with scalloped surfaces that make them look like giant avocados. The sheer fury of this spectacle can be so intimidating that guides have been known to sit on the scout rock for hours as they screw up the courage to return to their boats. But for a period during the golden age of river guiding, a marvelous corridor through all of this chaos opened up.

Not long after the debris flow that formed Crystal, a flash flood roared down Prospect Canyon, a large tributary drainage on the south side of Lava, and rearranged the submerged boulders in the center of the river. The shift was minor and subtle, but the new alignment pried open a subsurface channel that allowed a narrow stream of current to proceed smoothly downstream without folding back on itself or colliding against a rock. That stream was breathtakingly thin, and because it threaded through the most violent section of white water in the center of the rapid, it was impossible to discern. In fact, the only evidence that suggested it was there was a line of tiny bubbles that would pulse up at irregular intervals, burbling to the surface every few minutes and remaining visible for no more than fifteen seconds or so before disappearing again. The path that those bubbles delineated was so faint, so ill defined, so absurdly tenuous, that only the most careful and devoted observer would even take note of them and ponder their meaning. But one afternoon in the summer of 1971, Wally Rist caught a glimpse of the bubbles, decided to follow their line, and demonstrated that a viable run was indeed there.

In the spring of 1995, another flood would race down Prospect Canyon and tweak the configuration once again—and the bubbles would vanish for good. But for twenty-three years, that ephemeral trail marked the most mysterious and confounding run in the entire canyon. They called it the Slot, and a large part of its allure lay in its evanescence. Sometimes you could search for the bubbles and never see them. Other times you would *think* you spotted them, only to discover in the midst of your run that you had seen something else. But when they were there and you lined up your bowpost on the path they laid out, the ride was pure delight—an effortless glide in which you barely even touched your oars as you slid through the heart of the rapid while water exploded around you in every direction. If you executed a flawless run through the Slot, you wouldn't take on a single drop of water, which seemed so outrageously inconceivable that you would arrive at the bottom of the rapid half-convinced that the whole thing had been a dream. And therein lay the other part of the run's fascination. Although the Slot was a manifestation of the laws of fluid mechanics, it seemed to partake in equal measure from the realm of metaphysics. In some ways, the run offered a hydraulic affirmation of that wiggy paradox to which Zen masters refer when they talk about journeys and destinations: the notion that only by steering himself unflinchingly into those places he most fervently wished to avoid—in this case, one of the vilest patches of white water in the entire canyon—could a man hope to arrive at the place he truly needed to be.

You would never want to try the Slot in a motor rig—the gap between the rocks was narrower than the width of a big baloney boat. You could certainly pull it off in an oar raft, but rubber wasn't always the best tool for the job because it lacked the precision and the maneuverability that the run demanded. So the Slot became something of a dory specialty—even as other boatmen initially wrestled with the question of whether the run existed at all. Which was perhaps the most bewitching aspect of the Slot: the possibility that executing the run correctly might have less to do with actually being able to see the bubbles and more to do with your willingness to *imagine* that they were there. For the first several years, a handful of skeptics even started peddling the heretical but exquisite theory that perhaps the bubbles weren't anything other than just that—bubbles—and that the line the dorymen were surfing through the maelstrom during those enchanted years was nothing more than the glittering suspension of their own self-righteousness.

That was eventually disproved as the dories and later some intrepid rafters ran the Slot time after time. But if nothing else, the theory reflects what a special time this was on the river—an era of magical possibilities that briefly willed itself into existence and then, like most things of wonder and beauty, failed to sustain its own fire and winked out. Even when there was doubt it existed, however, the Slot offered the clearest possible window into the dory-men's desperation to find a way through the madness of Lava Falls and avoid the kind of catastrophe that was visited upon the *Emerald Mile* in the summer of 1977.

~

In July of that year, the Slot was wide-open, and the key that unlocked its entry was a narrow and continuously wriggling line of jade-colored water at the top of the rapid that squeezed through a small gap between the right-hand boulder garden and the keeper hole in the center. The trick was to allow your boat to drift down this tongue with the bow pointing slightly left and, at exactly the right moment, pull sharply on your right oar to pivot into the slower water and kill your momentum. A boatman who executed this move properly would emerge from the top of the rapid dry and happy, then find himself run through a sequence of enormous whaleback-shaped tail waves at the bottom. If you missed the entry for any reason, however, you would find yourself at the mercy of a complex series of events whose sequence and details didn't matter much because you were totally hosed. Which is exactly what happened to the *Emerald Mile* on the afternoon of July 23, when Stevie Sperm tried to follow Regan Dale and the rest of the boatmen through that narrow little keyhole.

Dalton was just a few feet to the right of where he needed to be, but that was enough. Instead of riding the magic carpet through the center, he was rudely hurled into the V-wave, a mountain of water created by two standing waves that crash continuously into each other. Here the river gathered itself into a fist and delivered a roundhouse punch straight over his bow, a haymaker of frigid water whose arrival felt like a truckload of wet cement. As Dalton's decks and foot-wells were swamped, the boat reeled helplessly under the shocking weight of more than two tons of water, then flipped—at which point the backside of the V-wave harpooned him straight into a murderous vortex along the right shore known as the Corner Pocket. When the Corner Pocket got its claws around the *Emerald Mile*, it began drilling the dory around and around, and with each rotation the boat was smashed into the side of a giant chunk of basalt called the

Black Rock, a series of crashes that swiftly began to dismember her piece by piece.

Dale, who had skated through without a hitch, was now tucked into a quiet eddy at the bottom of the rapid and thus unable to see what was happening upstream. But when he caught sight of several pieces of plywood with beryl-green paint bobbing down the river, he knew exactly what had happened and raced back along the shoreline to help. Unfortunately, he and the other guides could do little except gather on the tilted surface of the Black Rock and shout encouragement to Dalton, who was now clinging to the stern as he and the boat were repeatedly slammed against the side of the rock.

On one of those passes, Dalton made a grab for the rock and was pulled to safety. But the hapless dory continued to circle, ramming into the rock again and again, losing another chunk with each crashing gyration. The punishment continued without letup for at least twenty minutes—by which time the eddy was awash with shattered pieces of plywood—until Dale and the rest of the crew finally latched on to her carcass, levered her out of the water, and carried her bodily over the top of the Black Rock.

When they stepped back to assess the devastation, she barely resembled a boat. The stern was more or less intact, but her entire bow had been obliterated. The gunwales and bowpost were gone. Her front hatches were smashed or missing, and the front portion of her hull looked as if it had been lopped off by a drunken logger with a chain saw. Remarkably—and this was perhaps the most eloquent testament to the *Emerald Mile*'s resiliency and spirit—she could still float, largely thanks to the watertight hatches amidships and in her stern.

After taking stock of the disaster, the crew broke open the repair kits and got to work. They brought what was left of her side panels together across the front seat and anchored the ends together with baling wire. Then they started in with the duct tape, reinforcing the wire and closing up as many gaps as possible. When they were through, there was no question of applying a coat of paint or touching up her logo—she was now little more than a marginally buoyant piece of trash. The challenge was to devise a way of simply getting her down the river and out of the canyon.

Dalton, who had cracked several ribs when he was caught between the rock and boat during one of the brutal collisions, was in no condition to row. So after every piece of cargo had carefully been lifted from the hatches and transferred to other boats, her oars were handed to Rudi Petschek, a guide who had been on her maiden voyage back in the summer of 1971. While Dalton huddled in her stern, cradling his chest, Petschek applied himself to the delicate task of rowing her, backward, toward the end of the canyon.

The journey took three days and was touch and go the entire way. Under Dale's watchful eye, Petschek cheated every riffle between Lava Falls and the Grand Wash Cliffs, hugging the shore wherever possible and doing his best to dance between the waves. His toes and feet were awash in water the entire time, and at several points he was convinced that the boat was on the verge of sinking. Through perseverance and skill, however, he nursed her through—entirely oblivious to how the dory's saga was far from over and that he, along with Steve Reynolds up in distant Idaho, was ordained to play a key part in her final, as yet unwritten, chapter.

When they pulled into Pierce Ferry, the wreckage of what had once been the *Emerald Mile* was hoisted onto the back of Big Blue, the truck they used for transporting the dories, and Dale's weary crew started the long drive back to Hurricane. Along the way, they debated what to do with the boat, eventually conceding that the most sensible thing was to haul her off to the town garbage dump and give her a "Viking funeral"—setting her on fire, then pushing her off the back of the truck and into the rubbish pile. This, they all agreed, would offer a fitting farewell for what had once been the fairest member of their fleet—an homage to the seminal role she had played in the evolution of the dories and, simultaneously, a concession to perhaps the deepest and most sobering of the canyon's many lessons: that all earth's children—those whom she neglects and those whom she loves the most—are destined for oblivion. In the face of that truth, nothing was more practical or more poetic than consigning her to the flames.

So that was the plan. But when Big Blue finally pulled into the boatyard in Hurricane, a man everyone called the Factor stepped forward, cast his eye over what was left of the little boat, and declared that he had a better idea.

And in a single stroke, everything changed.

PART IV

The Master of the Emerald Mile

If a man is to be obsessed by something,
I suppose a boat is as good as anything,
perhaps a bit better than most.

—E. B. WHITE

Kenton Grua and his dory

10

The Factor

"And you really live by the river? What a jolly life!"
"By it and with it and on it and in it," said the Rat.... "It's my world,
and I don't want any other. What it hasn't got is not worth having, and
what it doesn't know is not worth knowing."

—KENNETH GRAHAME, *The Wind in the Willows*

AMONG the many odd members of Litton's crew, perhaps the most unusual was an eccentric and contrarian boatman who had mastered the art of Grand Canyon river running at the throttle of a motor rig before converting to the science of oars, who loved the rocks as deeply as he adored the water, and who, despite his upbringing in the astringent faith of Brigham Young, harbored an abiding fondness for top-notch reefer as well as Kessler, a bottom-shelf brand of hooch so cheap it was mostly sold in plastic bottles.

By the age of twenty-nine, Kenton Grua was so bald that his skull looked like a wind-blasted billiard ball, yet his shoulders supported a peltry of back hair that could have doubled as a shag rug. He was so short that he barely cleared five foot six on tiptoe, but his personality was large enough to generate its own weather. He was stubborn and combative and intensely playful; fiercely self-righteous and enormously sensitive to the needs of others; often inspiring, frequently ornery, never punctual, endlessly original, chronically cross-grained, and almost invariably a colossal pain in the ass. The cocktail of traits he presented was complex enough to evoke intense anger, weary exasperation, and genuine love—in equal measure, and often within the same instant—from the dory rats in whose midst he lived and worked for most of his thirty-three years on the Colorado.

Something insane, absurd, and at times a little frightening lurked in the depths of passion that Grua nurtured for the river and the dories. But a hint of something singular, a whiff of the extraordinary, wafted off the surface of those fixations too. More than anything, perhaps, he stood as an exemplar of the obsessions that can spontaneously ignite the tinder of a man's soul and then race like a wildfire through the upper branches of his spirit when he decides to surrender the entirety of himself, unconditionally and without reservation, to the narrow and seductive world at the bottom of the canyon.

He was born in Salt Lake City in the summer of 1950 and spent his first eleven years in the citadel of Mormondom, although the primary altars of worship that held his interest were the ski slopes in the Wasatch Mountains just outside the city. The year he turned twelve, his family pulled up stakes and moved 175 miles east to Vernal, a high-desert town in the northeastern corner of the state, where his father was starting up a small trucking company that specialized in hauling freight to the isolated outposts of Wyoming, Utah, and western Colorado. Cupped in the shadow of the Uinta Mountains and perched less than fifteen miles from the point where the Green River flows through Dinosaur National Monument, Vernal was remote, tight-knit, and deeply self-contained—the kind of place where if a man dislocated his shoulder after getting tangled up with his horse, it was written up in the newspaper. In Grua's eyes, Vernal's chief deficiency was that it lacked access to good skiing, and he initially disliked the place so much that when his birthday finally arrived, his father decided that his son needed not one present, but two: a ten-speed bicycle and a river trip.

They hired on with a local outfitter owned by two brothers, Ted and Don Hatch, who ran large motor rigs all along the Green and the Colorado, and whose head boatman, Shorty Burton, was a gifted and generous guide. Burton, who had four children of his own, took the boy under his wing as they floated down the Yampa to its confluence with the Green at Echo Park, the place that had so enchanted both Powell and Litton. By the end of the trip, having learned how to bake biscuits in a Dutch oven and having been given his first chance to row, Grua was utterly hooked. Later, when his father purchased an old army-surplus raft, he began disappearing on solo trips that took him through Lodore, Desolation, Split Mountain Gorge, and the rest of the canyons along the upper Green and the Yampa. By the time he graduated from high school, Grua was a full-fledged boatman.

The year he turned eighteen, he was given the opportunity to build the sort of life whose arc would probably have taken him far from Vernal and its rivers when Utah senator Wallace Bennett nominated him to compete with eighteen other candidates for a spot at the US Naval Academy in Annapolis. Failing to win the selection, he headed off to Salt Lake City to attend the University of Utah, where he intended to study mechanical engineering. But at the end of his first semester when he returned home for Christmas break, he had a chat with Ted Hatch about the possibility of working as a river guide the following summer in the Grand Canyon. When Hatch asked if he was available to start the following week, Grua immediately said yes, quit school, and signed on.

His first training run was in March of 1969, and on the very next trip he was in charge of his own rig, a set of thirty-three-foot bridge pontoons with a frame made from two-by-sixes and equipped with a twenty-horsepower Mercury outboard engine that hung off the back. Hatch was then one of the largest outfitters in the canyon, and the ten-day trips he ran in those tail-draggers were fast and highly profitable. They were also exciting, especially for the guides. The tail-draggers were long and highly flexible, and if you smashed through a large standing wave or plunged into a hole, the stern could kick up with enough force to catapult you straight over the bow. To prevent this, the Hatch boatmen lashed themselves to their sterns like rodeo riders. Grua was thrilled by the action, but what really caught his attention during that first summer, and what stayed with him later, had no connection with the motor rigs he was riding.

Sometime in August, he whisked past a pod of wooden boats led by an imposing figure in a black, nineteenth-century frock who was pretending to be John Wesley Powell. Those boats were graceful and intriguing, and the moment Grua spotted them, he knew he had to find a way to get himself into the driver's seat of one.

He wasn't sure exactly how to approach the man in the frock, whose smoldering antipathy toward motor rigs was widely known. And in any case, Grua understood that he first needed to get some experience with an oar boat. So two seasons later, he told Ted Hatch that he was quitting and joined up with another outfit that rented out part of its boathouse to Martin Litton.

For the rest of that summer, Grua watched in fascination as Litton's crews staggered off the water in boats covered in duct tape and then engaged in marathon repair sessions to get their battered dories ready for another go-around with Crystal, Lava, and the rest of the big rapids. The following spring, Grua strode across the warehouse and asked Litton for a job. The old man looked him over, hired him on the spot, and assigned him the *Chattahoochee*, an early knockoff of the *Emerald Mile*.

~

Grua's new colleagues didn't quite know what to make of him, but the thing they noticed first was the disproportion between his size and his strength. He was built like a wolverine, small and compact, but wired with quicksilver reflexes. He had small hands too, and when you watched him row, you could see that both of his thumbs were clubbed, a genetic condition that fortune-tellers call hammer thumb or murderer's thumb. He barely weighed 135 pounds, but every square inch of tissue inside his skin was pure muscle, with not an ounce of fat anywhere on his body.

The dorymen also noticed that he didn't sleep much, no more than four or five hours a night. If one of them awoke at 3:00 a.m., he would look over and see that Grua's headlamp was on and he was reading a book in his hammock, or rattling around in his boat, or quietly strumming on his guitar, or flossing his teeth. During the day, however, Grua had plenty of energy to power through the long hours of labor—the rowing and the scouting, the rigging and the loading, and the hundred-odd other tasks that made up a boatman's day. He was constantly gathering the clients together and leading them off on epic hikes up to spectacular vantage points high above the river or deep into the countless tributaries that branched off the river corridor. Once, when a river trip chartered by a group of alumni from Yale drank up all the booze within the first three days of their trip, Grua volunteered to hoof it all the way up to the South Rim for a resupply. He returned the following day, toting a backpack stuffed with $240 worth of hard liquor.

His colleagues noticed too that he understood the boats—their strengths as well as their limitations. This was as clear in the repair shop as it was on the river, and it was equally evident that he was good at reading water. Even though he often lagged behind the other guides when they pulled over to scout an upcoming rapid—usually because he was fixing something on his boat or explaining some aspect of geology or botany or hydrology to one of the passengers—they would hold off on forming a plan until he had arrived.

"Let's wait for the little man," someone would suggest, "and see what he has to say."

What the dorymen noticed more than anything else, though, was Grua's consuming fascination with the canyon. He was spellbound by the way it seemed so timeless and so eternal, yet also provided what he called "an instant flash picture" of how the earth had been formed. He couldn't seem to get enough of the place, and he regarded each journey as unique, except in one crucial respect: when it was over, he simply couldn't wait to get back to Lee's Ferry and start the whole thing all over. Each time he went through the canyon, the list of places he absolutely had to explore and the things he urgently needed to experience—a cool new cave he'd spotted here, a drainage he had yet to check out there, a special little grotto that, granted, he'd already visited half a dozen times but simply couldn't wait to show to yet another group of clients—grew longer and more compelling in a way that left him simultaneously bewitched and insatiate. "It just seems like it's going to go on forever and then—*boom*—it's over," he would grumble at the end of yet another three-week trip. "I want to do this again!"

Those were things his coworkers found endearing. But many other aspects of his personality also drove them nuts—in particular, the feverish intensity with which Grua insisted on flinging himself into each and every task to which he applied himself, oblivious to the needs of those around him. At 8:00 a.m., when the gear was stowed and the passengers were aboard the boats, expectant and eager, one might well look over and discover that Grua had emptied out his hatches and that every square inch of the *Chattahoochee*'s decking was stacked with tin cans, coils of rope, rubber dry bags, and sundry pieces of gear. When you asked him when he thought he might be ready to launch, he'd exclaim that he'd woken up in the middle of the night with a sensational new idea about how to redistribute the cargo in his boat so that the trim—the lateral balance— would be radically improved, and he was so excited by the possibilities that he needed to test the program *right now.* Two hours later, he'd have everything rearranged and pronounce himself good to go.

That intensity might have been less annoying—after all, each of the other dorymen had quirks of his own—if Grua hadn't been such an incorrigible evangelist. An outgrowth of his fervency, they discovered, was his conviction that there was an absolutely right way and an absolutely wrong way to do absolutely everything. He had rules about how you should boil the water for coffee in the morning, and rules about how to make a proper scarf cut when you were replacing a fractured side panel on a smashed boat. He had rules about the kind of wood you should collect for the evening campfire, where that fire should be built, and what needed to be done with the coals the following morning. Grua took it upon himself to codify those rules, and having done so, he then judged both himself and everyone else by the standards he had framed.

Most of the dorymen acknowledged that many of these rules were actually quite good. But Grua was never satisfied with outlining them just once, especially when he could hammer the point home by repeating the thing six or seven times. If he had something on his mind, he'd come up, look you straight in the eye, and keep telling you and telling you. And when he was finally done pounding his lesson home, you knew you'd have to listen to the very same homily all over again later that afternoon or the following morning or sometime next Tuesday when he decided to return to the subject.

What made all of this doubly onerous was that Grua's rules were constantly being improved and revised. Whatever tack he was on was the right way, the *only* way, and he would preach its virtues until something shifted and he realized that, no, the answer lay elsewhere. Then he'd march off in the opposite direction. Like the fierce winds that swept upstream through the canyon each April, his standards were subject to change without warning. Coffee was one of his fixations, but then, all of a sudden, he was off it and passionately inveighing against the perils of caffeine. When he somehow got the notion that using a toothbrush was damaging the enamel on his teeth, he threw it away and spent about a year cleaning his teeth by rinsing them with water. Then he abandoned that idea and focused instead on food, restricting his diet to protein shakes and eventually becoming a vegetarian.

In many ways, Grua seemed to approach not only his standards of behavior but his entire personality like an endless boat-repair project: modifying this or tweaking that, adding a new feature here or replacing one there, occasionally rolling up his sleeves and pulling everything apart for a complete overhaul. You could wake up one morning and find his language or his demeanor almost unrecognizable, and the new configuration would mean that you had to make some adjustments in your approach—the techniques you used to handle him. In that sense, he was a lot like the rapids of the canyon.

On the other hand, some things about him never changed. In the mornings, no one was more solicitous of the passengers than Grua. He would wake before dawn and, regardless of whether he was on kitchen duty or not, brew coffee and then pad silently through camp, leaving a hot cup next to everyone's sleeping bag. "He's the most considerate person I know," Wally Rist once said of him. "Kenton is a gentleman."

Despite such benevolence, however, Grua's dramatic, high-stakes, all-or-nothing demeanor could be abrasive and enervating. Even those who admired him most acknowledged that, at times, being around the man was downright exhausting. On any given day, half the folks in Litton's outfit were convinced that Grua was God's gift to the Grand Canyon, while the other half wanted his hide nailed to the boathouse wall. The park rangers found him especially insufferable, and nearly everyone tired of his single-minded tenacity and relentless sermonizing. "Christ, he could be impossible," recalls a boatman who worked with him for years. "We got into some arguments back in the seventies that my head *still* hurts from."

In the end, however, everyone conceded that Grua presented a complex combination of qualities that were charming, maddening, and utterly impossible to ignore. Sooner or later everybody in the canyon—those who loved him, those who couldn't stand him, and the large group in the middle that swung back and forth between those two extremes—eventually came to the same conclusion. Frequently inspiring, sometimes insane, always exasperating, Kenton Grua was a man with no antecedent: a Grand Canyon original who injected a uniquely wild-ass variable into the river equation that, like it or not, you simply had to factor in whenever he was around.

Hence, the name by which he came to be known.

~

If you spent any time working with the Factor, it wasn't long before you could discern contrary elements of his character that were mirrored in the terrain itself, which may have helped to explain why he was endlessly measuring and testing himself against the canyon's myriad challenges. High above Deer Creek Falls, for example, there was a gap between two cliffs of Tapeats sandstone whose width seemed just beyond the ability of a human being to jump across. One summer, he decided to give the leap a shot—and barely succeeded, cheating certain death by clawing at the opposing wall with his fingernails to prevent himself from toppling backward into the abyss. Once, for no reason other than that it seemed like an elegant thing to do, he decided to see if it was possible to row an entire trip without taking his oar blades out of the water. A few years later, he scaled a vertical face of limestone featuring a precarious footbridge that the Ancestral Puebloans had constructed more than six hundred feet above the river. Then, at a place called Elves Chasm, he decided it would be fun to see if he could ascend and descend a series of rock ledges and tight vertical passages along a chain of waterfalls without using his hands.

Those stunts may have seemed pointless, but they spoke to something at the center of who Grua was, and to the forces that drove him. He wanted to know and experience the canyon in its entirety—not simply the river or the rimrock or the trails in between, but the grand whole of the thing. What's more, he was determined to touch that essence as directly as possible, with the soles of his feet and the palms of his hands. This meant that, with time, he fostered a deeper relationship with the canyon than almost anyone else—scrambling along ledges and cliffs that no river guide would ever tread while developing a connection with the boats and the white water that no hiker, ranger, or naturalist would ever feel. Those around him saw clearly that he considered the canyon as necessary and essential as the air he breathed.

Perhaps the most eloquent expression of this addiction was that Grua so often acted as the canyon's self-appointed custodian and caretaker. At the end of a long day, when the rest of his colleagues were draped wearily across their decks, beers in hand, watching the light fade as the curtain of darkness came down the walls, they'd glance over and see Grua hard at work on some new project—building a stone cairn to mark an obscure trailhead, or shoveling a sand beach that the river was eroding, or pruning back the branches of a tamarisk tree that was offending his sense of the view. When they watched him perform those tasks, they speculated that perhaps Grua had become trapped in the emotional facsimile of a keeper hole. In those moments, it was evident to everyone that his feelings for the canyon were so potent that the current of his emotions had curled back on itself, reversing energy and direction and recirculating with such fury that neither Grua nor anyone else had the faintest idea whether he belonged to the canyon or the canyon belonged to him—or whether both things were true in a way that encompassed, in all the wonder and fearsomeness of the word, the full meaning of *possessed*.

In any case, as Grua prepared to enter his third season with Litton's company, the scattered forces whirling inside his heart—the moralism and the dogma, the testing and the sense of ownership—converged into a single beam of resolve that drove him to do something no one had ever before done.

~

One odd aspect of the Grand Canyon was that, although dozens of trails led into and out of the abyss from the rims—many of which followed pathways originally developed by the prehistoric Puebloans—there was not a single route on either side of the river that enabled a person to walk along the length of the canyon from Lee's Ferry to the Grand Wash Cliffs. Much of the shoreline was too convoluted to permit efficient trekking, and significant reaches had no shoreline at all because the cliffs dropped directly into the river. Anyone hoping to forge such a path would thus confront the ordeal of repeatedly descending and ascending through many different layers of rock to link together a network of passable ledges. As a further problem, one could not simply cruise along the biggest and most convenient terraces because they were located many hundreds of feet above the river, and therefore offered almost no access to drinking water.

Despite the obstacles, by the 1960s a handful of hiking fanatics had slowly begun to piece this puzzle together and force a line that ran the entire distance. The foremost expert, who did more work than anyone else, was Harvey Butchart, a mathematician from Flagstaff, who was also a friend of Grua's. Butchart had just unlocked the final segment of this elusive goal in 1968 when, to everyone's surprise, a popular book called *The Man Who Walked Through Time* was published by Colin Fletcher, an ex-British-marine commando who was also an avid backpacker. The jacket of Fletcher's book identified him as "the first man ever to have walked through the entire length of the Grand Canyon."

When Grua picked up Fletcher's book and read it during one of his first river trips, he scoffed with disbelief. Fletcher was a fine writer, but his claim was considerably less impressive than it seemed. When he conducted his transect, in 1963, Grand Canyon National Park stopped far short of encompassing the entire abyss. If you were floating down the river during those years, you would not actually enter the park until you reached a rapid called Nankoweap, more than fifty miles below Lee's Ferry, and you would exit the park farther downstream at a spot known as Tapeats, which was almost 145 miles above the Grand Wash Cliffs. The park's boundaries thus bore no relationship to the true size and scope of the canyon.

Fletcher hadn't lied about what he had done, which was to conduct a continuous backpacking trip along the length of the river corridor that was contained within Grand Canyon National Park. But he didn't exactly go out of his way to advertise that he had covered considerably less than half the length of the actual canyon. Moreover, seven years after the book's publication, when the boundaries of the park were expanded by an act of Congress to include almost the entire canyon at river level, Fletcher's claim was rendered moot. This was obvious to everyone on the river. But only Grua decided to do something about it.

"Somebody else needs to do it and do it right," he announced to a friend. And to no one's surprise, Grua had some rather strong ideas about the difference between doing it right and doing it wrong.

First, he declared, you had to start at the top and go to the bottom, walking *with* the river instead of against it; otherwise, you were doing the thing "backwards." Second, you had to pick either the north or south shoreline, and then you had to stick to that side of the river the entire way. (Tracking back and forth across the Colorado like an addled beaver was, in Grua's view, "cheating.") Also, it was essential to conduct the hike *lightly*, which meant traveling with a minimal amount of gear and carrying as little weight as possible. Grua wasn't sure what the exact weight parameters were, but he had no doubt that Fletcher's sixty-pound backpack violated this standard, and that he was therefore guilty of poor style.

All of those points were arbitrary, and one can all too easily imagine Grua changing his mind and passionately arguing the opposite point of view on any of these criteria. But everyone could recognize the truth of the final and most important element. To be the first person to truly walk the entire length of the Grand Canyon, you had to do the whole damn thing—all 277 miles—from Lee's Ferry to the Grand Wash Cliffs.

This was considerably more difficult than what Fletcher had pulled off, and length was only a small part of the reason. The most vexing problem was figuring out how to piece together a chain of exceptionally narrow ledges that would enable a person to traverse the high cliffs that lay downstream of Havasu, the point where Fletcher had started his hike.

The challenge essentially boiled down to geology. The hardest and most resistant rock strata—the limestones, sandstones, and schists—tended to form vertical cliff faces that were all but impassable. So the key lay in charting a route that would cut across the layers of shale that lay closest to the river, many of which were tilted and warped by fault lines. To solve this interlocked series of problems, you needed to be able to read the rock almost as well as the dorymen could read the water. In this respect, geology was a bit like hydraulics. It all came down to finding your line.

Grua started scoping out his route during his first season on the river, surveying the walls from the deck of his motor rig, plotting where he would go, and keeping careful notes on questionable spots that would require further study. In the areas where he was unable to conduct a proper evaluation of the terrain from his boat, he would make some excuse to pull over—announcing that it was time to eat lunch or for everyone to take a nap—then dash off on an inspection tour. In this manner, he was able to bring a large portion of the river corridor into alignment, although one segment had him completely stumped.

The stretch of river just downstream of Havasu featured a long line of cliffs that shot directly out of the river and soared upward at an eighty-five-degree angle for several hundred feet. Here, the rock—consisting of three separate layers of limestone known as the Muav, the Temple Butte, and the Redwall—was so resistant to erosion that there wasn't a single breach. After several seasons, Grua was still looking for a way past those escarpments. Then one autumn, he gazed up and spotted a family of bighorn sheep carefully picking its way across the face of the cliffs about 150 feet above the river. When he climbed up to confirm what he had seen, he spotted a ledge so narrow it was all but invisible, and he realized that the sheep had handed him the answer to his problem.

Convinced that he was now ready to embark, he was busy gathering together his gear in the fall of 1972 when he made a decision he would swiftly come to regret. At this point, Grua had taken a passionate dislike to modern footwear and was spending most of his days running around the bottom of the canyon in his bare feet. Although he didn't necessarily think it would be a good idea to attempt a full traverse without any shoes whatsoever, he liked the notion of trying to pull it off wearing moccasins.

Having purchased three pairs, he started along the south side of the river at Lee's Ferry that November. Within the first eight miles, he discovered that he had worn several holes in his first set of moccasins. By the time he reached Nautiloid Canyon, a tributary that enters the river at Mile 35, the holes had expanded, and when he accidentally stepped on a prickly pear cactus, the spikes penetrated deep into the ball of his right foot. Loath to give up, he stubbornly continued hobbling downstream. But a few days later, when he reached Eminence Break, a fault line at Mile 44, infection had set in. Out of options, he had to limp down to the edge of the river, stick out his thumb, and hitch a ride downstream to Lake Mead with a passing motor rig.

So much for teaching a lesson to Colin Fletcher.

~

The following spring, Grua joined Litton's company and entered a period of such intense learning and change that a full five years would pass before he was able to take another crack at the through-hike. But when the opportunity finally presented itself, he left nothing to chance. In the autumn of 1976, he began mixing up batches of homemade gorp and custom-blended dried soups in his kitchen, then funneling them into five-gallon honey jars. Later that winter, he selected six points along his intended hike route, climbed up to each of them from the river, and established a line of food caches.

He departed on the twenty-ninth of February, toting a small North Face rucksack with an interior frame and clad in a pair of sturdy, high-topped work boots with thick Vibram soles. The load on his back was astonishingly light—the weight of the pack would never exceed thirty pounds—and he hauled no more than a gallon of water at one time, even along those stretches where he was cut off from the river. (For drinking water, he would gamble on his ability to sniff out springs or to sip from potholes—cup-shaped indentations in nonporous layers of rock that often contain small pools of rainwater, as well as thriving colonies of tadpoles and copepods.) He carried little in the way of clothing and didn't even bother to bring along an extra pair of socks.

His daily routine was spartan. He would awaken early, well before it was light, make a fire, and linger for a few minutes to enjoy the predawn gloaming while stoking a cup of instant coffee and a bowl of granola mixed with water or dehydrated milk. He was usually on the trail by 5:00 a.m., then hiked all day without stopping, ranging up and down the layers as he moved downriver. Just before darkness set in, he would find a place to camp, boil some more water to brew up a batch of soup, drift off to sleep, and then restart his engines first thing the following morning. This ritual remained largely unchanged, except that the deeper he penetrated into March, the longer the days got, which meant he could spend more hours hiking between dawn and sunset.

Every five or six days he reached a spot where he had stashed one of his honey jars, and replenished his food supply while exchanging the socks he was wearing for a fresh pair (which had been wedged in with the food). When he set off again, he would leave behind the empty jar and a pair of stinky socks. In this manner, he covered between fifteen and twenty miles a day, a pace that is punishing to sustain even on terrain where there is a trail. On many days, he covered closer to twenty-five or even thirty miles.

It was 277 *river* miles from Lee's Ferry to the Grand Wash Cliffs, but the actual walking distance was far greater. Grua wasn't sure of the precise length of the entire traverse, but with the constant detours—necessitated by the fact that the contour lines of a ledge often took him into deep recesses before looping outward and returning to the Colorado—the total distance was almost doubled. His food caches had been placed correctly in terms of distance, but the extra miles he was covering meant he was burning an enormous number of calories and was constantly famished. By the middle of March, he was boosting his energy intake by stirring almonds and cashews into his soup at night.

Some sections were more difficult than others. Not surprisingly, the most dangerous ones lay along the limestone cliffs below Havasu, where the sheep had shown him the route. The bighorn ledges were extremely thin and often obscured by a steep wedge of scree that was as loose as ball bearings. The tracks of the bighorns told him that they kept to the outermost edge, which was often terrifying and demanded intense focus. Where the pathway was blocked by a dihedral—an L-shaped corner in the cliff—a gap would have to be jumped. The drop in those spots exceeded 150 feet, and a miss would have splattered him across the rocks at the bottom.

What buoyed his spirits was that along much of the route he found signs that the Puebloans had been there before him. Although there was never any sign of a continuous trail, he could see they had moved through the area in much the same manner as him—lightly, quietly, and without an audience. It was also evident that they had lingered, often for long stretches. There were mescal pits where they had roasted their agaves. There were granaries where they had stored their corn in clay pots, and they had carefully placed those pots inside alcoves that had been sealed with rocks and hand-plastered mud. When he looked closely at those lines of plaster, he could see the whorled prints of the men and women whose fingers had shaped the mud and nudged the stones into place some eight hundred or a thousand years before—and the intervening centuries seemed to snap together into an electric moment of connective immediacy when he gently placed his clubbed thumbs over those ancient imprints and noted, with wonder, that his hands were almost as small as theirs. It was a heady sensation to realize that he was at times moving in their actual footsteps.

He reached the Grand Wash Cliffs on April 4, five weeks to the day after he had started, and by his best reckoning, he had covered just under six hundred miles. This was the first time in recorded history that a human being had traversed the entire length of the canyon, and although he would have been justified in calling a press conference or trumpeting his astonishing feat, he did neither—nor did he ever bother to publish a single word about what he had achieved. For him, it was sufficient that he had made good on his declaration that somebody needed to "do it right."

Nevertheless, word leaked out within the guiding community, and for those who learned of Grua's navigational tour de force, his disinterest in publicity or profit was almost as impressive as the hike itself, if not more so.

There was, however, one important task he felt he needed to complete before he could call the job finished. Later that spring, he returned to each of his food caches, where he retrieved his empty honey jars and packed them out, making sure to collect his old socks when he did so. He wasn't willing to leave that sort of thing behind, even in a remote location that might never again be visited by another person. It would be poor style and just not right.

∼

After that, it was impossible to be on the river and not have heard about the Factor—although it could be hard to know exactly which portions of the stories being peddled about him were actually true and which were hype. Some people firmly believed that Grua had completed his marathon wearing nothing but flip-flops. Others insisted he had shunned modern footwear altogether and pulled the whole thing off in a pair of sandals modeled on what the Anasazi had worn. And another group declared that, no, he was actually naked the entire time.

It probably said as much about Grua as about the hike itself that all three versions of the story were completely believable. And so these tales took their place among what would eventually become an epic anthology of narrative hyperbole—anecdotes, yarns, whopping lies—that was recounted in the bars of river-guide towns from Flagstaff to Lewiston, and often what was even more entertaining than the stories themselves were the larger arguments they provoked over where the truth about Grua ended and the legend began. He was rumored, for example, to be the only doryman ever to have his boat flip upside down in one wave, then have a second wave flip him right side up so fast he was still at the oars. (True, and verified by witnesses.) There was another tale about how a wave had exploded beneath him in Lava Falls with enough force that the *Chattahoochee* had performed a double backflip. (Utterly false.) And one account suggested he had once saved himself from flipping by leaping over the shoulders of a passenger into the bow to counterbalance his boat. (Probably true, but still debated to this day.)

Hearing those stories, one had to speculate that, among many other things, Grua might be more than a little crazy. He wasn't the sort of person who could simply be dismissed as a crackpot, but the tales provoked a compelling question: What the hell was it that drove him?

One possible answer resided in the notion that all of Grua's achievements in the canyon—the six-hundred-mile traverse and the death-defying leap at Deer Creek and the rest of his feats—may have been inspired by something considerably more complicated, and infinitely more treacherous, than simple lunacy.

Grua's fascination with the smallest details of the world beneath the rim— his eagerness to test his skills against each of its features, as well as the unhinged exaltation that those trials evoked in his heart—was the hallmark of a man smitten by every facet and curve on the face of the river and the canyon that contained it. A man who, having permitted this place to seduce him so thoroughly, had become, in a literal and a symbolic sense, both its steward and prisoner. Therein, perhaps, lay the insight that unlocked an understanding of the complex torrent of forces that ran through the center of his soul.

There may well have been more sophisticated psychological explanations for who Grua was and what fueled him: the disruptions that a wrenching family move had inflicted on the mind of a twelve-year-old boy; the nagging insecurities of a man who had failed to finish college; even the possibility that he may have suffered from some sort of obsessive-compulsive disorder during an era when such afflictions lacked even a name. Ultimately, though, those theories were nothing more than bubbles. Like the Slot run at Lava Falls, they offered an ephemeral trail you could try to follow, but they were not the thing itself.

In the end, only one line cut smoothly through the confusion and contradictions that characterized Grua's inflamed response to the Grand Canyon. As hokey as it may sound, he was in love. And the force of that love, a passion as wild and as turbulent as the river itself, was about to inspire in him a gesture that would connect his name to the river as indelibly as the dories themselves.

11

Speed

And so in time the rowboat and I became the same—
like the archer and his bow or the artist and his paint.

—RICHARD BODE

LTHOUGH it was a given that everybody on Litton's payroll was
bewitched by wooden boats, no one came close to Grua's obsessed
fixation with the dories, and a large part of that fascination was
rooted in intimacy. The dories rode closer to the surface of the water than any
other commercial craft, putting you in direct contact with the river—not only
with its nuances and its quirks but also with the swelling powerhouse of its
energy—in a way that simply wasn't possible in a raft or a motor rig. And like
all forms of intimacy, that closeness also made you vulnerable in ways that were
both unnerving and seductive.

If you were at the helm of a motor rig or behind the oars of a rubber
raft, you knew that regardless of what the river might try to do, you were
probably going to muddle through one way or another, even if things got
messy. But in a dory, you had to be on your toes every single second. If you
failed for any reason to anticipate, to react, to assemble the proper sequence
of moves—pivoting and squaring up in perfect sync with the waves and,
above all and always, reading the current and going with the flow—you'd find
yourself upside down in the blink of an eye. As Grua never tired of pointing

out, it took something extra to get a small wooden boat through, which not only called forth excellence but also injected an additional charge: a frisson of energy stemming from the awareness you were piloting an eggshell that could break into pieces.

For Grua, however, even that didn't fully capture the essence of the dories' magic, which lay in something he called touch. The dories simply felt different, and it wasn't just a matter of their exquisite sensitivity, the alacrity of their responses to the shifting dynamics of the water. It was the feelings they transmitted to you, the subtle vibrations they were constantly broadcasting up through their hulls and their chines and the shafts of their oars. They were sort of like floating mandolins, delicate little instruments that vibrated in tune with the harmonics of the river at a frequency that was impossible for the ear to discern, but which you could sense in your forearms and your wrists and, most especially, in the palms of your hands. If you attuned closely enough and with your whole body, you realized that the boats were singing to you, and that the music they made wasn't a by-product of white water alone. You could sense their music in the flat water as you slid back and forth across the laced and undulating patterns of light and shadow that shifted with a mysterious cadency known only to the river. You could even hear the music when you were asleep, rocking gently in the eddies at night.

For Grua, the dories were luminously alive in a way that no other kind of boat could be—and if that weren't enough, there was also the spectacular bonus of what they could achieve inside the hydraulics when they were properly handled. Like the fact that if you arrowed out of a heavy eddy at just the right spot and with precisely the right angle, you could spear into the current and skim ten or twenty or even thirty feet across the river without taking a single stroke. Or the way you felt when you dove into the trough of a giant haystack such as, say, the #5 wave in Hermit—the way you could see the wave swelling and building and then opening for you, and if you had your bow square and everything was truly dialed, you would plunge down that trough and up the front side of the wave, and when you reached the crest, the boat would seem to just shoot into the sky. In that moment, it would feel as if the strings of gravity that were supposed to keep you tethered to the river had briefly parted and left you free, hanging on to your oars, for a delicious moment of pure weightlessness in which you were *actually flying*. And then, in the next instant, your bow would crash down over the top of the wave and you would head into the next sequence, up one crest and down another, on and on until you came out at the bottom, soaking wet and awash in the kind of giggling delirium you hadn't tasted since you were twelve years old.

Grua was among the first to concede that to someone who had never rowed a dory, this probably sounded a bit infantile. But that didn't make the appeal any less real, and the potency of that appeal achieved perhaps its most exuberant expression when he struggled to put his feelings into words and found his thoughts tumbling over themselves in a kind of jumbled poetry that mirrored the looping chaos of the water itself.

"You could do this until you died, and then you could get born again and do it another ten, twenty, *fifty* lifetimes," he once exclaimed when his good friend Lew Steiger asked him to explain his feelings for the boats. "You could do it straight through the year, all year long, and you'd never, ever get tired of doing it—*never*," he said, laughing. "I mean, they're too much fun to row down there. It's the funnest thing there is to do, and you could never do anything else once you start doing them—and at least be happy. You might do something else because you felt *guilty*, because you weren't really doing anything with your life, you know? But between them and being in the Grand Canyon? Yeah— you could just never do anything else once you start rowing dories. . . . It's just like—*God*, there's just nothing better. Once you've been in a dory, that's it. And the only way to really know it is to do it. . . . It'd be the best thing if every boat-man down there—every boatman that's really a true boatman that loved the Grand Canyon, motorboatmen especially—could at least once—of course you can't do it once!—could row a dory through the Grand Canyon."

To Grua, it was "the best drug in the world." And thanks to that feeling, by the end of the 1970s he was perhaps the only boatman on the Colorado who could row a dory the way Louis Armstrong had once played the trumpet—with the kind of ferocity and joy that bordered on madness.

~

Other guides on the river possessed skills at the oars that certainly matched and may even have surpassed Grua's. But almost everyone acknowledged that the Factor had something special, a feel for the boats that seemed to flow directly from the wellspring of his connection to the river and the canyon. He commanded an uncanny sense not only of what the dories could and could not do, but also of what they wanted to do—and unlike many of his colleagues, he relished taking risks to explore the outermost frontier of the boats' potential. Although this often got him into trouble (he didn't always have a golden trip), he was willing to push the limits further than anyone else, and this willingness took him to places few were prepared to follow. Especially when it came to the rapid that enthralled him most.

Of all the nasty pockets of white water on the Colorado, Crystal was Grua's favorite. He had come to the river only two years after the debris flow at Mile 98, so he and the rapid had become a part of the canyon together. He was fascinated by the way it linked together so many exceptionally challenging elements—the deceptive entry, the huge current, the massive hydraulics. But the main reason he found it so irresistible was that, unlike with Hance or Granite or Horn Creek or even Lava Falls, he was never able to find the master key to its secrets, the solution that would unlock all its doors.

Over the years, the search for that cipher had taken Grua on some strange journeys. In the midseventies, he and a handful of his colleagues got it into their heads that somewhere deep inside the Big Hole lurked an invisible seam where something abnormal was taking place. That hole had a spine running through the middle of it, with water rooster-tailing off to the side in both directions, and at that one spot, according to the theory, several teaspoons of current were passing smoothly through the vortex and over the haystack behind it. If a guide could put the center of his bowpost into that exact spot at precisely the right angle with pitch-perfect momentum, the boat might simply whoosh through the tourbillion and materialize, intact, on the downstream side of the hole. (Basically, this was the equivalent of the Slot run at Lava Falls, but even more mysterious and phantasmal.) Unlike the rest of the dorymen, however, Grua was also convinced that, with enough practice, an oarsman could perform this trick not just once, but every single time, a hypothesis that he set out to test by repeatedly attempting to drive the *Chattahoochee* straight through the worst part of the Big Hole.

In addition to some spectacular wipeouts, this had produced a sequence of ferocious arguments between Grua and Regan Dale, who was in charge of most of the expeditions on which Grua pursued this quest, and who also had an exceptionally complicated relationship with the Factor. Having joined the company the same year, each man was the other's oldest friend; but because they had taken fundamentally different approaches to rowing dories, they were also rivals and, where their visions collided, adversaries. Dale had polished his style of steely minimalism and finesse to near perfection, partly because it suited his personality and partly because it represented, in his view, the most responsible way to handle dangerous white water when the lives of passengers were in his hands. In Dale's eyes, the demented experiments that Grua was conducting inside Crystal not only violated his sense of guiding ethics but also challenged his authority as the TL, and it incensed him.

Kenton, these people aren't our guinea pigs—we're responsible for their safety, Dale would exclaim, outraged that Grua's runs required him to persuade at least one passenger to accompany him to counterbalance the boat. Those passengers, Dale would point out, had signed on with Litton's company in the belief that they were likely to emerge alive at the bottom of the canyon because the boatmen actually knew what the hell they were doing.

Grua couldn't have cared less. On one trip when Dale had flat out forbidden him to solicit volunteers among the dory clients, Grua planted himself at the little harbor at the top of Crystal and beseeched those on other river trips until he found someone to ride shotgun with him. What bothered Dale even more than the insolence and the insubordination was the ego behind these games. What made Grua think it was acceptable to put the lives of other people in danger like that? Dale would demand, still angry at the recollection many years later. How could he have been so selfish?

What Dale could neither comprehend nor condone was that although safety was a genuine concern for Grua—who generally did his best to protect the welfare of his passengers—this was ultimately superseded by two things that mattered even more to him: his curiosity and his sense of wonder. In his mind, Crystal justified the risks he was courting, both to himself and to others, because it confronted him with the same allure that an equation holds for mathematicians when it refuses to yield up a neat and elegant solution. What's more, the possibility that there simply might not have *been* a solution to Crystal's conundrum only deepened Grua's fascination, perhaps because he found this notion to be simultaneously so grotesque and so sublime. Crystal beguiled him because it threatened to undermine the principle that a river possesses inherent symmetry and coherence, thereby raising the heretical possibility that a dory's magic might not, in all circumstances, enable it to merge with the mysterious mechanics of white water. Yet, in committing this offense, Crystal also offered up some compellingly graphic testimony to the notion that the river and the canyon conformed to their own definitions of symmetry and coherence—and that perhaps those principles could never truly be understood or controlled by anyone.

The tension between these competing truths meant that Grua simply found it impossible to let Crystal go. To him, it was the single greatest unsolved puzzle on the river, a riddle whose answer always seemed to lie just beyond his reach. When it came to the dories themselves, however, most problems surrendered to his persistence. And it was in this arena more than any other—the black arts of designing, building, and improving wooden boats—that he made his most lasting contributions.

The innovations that Grua conceived transformed Litton's outfit in ways both large and small. Some of his ideas were rather absurd, such as the notion of stuffing air bags into the bow and the stern of a dory to render the boat unflippable. But many of the schemes he concocted were quite brilliant. It was Grua's idea to teach passengers to "high-side" vigorously when a dory was out of kilter in the big waves, thereby preventing innumerable flips. He came up with the notion of using a sawed-off oar shaft in the footwell as a brace so you could hook your toes around it and gain leverage while rowing, and he was the first to employ inflatable tubes for rolling dories onto and off a beach.

It was also Grua who perfected the technique for righting upside-down boats in midstream instead of pulling them onto the rocks at the side of the river. He developed an elegant system for waterproofing the hatches using aluminum channels and piping that ran through the boat, which kept supplies dry. In his boldest experiments, he modified the entire concept of rowing, first by designing a dory with a sliding seat like an Olympic rowing shell, then later (and most radically) by building another boat with a deep footwell and raised oarlocks so that he could row while standing up. Most of his colleagues dismissed this as ludicrous. But on certain stretches of the river he could row circles around the rest of the crew.

The list of his contributions was endless, and in addition to his design and performance innovations, no one had a better sense than Grua of the best ways to repair damaged boats. If you came off the river with a smashed chine or a hole in your stern, you turned to the Factor for advice. He was a wizard in the boathouse, able to tear a boat apart and put it back together better than almost anyone else, and his skills as a carpenter were unrivaled. So it seemed somehow fitting and right that when Regan Dale's crew pulled into Hurricane during the last week of July 1977 hauling the mess that used to be the *Emerald Mile*, the Factor stepped out from behind the boathouse, put his hands on his hips, and announced that there wasn't going to be a Viking funeral.

Instead, Grua intended to gather up what was left of the stricken dory, put her back together, then take her for his own. And like everything else he set his mind to, that's precisely what he did.

~

For a man whose passions raced like wildfire, the Factor was oddly slow, especially when he was solving problems. His willingness to stick with something until the job was done, moving methodically and refusing to be rushed, could be both exasperating and deeply impressive. If the rig truck broke down in the middle of the desert on the way to Lee's Ferry because of some complicated electrical snafu that no one, including Grua himself, had the faintest idea how to fix, the Factor would disappear under the dashboard, carefully tracing the wires while everyone else stood around wondering if it wouldn't make more sense to start hiking to a pay phone. Three hours later, he would reemerge, calmly insert the key into the ignition and start the truck, then head off down the road without a hint of irritation or bother.

So it surprised no one that when he broke out his tools and applied himself to bringing the *Emerald Mile* back from the dead, the work unfolded at a glacial pace. The project started in the autumn and went on throughout the winter and the better part of the following spring. In the process, he introduced some bold changes to the boat, some of which had never before been seen in a canyon dory. To enable the boat to handle large waves from both directions, he got rid of her tombstone-shaped transom and transformed her into a double-ender with a pointed stern that mirrored the profile of her bow. He increased her potential for speed by adding a second set of oarlocks to enable her to be rowed by two people at the same time. He also installed false flooring in the footwells, then punched drain holes through the hull so she was completely self-bailing.

As with all things, each of these advances was purchased at a cost. The passenger seats in the bow and the stern were awkward and exceptionally uncomfortable. The self-bailing footwells raised the boat's center of gravity, which made her less stable. But in bringing her back to life, Grua demonstrated what can happen when obsession, discipline, and a touch of madness combine to form art.

When he finished, the little dory was both a restoration of her former self and something entirely new, the Lazarus of the river. She had been transformed from a battered guest boat into a streamlined instrument that had some problems but was nevertheless very much ahead of her time. She was also a tool through which Grua could continue to answer the call that had already driven him to challenge his own limitations by climbing up to the Puebloan footbridge, leaping across the Deer Creek Narrows, and undertaking his epic mega-transect of the canyon. The quest to which he harnessed himself next would be odder and more irrational than all those things put together. But it also had the potential, in ways that were obvious and ways that were not, to transcend them all.

~

At the center of this new quest lay a narrative that dated back more than a century, starting with John Wesley Powell's last sack of flour and extending like a thin, improbable filament through the subsequent history of boating in the canyon: the element of speed. To fully understand how this dovetailed with the story Grua was about to write, one has to know a few things about the history of Grand Canyon speed runs.

During the years that followed the one-armed Major's original trip, the canyon witnessed a thin trickle of rather bizarre boating schemes, several of which achieved impressive levels of misery, carnage, or farce. In 1889, an ill-conceived effort to survey the bottom of the canyon for a river-level railway ended in disaster when three members of the expedition drowned less than thirty miles below Lee's Ferry. (This was the trip that produced Robert Brewster Stanton's striking description of a debris flow as he and the other survivors clawed their way toward the rim.) That tragedy was later followed by some rather comical attempts to shoot motion pictures on the river, one of which included a former tenant of the Central Park Zoo named Cataract and a "mostly Airedale" mutt from the Salt Lake City pound named Rags. Together, they became the first bear cub and the first dog ever to boat through the Grand Canyon. Then in the winter of 1928, a pair of newlyweds from Idaho headed downstream in a cumbersome wooden scow accessorized with a kerosene-burning stove, a mattress, and a set of box springs, which was later discovered floating in an eddy forty-seven miles from the end of the canyon. (The bodies of the couple, Glen and Bessie Hyde, were never found, and the details of their disappearance remain a mystery to this day.)

As dramatic as those ventures may have been, none involved an effort to sprint through the canyon in the manner that Powell and his starving crew were trying to do as they completed their "race for a dinner" during the desperate weeks of August 1869. But finally, in the summer of 1949, the second chapter of this subchronicle was composed by an overweight pharmacist from Paso Robles, California, named Ed Hudson. On the morning of June 12, Hudson and a group of friends pulled out of Lee's Ferry in a motorboat called the *Esmeralda II*. They had two goals in mind: to test-drive the boat, and to stash gasoline supplies in preparation for returning the following year when Hudson planned to take a bold stab at running the entire canyon backward by charging upstream from Lake Mead to Lee's Ferry—an audacious vision that, as he would discover, would prove impossible until the advent of the water-jet engine.*

The *Esmeralda II*, which Hudson had cobbled together in his garage, was unlike anything ever before seen in the canyon. Nineteen feet long and built of plywood, she was modeled along the lines of a Higgins landing craft, a vessel that had been used extensively during World War II for amphibious landings in the invasion of Normandy and throughout the Pacific Islands. On the Colorado, the *Esmeralda II* represented an invasion of a different sort. Propelled by a seventy-five-horsepower inboard engine, she was the canyon's first-ever motorboat, and the roar of her four cylinders heralded the wave of internal-

---

*In July 1960, a New Zealand inventor named Bill Hamilton led a squadron of three jet boats equipped with propulsion-driven engines from Lake Mead to Lee's Ferry, the first and only time the canyon has ever been run in reverse. Several years later, the Park Service declared it illegal to drive motorboats upstream inside the canyon. The ban remains in effect to this day.

combustion-driven rigs that would soon dominate the world at the bottom of the canyon.

Although Hudson and his crew stopped to camp each night along the shore and also suffered a daylong delay at Phantom Ranch because the mules that were hauling in their resupply of gasoline had stampeded and strewn fuel cans all over the trail, they nevertheless made excellent time, clearing the entire stretch from Lee's Ferry to Pierce Ferry in five days and ten minutes. This was the shortest trip in history from the head of the canyon to the Grand Wash Cliffs. Which meant that in addition to having pulled off the first successful motorized run down the river, Hudson had decisively established a Grand Canyon speed record.

That benchmark immediately caught the attention of two brothers who had already carved out places for themselves within the river-running community. Jim Rigg, the older of the pair, was an ex-soldier and a talented aircraft mechanic from Grand Junction, Colorado, who had become a partner in a company that conducted commercial river trips on the Green, the San Juan, and the Colorado. Jim's younger brother, Bob, joined the outfit in 1951. The two men were natural athletes who had a gift for rowing and a solid feel for white water. They were also fond of adventure. So that year they decided to see if they could smash Hudson's motor-driven speed record using nothing more than the muscles in their arms and a pair of oars.

Actually, adventure was only part of the Rigg brothers' motivation. As partners in a fledgling river company, one of the concerns that kept them awake at night was what they would do if one of their passengers suffered a traumatic injury and had to be evacuated from the canyon. At the time, there was virtually no means of summoning outside help, aside from hiking to the rim or attempting to flash a passing aircraft with a mirror, and helicopter extraction was still in its infancy. So if something truly awful happened to one of their clients—a broken femur, a fractured skull, a ruptured spleen—and they absolutely *had* to get that person to a hospital as fast as possible, how long, the brothers wondered, would it take to row out of the canyon?

Intent on finding an answer to that question while also inscribing a new entry in the record books, they pulled away from Lee's Ferry at 7:20 on the morning of June 9, 1951, aboard a wooden boat called the *Norm*, carrying only their "emergency supplies"—a pair of sleeping bags, a screwdriver, a section of plywood patching, their water bottles, and two glass jars, one filled with peanut butter and the other with jelly. Their plan was to run almost every rapid "wide-open," which meant they would not be stopping for a single scout, except at Lava Falls. They took turns at the oars, each brother rowing for about an hour at a time, and they moved with unbelievable speed, passing beneath the metal footbridge at Phantom Ranch late on the first afternoon and anchoring to set up camp just above a tributary drainage called Bass Canyon, 108 miles from Lee's Ferry, around 8:00 p.m. that night.

The following morning they were back on the water at dawn, and by early afternoon they were pulling over at the top of Lava Falls. After taking a quick look at the rapid, they agreed to tackle it by threading through a narrow chute on the left-hand side that featured a sharp drop-off. As they hurled down the tongue, Bob, who was at the oars, felt a series of harsh bangs reverberating up from his blades. "Man, we got rocks on the oars!" he cried.

"You're doing great," declared Jim, who was riding "fish-eye," splayed across the deck. "We're going the right way!" Indeed they were. A few seconds more and the little boat had been spit out of the bottom of the rapid and was rocketing through the tail waves without a scratch.

When darkness descended a few hours later, they kept right on rowing, dodging the rocks by sound until just before midnight, when they finally eddied out, wolfed down another ration of peanut butter and jelly, and snatched a few hours of sleep.

They peeled through the final stretch of river on the morning of the third day, reaching the Grand Wash Cliffs shortly before 11:00 a.m. and establishing three separate historic precedents. This was the first time that all but one of the rapids had been run wide-open in succession, a testament to the skill of two extraordinary young men who had a total of only three previous Grand Canyon trips between the pair of them. They had also set a brand-new speed record of fifty-two hours and forty-one minutes. And they had proved that a hard-hulled, wooden oar boat could more than hold its own against motors.

The Rigg brothers' run is justifiably remembered to this day as one of the most impressive feats of boatmanship the canyon has ever seen. To run the whole 277 miles in just over two days seemed nothing short of miraculous, an accomplishment that evoked both admiration and envy within the guiding community. But it also raised some stark questions about whether racing down the Colorado might not cut directly against the grain of what was emerging, among those who knew the river world the best, as a consensus about the most fulfilling and exemplary way to experience the canyon.

~

Of the many attractions that draw people to the bottom of the canyon, perhaps the most potent and beguiling is the realization that the experience is the *opposite* of a race—the antithesis of rushing from where you are toward someplace you think you would rather be, only to discover, once you arrive, that your true goal lies somewhere else. That is a defining characteristic of life in the world *above* the rim, and if there is a point to being in the canyon, it is not to rush but to linger, suspended in a blue-and-amber haze of in-between-ness, for as long as one possibly can. To float, to drift, savoring the pulse of the river on its odyssey through the canyon, and above all, to postpone the unwelcome and distinctly unpleasant moment when one is forced to reemerge and reenter the world beyond the rim—that is the paramount goal.

For the guides who worked in the canyon during the heyday of the 1970s, this was more than an abstract concept, the sort of beautiful ideal that people pay lip service to but never take seriously. Some of the most treasured moments in that era occurred when the trip leader announced that an expedition would be camping in the same spot for two nights, which meant an entire day could be spent hiking, reading, or simply staring up at the walls and watching the pageant of light play across the vertical amphitheater of rock. These "layover days" were coveted like gold coins because they enabled one to touch the best of what the canyon had to offer. The rapids were undeniably thrilling, but for boatmen privileged to return to the canyon again and again, the excitement of white water began to take a backseat to the hours of pure, unvarnished perfection that opened themselves to those who were not in a hurry.

Only during these interludes could one nap amid a bed of hellebore orchids and scarlet monkey flower, or listen to the hollow, head-knocking clonks of the bighorn rams as they battled along the cliff faces during their rut. Only in those moments could one peer into a Puebloan granary stuffed with dried cobs of corn that had been harvested when Saracens were battling Crusaders on the walls of Jerusalem, or hike to the base of Mooney Falls, a waterfall higher than Niagara, and watch it plunge into a pool whose color was deeper than that of a chunk of freshly mined lapis lazuli. Only in those intervals could one fathom the deepest wonders of the river world by disappearing into the aboriginal dreamtime, the *real* Stone Age, and truly comprehend how the canyon held in its fist a crazed and cracked beauty whose brutishness could strike with the force of a landscape from another planet.

This was the reason why, among all of the outfitters and boatmen, the oarsmen were considered the aristocrats of the canyon. Motor guides made considerably more money, moving swiftly downstream, racking up one six-day trip after another and merrily pocketing their tips at the end of each run. But the motor trips rarely had layover days; they moved too fast to linger, and the most you might get would be an extra morning or afternoon. The oar guides' wealth was envied because their riches were calibrated not in dollars but in time. A trip in an oar raft lasted at least two weeks, sometimes as long as three—and it stood as a point of fierce pride among the dorymen that they could extend that schedule even further. Sometimes running twenty-three days, Litton's were the longest commercial expeditions in the canyon. Yet even that deliciously languorous pace was trumped by the luckiest people of all—the private boaters on noncommercial expeditions in which small parties, unconstrained by any timetable but the ticking of their internal clocks, could take as long as they liked.

Those private ventures were so appealing that during the 1970s several groups, many of them composed of river guides who were on vacation, launched a series of extended marathons that stretched the principle of slow-boating to its outer limits. One of the first of these, which lasted for forty-two days, was eventually followed by an even longer trip, a seventy-seven-day whopper that would probably have set some sort of record, had it not been surpassed by yet another endurance run in which six friends left from Lee's Ferry in the winter of 1976 and didn't emerge from the bottom of the canyon for *a hundred and three days*—a hiatus that afforded them the space and the freedom to do things they had dreamed of doing for years and were finally taking the time to try.

They brought along a metal box filled with wheatberry and a stone grinder so that they could bake their own bread, just as Powell and his men had done. They hiked every side canyon they wanted to, those with names and those without, exploring some of the most exquisite and inaccessible springs and oases in the canyon. At their favorite camps, such as Eminence Break and Nankoweap and Bass, they planted themselves for a week or more and simply watched the water flow past. These vantages enabled them to observe the river world unfurling not merely for a fortnight or even a month but across the arc of an entire season. As the air warmed, they watched the ice melt from the canyon walls and the snow line retreat farther upward toward the rim with each passing day. Then they saw the ocotillo and the redbud blossoms emerge, and the naked cottonwood branches cloak themselves in the acid-green leaves that herald the arrival of spring. They bathed beneath the glow of the moon as it waxed and waned and waxed again, three times over. They were serenaded by peeping choruses of frogs. And on the beaches where they had camped, they played cards and read by lantern light while watching the meteor showers rain down and the constellations wheel across the sky.

The trip would stay with them for the rest of their lives, and when it was finally over, it took its place in canyon lore. Years later when stories of legendary river expeditions were traded, none was more revered or more envied than the Hundred Days Trip—especially after the Park Service revised the canyon's boating regulations to render another such excursion impossible, a thing that could never be repeated. It was also the polar opposite of what the Rigg brothers had achieved in 1951, and when you compared those two ventures—the speed run and the Hundred Days Trip—there was really only one question you had to ask yourself: Why, in God's name, would anyone who wasn't hurt or starving or insane ever want to *race* through the Grand Canyon?

~

One way of teasing out the shallowness of conducting such a sprint is by turning to Bernard Moitessier, the great French yachtsman who took part in the Golden Globe, the legendary single-handed sailing race designed to reward the first sailor ever to circumnavigate the earth alone, without assistance and without stopping. Moitessier cast off from Plymouth, England, in August 1968 aboard *Joshua*, his thirty-nine-foot steel ketch. By the following February, having survived a series of gales and other trials, he was rounding Cape Horn at the tip of South America when he underwent a startling epiphany. Only another month or two separated him from Plymouth, and thanks to his position he stood an excellent chance of winning. Although victory would forever have inscribed his name in the annals of sailing, Moitessier decided that he neither needed nor wanted to finish the race. Instead, he turned south and kept sailing, rounding the Cape of Good Hope off the tip of Africa, then jacking far down into the Roaring Forties and eventually out into the reaches of the southern Pacific. When he finally stopped in Tahiti, he had been alone at sea for ten months and had never once touched land.

The book that Moitessier later wrote about this experience, *The Long Way*, chronicles an odyssey that was as much spiritual as it was physical. He wrote that leaving from Plymouth and returning there seemed "like leaving from nowhere to go nowhere." He also declared that he was "a citizen of the most beautiful nation on earth—a nation whose laws are harsh yet simple, a nation that never cheats, which is immense and without borders, where life is lived in the present." But perhaps his most provocative discovery was the realization that winning a race had no connection with his true goal, which was to reach a point in space and consciousness that would enable him to bear witness to the beauty and the complexity of the natural world—and to glimpse, however briefly, the sort of person he might become if he permitted himself to cross a kind of international date line of the soul and merge with those things. In the end, he realized, the journey itself was the destination.

Intriguingly, Moitessier's words echoed a comment made almost three decades earlier by one of the most legendary boatmen in the Grand Canyon. In the autumn of 1937, an Oregon gas-station attendant named Buzz Holmstrom took a handmade wooden boat all the way from the upper reaches of the Green and down the Colorado to Lake Mead, becoming the first person to row every rapid on both rivers, as well as the entire Grand Canyon, alone and without aid.

Toward the tail end of his trip but still twenty-eight river miles upstream from the Grand Wash Cliffs, Holmstrom made his final camp inside the canyon and noted that this would be the last night he would sleep next to the moving river and look up at the stars through the narrow canyon walls. He knew that when he rowed across Lake Mead and allowed the bow of his boat to tap the concrete surface of the newly completed Hoover Dam, his achievement would make headlines across the country. But now that the journey was coming to an end, he wasn't sure the fame and the opportunities that awaited him had any value. "I had once thought—once past here—my reward will begin," he wrote in the pages of his journal that night. "But now—everything seems kind of empty & I find I have already had my reward—in the doing of the thing."

When viewed from the perspective of these two boatmen, the idea of racing through the Grand Canyon might not only begin to seem rather absurd and pointless but could also appear to violate, at some fundamental level, the very essence of the place. In light of what Moitessier and Holmstrom and the members of the Hundred Days Trip underwent, a speed run can seem just plain wrong. But there is another perspective, a way of looking at the same issue from an entirely different angle, and when one considers this point of view, the conclusion one reaches is something else entirely.

Of all the writers who have attempted to explain the obsessions that fire extreme mountaineers, one of the most eloquent is the novelist James Salter. In 1979, Salter published a novel called *Solo Faces*, which is loosely based on the life of Gary Hemming, a remarkable American climber who, in 1962, put up the first ascent of a route called the American Direct on the Aiguille du Dru, a spire in the French Alps whose profile is so sheer that for many years it was deemed impossible to scale. At the center of the book is a scene in which Hemming (who is given the name Rand) finds himself staring up at the Dru while he contemplates the challenge before him. The ascent he has selected is so dangerous it verges on suicide, but it is also intoxicating—and Salter's explanation of why that line holds such irresistible appeal bears on the matter at hand. "There are routes the boldness and logic of which are overwhelming," Salter writes. "The purely vertical is, of course, the ideal. If one could ascend, or nearly, the path that a pebble takes falling from the top and climb scarcely deviating to the right or left, impossible as it may seem, one would leave behind something inextirpable, a line that led past a mere summit. The name of that line is the direct."

As it turns out, the appeal of the American Direct and the appeal of a Grand Canyon speed run have much in common. The allure of both lies in the notion that both lines possess such shining simplicity that the path they inscribe on the imagination is a statement of daring and beauty—a thing whose boldness and clarity are too overwhelming to be ignored. An added part of its power also resides in the subversive fact that such a line has no reverse gear, because if you have thought of it once, you simply cannot dismiss it. Once the genie has been let out of the bottle, there is no way to coax it back in. You cannot blink it away or run the film loop backward until it is expunged from your brain. If you have conceived such a line, even for a second, it is there forever, beckoning and urgent, a standard and a goal to test yourself against. It is so compelling that it cannot be turned away from—compelling enough that it may even be worth risking the possibility that the course you have charted might contradict or transgress the spirit of the place itself.

This is precisely why the notion of another speed run formed a major topic of discussion among Grua and the other dorymen during the golden age of guiding in the midseventies. They returned to the topic again and again because, among other things, the practical questions it raised were so endlessly intriguing. How could the Rigg brothers' record ever be broken? The river level that had borne Jim and Bob on its crest—more than 40,000 cfs—hadn't been seen in almost fifteen years. That flow must have boosted their velocity by nearly three miles an hour, which meant that you'd have to be rowing almost twice as hard as they were. The only way to even have a chance, everyone agreed, would be to row through some of the biggest rapids at night, something that had never before been tried. But even if you were willing to tackle all that white water in the dark, how would you cope with the engineers at the dam, who were constantly ramping the river up and then throttling it back down again every twenty-four hours? If you set out on the surge, you would row yourself smack into the ebb, and how would you get past that? And what *else* would you need to pull it off? What kind of boat? How *many* boats? How many boatmen? What would you take and what would you leave behind? And how would you get around the Park Service, whose ever-expanding litany of regulations was another thing Ed Hudson and the Rigg brothers had never had to worry about?

Inherent within those questions lay the recognition of an intriguing paradox. Bernard Moitessier's epiphany seemed to suggest that a race was fundamentally anathema to obliterating the barriers between oneself and the natural world. But when you thought about it, that wasn't entirely true—or, to frame the idea with slightly more nuance, it *could* be true but it didn't *have* to be true, because the line that separated those two things boiled down to nothing more (and nothing less) than intention: the spirit with which you embarked on the enterprise. If you were gunning for fame or fortune, it was pretty much a given that you would never arrive at the place Moitessier and Holmstrom had. But what if the idea of setting a record was ancillary, maybe even irrelevant, to the true goal? What if the summit on which you had set your crosshairs had absolutely nothing to do with trying to elevate yourself above another man's achievements, and everything to do with forging a connection inside *yourself*—in this case a connection with the river and the canyon that might deepen the intimacy that bound you to both? What if the reward that you were chasing lay not in the result to which you were ostensibly striving, but in the simple doing of the thing?

That may well sound like a twisted rationalization, but there was some hard truth at the core of it. Because when you have fully given yourself over to a landscape, without condition or reservation, and when you have come to love that place deeply and with all of your heart, you will do almost anything to celebrate and extend your connection to it. Going slow was a good way of doing that, perhaps the best way of all. But going fast was another way—and if you did it right, if you went fast enough—it might take you to the same destination.

If you looked at the matter from this angle, sooner or later you were forced to concede that there was really no difference at all between slow and fast; that the Hundred Days Trip and a speed run were simply different facets of the same quest. The essence of both actually had nothing to do with velocity and everything to do with depth—and thus what appeared to be a paradox was, in fact, not a paradox at all. At the heart of both approaches lay the dream of forcing open a doorway to a dimension that would enable you to fully explore what it meant to transcend your limits—to arrive at a destination in time and mind where the dichotomy that separated you from the natural world collapsed, where you and the thing became one.

For Grua, that last element must have seemed especially seductive.

Later, the idea of a speed run—its meaning and purpose—would come to acquire new layers of understanding, both in Grua's mind as well as in the minds of those who witnessed what he set out to do. But this was where Grua's fascination with speed in the Grand Canyon began. And it was the reason why, when a group of his friends and coworkers finally saw an opportunity to try to break the Rigg brothers' record, he had no hesitation about declaring himself fully on board with the program.

12

Thunder on the Water

Once it was a boat, quite wooden
and with no business, no salt water under it
and in need of some paint. It was no more
than a group of boards. But you hoisted her, rigged her.
She's been elected.

—ANNE SEXTON

As the 1970s came to a close, the Glen Canyon Dam was approaching an important milestone. Ever since the headgates to the dam's diversion tunnels had been slammed shut in the winter of 1963, Glen's discharges had been calibrated with one paramount goal: filling Lake Powell. Minimal amounts of water had to be released to generate electricity and to meet the water rights of the states located downstream, but the bulk of the Colorado's flow was held back in an effort to fill the enormous bathtub directly behind the dam to the brim. This process had continued for more than sixteen years until, early in the spring of 1980, the numeric gauge in Glen's Control Room, the instrument that measured the depth of the reservoir, indicated that Powell was just a tick or two shy of "full pool."

To commemorate this event, many of the major politicians who had pushed for the dam's construction, including Colorado's Wayne Aspinall, traveled to Page, Arizona, for a special ceremony on June 22. Aspinall, who had fought so fiercely to authorize the construction of the two additional dams inside the Grand Canyon, had his picture taken next to the gauge at the exact moment the fill was complete. A host of local and regional dignitaries was also on hand to take part in the event and tip their hats to the reservoir that bore the name of John Wesley Powell. And as an added bonus, the engineers decided that this would be a good time to conduct a partial test-drive of the spillways by sending a bunch of water down the intakes, through the tunnels, and into the canyon.

The release was relatively small. Each spillway tunnel was designed to handle more than 100,000 cfs, but the test run would generate a maximum combined flow of less than 46,000, which would last for only three hours and fifty-three minutes. Then they planned to lower the gates and crimp the flow to a steady 34,000 and let that run for about a week—just long enough to create a buffer that would enable the reservoir to absorb additional spring runoff. This wasn't remotely close to the amount of water that Glen's spillways would be required to handle under full flood conditions, but it would nevertheless bring the river to a level that hadn't been seen inside the canyon in almost twenty-five years. The window of opportunity was narrow, but when it opened up, Litton's dorymen were ready.

By this point, they had already worked through most of the details of another speed run, driven primarily by Wally Rist, who had first conceived the idea of breaking the Rigg brothers' record. Grua, however, was an equal collaborator because the features he had incorporated into the *Emerald Mile* meant that she was, by far, the best tool for the task. Her self-bailing footwells would save her high-siders from having to worry about bailing and enable them to concentrate exclusively on keeping the boat upright. Meanwhile, her double-ended bow and stern would enable her to punch into the hydraulics backward or forward, which would give whoever was at the oars a wider range of options in maneuvering.

After some lengthy discussion, Rist and Grua had decided that the trip would have to be a private venture conducted on their own time that did not endanger the lives of commercial clients. Only three expert boatmen could take part, and each member of the crew would have to row. The participants would rotate—one man at the oars, pulling as hard as he could, while the other two served as spotters. When it came to filling out the third slot on the crew, both men agreed that there was really just one choice. Rudi Petschek had not only taken part in the *Emerald Mile*'s maiden voyage back in the summer of 1971 but had also rowed her remains out of the canyon six years later, after Steve Dalton had all but destroyed her in Lava Falls. In addition to his special connection to the boat, Petschek's unusual background had imbued him with a special set of skills that would prove crucial to the venture.

Petschek had been born into a family of elite Jewish industrialists and bankers who had established their fortune in Bohemia at the end of the Hapsburg Empire, then later moved to Prague. There Otto Petschek, the family's patriarch, had built an elaborate mansion for his residence and another building, known as the Petschek Palace, that served as the headquarters of the bank. In 1938, just as the Nazis were coming to power in Central Europe, the Petscheks had liquidated their holdings and fled to London, where different branches of the family then scattered to various capitals around the world.* Rudi's parents had opted for Argentina, and there, in the Highland Lakes region to the southwest of Buenos Aires, he developed his passion for rowing small wooden boats, an interest that stayed with him when he headed off to the University of California at Berkeley, where he obtained a PhD in physiology.

His graduate thesis, for which he put rats in refrigerators to analyze the way their brain functions responded to the cold, bored him so profoundly that he typed out the entire thesis by hand, with the margins of each paragraph justified on both the right and the left sides, in an effort to keep himself engaged. That rather pointless exercise said a lot about the way Petschek's mind worked. He was thorough, patient, even-tempered, and delighted in applying himself to tiny details—traits that served him well when he tossed his career as a scientist out the window, found his way to the Grand Canyon, and devoted himself to the life of a dory guide. On the river, he was renowned for his meticulousness and his precision. (He was so obsessed with maintaining perfect trim on the *Ticaboo*, the dory he captained, that he glued a carpenter's level to the bowpost so he could monitor her lateral balance while he rowed.) For all of those reasons, he was also a superb oarsman.

Petschek's love of analysis, experimentation, and problem solving were all qualities he shared with Grua, and by the spring of 1980 the two men had become close friends. So Petschek was easily the best choice when Grua and Rist realized they needed to fill out their crew with a boatman who, among other things, was capable of helping Rist work through the calculations for how the trip should be paced. This issue was complicated by the need to optimize their daylight hours in order to minimize the challenges of rowing at night. They knew they wanted to be inside the Granite Gorge, where they would encounter some of the biggest white water, while there was still plenty of light. But they also knew that they didn't want to tackle Lava Falls, which lay far

---

*While the Petschek family mansion was initially seized by the Nazis, who used it for housing high-ranking officers, the palace later became the headquarters of the local Gestapo. The interrogation, torture, and execution of Czech resistance members took place in its vaults.

below the gorge, in darkness. The problem boiled down to one question: Given how fast the current would carry them and the additional speed they would generate with their oars, when should they launch?

When Petschek and Rist sat down with their notebooks and ran the numbers, they calculated that the trip would have to begin sometime in the late afternoon, and the launch should take place as close to the full moon as possible. To help them get through the darkness, they also realized that they would need to equip themselves with a set of large waterproof flashlights. Meanwhile, Grua set about getting sanction from the boss and wrangling permission from the Park Service. Litton didn't present a problem—although a speed run certainly cut against his philosophy of how the canyon should be run, he wasn't in the business of telling his employees how to do things, especially on their own time. The rangers, however, were another matter.

The river was now under tight government control, and it was no longer possible to simply barnstorm downstream without proper authorization. They would need a special permit, and Grua and Rist both suspected that telling the Park Service that they were seeking to break the speed record probably wouldn't pass muster. In the end, the solution had a familiar ring, a theme that echoed all the way back to the Rigg brothers. They would submit an application to "test evacuation procedures" in order to update the data on how long it would take to row a severely injured passenger out of the canyon.

Surprisingly, the Park Service actually bought this logic, and by the time Aspinall was posing for his picture next to the reservoir's water-level gauge, they had their paperwork in hand and were ready to go.

~

They launched at just after 4:00 p.m. on the afternoon of Monday, June 30, one day after the full moon, and things began going off the rails from the start. A massive weather system was lumbering across northern Arizona, and when they arrived at the ferry, it was already raining so hard that they had to meet with Tom Workman, the ranger who reviewed their paperwork, inside the cab of Petschek's truck. While Workman completed their checkout procedures, the rain pounded down on the roof like ball-peen hammers.

When a storm of this magnitude strikes the canyon, it is nothing short of biblical. As the water runs over the rimrock, it funnels into hundreds of waterfalls that stream over the lowest band of cliffs and splatter into the river. The effect is breathtakingly gorgeous and spectacularly violent, a line of miniature Niagaras discharging to the left and the right, extending as far downriver as the eye can see. To avoid being shotgunned by those waterfalls, Grua and his crew had to hew as close to the center of the river as possible.

By the time they tackled the first several miles along the upper stretch of the canyon, the rain had tapered off, but the sky remained an angry shade of eggplant. By the time they reached Redwall Cavern, at Mile 33, night was upon them and the storm clouds had thoroughly obscured the moon. This was where Grua took over the oars, and during the next several hours he truly came into his own as the captain of the *Emerald Mile.*

As Rist and Petschek peered into the darkness from their posts in the bow and the stern, they marveled at his mastery of the river's dynamics. He ordered them to direct the beams of their flashlights at the walls—Rist to the right and Petschek to the left—and although neither man could fathom where they were, Grua calmly called off the rapids and the mileage numbers. His ability to navigate without any visual cues seemed remarkable, until they realized how extensively he had done his homework and prepared for this part of the trip, memorizing each twist and turn of the canyon so thoroughly that he was steering by the blueprint inside his head.

In this way, he took them past 36 Mile Rapid, where the current heads straight toward the wall, and past Kwagunt at Mile 54, which features a huge, haystacking hole in the center of the main current that he skirted by cambering smoothly to the right. Grua had never rowed or even seen the river at 34,000 cfs, but it made no difference. He knew exactly where he was and precisely where he wanted to be, and he tackled the entire night completely on his own, rowing for seven hours in total darkness until they reached Unkar at Mile 71, the gateway to the big water, where he finally pulled in at the top of the rapid so they could brew up a pot of coffee and wait for first light.

Forty-five minutes later they were off again, and with the arrival of daylight they picked up the pace, each man rowing hard for twenty minutes before rotating to the bow or the stern as they began smashing through the hellbenders: first Hance, then Sockdolager, followed in swift succession by Horn Creek and Granite and Hermit, until they finally reached Mile 98, where, to no one's surprise, Crystal threw them for a loop. They didn't flip, but the hole in front of Big Red, at the top of the Rock Garden, struck them hard enough to catapult both Grua and Petschek into the river. Fortunately, they slid past Big Red without mishap, and Rist was able to pull his comrades back aboard a few seconds later.

They had barely missed a beat and were on their way through the Jewels, past Waltenberg, and across the long straight stretches at Stephen Aisle and Conquistador Aisle. They were really moving now—through Specter and Bedrock and Dubendorff—when, just above Tapeats Creek at Mile 133, the weather returned and hammered them once again.

The fury of the storm was unbelievable. Hail came down hard and dense, and an upstream wind flung it straight into their faces like buckshot. It was impossible to see anything downstream, even though it was the middle of the afternoon, and a few minutes after the storm struck, the waterfalls returned— big and brown and menacing. The combined effect was enough to cut their pace in half while draining the energy they had been hoping to hold in reserve for their second night.

When the storm finally passed, they picked up the pace again, and by 5:00 p.m. they had reached Lava Falls, which, they were pleased to discover, was entirely runnable. Grua was once again at the oars and they whooshed through without a hitch. From there, they continued cranking hard, racing through the first stage of the lower canyon in the remaining hours before darkness returned. Night caught them just above Pumpkin Spring at Mile 213, and there their fuel tanks ran dry.

They had now been rowing for more than twenty-four hours virtually without pause, and they were hungry and wet and utterly drained. When they saw the lights of a commercial trip winking through the darkness on the left side of the river, they pulled into the camp, curled up on the decks, and went to sleep. When the rain returned later that night, they slept on, too tired to care.

They were back on the water before dawn, and the final segment was miserable. They didn't reach Separation, the side canyon where three members of Powell's crew had lost all hope and abandoned the expedition, until lunchtime, and when they reached the Grand Wash Cliffs and laid down their oars, it was well into the afternoon.

By this point Rist and Grua were too tired to do the math, but when Petschek told them the news, their spirits rose. Even with the waterfalls and the hail and the night spent sleeping in the rain, they had maintained a superb pace. So remarkable that their total elapsed time was forty-six hours and fifty-six minutes. They had beaten the Rigg brothers by almost six hours, and the record was theirs.

~

That should have been enough—and for anyone other than Grua, it surely would have been. They had achieved something remarkable, snatching the record while upholding the marvelous and immensely satisfying principle that when it came to speed in the Grand Canyon, oars were still superior to motors. What's more, they had pulled it off in a little wooden boat that less than three years earlier had almost been condemned to a Viking funeral, which was almost as miraculous as the run itself.

When they returned to Hurricane, their coworkers were thrilled by what they had accomplished, and even Litton seemed pleased. He was still unconvinced of the merits of racing down the river, but he couldn't conceal the pleasure he took in the knowledge that the record now rested in the hands of one of his dories, although he did his best to hide his satisfaction. ("Well, did you do it?" he demanded, and when they said they had, he nodded crisply and walked away.) By almost any yardstick, the task was finished and they were entitled to congratulate themselves on a job well done. Grua, however, didn't quite see it like that.

In the same way that Colin Fletcher's shortcut through-hike had rankled Grua's sense of correctness, he was nagged by some troubling thoughts that refused to go away. The three men may have smashed the record, but they hadn't pushed the outer limits of what was truly possible, certainly not in Grua's mind. What's more, they had made no secret of the obstacles that had slowed them down—the weather delays and their extended nap at Pumpkin Springs—and since this was now known within the river community, it was only a matter of time before someone got it into his head to run the damn thing even faster than they had, claiming the record and reducing the *Emerald Mile* to a minor footnote tacked onto another person's achievement.

Those thoughts slowly ate away at Grua for the next two years, until the winter of 1983, when the weather started to do something strange. By now, Rist had left the company to pursue a real estate career in St. Louis and was no longer connected to events in the canyon. But from the house that Petschek shared with his wife in the foothills of the California Sierra, he took note of how one storm seemed to follow another and the snow refused to stop. Meanwhile, Grua listened to the radio from his Airstream trailer in Hurricane and was intrigued to hear that flooding was popping up all along the lower elevations of the Great Basin.

At first, Grua wasn't sure what to make of this odd turn. But as the winter deepened and the snowpack in the Sierras and the Rockies built into something epic and laden with cold promise, the Factor began turning a provocative question over in his mind. Was it possible, he asked himself, that the universe was aligning itself in a manner that might allow his resurrected boat, the Lazarus of the river, to seize hold of the bar and set it so unreachably high that no one could ever even think about contesting her achievement again? Could it be time for the *Emerald Mile* to carve out an abiding place for herself in the history books—not a provisional and temporary perch to be shoved aside at the next big event, but, like the canyon itself, permanent and lasting, something for the ages?

PART V
The Gathering Storm

And farther off, where darkness met it,
the light was broken into scallop-shells of gold,
it swam and shimmered in a billion winks of fire
like a school of herrings on the water,
and beyond all that there was just the dark.

—THOMAS WOLFE

Clouds gathering over Maricopa Point on the South Rim of the Grand Canyon.

13

Deluge

Even this may be the eventful year,
which will drown out all our muskrats.

—Henry David Thoreau

T HE massive storms that drew Grua's and Petschek's attention during the winter of 1983 were the handiwork of something enormously complex and fantastically remote—a meteorological anomaly that had been triggered seven months earlier on the far edge of the Pacific Ocean, more than eight thousand miles to the west of the Grand Canyon. The ripple effects of that event would spend the better part of a year cutting almost halfway across the globe, playing havoc with weather systems from the jungles of South America to the Canadian Arctic. But nowhere would the repercussions be greater than in the western United States—especially within the Colorado River basin.

The prevailing weather in the southern reaches of the Pacific is typically governed by an immense barometric gradient in which areas of low pressure are concentrated off the coast of Australia, while zones of high pressure are restricted to the Pacific coastline of the Americas. Normally, the trade winds of the tropics ride this vast gradient, blowing from the Galápagos toward Australia, and as these gusts drive west they tend, like an immense plow, to push the warm water that lies on the surface of the ocean before them. The effect is so pronounced that the sea levels around Indonesia and Australia are generally about a foot and a half higher than those off the coast of Peru.

Roughly every five years, for reasons that are still not clearly understood, this pressure gradient weakens or disappears, touching off a shift in what is known as a southern oscillation. Within weeks, the trade winds taper off or even reverse direction, in which case they drive toward the Americas, pushing the ridge of warm surface water east instead of west, and generating a sequence of dramatic weather disruptions. When the weather stations in Darwin, Australia, registered this type of pressure shift in April of 1982, it provided the first indication that another swing in the southern oscillation was about to unfold. Although no one realized it at the time, the most massive El Niño event on record had just been set in motion.*

After weakening considerably in April, the trade winds collapsed and died in early May. Then they started blowing in the reverse direction, pushing an immense pool of warm water eastward along the equator and pulling a series of storm systems in their wake. This ushered in a period of almost unprecedented drought across the western end of the southern Pacific. During the next several months, the city of Melbourne would suffer its worst wildfires in two hundred years, while sea levels around the Great Barrier Reef would drop by fifteen inches, exposing large parts of the reef to direct sunlight and killing off vast sections of coral.

In June, thermal readings on the surface of the ocean were starting to rise across the middle of the Pacific. By July, atmospheric temperatures along the international date line had also spiked and isolated tropical islands such as Fanning and Jarvis, which normally bake beneath cloudless skies, found themselves blanketed in deep banks of fog. On Christmas Island in the Republic of Kiribati, the rain started pouring down and refused to stop. More than seventeen million terns, petrels, and shearwaters that used the island as their primary breeding site were forced to abandon their young and disappear in a desperate search for food. Several of these species would never return.

As the warm water continued sluicing east, storms started battering islands that are renowned for the stability and mildness of their climate. By November, Tahiti had been clobbered by five of the biggest cyclones it had experienced in decades, while Hawaii suffered its first significant hurricane since gaining statehood in 1959, with winds that reached 120 miles per hour. A tornado was reported on Oahu, and the waves on Kauai surpassed thirty feet in height, sinking forty-four of the forty-five boats moored in the harbor of Port Allen

---

*Although the El Niño of 1982–83 was the largest on record up to that point, it has since been surpassed by several subsequent southern oscillation events.

and knocking out power across the island. That Thanksgiving, thousands of Hawaiians without electricity were forced to cook their turkeys on barbecues or outdoor grills.

By early December, the mass of warm water was slamming into the continental shelf off the coast of South America and splitting into two vast plumes. The southern plume raised sea levels by more than a foot and devastated marine ecosystems off the coast of Peru that depend upon a rich supply of deepwater nutrients, primarily nitrates and phosphates, which are normally conveyed to the surface by a rising column of cold water. Within weeks, the commercial anchovy and sardine fisheries, key components of the economies of both Peru and Ecuador, had collapsed.

Meanwhile, the northern spool of warm water was sliding up the Pacific coastline toward California and British Columbia. As temperatures rose, fish began migrating north in vast numbers. As Christmas approached, tropical species such as barracuda and red crabs appeared off the shoreline of Monterey, while marlins and sea horses, creatures normally found at the latitude of Mexico, were showing up outside the entrance to San Francisco Bay. The most dramatic impact of these changes, however, was on the engine that drives the winter weather across the western part of the United States.

～

Simply put, the Pacific jet stream is a celestial river of air that flows over the troposphere, the lowest layer of the earth's atmosphere, from Japan to California at an altitude of roughly forty thousand feet. Like the lower reaches of the ancestral Colorado, the jet stream refuses to be confined to a single channel; instead, it swishes back and forth like a loose fuel hose on the deck of an aircraft carrier, banging off the high-pressure zones and convulsing toward the lows. In the late autumn, when the surface water off the western coast of the United States began to heat up, this roiling current of cold air began gathering energy as it inhaled immense drafts of warm, moist air. This, in turn, sent a series of gales catapulting directly toward the coast of California.

The first of the '83 El Niño superstorms made landfall on Saturday, January 22, striking the entire coastline with torrential rains and gale-force winds. A man-made offshore island dotted with 120 oil wells was demolished by a towering train of sixteen-foot-high waves, which went on to tear apart the Santa Monica Pier and wreck at least sixteen thousand homes. San Diego received nine straight days of rain, and in the coastal mountains directly to the east, cross-sections of saturated soil on the hillsides lost their cohesion and began disintegrating, sending semiliquid avalanches slumping into the lowlands, which killed sixteen people and left more than ten thousand homeless. Those storms also disrupted the travel schedule of perhaps the last person in the world one might imagine being put off by lousy weather. In late February, the queen of England was forced to scuttle her plans to sail from Los Angeles up to Santa Barbara, where she was hoping to celebrate President and Mrs. Reagan's thirty-first anniversary. The eighteen-foot seas and the fifty-mile-an-hour winds were deemed too much even for *Britannia*, the royal yacht.

By the end of that month, the storm systems were relentlessly bludgeoning the Sierra Nevada. In Yosemite Valley, the Merced River overflowed, and the campgrounds and parking lots at Tuolumne Meadows went underwater. Echo Summit, ten miles south of Lake Tahoe, was buried beneath sixty-two feet of snow, the largest accumulation since record-keeping had started in 1906. Several weeks later, when an enormous mudslide triggered by that melting snow cut off six remote mountain towns, the US Postal Service would be forced to take the unprecedented step of actually *restarting* the Pony Express. For six weeks, thirteen riders carried more than twenty thousand pieces of mail to and from the stranded communities by horseback along the 115-mile relief route, parts of which paralleled the original Pony Express route, in an effort to ensure, among other imperatives, that residents' April 15 tax returns reached the IRS on time.

The High Sierra, the loftiest range in the Lower 48, is often able to wring dry most of the storm cells that pass over it, but the winter of 1983 broke all the rules. By March, much of the Great Basin, an arid hardpan that typically receives scant precipitation, found itself awash in torrential downpours. In western Nevada, a forty-acre section of rain-saturated dirt gave way and slid into a mountain lake, a mudslide that one witness described as "a huge wave of chocolate pudding." Farther east across the state line in Utah, bone-dry depressions began filling up with water. The Great Salt Lake rose by four and a half feet, nearly doubling its surface area and sending brackish currents sluicing across Interstate 80, twenty miles from its shoreline, and forcing work gangs to elevate the Union Pacific's railroad bed to keep the train tracks from being submerged.

Meanwhile, the frontal systems that had created this mess continued lumbering eastward. When the storms reached Colorado and smashed against the southern Rockies, the snow started falling in earnest, and it didn't stop until the summits were entombed beneath a thick and frozen blanket. At Crested Butte in the Elk Mountains, it snowed for forty-five days straight, forcing the lift operators to get to their posts by 4:00 a.m. to start shoveling so that the lifts would be ready for skiers at 9:00.

On March 10, a huge storm took the snowpack in portions of the southern Rockies past seventeen feet. Two days later, an even bigger storm dumped another two feet on top of that. In this case, it wasn't the levels of snowfall that were so exceptional, but the fact that the storms tamped the temperatures down well below freezing and thereby delayed the start of the spring runoff. As April approached, resorts from Salt Lake City to Denver were preparing to continue hosting skiers past Memorial Day, and their snowfall gauges were registering as much as 825 inches, three times more than normal for that time of year.

As delightful as this may have been for the managers of those resorts and their clients, these weather developments elicited a radically different response from officials at a host of federal agencies who would be responsible for dealing with all of that snow when the runoff finally arrived. "All that we can hope and pray for," announced Robert Vickers, a regional director of the Federal Emergency Management Agency, "is that we have a normal melt."

If God took note of Vickers's prayers in the spring of 1983, he apparently decided to ignore them.

~

In the southern Rockies, the snow typically starts to taper off in late March, and by April Fools' Day, a warming trend—a *gradual* warming trend—has set in. The mechanics of a normal melt-off roughly mirror what happens when a child accidentally drops an ice cream cone on a hot sidewalk. As ambient temperatures slowly increase, the snowpack loses its rigidity and slumps to a gooey liquid at a gently measured pace, which ensures that the runoff doesn't suddenly come roaring down off the mountains all at once.

During the early 1980s, the job of tracking this process within the Colorado River basin fell on the shoulders of two obscure government agencies. At higher elevations, the US Soil Conservation Service, a little-known division of the Department of Agriculture, maintained a network of snow-telemetry devices that monitored the depth of the snowpack. Meanwhile, the National Weather Service, which was part of the Department of Commerce, operated a system of precipitation gauges at lower elevations. In the same manner that the Colorado and the Green merge at their confluence, these two streams of data flowed together and became one inside a rust-colored building located on the edge of the Salt Lake City airport, where a team of seven hydrologists ran the Colorado Basin River Forecast Center, one of thirteen offices around the country that are responsible for monitoring major river basins in the United States.

The center was run by a sandy-haired maverick named Gerry Williams, who enjoyed hunting deer and javelina in his spare time, and was fiercely defensive about his office's prerogatives. The walls of Williams's office were thickly plastered with large satellite maps that spit through an oversize facsimile machine each hour, providing blueprints of weather systems stretching from the Bering Sea to Japan and across the entire western United States. Thanks to those maps, Williams and his team enjoyed a highly refined picture of a world that extended far beyond the northern quadrant of Utah—but had almost no direct connection to the river system that was driven by the weather that they monitored and analyzed. In the spring of 1983, however, all of that changed.

Williams was a veteran with more than twenty years of experience, and the information that was streaming into his office was unlike anything he had ever seen. In the mountains and valleys of the upper Colorado basin, the snowpack in January had burgeoned to 14 percent above normal, but in February and March little new snow had fallen and the snowpack actually dropped to about 5 percent *below* the average. In April, however, the snowpack increased again, and then in May the train started running off the rails. As late-season storms dropped their loads while keeping temperatures well below normal until halfway through the month, the snow-telemetry gauges indicated that the snowpack was increasing dramatically. Then on Saturday, May 28, as if someone had flipped some sort of meteorological switch, the temperatures abruptly shot into the high eighties, rousing all that snow from its cold slumber and sending it racing downhill. One of the places that bore the brunt of this initial onslaught was Salt Lake City.

During the first week in June, every major stream in the Salt Lake Valley was overflowing. Up in the foothills of the Wasatch Mountains, on the eastern edge of town, residents attended to the sinister sound of boulders pounding down the channels as the torrents of snowmelt rearranged the streambeds. Realizing that this onrush was heading directly for the center of town, local officials put out an emergency call for volunteers, and within hours some six thousand citizens—schoolteachers, bus drivers, off-duty firefighters, and anyone else who was prepared to lend a hand—got in line and started diking both sides of Salt Lake's three main thoroughfares with a wall of nearly a million sandbags. City engineers then routed the floodwaters into these canals, instantly transforming the capital of Mormondom into a desert version of Venice. For the next week, pedestrians would make their way across the center of town along a series of wooden footbridges while kayakers merrily paddled down the midstream current.

Williams and his hydrologists were forced to circumvent the morning traffic snarls created by those makeshift rivers on their way to work, and when they arrived at their office, they were confronted with further evidence that the phenomenon unfolding before their eyes had no precedent in the thirty years during which anything approaching accurate and detailed weather records had been kept in the upper Colorado River basin. Never before had so much snow fallen so late in the season. Never before had it melted off with such shocking abruptness.

These developments presented Williams with two problems. First, the events lay well beyond the range of statistical possibilities embedded in the multiple-regression models that his team was using to predict the river's flow. Second, it was painfully evident that the government simply had not placed enough snow-and-rain telemetry monitors and precipitation gauges to build an accurate assessment of the speed and volume of the runoff. Moreover, because much of the snowpack had accumulated in the late spring, far less water had been lost to evaporation and infiltration. All of this meant that as the melt-off accelerated, Williams's computerized programs could neither keep pace with these changes nor integrate them into any meaningful predictions about how much water was actually funneling into the Colorado. "Our models are among the best in the world, but they are only as sophisticated as the current data network," Williams informed the *Denver Post*. "You can't go in and completely model an entire basin in a two-week period."

In effect, Williams and his hydrologists were trapped in a losing game of catch-up that had started at the end of March and refused to level out. In the past, the runoff had been so predictable that the River Forecast Center had not even bothered revising its forecasts beyond the first of May. Now, in early June, they were putting out revisions every seventy-two hours—yet each stream-flow forecast they issued was immediately rendered inaccurate by a deluge of more snowmelt. The amount of water that was racing through the river system was building by leaps and bounds, and Williams's forecasts—which, among other things, provided the basis on which officials at the Bureau of Reclamation were deciding how much water to release downstream from each of their dams along the Colorado—bore almost no resemblance to what the river was actually doing.

~

The exodus of snowmelt began in the Never Summers, a cluster of high peaks located fifty-three miles northwest of Denver in the heart of Rocky Mountain National Park, where an idyllic meadow cups the headwaters of the Colorado. Swollen with frigid inflow from countless freshets and small creeks, the river rapidly built into a torrent whose strength and volume increased as its down-stream tributaries added their own discharges to the main current: the Fraser and the Muddy, the Blue and the Eagle, the Roaring Fork and the Fryingpan and the Crystal.

After blasting out of the mountains and jetting across the orchard-studded piedmont of western Colorado, the river reached the town of Grand Junction and picked up the Gunnison. Then it turned left and made a beeline toward the Utah badlands, hurtling through Westwater Canyon and gathering up the waters of the Dolores and the San Miguel, before rushing past the town of Moab and boring into the heart of Canyonlands National Park. There, beneath a towering mesa called Island in the Sky, the Colorado picked up the entire discharge of the Green, which was hauling the runoff from its own network of tributaries whose waters extended all the way to Wyoming.

Below this confluence, the Colorado throttled through Cataract Canyon, then drilled its way toward the Escalante, the last northern tributary above the entrance to the Grand Canyon. By this point, the fourth-longest river system in the continental United States had become a watery express train freighting the runoff of a region whose landmass approached the size of Poland. The National Weather Service's river gauges indicated that this torrent was now approaching 100,000 cfs, which was something to behold. A flood of such magnitude had not been witnessed anywhere on the Colorado in more than a quarter of a century—although that figure had some important qualifications.

Before the Bureau of Reclamation constructed its phalanx of dams on the Colorado and its major tributaries, spring runoffs with a peak discharge of 120,000 cfs occurred, on average, once every three years—and floods of considerably greater magnitude were hardly unusual. In the summer of 1921, for example, the Colorado had reached 170,000. And on July 8, 1884, thanks to torrential rainfall triggered by the severe atmospheric disruptions following the eruption of the volcano Krakatoa, the flooding may have surpassed 240,000, the highest level ever recorded. (A precise calibration of this discharge was impossible because the gauges were submerged by the current; but a cat trapped in an apple tree enabled experts to make some credible extrapolations.) Moreover, historical debris deposits reveal that even larger floods have taken place in the distant past. On roughly a dozen occasions during the last forty-five hundred years, the Colorado has approached 300,000 cfs. At least once, the river may actually have flirted with 500,000, a level comparable to the average discharge of the Mississippi.

As these numbers illustrate, the size of the runoff making its way toward the Grand Canyon in early June of 1983 was hardly a record-setter. But two additional conditions rendered what was about to unfold both unique and rather chilling. First, it was rare to see the runoff explode out of the mountains so swiftly and materialize as a single, solid rush. Second, and equally significant, just downstream from the mouth of the Dirty Devil, the Colorado's current abruptly collided with the northernmost tentacles of Lake Powell, at the far end of which the river's progress was impeded—for the moment—by the 710-foot-high ramparts of the Glen Canyon Dam.

In its twenty-year life span, the dam had never been required to handle an onrush of this magnitude, and thanks to the speed with which it had arrived—together with the fact that the entire system of reservoirs on the Colorado was virtually full—the Bureau of Reclamation was caught completely flat-footed. Having failed to draw Lake Powell down to a level that would accommodate this flood, Reclamation would now be forced to confront the unpleasant reality that the snowmelt was pouring into the top of the reservoir almost twice as fast as it could be drained through the dam's penstocks and river outlets. With each passing day, the surface of the water was inching closer and closer to the concrete lip on the parapet of the dam. Moreover, as the team of men who were in charge of that dam were about to discover, the only tool at their fingertips for handling this emergency was about to suffer a catastrophic breakdown, pitching them into a crisis that had no precedent in the history of hydroelectric engineering.

Among the sixty-four Reclamation employees who worked at Glen—the operators on Dick White's Control Room team, the power-system electricians and the machinists, the work foremen and the heavy laborers, the secretaries and maintenance personnel—the challenges of that crisis would fall most heavily on the shoulders of one person, the man who was in charge of the entire billion-dollar, ten-million-ton edifice.

14

Into the Bedrock

Rivers, rivers, we can never—
well, hardly ever—have enough of them.

—Edward Abbey

T OM Gamble was a trim, forty-six-year-old Californian with wire-rimmed glasses and a shock of brown hair that was well on its way to becoming white. By June of 1983, he had been serving as Glen's field division chief and power operations manager for nine years, and as the Bureau of Reclamation's top man at the dam, the buck stopped with him—an arrangement that suited his personality rather well.

Unlike Kenton Grua and the rest of the boatmen who had fallen under the spell of the Colorado deep inside the Grand Canyon, Gamble placed little value on the charms of free-flowing rivers. His interest in running water was pragmatic—rooted in neither aesthetics nor romance, but in a hard-nosed sense of appreciation for the energy that rivers contain and a deep respect for the discipline and skill it takes to harness that power for the benefit of human beings. In Gamble's view, there wasn't a stretch of white water anywhere whose excitement could match the thrill of watching eight Frances turbines transform the mechanical energy of the Colorado into pure electricity. For him, Glen wasn't simply a magnificent machine that brought a wild river under control. This was where power was *created*.

As the son of a self-taught electrician who spent much of his career managing lumber mills in Oregon and California, Gamble's childhood had unfolded in a series of industrial encampments where the trunks of towering trees were transformed into raw lumber. He started work at a young age: by his early teens he was driving a forklift on weekends and loading massive trucks at night. During those years, he acquired a passion for the tools and the accoutrements of the trade—the sledgehammers and the giant band saws, the hydraulic jacks and the steel-toed boots, the draglines and the knuckle-boom loaders. With time, he also formed an abiding affinity for the men (and they were invariably men) who made their livings with those tools: the furious bursts of energy they flung into their jobs; the ingenuity of their problem solving, especially when it came to fixing heavy machinery; and the values they forged and instilled through brute labor.

The logging mills of Oregon weren't pretty places. The noise, the dirt, and the mechanized ferocity of the work could be harsh and ugly. But to Gamble those mills were helping to assemble the building blocks of civilization, and the people who toiled in them belonged to a brotherhood that was responsible for turning the world and making it run. Somewhere in his late teens, he realized that he didn't merely respect this enterprise. He also wanted to be a part of it.

After studying electrical engineering at Chico State University, he discovered that his boyhood interests dovetailed perfectly with the oversize machinery inside the giant hydroelectric dams of the West. His first field posting was at Shasta, a massive bulwark on the Sacramento River. When it was completed in 1945, at the apogee of the great dam-building boom, Shasta stood as one of the Bureau of Reclamation's jewels, the second-tallest dam in the country behind Hoover and a marvel of engineering. Although Gamble didn't know it at the time, his appearance at Shasta in the summer of 1962 coincided with the start of a new phase in the bureau's mission and ethos.

By this point, many of the West's colossal hydroelectric dams had been cranking at full capacity for the better part of two decades, and their components were now beginning to wear out and break down. Shasta was an exemplar of this trend. When Gamble arrived, it was painfully evident that much of the instrumentation and machinery would need to be rebuilt or replaced. Almost no one had the faintest idea how to handle these tasks. Not only had the men who had designed and built Shasta long since retired, but their expertise had resided almost exclusively in the art of putting the structure together, not taking it apart. As a result, the current generation of young engineers would be summoned to grapple with these challenges on their own, largely by the seat of their pants.

Gamble began by exploring every square inch of the dam. He methodically walked through Shasta's entire network of tunnels and adits—the narrow and dripping passageways that ran through its interior. These sorts of places were rarely accessed, and most people at his pay grade never bothered to go there. But Gamble wanted to see and touch each facet of the structure for himself. By the end of his first year, he had immersed himself in every piece of machinery there was—the transformers and the turbines, the generators and the penstocks, the cooling coils and the dynamos. He would come down to the power plant clad in his collared shirt, change into a set of coveralls, and start crawling around the top of the stator windings, the electromagnetic conductors on a generator, while the mechanics and the machinists stood around and scratched their heads.

This wasn't the way that supervisors had conducted themselves in the past, and several of the older technicians, men who had developed some firm opinions about where bosses belonged and where they didn't, regarded this behavior as unnecessary and somewhat bizarre. Gamble didn't care what they thought. He was learning by doing, and he found the challenges before him invigorating. Something about fixing and maintaining things was seductive, especially when you had to feel your way through the process on your own. The calling may not have been as heroic as raising the dam in the first place, but the rewards were there. Tearing apart giant machines, repairing them, then putting them back together so well that they ran better than they did before was not merely satisfying and fun for Gamble; it also framed his ethos about how things should be done.

Running a giant hydro dam and a power plant was serious business. The forces that drove the turbines and the generators were absolutely enormous. The simple action of closing the 230-kilovolt air-blast breakers on a transmission line—a routine act that could happen several times a week—sounded like a bomb going off, and the shock it would administer to a two-thousand-ton rotor made it seem as if the entire unit had been smashed with a sledgehammer. If you were responsible for technology like this, you handled it with extreme care, because when things went wrong the consequences could be horrific.* So when Gamble encountered even minor lapses in duty—when, say, he spotted water dribbling out of a set of dresser couplings because no one had bothered to replace them—he was incensed. He couldn't fathom what went through the mind of a manager who would tolerate that kind of thing.

When his stint at Shasta was over, Gamble took this philosophy to Folsom, another large California dam located on the American River. By now, his ideas

---

*In August 2009 when a single turbine spun out of control at Russia's Sayano-Shushenskaya Dam on the Yenisei River, a generator was torn from its bearings and hurled through the wall of the plant, flooding the generator room, triggering an underwater explosion that shut down the power plant and released forty tons of oil downstream while causing a blackout over the entire region. Seventy-five people were killed.

about integrity in the workplace were firmly established, and in an odd way, they echoed Grua's approach to river guiding (a comparison Gamble probably would not have found flattering). There was a right way and a wrong way to do things, and, like Grua, Gamble judged himself and his coworkers by their willingness to adhere to those standards. Among the rules that were nailed to the wall of his mind, at the top of the list was "Be prepared, because you never know what's gonna happen."

Shasta and Folsom had both run well under his leadership, and by the time he received his next big promotion in 1974, Gamble saw himself, with some justification, as a hotshot manager. By actively working to get rid of people he thought weren't performing, he had made more than a few enemies along the way, several of whom had tried to thwart his promotion up the ranks. But he had left Shasta and Folsom in better shape than when they were handed over to him. Now he was being given the keys to one of the largest structures in the entire system, a first-rate facility in a setting of unrivaled grandeur—the most remote and, as he was about to discover, the most notorious dam in Reclamation's fiefdom.

∼

Heading up the Glen Canyon Dam wasn't the premier assignment in the bureau—that distinction was reserved for the managers in charge of Hoover and Grand Coulee. Nevertheless, Glen shared at least some of the glory of those two icons. Unlike most of the dams that had been built during the astringent, cost-cutting years of the 1960s, Glen was the personal baby of Floyd Dominy, Reclamation's hard-charging commissioner, and therefore a showpiece. Glen had none of the fancy artistic touches such as the sculpted Art Deco turrets that rose seamlessly from Hoover's face or Coulee's arresting visitors' center, which was designed in the shape of a giant turbine rotor. But the generator hall in Glen's power plant was gargantuan, and many of the floors, especially in the places where visitors were allowed to go, were done in polished terrazzo. Perhaps the most impressive of all the dam's attributes, however, was the magnificent austerity of its surroundings.

The tiny town of Page, which was perched on a dust-blown bluff on the eastern rim of Glen Canyon, had been carved out of a remote corner of the Navajo reservation, one of the most isolated regions in the Lower 48. Phoenix was nearly a six-hour drive; Salt Lake City took seven. If you enjoyed fine dining and first-class entertainment—which Gamble certainly did—Page could feel like the dark side of the moon. On the other hand, Lake Powell lay directly on the town's doorstep, and Gamble took full advantage of its wonders by purchasing a twenty-two-foot boat. On his days off, he and his wife, Claudine, would put together a picnic basket and roar out across the reservoir. In twenty minutes, they could be anchored inside their favorite side canyon on an isolated beach, fishing the deep-blue waters for bass, or staring up at the stone palisades that towered a thousand feet above. The sky out there was immense, and the way the clouds and the light moved across the surface of the lake was enough to take one's breath away. At sunset, they would watch as columns of light pierced the clouds and illuminated the sandstone, bathing the rock in a lantern glow that made it seem as if the walls were being lit from within. At night, the heavens were so black and so fathomless that they actually got dizzy staring into the cosmos. There were more stars out there than Gamble had ever thought possible.

By the end of his first summer, he had come to believe that Lake Powell was one of the most sublime places on the planet. Regardless of how wondrous the canyon at the bottom of that reservoir might once have been, Gamble was convinced that the splendors of Glen could never have surpassed the unspeakable loveliness of the reservoir that had replaced it. All of which made it not simply puzzling but downright offensive when he began to grasp just how deeply the lake, the dam, and the engineers who worked for the Bureau of Reclamation were loathed by the people who had inherited David Brower's and Martin Litton's anger over what had been done to Glen Canyon.

Gamble got his first real glimpse of that hatred early one Saturday morning in the spring of 1981, when five members of a newly formed environmental organization called Earth First! climbed over a fence and raced across the dam's parapet hauling a tapered sheet of black plastic roughly three hundred feet long, which they unfurled down the face of the dam, making it seem as if a giant crack had appeared in the concrete. Minutes later, while more than a hundred cheering onlookers stood in the parking lot of the visitors' center, a bearded figure clad in blue jeans and cowboy boots climbed into the back of a Chevrolet pickup and started to give a speech.

The man in the truck was the writer Edward Abbey, who had, several years earlier, published a novel called *The Monkey Wrench Gang*, which offered an irreverent portrait of a group of activists who defended America's wilderness through acts of industrial sabotage and vandalism that included burning down billboards, crippling bulldozers, and pulling up survey stakes across the once pristine Southwest. Although Abbey detested technocracy in all its forms, he reserved a special malice in his novel for the Glen Canyon Dam—a theme that was echoed in his earlier and even more famous work, *Desert Solitaire*, perhaps the single most influential document ever written on Glen Canyon. Abbey's depiction of that canyon, which he had floated through in a state of inebriated rapture aboard a drugstore raft back in the late 1950s, was gorgeous and evocative and deeply haunting.

I was one of the lucky few . . . who saw Glen Canyon before it was drowned. In fact I saw only a part of it but enough to realize that here was an Eden, a portion of the earth's original paradise. To grasp the nature of the crime that was committed imagine the Taj Mahal or Chartres Cathedral buried in mud until only the spires remain visible. With this difference: those man-made celebrations of human aspiration could conceivably be reconstructed, while Glen Canyon was a living thing, irreplaceable, which can never be recovered through any human agency.

By 1981, *Desert Solitaire* had emerged as a kind of miniature pocket bible for a generation of young people—backpackers, river rats, and wilderness advocates—who had come to love the canyons of the Colorado as deeply as Abbey. Although most of these readers had never laid eyes on the wonders entombed at the bottom of Lake Powell, they had come to regard the lost world of Glen as a stolen birthright and the dam as something to be reviled, a repugnant symbol of bureaucratic overreach and the gratuitous destruction of beauty. Among those who were directly inspired by Abbey's ideas were the founders of Earth First!, who had organized this protest, and now the author was about to air his views in person.

While Gamble's team of security guards moved across the parapet to cut down the plastic sheet, Abbey laid into the evils of the dam. "No man-made structure in modern American history," he shouted, "has been hated so much, by so many, for so long, with such good reason." He declared that the canyon beneath the waters of "Lake Foul" was a national treasure that had been snatched away from ordinary Americans by politicians and developers "in order to pursue and promote their crackpot ideology of growth, profit, and power." He urged the crowd to "oppose, resist, and subvert," and he concluded by announcing the launch of a nationwide petition demanding the immediate razing of the dam.

Videos of the event, entitled *The Cracking of Glen Canyon Dam*, were soon distributed all across the West, and within weeks minor acts of protest and vandalism were cropping up. College students would drive from as far away as Oregon to urinate off the parapet and plaster *Bomb the Dam!* stickers on every surface they could. Several months later, the threats started. One night, Gamble's phone rang at 1:30 a.m. An FBI agent in Denver was calling to let him know that a man at a bar had been bragging about how his friends had loaded a houseboat with TNT and were motoring down the lake with the aim of ramming it into the top of the dam.

Nothing ever came of such threats, but they left Gamble sobered and mystified by the dark currents of anger out there. Why, he wondered, were these people so *pissed off*? What the hell was their problem?

For the next year or so, he tried to engage in dialogue with members of the conservation community in the hope of offering them another perspective. When he received angry letters or phone calls, he wrote long and polite responses, patiently explaining the benefits of clean hydropower and the important contributions made by all of the Colorado River dams—to flood control, to irrigation, to the Southwest's electrical grid. None of those letters was answered. He attended a river runners' conference in Flagstaff, where he was publicly embarrassed in front of his wife by a singer who performed a raucous song that ridiculed him and the bureau. He even approached Edward Abbey at a book-signing event and made an offer (which was never accepted) to give him a personal tour of the dam. Rebuffed at every turn, Gamble was eventually forced to conclude that these were people who had no interest in exposing themselves to information that might complicate or add nuance to the picture they had drawn for themselves.

His patience was now gone. From what he'd seen and heard, it was clear to him that the environmental community was willfully blind and self-deluded. Yes, a marvelous canyon had been lost, but plenty of other canyons were left, including the grandest of them all. And in addition to providing reliable electricity and sound water management, Glen had created a lake of unmatched beauty, which was now enjoyed by millions of people who flocked to a region that had previously been visited by almost no one. Despite those gains, the dam's opponents insisted on complaining about how terrible flat water was and how important it was for rivers to be *free* and *flowing*. To anyone who shared Gamble's sense of pragmatism, this made no sense. What was even more infuriating was that every one of those protesters happily consumed affordable electricity, clean drinking water, and fresh winter vegetables while ignoring that such benefits came at a cost. Something hypocritical lay in the refusal to acknowledge that trade-off—a level of sanctimony that, in Gamble's mind, rendered the entire subculture of environmentalism naive and rather childish. To him, this was a group of misguided people who couldn't bring themselves to sort through the compromises that went with being a responsible citizen.

As the spring of 1983 unfolded, however—as the runoff surged uncontrollably out of the mountains and the surface of the lake that he loved so deeply climbed inexorably up the face of his dam—Gamble was forced to admit the possibility that if he and his team didn't get a handle on this crisis, Abbey and his ragged band of monkey wrenchers weren't going to need a houseboat stuffed with dynamite to roll back the clock on the Glen Canyon Dam. The river would do the job for them.

~

Managing a reservoir as large as Lake Powell is typically a balancing act to satisfy three competing objectives: keeping as much water in the lake as possible as a hedge against drought, maximizing electricity-generation revenue, and leaving *just enough* room in the reservoir to accommodate the spring and summer runoff. Each winter, these conflicting demands force officials at Reclamation's regional headquarters in downtown Salt Lake City to play the role of gamblers in a high-stakes hydrology casino by placing bets on how much water will arrive when the weather warms up, drawing the reservoir down far enough to accommodate this snowmelt, then praying they got things right.

In 1983, the bureau's guesses were based almost exclusively on the weekly and monthly reports issued by Gerry Williams and his team at the River Forecast Center out at the Salt Lake airport, and as the spring ran its course, it was becoming painfully obvious to everybody that this year's wager had backfired.

In late February, Lake Powell had enough storage space to absorb well over a million acre-feet of runoff. In March, however, the reservoir was hit by the first surge of massive inflows. Despite the fact that an entire river's worth of water was already roaring down the penstocks into the turbines and even more water was hurtling through the river outlets—the four intake tubes running inside the dam that bypassed water around the power plant—the lake was steadily climbing toward the top of the dam.

From the beginning of March through the first week of April, the reservoir ascended at roughly an inch a day. On April 10, it paused and dipped briefly before resuming its climb, rising nearly half an inch a day from April 22 to May 31. By Wednesday, June 1, the surface of the lake was less than three inches from the top of the spillway gates. That afternoon, the officials who were in charge of the river gathered in Boulder City, Nevada, and conceded that additional water would have to be released, even if it meant the loss of future power revenue. It was time to open the spillways.

A spillway is a feature designed to shunt excess water around or over a dam without inflicting damage on the structure itself. Most spillways are pressed into service only during floods, and the configuration that engineers most prefer involves an inclined, open-air chute or trough that channels floodwater either along the side of a dam or directly over its crest. But when a large hydroelectric dam has been wedged inside a narrow canyon and the power plant is located at the base of the dam, often no room is left for an open-air spillway chute. Instead, sharply inclined tunnels must be drilled into the abutments on either side of the dam to convey water to the river downstream.

Glen was equipped with two such tunnels, and they were enormous—twin boreholes more than forty feet in diameter, three times the size of the London Underground, and large enough to handle 276,000 cfs, sufficient for all but the most colossal floods on the Colorado. The entrances to both spillways were protected by a set of gates notched into the sandstone cliffs along the upper surface of the reservoir a few hundred yards upstream from the wall of the dam.

At 1:00 p.m. on the afternoon of Thursday, June 2, the east tunnel gates were opened for the first time since 1980, when the spillways' initial test-drive had enabled the crew of the *Emerald Mile* to break the Grand Canyon speed record. As the water passed into the mouth of the east spillway, it was carried through the sandstone abutment supporting the shoulder of the dam, descending at a steep angle for five hundred vertical feet. During this descent, the water rapidly accelerated. When it reached the tunnel's portal, traveling at 120 miles per hour, it shot into an open trough and passed over a flip bucket, a wedge of concrete shaped like a ski jump that flung the water high into the air, allowing its energy to dissipate before falling into the river.

At first, everything proceeded smoothly. The water was sliding under the gate, through the tunnel, over the flip bucket, forming a graceful white plume that arced for almost a hundred feet before plunging into the river. Spray filled the air, and as the bright sunshine was refracted through the shifting patterns of mist, dozens of rainbows formed and disappeared, then returned again. The spillway was performing so flawlessly that after monitoring the flow for twenty-four hours, Gamble and his bosses in Salt Lake City decided to raise the gates by another two inches to ramp up the discharge. They planned to hold it there over the weekend, then jack the gates up by another inch and a half at 9:00 a.m. the following Monday, June 6, to increase the flow even further.

Late on Sunday night, however, something bizarre happened deep inside the dam.

~

When the pair of operators who were tasked with manning the dam between midnight and 8:00 a.m. arrived for the graveyard shift, water was thundering through the east spillway tunnel at 20,000 cfs. While the head operator settled into his chair at the steel desk in the center of the Control Room on the ninth floor of the power plant, his assistant took the elevator down to the generator hall, walked across a concrete breezeway toward the base of the dam, and got started on a job that called for a special sensitivity.

The interior of the dam, as well as a portion of the cliffs on either side, was laced with a network of narrow passageways known as galleries and adits, which enabled operators to access the instrumentation that monitored the performance of the dam and to conduct physical inspections throughout the structure.

It could be eerie walking through those passageways, especially at night when you knew that you were the only person moving through the hulking edifice of the dam. Most of the tunnels were five feet across and seven feet high, and they felt like the inside of a mine whose interior had been lined with concrete. The only source of illumination was a long string of metal-caged lightbulbs suspended from an electrical conduit that ran along the domed ceiling. The air was cool and dank, and moisture was everywhere—dripping down the walls, dribbling through the drain holes, offering a constant and ominous reminder that a wet curtain of concrete was the only thing that stood between you and nine billion gallons of water whose weight was insistently pressing against the upstream wall. But the job was vital because if anything was amiss, the odds were good that the first place where the problem could be detected was inside those passageways, and the single most effective diagnostic tool was one's sense of hearing.

This was the assistant operator's task—to attend to the quirky music of the tunnels—and that night he had been instructed to pay particular attention to the eastern shoulder of the dam, where the adits penetrated so far into the cliff that no more than seventy feet of sandstone separated the floor of the passageways from the crown of the east spillway. This was the place to listen most closely.

A lot of water was inside the adits—it seeped through hundreds of drain holes that had been bored into the sandstone and collected in a narrow gutter that ran along the floor, which meant that the passageways echoed with a soft trickling. But as he made his way toward the abutment the assistant operator heard something else, a sound that must have made his heart pause and skip a beat. Over the noise of the water in the trough, he could discern something strange coming through the rock. It was subtle and low—he actually had to put his ear to the side of the tunnel to be able to detect it. When he did so, it sounded weird and mysterious: a faint crackling and popping, the kind of thing you might pick up if you awoke in the upstairs bedroom of your house and someone was downstairs in the kitchen frying bacon.

At first, the assistant was puzzled. The galleries were spooky enough that perhaps his imagination was playing tricks on him. But after pressing his ear to the concrete again, it was clear that something was definitely going on—and further, the sound was more complex than it initially seemed. The crackling and popping registered toward the middle end of the scale, but layered beneath that descant was something deeper and more sinister—a soft, rumbling boom, like the indications of a thunderstorm in the distance. Also like an approaching storm, the booming was not continuous. There were long silences, and then, at irregular intervals, the rumbling would start—*boompa-boompa-boom*—before vanishing again.

Whatever was making those sounds was coming from deep inside the spillway. To the assistant, it almost sounded as if something was tumbling through the water, banging back and forth between the walls of the tunnel with great violence. Disturbed by what he had heard, he made his way back to the power plant and told his supervisor, who immediately seized the phone and dialed the home number for his manager, Dick White.

A call at this hour of the night was not at all unusual for White. As the man in charge of Glen's Control Room, he was accustomed to receiving three or four such calls a month, and often the question was simple enough that he was able to mumble some instructions over the phone, go back to sleep, and check back in with his operators when the shift changed in the morning. But when he heard about the mysterious noises coming from the east spillway, White knew that he needed to get down to the dam as quickly as possible.

Moving softly to avoid waking up his wife, he got dressed, stepped outside, and climbed into his government-issue station wagon with a Bureau of Reclamation sticker on the door. He threaded through the darkened streets of Page, then turned onto the access road leading to the base of the dam, which ended at a parking lot next to the machine shop.

A powerful spotlight was mounted on the roof of the station wagon, and when White reached the far end of the parking lot, he trained the beam on the left side of the canyon walls in the hope of answering the most pressing question raised by the telephone call: Was anything coming out of the spillway tunnel that might explain the strange rumbling from inside the rock?

Despite the spotlight, it was far too dark to see anything: the plume of water was nothing more than a ghostly gray blur. A visual assessment would have to wait until daylight started seeping into the canyon. In the meantime, it was clear to White that this wasn't something he could handle by himself. He went up to the Control Room and placed a call, then took the elevator down to the generator hall, walked out to the transformer deck, and stood there staring at the river while he waited for his boss.

$\sim$

Tom Gamble wasn't quite as used to getting woken up in the middle of the night as White, but when the summons came, he got into his car, made his way down the access road, and joined White on the transformer deck, a concrete platform that formed a kind of balcony over the swirling surface of the river. In the glow of the dam's arc lights, the two men could see the currents swirling in confusion beneath their feet—twisted eddies and strange boils created by disoriented water that had just passed through the turbines in the base of the power plant. Then they walked back into the generator hall, through the machine shop, and out along the base of the east abutment until they were standing next to the flip bucket, where the jet of high-speed water was arcing into the shank of the arriving dawn.

Of all the places where one could stand at the dam, this was perhaps the most dramatic. Two sounds predominated: the thunder of the jet as it exited the portal of the spillway, and the hiss of the plume soaring almost half the length of a football field into the river. The combined roar was loud enough that the two men had to shout to be heard, so they mostly stood in silence gazing into the gray, early-morning light. They waited patiently for about ten minutes as the darkness muted and the arc of water slowly materialized. Then it happened: something dark appeared to fly over the flip bucket and catapult out toward the river.

The object seemed to be about the size of the chair at the desk in the Control Room, but it was difficult to be certain because the projectile was propelled with such extreme force and speed. Even though it must have weighed hundreds of pounds, it shot into the air and then, like a flash, was gone, vanishing so swiftly that neither White nor Gamble was sure of what he had actually seen. The two men turned to each other with a look that said, "Did you see that?!"

The canyon was still half dark and the light was tricky. Perhaps they had imagined it. They turned back to the plume of water and resumed their vigil.

By now, the sun was just topping the rim and light was finally starting to pour into the canyon. As the first beams illuminated the spillway arc, White and Gamble registered a visual shock in the same instant. The plume was not a uniform blast, but a series of spitting coughs. Every few moments, the sweep would waver slightly. Then a cough would come as a load of debris spewed forth—half-digested gobbets of gravel, along with shards of concrete and thin, twisted objects that appeared to be pieces of rebar. But what disturbed them most wasn't the material that was being vomited from the portal of the spillway; it was the color of the water.

When the sun hit the stream directly, they could see the plume was neither white nor green, but a pastel shade of pink—a hue halfway between orange and maroon that both men realized with a chill perfectly matched the color of the Navajo sandstone that formed the walls of the canyon cliffs.

The conclusion was inescapable. Somewhere deep in the east spillway, the water had excavated an entire section of the tunnel's steel-reinforced concrete lining, exposing the porous sandstone walls to the full fury of the river.

Good God, thought White. *It's into the bedrock.*

While White pondered the implications, Gamble headed for his office. He needed to get on the phone to Denver and call in the cavalry.

15

The Mouth of the Dragon

No matter how full the river, it still wants to grow.

—AFRICAN PROVERB

THE Denver Federal Center is a heavily guarded, one-square-mile enclosure that hosts the largest concentration of federal agencies anywhere in the country outside of Washington, DC. Here, in the shadow of the Colorado Rockies just west of Denver, twenty-six branches of the government ranging from the Fish and Wildlife Service to the FBI are spread across a miniature city gridded with streets and parking lots that are patrolled each night by foxes, deer, and coyotes. The biggest structure within this enclosure, by far, is a fourteen-story glass-and-concrete monolith known as Building 67, which serves as the headquarters of the Bureau of Reclamation's Engineering and Research Center. Whenever something goes wrong at one of the bureau's 467 dams, which are spread across seventeen western states, and somebody decides it's time to dial 911, this is where the call arrives.

When Gamble got through to the E&R Center on Monday morning, he kept calm and restricted himself to the facts. He offered no dramatic pronouncements about the spillway tunnels collapsing, nor did he indulge in any feverish speculation about the possibility of a tsunami tearing through the Grand Canyon toward Lake Mead and southern Arizona. His tone was measured and the gist of his message was simple. *Something has gone wrong inside our spillway* and we need for you to get a few experts out here to have a look. And if possible, we would really like you guys to try to make that happen *right now.*

That last part caught their attention. When the captain of a flagship dam such as Glen Canyon said that he needed something to happen fast, Reclamation was capable of switching from a ponderous bureaucracy whose pacing mirrored that of the IRS to an operation of military efficiency and dispatch. The expertise of the scientists, technicians, and bureaucrats in Building 67 and a handful of satellite offices just a few steps away encompassed everything from mechanical engineering and electrical design to power transmission and geosynthetic corrosion monitoring. When a dam was in trouble, every one of those people shelved their priorities and brought everything they had to bear on the matter at hand.

Gamble's call was swiftly passed to Bruce Moyes, who headed up a division that specialized in the structural analysis of concrete, and would spearhead the crisis team. A bearded engineer with a gruff sense of humor, Moyes had a range of responsibilities, among which was a long-term assignment to track the performance of Glen's concrete as it aged. Thus he was intimately familiar with the dam and tended to speak of the structure as if it were alive, a cantankerous creature whose temper and moods—not unlike Moyes's own—shifted and changed with time, temperature, and a host of other variables. The two things Moyes cared about most deeply were evident every time the phone in his office rang and he barked into the receiver, "Concrete dams!"

Moyes had direct access to all of Glen's blueprints and schematics, and the team that he could assemble within Building 67 was capable of tackling virtually any challenge arising from a problem with the valves, gates, penstocks, turbines, generators, pumps, or any other mechanical component of the dam. Those experts, however, did not necessarily have a handle on the forces at work inside Glen's spillway tunnels. For that, Moyes needed to talk to the folks across the street at the Hydraulics Lab.

Building 56 was a squat, two-story redbrick structure where the Remington Arms Company had manufactured ammunition during World War II, and the lab it housed was enormous—sixty-five thousand square feet, almost half a city block, with thirty-foot ceilings and a floor so vast that the staff kept a little fleet of bicycles next to the door, two for the engineers and three for the shop technicians. Along the floor, a network of trenches and pipes could funnel up to a quarter of a million gallons of water to the scale models that were used for testing and research. The man in charge of the lab, Phil Burgi, had spent two years working as a civil engineer and teaching math with the Peace Corps in Chile before joining the bureau in 1969. His specialty was hydraulics, and his point man for this emergency was Dr. Henry Falvey, a gifted scientist who had completed his doctorate on hydrodynamics in Germany.

When Moyes summoned Burgi and Falvey, the three men conducted a quick huddle to grapple with the most immediate question, which was to figure out which of them lived closest to the Jefferson County airport. Falvey's house was up in the mountains, and Moyes lived in the opposite direction, but Burgi's place in Wheat Ridge was less than ten miles from Jefferson. Moyes ordered him to drive by his house to grab his steel-toed boots, then make a beeline for the airport and get himself down to the dam so he could start feeding information back to the lab.

Burgi left immediately. When he got to the airport, an Aero Commander 500 was on the tarmac and the pilot was waiting. They were in the air in less than two minutes.

~

Denver sits on the east side of the Rockies, and all of the rivers that flow off the Front Range—the Platte, the Arkansas, the Republican—drain east toward the Mississippi. But within the first twenty-five minutes of the six-hundred-mile flight, the little Aero Commander had vaulted over the Continental Divide and was charting a path that roughly paralleled the upper Colorado River. This offered Burgi a bird's-eye view of the mountain snow cover and a portion of the runoff that had placed Gamble and his team in such a fix.

Far below, on the Gunnison, he could see that the Blue Mesa Dam was spilling spectacularly, and so too were Morrow Point and Crystal, a pair of sister dams that lay just downstream. A few minutes later, they were directly over the waters of the San Miguel and its main fork, the Dolores. Both rivers were swollen with snowmelt. And just off his left shoulder lay the San Juan, which was freighting its own heavy load of runoff from the Animas, La Plata, and the Mancos. Every drop of water in each of those rivers was heading directly for Lake Powell.

Burgi was not a pilot but he shared some of a pilot's passion for flying. He had always taken pleasure in staring out the window of an airplane and observing the landscape unfurl beneath him, and he studied the terrain closely as they passed over the Colorado border, swung into the southeastern corner of Utah, and entered the crystalline airspace above John Wesley Powell's Plateau Province. By now they were approaching the "sky islands," the isolated pockets of desert mountains that dot the canyon country, and he was able to pick out the Abajos, La Sals, and the Henrys. Along the empty and desiccated stretches between their snowcapped summits, he watched as the land turned dry and sunbaked and deeply incised. Then he spotted something strange.

What caught his eye was a patch of blue so intense, so impossibly vibrant—especially when cast against the toasted browns and the charred oranges of the canyons—that it almost looked fake. But what struck him with even greater force than the way the color clashed with the surrounding terrain was the overwhelming size of this thing. It seemed to go on forever, extending far beyond the field of vision afforded by the windows of the plane. He'd never seen a reservoir so flagrantly immense.

Reservoirs come in almost every configuration imaginable. Some are thick and others are thin, but most have a kind of cardinal integrity to their shape. Lake Powell wasn't like any other reservoir that Burgi had ever known. Perhaps the best analogy—an image that captures with uncanny accuracy the appearance of the reservoir as seen from the air—was a comparison invoked by the writer John McPhee, who once likened it to the human lymphatic system. The reservoir wasn't so much a body of water as a tessellated mosaic of squiggly lobes and nodules connected by long, thin tentacles.

As Burgi flew over this azure labyrinth, he marveled at both the reservoir's surreal shape and weird beauty, and at how much water must be stored within that huge and intricate lattice of sandstone. Then, tucked at the far southern end, something else caught his eye.

Standing out defiantly against the blues and the browns was a thin and curving white line. This, Burgi knew, was the top of the Glen Canyon Dam, and from his vantage, it appeared exquisitely slender and delicate—a feature whose scale, in the surrounding landscape, was no less tiny than the leading edge of a baby's fingernail. He was struck too by the starkness of the division created by that alabaster curve. On one side loomed the immense and deceptively placid man-made sea. On the other side lay a great canyon whose dark declivity cut across the plateau in a series of loops and bends that faded into the purple distance far to the south and west.

Burgi didn't spend much time peering toward the Grand Canyon. As the Aero Commander initiated its descent, he fixed his attention instead on the emerging features of the dam. He could see the keyways in the sides of the canyon, where the east and the west ends of Glen's wall notched deeply into the orange sandstone. Next he spotted the rectangular-shaped power plant crouched at the toe of the dam, and just downstream, a plume of water soaring into the river from the portal of the west spillway tunnel. Finally, he took in the switching yards on the west rim, just beyond the visitors' center, and the little town of Page huddled on the opposite rim. From these details alone he could put together, in his mind's eye, at least a part of what had been done to the concrete lining of the east spillway.

That was because, like the boatmen of the Grand Canyon, he had a thing for water.

Burgi had been obsessed with the personality of water ever since he'd first studied civil engineering at the University of Akron. He had devoted his career to studying the myriad ways in which water moved and behaved, particularly when it was coursing through a structure. And he didn't really care whether that structure was the headgate on a beet farmer's irrigation ditch or the jet valves on a giant hydroelectric dam, because both revealed the property of water that he found most mysterious and intriguing.

Those who have mastered the exceptionally complicated mathematics of fluid dynamics understand that the movements of water can be quantified and predicated with beautiful precision, but only up to a point. Beyond that point, a threshold known as turbulence, something unstable and nonlinear takes over, and water—along with most other fluids and gases—stubbornly refuses to yield up its secrets, even to some of the sharpest minds in the history of the human race. As the legendary quantum theorist Werner Heisenberg lay on his death-bed in 1974, he declared that when he met God, he anticipated asking two questions:

"Why relativity? And please explain turbulence."

One version of this story includes a coda in which Heisenberg commented on what he expected to learn from God.

"I really think," he said, "that He may have an answer to the first question."

Hydraulic equations remain some of the thorniest unsolved problems in physics, and for Burgi the mathematics of nonlinear systems and its related field of chaos theory lay far beyond his purview as a civil engineer. But he understood that a peculiar and insidious manifestation of turbulence was taking place inside the east spillway—and in a few minutes his job would be to climb down into that tunnel and diagnose its nuances.

∼

It was already midafternoon when the Aero Commander touched down at the airport in Page, and a visibly anxious Tom Gamble scooped Burgi up in his station wagon. Time was running out, Gamble explained as they completed the six-minute drive, and when they arrived at the reservoir, Burgi began to grasp why.

From the window of the plane, it had been impossible for him to form an impression of just how full the lake actually was. He got his first clue when Gamble drove them out along the east side of the canyon to a parking lot about six hundred yards upstream of the dam, where Burgi stepped out and saw the gates.

The east spillway tunnel intake was controlled by a pair of steel radial gates, each of which weighed 174 tons and resembled the letter *T* tipped on its side. Each gate was fifty-two feet high and rotated on a trunnion supporting a set of girders that formed the base of the *T*. The gates were operated by a set of cables connected to a drum hoist. The cables lifted the gates in a shallow arc, permitting the water from the lake to surge beneath the bottom of the gates and spill into a concrete trough. This configuration initially seemed odd, but anyone looking at the gates closely could grasp the logic behind their design. While the trunnion arms braced the gates against the pressure of the reservoir, the drum hoist enabled the dam's operators to calibrate the precise volume of water they wanted to send into the tunnel.

Running across the top of each gate was a concrete bridge about twenty-five feet above the intake. When the gates were opened, twin streams of water (one from each gate) rushed along a sloping channel toward the mouth of the tunnel, an oval-shaped opening in the sandstone looming several yards below. The bridge thus enabled one to look down on the gates, the intake, and the surface of the lake. This view gave Burgi pause.

For the better part of the past three months, as the runoff had poured into the head of the reservoir more than 186 miles to the north, the surface of the lake had been nudging its way up the face of the spillway gates, and the water was now lapping less than three inches from the tops of the gates. This meant that Gamble's team had only a narrow window to do what they needed to do. Having closed the gates to prevent water from flowing through the tunnel, they would attach Burgi to the end of a long steel cable, guide him into the mouth of the spillway, and lower him through five hundred vertical feet of rock to see what the water had done to the inside of the spillway. Once Burgi had assessed the damage, they'd fish him back up—ideally before the surface of the lake reached the tops of the gates.

Aside from whatever misgivings he may have harbored about being lowered into a giant drainpipe, Burgi had two other things to ponder during his brief walk out to the middle of the bridge. First, if the steel cable malfunctioned, he could well find himself stuck, with no way of climbing out or lowering himself down. Second, nearly fifty-two feet of water was now pressing against the face of those gates, and if they failed for any reason—or if the reservoir overtopped the gates before he could be extracted—the upper layer of Lake Powell would roar into the mouth of the spillway, snatch him up on its way down the tunnel, and spit him out the portal at the base of the dam, where the flip bucket would send whatever was left of him catapulting over the Colorado like a champagne cork.

Mercifully, perhaps, he wasn't given much time to contemplate any of this.

At the center of the bridge was a white dual-axle flatbed truck equipped with an air compressor and a large winch. Here, Burgi discovered that he didn't need his steel-toed boots after all. Gamble's team handed him a pair of rubber irrigation boots, a set of rain gear, a plastic hard hat, and a portable, battery-operated light. While he donned the gear, he cast a glance into the sloping channel and spotted what was attached to the truck's winch. The odd-looking metal contraption looked like a cross between a go-kart and an elevator cage— a square platform surrounded by a set of guardrails, equipped with four small wheels, and featuring a tie-off pulley attached to the winch cable.

Extending from one corner of the guardrail, like a parasol stuck in a cocktail glass, was a pink umbrella. And across the face of the cart, which was painted bright yellow, someone had stenciled a phrase as a dare to anyone contemplating descending into the spillway tunnels in this contraption:

I Challenge U 2

After donning a nylon safety harness, Burgi jammed his notebook into his belt and started down a metal ladder to the surface of the sloping channel. He couldn't help but notice that thin jets of water were squirting beneath the bottom of the closed gate and around the sides, forced through the cracks by the pressure of the reservoir. An awful lot of lake wanted to get through that steel plating.

When he stepped off the final rung of the ladder and onto the surface of the sloping channel, the shallow stream raced over the soles of his boots. He made a mental note about how slick the wet concrete surface appeared—one slip would send him skidding down the intake toward the mouth of the spillway, which loomed downstream like the entrance to a mine shaft. But Gamble's team was prepared for his arrival.

Three men were already standing in the channel, each anchored to a safety line. Burgi was handed off from one man to the next in a kind of shuffling dance until he reached the cart and stepped on board.

Waiting inside were two technicians, one of whom carried a waterproof radio. His job would be to relay instructions to the operator of the cable hoist on the bridge. This would be their sole means of controlling their progress into the spillway and back out again. The other member of the team used a carabiner to clip Burgi's safety harness to a stanchion on the side of the cart.

If this gate fails, Burgi thought, casting a glance up at the leaking bulwarks of steel, *I'm gone*. With that, the cart began its journey into the mouth of the dragon.

∼

The cart was about five feet wide, and the wheels canted outward to stabilize the vehicle while also discouraging it from climbing up the rounded sides of the spillway tunnel. As the winch paid the cable out, the cart slowly passed from the blinding sunlight of a June afternoon into the clip-edged shadow that marked the entrance to the tunnel, whose crown arced forty-one feet above. As they approached this threshold, the slope of the tunnel increased dramatically, angling from fifteen to fifty-five degrees, and the front of the cart suddenly

The Grand Canyon barely made an impression on Don García López de Cárdenas, the Spanish conquistador who became the first European to stumble upon the great chasm in the autumn of 1540, eighty years before the Pilgrims arrived on the *Mayflower* and almost two centuries before the birth of George Washington. The abyss carved by the Colorado River (seen here from the Toroweap Overlook on the North Rim) was so impassable that more than three hundred years would elapse before anyone attempted to penetrate its mysteries.

1

2   3

A man described by one of his biographers as "a stick of beef jerky adorned with whiskers," Major John Wesley Powell lost his right forearm to a Confederate minié ball while commanding a Union artillery battery at Shiloh (note the hole in the sleeve of his jacket). In light of that handicap, Powell's greatest achievement is nothing short of astonishing: leading a tiny fleet of wooden rowboats (one of which is pictured at right, with the Major's armchair lashed to the deck) on two trips, in 1869 and 1871, down the most ferocious river in the West in order to unlock the secrets of the Grand Canyon. When Powell died in 1902, the *Washington Post* ranked him with Columbus, Magellan, and Lewis and Clark.

In the annals of the Grand Canyon, Martin Litton stands as something unique: a tornado of soaring eloquence and distempered fury who helped to shape the destiny of the most iconic natural wonder in North America. After barnstorming into Holland and France as a WWII glider pilot, Litton came home and flung himself into a series of conservation battles along the Colorado River, where he and his white-water dories played a key role in the fight to prevent the hidden paradise at the bottom of the canyon from being destroyed by the US government.

4

From the moment the headgates to the Glen Canyon Dam were closed in 1963, the river that flowed through the Grand Canyon may have seemed wild and dangerous and free, but every drop would now be metered and rationed by engineers and bureaucrats.

5

By the mid-1960s, the Bureau of Reclamation's mission to bring the Colorado River under total control was almost complete. The only remaining untamed section lay deep inside the Grand Canyon, where the steep gradient and soaring walls afforded prime sites for two giant hydroelectric dams—until Litton and a host of other conservationists launched a campaign that roused the fury of the American public, provoking editorials and other protests, like this 1966 cartoon in the *Los Angeles Times*.

6

Braced between the flanks of a narrow gorge at the head of the Grand Canyon, Glen Canyon Dam soars more than seven hundred feet from its foundation in the bedrock beneath the river. Pressing insistently against that ten-million-ton wall of concrete is one of the longest reservoirs on earth.

7

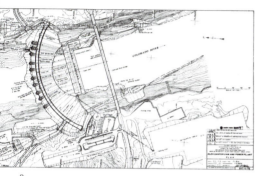

The schematics of the dam, as seen from above, capture key features of one of the largest machines on the planet. Here one can see the eight penstocks that direct water from the reservoir into the power plant at the base of the dam and the four river-outlet tubes, which bypass the power plant and hurl their discharge directly into the river. Along either side of the dam run the spillways, two massive tunnels bored through solid sandstone that are designed to serve as the dam's safety valve during exceptionally large runoffs.

8

9   10

From the intakes of the dam's penstocks, water plummets more than three hundred vertical feet and is funneled into Glen's turbines, each of which is paired to one of eight generators (shown here) that convert the mechanical energy of the river into electricity, which is distributed across the desert and released to civilization: lighting homes, powering air conditioners, and zapping frozen microwave dinners in cities from Utah to southern Arizona.

Every aspect of the dam's Control Room upholds and reinforces the principle that here, in Glen's nerve center, human beings are the indisputable masters of a renegade river that was once the scourge of the Southwest. In the spring of 1983, thanks to the most massive El Niño event on record at that time, that principle would be turned on its head.

When the spillway tunnels at the Glen Canyon Dam were opened in June 1983 in response to a massive spring runoff, the dam's operators stood by as rocks and jagged pieces of concrete were ejected at 120 miles per hour from the mouths of the tunnels. Realizing that something had gone terribly wrong, they were forced to lower a lone engineer into one of the spillways with the hope of diagnosing the problem. The photo on the left captures Phil Burgi on his harrowing inspection tour aboard a tiny, wheeled cart attached to a long steel cable. (Extending from one corner of the cart, like a parasol stuck in a cocktail glass, was a small umbrella to protect Burgi from the water cascading through the tunnel's weep holes.) Deep inside the spillway, he discovered that the raging water had excavated a series of jagged holes along the surface of the tunnel.

11

12

13

With the spring runoff pouring into the head of Lake Powell faster than it could be discharged, and with the tunnels now crippled, Glen's engineers confronted the prospect of an "uncontrolled release." To prevent this, they hastily erected a bulwark of plywood flashboards atop the massive steel radial gates guarding the intakes to the spillways. As a watertight barrier, the plywood was hopelessly inept; in the photo above left, powerful jets can be seen spurting through the gaps. Nevertheless, the flashboards bought the engineers some desperately needed time to troubleshoot their stricken dam—all the while sending enough water downstream to create the largest flood the Grand Canyon had witnessed in a quarter of a century.

Kenton Grua stood as an exemplar of the obsessions that can ignite the dry tinder of a man's soul and then race like wildfire through the upper branches of his spirit when he decides to surrender the entirety of himself, unconditionally and without reservation, to the hidden and seductive world at the bottom of the Grand Canyon.

14

There were different theories about why the dories of the Grand Canyon (seen here in Martin Litton's boathouse in Hurricane, Utah) were so bewitching. But an unspoken consensus held that the boats' appeal was rooted in the blending of three elements: simplicity, balance, and ruthless reductionism.

15

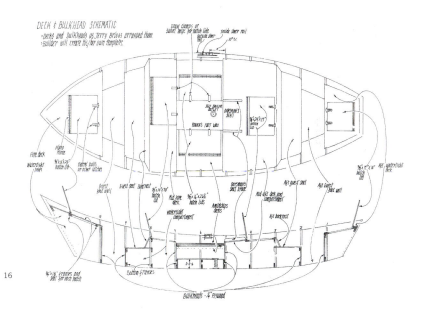

16

For the little dory that was made for Litton in the summer of 1971 (whose schematics are seen here), he selected perhaps the most beautiful name of any boat in his fleet—a gesture of remembrance to honor a towering stand of old-growth redwoods tucked deep in the coastal forests of Northern California that had been clear-cut during the early 1960s. "Truly something to cry about," Litton raged. And so she became the *Emerald Mile*.

In 1977, when the *Emerald Mile* was extracted from the rocks at the edge of Lava Falls, the largest rapid in the Grand Canyon, following her brutal accident there, she barely resembled a boat. The damage was so terrible—her bow had been completely destroyed and several key pieces of her hull had disappeared down the river—that she was slated to be set on fire as her carcass was pushed off the back of a trailer into a municipal garbage dump.

17

After stepping in to put a stop to the *Emerald Mile*'s "Viking funeral," Grua declared that he would claim the stricken dory as his own and bring her back to life. Here, he pauses for a sandwich break during the months of restoration work that followed.

19

18

When Grua completed his rehabilitation project, the *Emerald Mile* was both a restoration of her former self and something new: a streamlined instrument of speed and grace, as well as the Lazarus of the river. The morning that Grua launched her into the shallows at the head of the canyon (above) and rechristened her with a bottle of champagne (right), she was poised for the final and most dramatic chapter of her story.

20

Steve Reynolds, known to his friends as Wren, was the kind of boatman that river folk sometimes refer to as a "looker"—an oarsman who took an almost preternatural joy at being able to row a complicated stretch of current without hitting a damn thing. It was not unusual for Wren to rack up ten or fifteen flawless trips in his dory, the *Hidden Passage* (below), skating past rocks and through white water with a seamless perfection that made his colleagues shake their heads with envy. In the spring of 1983, Wren sensed that Grua was contemplating a speed run in the *Emerald Mile* and pulled him aside with a special request. "If anything happens," he declared, "I'd love to be a part of it."

21

22

23

Rudi Petschek was one of the most unusual boatmen ever to run the Colorado, a Jewish refugee whose path to the river had drawn him from Nazi-occupied Europe, through the lakes of Argentina, and then to the laboratories of Berkeley, where he abandoned a promising career as a scientist, went to the Grand Canyon, and found his true home on the decks of a seventeen-foot wooden dory. At age forty-nine, Petschek was by far the oldest member of the speed-run crew. Yet it was he who would see them through the darkest hour of their journey.

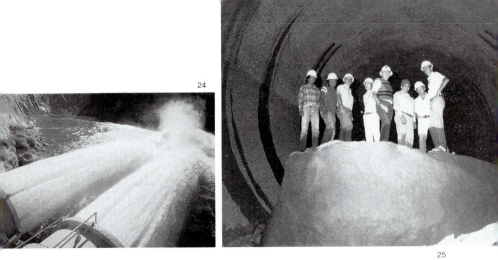

24

25

Thanks to the damage inflicted on the spillway tunnels, the operators of the Glen Canyon Dam were forced to send excess water through the dam's river-outlet tubes (left) in a nonstop torrent that lasted for months. The thunder of the discharge emerging at the mouths of those outlets could be heard from the dam's parapet, more than five hundred feet above.

Responsibility for overcoming the spillway crisis fell on the shoulders of Tom Gamble, the man in charge of the dam, who is seen above (center) standing atop House Rock, a massive boulder that lodged in the east spillway. After the runoff crested and Gamble's team was finally able to enter the spillway tunnels, they were stunned by what they encountered. At the elbow of the east spillway tunnel (left), the water had carved out a jagged trench, ripping away the concrete and excavating material from the sandstone cliff to a depth of three stories.

26

Only after workers had drained the tunnels and removed the rubble (right) could the job of repairing the spillways get under way. The cost of the spillway crisis came to more than $32 million, a hefty price for the Bureau of Reclamation's decision to fill Lake Powell to capacity while failing to leave sufficient storage space to accommodate the runoff. It also offered a graphic testament to the power of the Colorado River.

27

swung downward to become the floor—a transition that Burgi and his two companions negotiated with some awkward shuffling.

A six-hundred-foot incline now loomed between the men in the cart and the bottom of the tunnel. The fall wasn't vertical, but when Burgi leaned over the rail and gazed down into the black maw yawning between the toes of his boots, it was steep enough to take his breath away. What thrilled and terrified him even more was his growing sense of the sheer size of the spillway. As they rolled down its throat, he was reminded of the biblical story of Jonah and the whale—but then he realized that the spillway's diameter far exceeded the size of even the largest marine creature. The tunnel was *enormous*.

Within the first fifty feet, the oval-shaped patch of sky above winked out and the cart was cloaked in darkness, which only seemed to heighten the spillway's immensity. But as the light disappeared, Burgi's other senses began to take over.

The first thing he registered was the temperature drop. The coolness on his skin made him shiver. Another thing he noticed was the smell. He could detect the chalky odor of wet concrete, but even stronger was the clean smell of rain. Finally, there were the sounds—or more specifically, the absence of them. There were no mechanical noises—no churning turbines or whirring generators, no clanking of gate hoists or grinding of gears. Aside from the chatter between the radio operator and the folks up on the surface, all he could hear was the flow of running water—a lot more water than Burgi had expected.

The leakage from the spillway gates converged along the invert, the tunnel's rounded centerline, to form a powerful stream that created a constant spray. In addition, every few feet the cart was also passing beneath a thin waterfall pouring from one of the many weep holes that had been drilled into the crown of the tunnel. These were designed to drain the moisture that seeped through the sandstone surrounding the outer lining of the tunnel, and as the distance from the top increased, so too did the intensity and speed of all this falling water. At the halfway point of their journey, three hundred feet into the spillway, the water in the centerline was whooshing between the wheels of the cart at nearly eighty miles per hour.

The umbrella wasn't much help. The torrents pouring through the weep holes swiftly punched out several panels of fabric, so Burgi and his two companions gave up trying to huddle beneath it and concentrated on dodging the waterfalls. Some of these they were able to spot ahead of time and avoid; others caught them by surprise in the darkness. By the time they reached four hundred feet, all three men were soaked.

About eight minutes into their descent, Burgi noticed that the darkness seemed to be abating. At first, the illumination was so faint and pale that it seemed like a mirage. But as the light grew in strength and took on shape, a half oval, he realized that he was about to get his first glimpse of a peculiar quirk in Glen's spillway tunnels—a feature that was a by-product of a decision made many years before, and that now played a key role in the problem he was attempting to diagnose.

When work on the dam began in 1956, a set of diversion tunnels had been drilled at river level through the sandstone cliffs on either side of the river. By shunting the Colorado into these horizontal tubes, the construction site was kept dry while the dam was being built. Then, six years later, as work on the concrete edifice was nearing completion, the construction crews had to bore a *second* set of tunnels through the cliffs to serve as the spillways. Drilling through solid rock was extremely expensive, so Glen's design team had opted to save some money by allowing the steeply inclined spillway tunnels to intersect with the lower ends of the nearly horizontal diversion tunnels. (This configuration can easily be visualized by placing one's arm on a desk: the bone that runs from the shoulder to the elbow represents the new spillway, while the forearm between the elbow and wrist represents the lower portion of the old diversion tunnel.)*

This was an efficient arrangement, but it forced the water flowing through each spillway to negotiate a significant bend at the elbow, where the two tunnels met. Moreover, as the water thundered through the tunnels, it picked up enormous speed, which meant that the most violent hydraulic forces were concentrated at this elbow joint. The faint illumination that Burgi discerned as the cart descended was coming *up* the bottom of the old diversion tunnel, and reflecting off a pool of water that had collected directly at the elbow.

By now the cart had been trundling down the incline for almost ten minutes, and they were roughly 80 percent of the way to the bend. Here, something on the surface of the invert caught Burgi's eye. He told the radioman to order the cable operator to stop the winch, then flicked the switch on his portable light and peered through the mist. On the surface of the tunnel, where the concrete should have been solid and smooth and unblemished, he could see something that had no business being there: a jagged, ugly-looking hole.

Phil Burgi wasn't the sort of man who condoned the use of profanity, ever—even when the situation seemed to beg for execration. So when the words "Jiminy Christmas" escaped his lips in a low murmur, what he was really saying was *Holy mother of God.*

～

Burgi thought he had a pretty good idea what might have caused that declivity to form, and to confirm his suspicions, he trained the beam of his light just

---

*If you cup your palm and turn it upward, you've also neatly captured the flip bucket.

above the hole. Sure enough, there it was: a bump on the tunnel surface. It was tiny—only about a quarter of an inch high and small enough that he could have covered it with a poker chip. But as Burgi knew, that bump was connected to a story that, much like the narrative of the elbow joint, went back more than twenty years.

During the final phase of the dam's construction, the interiors of the tunnels were lined with concrete, and sometime after the concrete had set—it was impossible to know precisely when—a small protuberance had formed on the rounded invert of the tunnel's steepest section just inside an area known as Station 25.00, where Burgi was now suspended. Here, two separate sections of the tunnel's lining had butted together to form a joint, and the bump that had taken shape along that joint was anchored directly on the centerline of the tunnel. Composed of calcite, a crystallized mineral formed of calcium and carbon ions, the bump was generated by excess moisture rising to the surface through cracks in the concrete, the same process that produces powdery deposits on basement walls and the sides of swimming pools (and which also creates stalactites on cave ceilings). This nodule wasn't the sort of thing that an inspector would have been able to spot unless he was searching for it. It was about the size of a barnacle on the hull of a ship—and, like a barnacle, the calcite was extremely hard. Knocking it off would have required a hammer and a cold chisel.

This was the cause of all the trouble, although the mechanism was complex and stemmed from a peculiar property of moving water—one of those quirky and chaotic elements that made hydrodynamics so fascinating to Burgi.

When water traveling at high velocity strikes an irregularity on the surface over which it flows, tiny vacuum bubbles radiate downstream. When the bubbles implode, they send out miniature shock waves that reverberate through the water column. Each concussion is minuscule, but when the effect is multiplied by thousands of bubbles collapsing simultaneously over a sustained time, it can generate surprising impact. The effect is similar to what might be created by tapping away with hundreds of tiny ball-peen hammers. This force, called cavitation, was first identified by the British Royal Navy when the propellers of its warships and submarines began to sustain heavy damage during World War II. As the British discovered, when cavitation runs unchecked for days or weeks, it can inflict severe damage on hard metals such as iron and steel.

Concrete doesn't stand a chance.

Although the engineers who designed the Glen Canyon Dam were generally familiar with the challenges posed by cavitation, they had been unable to devise a solution to the problem. But by the summer of 1983, Burgi's team at the Hydraulics Lab in Denver understood cavitation more deeply than anybody else in the world: what triggered it, the damage it could wreak, and the steps necessary to contain it. The lab's roster of fancy gadgets included an enormous vacuum cavitation chamber, painted baby blue, that looked like the pilothouse of a ship perched on steel legs. Thanks to the research Henry Falvey and a handful of his colleagues had conducted inside that chamber, Reclamation had actually come up with an answer to the problem—an expensive but elegant fix in which a cushion of air was injected into a spillway's water flow to absorb the shock waves and neutralize the force of the collapsing bubbles. Because of budgetary constraints, however, this fix had been back-burnered in the bureau's dams across the arid Southwest on the grounds that their spillways were so seldom used. In a grotesquely ironic twist of timing, the discussions for implementing this repair at Glen Canyon had been scheduled to start on June 1, one day before the spillway gates had been opened. Now, as Burgi discerned, it was too late.

By the time Burgi located the calcite nodule, cavitation had been eating away at the east tunnel's concrete lining for five days. The hole just beneath the nodule was small—only about five inches deep and barely big enough to hold an orange. But Burgi could see that it contained a small pocket of wet gravel, which was as disturbing as the discovery of the hole itself. At higher velocities, the water in the spillway would cause those bits and pieces of broken concrete to swirl around the bottom of the hole like loose marbles, scouring the edges and rapidly causing the hole to widen. As it expanded, so too would the violence of the scouring. Engineers call this a positive-feedback loop—a system that builds in intensity by feeding on its own effects. But what was even more disturbing to Burgi was that this damage had probably triggered a chain reaction along the lower sections of the tunnel.

By creating a disruption in the water train that was quite a bit larger than that from the original calcite nodule, the orange-size cavity had almost certainly generated a second and considerably larger explosion of cavitation-inducing bubbles. Here lay the start of a different sort of positive-feedback loop—one that, if the theory was correct, would create a sequence of ever larger holes deeper inside the tunnel. Sure enough, when Burgi tested this theory by aiming the beam of his light into the darkness below, he could spot the shadowy outline of the next link in the chain. The concrete immediately below the first hole was undamaged, but eighteen inches farther down was a second cavity, at least twice as wide as the first and nearly a foot deep.

The second hole was followed by another intact section that ran for several feet and yet a third hole, then an even longer gap and a fourth hole, whose circumference was bigger than that of all of the others combined. Inside each impact zone, the damage grew radically worse—the scouring had penetrated deeper into the concrete, and each deposit of gravel was larger and coarser than the next. As the cart continued its descent, Burgi discovered a total of six holes, each wider and deeper than the one directly above it, the lowest of which was so extensive—penetrating nearly four feet—that twisted pieces of rebar were poking through the rubble.

Finally, the cart could go no farther. They had not yet reached the elbow joint at the bottom, but the size of the sixth hole exceeded the width of the cart's chassis and thereby blocked their progress.

As he hung there in the darkness, huddled under what remained of the shredded umbrella, Burgi pondered the scene before him and pieced together what had taken place. The cavitation had essentially leapfrogged its way down the tunnel with ever-expanding fury, creating a widening triangle of destruction. This was the source of the hollow thumps and the mysterious frying-bacon sounds that the Control Room team had picked up late on Sunday night.

The pattern of damage that had resulted was a classic double-echelon that hydraulic engineers refer to as a Christmas tree—with the giant hole at the base and the calcite deposit as the star. This came as no surprise to Burgi. But he was astonished by the extent of the destruction. The size of the holes, and even more shocking, the speed with which they had formed were far worse than he had anticipated. Moreover, if his hunch was correct, the area of worst damage wasn't even visible.

Somewhere within the nebulous depths of the pool at the base of the incline, down where the tunnel formed its elbow, a truly colossal breach was being excavated. Just how deep that hole might penetrate was impossible to say. But this, Burgi had no doubt, was where the spillway jet had drilled all the way through the concrete lining of the tunnel and begun mining out the soft sandstone of the canyon wall that supported the eastern abutment of the dam. Here lay the source of the orange-tinted discharge, as well as the chunks of debris that Gamble and White had witnessed flying off the end of the flip bucket and arcing into the Colorado.

The idea that such a minor aberration—a mineralized globule half the size of a walnut—could have initiated the dismantling of something as immense as the spillway of the Glen Canyon Dam was hard to believe. But the evidence was clear.

Dismayed by what he had seen, Burgi pulled out his notebook and, doing his best to shield it from the cascade, made a quick sketch of the Christmas tree with his best estimate of the measurements and dimensions. Then he told the radio operator to order the folks on the surface to start hoisting them back to the top. It was time to get out of the tunnel and give Gamble the bad news.

16

Raising the Castle Walls

The distant lightning glowed mutely
like welding seen through foundry smoke.
As if repairs were under way
at some flawed place in the iron dark of the world.

—CORMAC McCARTHY

A s the cart ascended toward the top of the tunnel, Burgi concluded that using the spillways was no longer an option. The moment they reopened the gates and permitted the flow to resume, the cavitation damage would resume. Judging by what he'd just seen in the east tunnel, a similar process was surely unfolding in its counterpart on the west side of the canyon, which was still passing water. In Denver and Salt Lake City, however, Burgi's superiors had drawn precisely the opposite conclusion: it was no longer an option *not* to use the spillways. Even as Burgi clambered from the cart and climbed the ladder back to the dam's parapet, Gerry Williams's team at the River Forecast Center was once again increasing its estimates for the amount of runoff pouring into Lake Powell.

This left Gamble in a terrible predicament. With barely two inches of freeboard left on the spillway gates, the man in charge of Glen had roughly twenty-four hours to ponder his options before the river made the decision for him. If the gates remained shut, sometime on the night of Tuesday, June 7, the first surge would come sluicing over the top of the gates and form a fifty-two-foot waterfall at the upper end of the tunnel intake. The gates weren't designed to handle such a cascade, which would tear out the cable hoists and damage the trunnion arms. Then, with no way of raising the gates, Gamble and his team would be robbed of their ability to control the flow into the spillway tunnels, where the water would resume its stripping away of the concrete lining and drilling into the sandstone.

Clearly, the situation called for out-of-the-box thinking. What they really needed was for some kind of river fairy to fly over the surface of Lake Powell, wave her wand, and expand the size of the reservoir by a couple of million acre-feet so they could store some extra water while figuring out what the hell to do next.

That was a tall order. But as it turned out, Gamble and his team had something in mind.

~

Shortly after lunch break the following afternoon, the foreman of the dam's maintenance department summoned his crew together for a quick huddle. Leon Swapp's group wasn't big—they rarely had more than six or seven men—and they were responsible for a range of duties that ran from the exciting to the banal. If you worked for Swapp, you might find yourself starting off the workweek pulling components from one of the generators in the power plant using the three-hundred-ton overhead crane. By Friday, you could be scrubbing out a clogged toilet in the visitors' center or scraping up the remains of a ringtail cat that had accidentally incinerated itself in the switching yards. (The dam had a real problem with ringtails, desert mammals resembling raccoons that liked to plunder the eggs of birds nesting in the switching yards; if a ringtail was unlucky enough to pause atop a sixty-nine-kilowatt transformer while putting its paws on a conductor, the cat would literally explode.) On any given day, Swapp's crew encountered things that went quite a ways beyond the average maintenance person's duties. But the orders he issued on Monday afternoon left even the veteran members a bit mystified.

"I want most of you guys to get up to the warehouse and start grabbing all the angle iron you can find," Swapp told his crew in a tone that demanded this happen immediately. "The rest of us need to start calling up lumberyards—we're gonna need to round up every piece of marine-grade plywood we can get our hands on."

Richard Parsons was one of the men on the angle-iron crew, which rushed over to the dam's warehouse and started to cut lengths of two-inch steel into four- and eight-foot pieces with a torch, then loaded them onto the back of a truck that began shuttling loads to the radial gates at the top of the dam. Meanwhile, the rest of the team raced in to Page and bought up every piece of three-quarter-inch plywood in town.

As they completed these tasks, Glen's other crews were also mobilizing. While a team of electricians set up service lights on the bridge over the tunnel intakes, the dam's high-scalers rigged a safety system along the tops of the two sets of spillway gates. This was tricky. The tops of the gates were more than two feet wide, which was plenty of room to move about; but the consequences of a misstep would be severe. On the downstream side loomed the fifty-two-foot drop to the sloping channel and the mouth of the tunnel. On the upstream side was the reservoir, where the water was nearly five hundred feet deep. Knowing that time was of the essence, the high-scalers strung a single safety line across the top of the gates, then hastily tethered a dozen life jackets on the reservoir side.

By sunset, everything was in place, and Henry Dhieux, the foreman of the mechanics crew, summoned his five welders. Together they would tackle the most hazardous part of this job. "Let's grab our gear, get out on those gates, and tie off," ordered Dhieux (whose name was pronounced *Dewey*). "We're gonna start welding up some braces."

When Dhieux's team was in position with their rods and hoods, the maintenance crew began lowering sections of angle iron to the welders, who affixed a line of L-shaped supports to the tops of the gates. Onto those supports they attached a bottom rail and a top rail to create the skeletal frame of a four-foot-high breastwork that ran all the way across. Then it was time for the plywood. Each sheet was tied off and carefully lowered by hand, with care taken to avoid knocking off the welders, who laid the pieces lengthwise, butted them end to end, and bolted them onto the supports.

As one hour bled into the next, the pace never slackened. Although they had by now raised the spillway gates slightly to provide a bit of freeboard, the water was inching inexorably closer to the tops of the gates. Then, shortly after midnight, the wind came up and the surface of the lake grew agitated. Every few minutes, a wave would slap against the gates, forcing Dhieux and his men to raise their welding leads above their heads to keep from being electrocuted. In the midst of one of these splashes, Dhieux accidentally knocked his helmet off the gate and watched it go skittering down the dark channel and into the mouth of the spillway. As he turned back to his work, he spied a school of carp that had been drawn across the lake by the string of service lights. The carp were hovering in the water less than an arm's length away, little orange zeppelins with papery fins whose shivering undulations mirrored the strange and invisible currents of the reservoir. He stared at them for a moment, fascinated by their ghostly forms. Then he returned to the brace he was welding and sent a furious fantail of hot, blue sparks arcing into the darkness.

The teams worked straight through the night, and when the welders finally untied and climbed away from the gates at 4:45 a.m., just before dawn, the spotlights illuminated a wall of flashboards extending across the tops. When they lowered the gates to prevent the reservoir from flowing into the spillway tunnel, jets of lake water were spurting between every crack and seam.

As a watertight barrier, the flashboards were cartoonishly inept, a jerry-rigged patch that appeared to have been cobbled together by a band of amateur carpenters and shade-tree mechanics. But that didn't matter because, despite the leaks, the flashboards had effectively raised the upper edge of a nine-trillion-gallon swimming pool by four feet. In a single stroke, Gamble and his men had expanded the capacity of Lake Powell by conjuring roughly 645,000 acre-feet of additional storage space out of thin air.

Everyone was too exhausted to note that this marked an unusual moment in the annals of hydroelectric engineering. The Bureau of Reclamation, the world's premier dam-building agency and a colossus of cutting-edge technological know-how whose resources and budget exceeded the GNP of several small countries, had temporarily stemmed the flood crest of the greatest river in the Southwest with a makeshift fortress of *plywood*.

~

The fix had bought the dam's operators some desperately needed time, but a host of new problems were now popping up all over the dam, the first of which started the moment they opened up the river outlets, the four steel tubes running through the interior of the dam that bypassed water around the power plant. Within hours, the outlets' expansion joints were leaking, creating enough pressure to pop several manhole covers in the parking lot next to the machine shop and drive the concrete slab around them more than two inches into the air. A galvanized-metal shed where the maintenance crew stored their supplies also heaved upward and began to tilt. When the crew unbolted the manhole covers to see what might be causing this movement, a column of water came whooshing out in a powerful blast that refused to subside.

Gamble had no choice but to order the river-outlet works shut down so the couplings could be repaired, a job that would take two or three days. During that interval, the discharge they were sending through the dam would decrease by almost 30 percent. Now the reservoir would rise even faster.

Meanwhile, a number of people noted something even more disturbing than leaking couplings or heaving concrete: the dam itself appeared to be shaking. Many years later, people's memories of this would conflict. Glen's vibration monitors registered no unusual movement, but over the next several days, it was clear to everyone on site that *something* was being rattled. By now, they had been forced to resume sending a limited amount of water through the spillways, and the worsening cavitation—particularly in the east tunnel—was sending tremors through the sandstone. Those vibrations were especially noticeable in the lunchroom, which was tucked next to the machine shop and the #8 generator on the east side of the dam. During their breaks, the crews could hear an ominous rumbling and crackling, punctuated by an occasional hollow boom. One worker, who had served in Vietnam, would later liken this to the sound of distant artillery. Another would recall having to hold on to his sandwich to keep it from moving around on the lunch table. By the second week of June, the vibrations were causing the roll-up doors on the machine shop to shake so violently that they had to be braced with two-by-fours.

It was around this time that Gamble began growing concerned about his manpower. His crews were working double shifts, and although the majority of them seemed to be holding up well, a handful were getting jittery. The worst of this group was a welder in the mechanics crew who had taken to walking out onto the transformer deck, staring at the spillway portals, then wandering back inside the power plant and asking his coworkers if the dam might collapse.

Fearing that such anxiety could be infectious, Gamble ordered Swapp to start assigning the nervous welder to tasks that would keep him indoors. This kind of behavior, Gamble knew, was not merely unhelpful, but also displayed a fundamental misunderstanding of how well built Glen actually was.

On the other hand, however, such fears weren't entirely irrational. Especially when one considers what takes place when a dam fails.

~

There is something about a dam break that seems to awaken an almost atavistic terror in the human mind—perhaps, in part, because the litany of such disasters extends so far back in the history of civilization.

Although no one knows who built the first dam, the oldest structure for which evidence remains is Sadd el-Kafara, a seventy-eight-foot-wide structure filled with sixty thousand tons of gravel that the ancient Egyptians raised on the Nile about twenty miles south of Cairo around 2600 BC, about the time they were building the first pyramids. Sometime after its construction (the records are sparse on this point), the dam was overtopped and destroyed during one of the Nile's annual floods. Historians aren't able to say much about what kind of havoc this caused—how many crops were wiped out, how many lives might have been lost. But after Sadd el-Kafara's breaching, the Egyptians shied away from building large dams for a *very* long time. They didn't tackle another big engineering project on the Nile until they teamed up with the British to build the Aswan Low Dam, which was completed in 1902.

In the meantime, a host of other cultures experimented with dams in the hope of harnessing their benefits while mitigating their potentially catastrophic costs. Among the most successful were the Mesopotamians, who laid out a vast system of irrigation fed by numerous earthen dams on the Euphrates River during the reign of Hammurabi, who ascended to the throne of Babylon in 1792 BC. The maintenance of those dams was taken so seriously that Hammurabi's famous set of 282 laws—the world's first written code of public justice—flatly stated that if a flood occurred as a result of a dam break, "then shall he in whose dam the break occurred be sold for money, and the money shall replace the corn which he has caused to be ruined." As the author Bruce Barcott has pointed out, it was not the owner's assets that would be sold to pay for the damage, but the owner *himself*—a powerful testament to the consequences of dam failure.

Centuries later, a more graphic illustration of this principle unfolded nearly two thousand miles to the south when the Great Dam of Marib, an enormous bulwark on Yemen's Wadi Adhanah that was one of the engineering wonders of the ancient world, failed in either AD 570 or 575. The damage was so extensive—more than fifty thousand people were forced to abandon their homes and move away—that the dam collapse is actually mentioned in the Koran. Among other things, the failure of Marib underscores that, with the notable exception of warfare, nothing that premodern human beings created harbored more potential for destruction than a dam failure.

The surge of water from a collapsing dam is called a dam-break wave, and it can move with astonishing speed while generating unimaginable havoc. Even in modern times, it's hard to beat the raw and visceral impact of such a wave. Proof of that came in May of 1889, in a mountainous valley just east of Pittsburgh, Pennsylvania, where a group of wealthy steel-industry magnates had established a private hunting and fishing retreat around a dam and reservoir above a thriving community known as Johnstown. Following a series of ferocious rainstorms, the seventy-two-foot-high earthen dam—a structure only thirty-five feet higher than Sadd el-Kafara—abruptly gave way, sending some twenty million tons of water cascading through the Conemaugh Valley toward Johnstown. The main wave traveled at more than fifty miles per hour and scooped up everything in its path—trees, buildings, horses, cows, even a locomotive that was racing down the tracks as fast as it could go, its whistle tied down by the engineer in an effort to warn the town.

Minutes later, the roiling mountain of water plowed into the Cambria Iron

Works, where it picked up a load of railroad cars and barbed wire. When that mass of debris finally piled up against a massive stone bridge in the center of Johnstown, the wreckage caught fire. Many residents who had not drowned in the initial surge found themselves trapped inside an inferno and burned to death. The fire raged for three days, and the tangled wreckage eventually had to be blown to pieces with dynamite. Even for a generation inured to suffering by the carnage of the Civil War, Johnstown was appalling. The death toll, which included ninety-nine entire families, came close to the number of lives that would later be lost in the bombing of the World Trade Center. It was the largest loss of life in a civilian disaster in US history up to that point.

If Johnstown wasn't enough of a cautionary tale, other reminders have since occurred. In March of 1928, the St. Francis Dam, a 195-foot-high concrete structure about forty miles northwest of Los Angeles, gave way in the middle of the night, releasing a reservoir that held thirty-eight thousand acre-feet of water. The dam-break wave, which was at least 125 feet high, traveled fifty-four miles before discharging into the Pacific. The bodies of some victims were wedged into deep underground caverns, while others were carried into the ocean and washed ashore as far south as the Mexican border. The exact number of victims is still unknown—remains continued to be discovered throughout the 1950s—but is estimated at more than six hundred.

In the decades after that disaster, civil engineering made tremendous strides, but flawed design, shoddy construction, and inept oversight continued to take a toll, even as recently as 1976. On the morning of June 5 of that year, a stream of water began erupting on the face of a large earthen dam on the Teton River in southeastern Idaho. A pair of bulldozers failed to plug the leak, and in less than two hours the embankment had washed out, both dozers were engulfed, and their drivers had to be pulled to safety with ropes. Forty-two minutes later, a third of the dam wall disintegrated, and the entire reservoir gushed through the breach. By eight o'clock that night, the Teton reservoir was empty and eleven people were dead, along with thirteen thousand head of cattle.

Johnstown. St. Francis. Teton. Those events were stamped into the mind of every engineer, technician, and manager within the Bureau of Reclamation. And although the team confronting the crisis at Glen Canyon in the summer of 1983 were far too busy to worry about drawing historical analogies, every one of them would readily have conceded that those incidents raised a rather terrifying specter, given that the stakes on the Colorado River were so much greater.

Glen was almost ten times higher than the dam whose collapse caused the Johnstown flood, nearly four times higher than St. Francis, and well over twice the height of Teton. But far more sobering was the sheer amount of water in Lake Powell. The reservoir's myriad tentacles and arms, its countless alcoves and bays, extended along a shoreline that covered nearly two thousand miles, and the nine billion gallons of water within that sandstone labyrinth was ninety-four times bigger than the volume of Johnstown, St. Francis, and Teton *combined*. What would happen if a catastrophic flood surged out of the headwaters of the upper Colorado River basin, wiped out the Glen Canyon Dam, and sent all of that water racing through the Grand Canyon?

As it happens, the Bureau of Reclamation has studied that question, and the details make for a sobering read.

The initial dam-break wave, traveling about twenty miles an hour, would begin sweeping through Lee's Ferry sometime between thirty-six and forty-two minutes after the dam failed. Within six hours, the ferry itself would be under 520 feet of water, the height of the Standard Oil Building on the southern tip of Manhattan. Meanwhile, the peak stage of the dam-break wave would continue moving downstream, in the process taking out virtually every piece of infrastructure within the canyon.

Four miles below Lee's Ferry, the steel girders of Navajo Bridge, the only highway crossing between Lake Mead and Lee's Ferry, which sits 460 feet above the river, would be swatted aside like a spiderweb. Phantom Ranch, along with the pipes that supply all of the freshwater on the South Rim, would be inundated and destroyed. So too would every mooring spot, camp site, and Puebloan ruin along the river.

It would take almost a full twenty-four hours for the peak stage of the flood to reach Lava Falls, and ninety-eight miles beyond, the water would begin spreading across the surface of Lake Mead. Meanwhile, the effects of the surge within the canyon would be severe and lethal.

"Anyone still on the river," notes the report, "would have to climb the equivalent of a 40-story building, at a minimum, to have any hope of surviving."

~

Glen's chief designer was an engineer named Louis Puls, who had been born in the nineteenth century and whose wardrobe and habits—he dressed in jodhpurs and enjoyed smoking a corncob pipe—seemed lifted from that distant era. One of the finest dam designers the bureau had ever produced, Puls was legendary for being meticulous and for refusing to take chances. Even those who hated his dam or were convinced that its sandstone abutments offered a poor anchorage readily conceded that the structure itself was exceedingly well made.

When he began his assignment, one of Puls's most important decisions was what type of dam Glen would be. He had two choices. The first was a gravity structure—essentially an enormous pyramid that was wide at the bottom, narrow at the top, and would sit at a right angle across the river, directing the force of its reservoir downward into the dam's foundations. Squat and ponderous, a gravity dam's stability derives from brute mass: its sheer weight prevents the wall of water behind the dam from shoving it downstream. The alternative was an arch-type dam, a dam far more elegant and potentially even stronger (and which, as the name suggests, was invented by taking the kind of arch that the Romans had conceived and flipping it on its side). Instead of relying on its own bulk, an arch dam transfers the pressure of the water across its convex face and concentrates those forces in the abutments that anchor the structure to the walls of the canyon. Quite literally, the dam commandeers the rock walls to support its own aim. The harder the water pushes against the walls of the canyon, the harder the walls push back and the more resistant the dam is to failure.

Arch dams can be far thinner than gravity dams, but they require exceptionally dense and stable rock because the stresses on the abutments can be tremendous. Inside the canyon where Glen was going to be built, Puls knew that those forces would exceed the tolerance of the brittle Navajo sandstone. For this reason, as the writer Russell Martin has explained in *A Story That Stands Like a Dam*, his definitive chronicle of Glen's planning and construction, Puls ultimately opted for a hybrid design: a gravity dam that had a double-arched curvature.

When viewed from the side in cross-section, Glen was shaped like an enormous traffic cone, three hundred feet thick at its base and twenty-five feet at its crest. From above, however, the structure looked more like the rind on a slice of watermelon—an arc that bent more than a quarter mile from keyway to keyway. Puls's design ensured that the weight of the dam would relieve some of the stress on the sandstone walls while still retaining the strength of an arch. As a result, Glen was spectacularly strong.

Knowing this, almost none of the foremen and supervisors who were in charge during the spillway crisis feared that the dam itself was in any danger of suffering the kind of catastrophic breach witnessed at Johnstown, St. Francis, or Teton. However, a number of the Denver engineers did harbor concerns about what might unfold if things started to spin out of control. What vexed them most deeply was the integrity of the spillway tunnels and whether the cavitation damage might, in a worst-case scenario, impair the dam's ability to hold back the lake. This concern had its roots in one of two nightmare scenarios that were possible.

The first—overtopping of the dam—was rather straightforward. If the damage worsened to the point where the tunnels collapsed or were blocked by debris, the penstocks and the river outlets would be unable to cope with the runoff and the lake would rise uncontrollably toward the crest of the dam.

Eleven feet above the tops of the spillway gates, the surface of the lake would sluice over the parapets and begin sliding down the concave face of the dam. As the lake rose higher, the thickness of that waterfall would increase, and so too would the force with which a portion of it would be deflected squarely against the rear of the power plant. As hours turned into days, the plant's concrete superstructure would start to give way. When the walls and the concrete support pillars were gone, the eight generators would be exposed to the full fury of the cascade and eventually be shorn from their mountings, along with the turbines and the ninety-ton transformers, all of which would topple into the current and form a tangled wreckage at the bottom of the river.

The damage would be enormous and the repairs would be horrendously expensive. But the overtopping of the dam was largely a self-limiting disaster. Sooner or later, the runoff would peak, the lake would subside, and the destruction would cease. This scenario thus paled in comparison with the *real* nightmare, one whose mechanism hinged on the most vulnerable part of the dam—the elbow joint, where Phil Burgi had surmised that the worst of the cavitation damage was unfolding.

～

When Louis Puls and his team had opted to save some money by marrying the spillway system to the diversion tunnels, they traded a fiscal problem for a structural one. While they wanted to leave the lower portion of the diversion tunnels open to accept water from the spillways, they had to find a way of blocking off the upstream sections. Failing to do so would have created two drain holes at the bottom of the reservoir, which is why they sealed each of the upstream sections of the diversion tunnels with a massive plug of concrete. Each plug was 150 feet long and notched into the tunnel wall in such a way that no amount of water pressure could dislodge the concrete from the surrounding rock. However, as the Denver engineers now recognized, the position of those plugs was vaguely unsettling. Just in front was the elbow joint that was sustaining the bulk of the cavitation damage. And directly behind the plugs lay the bottom of Lake Powell.

This raised a disturbing possibility. The sandstone abutments were riddled with fissures, and if the cavitation damage eroded the sandstone *around* the concrete plugs enough to establish a connection with the water at the bottom of the reservoir, the pressure on that leak would be enormous, causing the leak to expand like cancer and, ultimately, the abutment to fail.

During the initial phase of the spillway crisis, the Denver engineers had weighed this possibility before dismissing it as absurd. The length of those concrete plugs and the manner in which they had been notched into the rock made it highly unlikely they could ever be dislodged. Moreover, the forces inside the spillway tunnels were almost certainly being directed *downstream* and away from the concrete, rendering the scenario even less likely. But a document in the bureau's own archives suggests that this remained a concern in the minds of the Denver engineers.

"The inherent stability of the dam and its ability to bridge openings in the foundation gave us confidence that no sudden loss of reservoir was possible," stated the report, "but any direct connection would lead to erosion of the sandstone, and the potential for uncontrolled release into Lake Mead was a real concern." Later, the report echoed this same anxiety that "a lateral progression of any damage pattern near the elbow" might, in a worst-case scenario, create "a direct opening to the reservoir."

The author of that report, Bruce Moyes, was raising a possibility that engineers and students of risk theory refer to as a low-probability, high-impact event—an incident that is extremely unlikely to occur, but whose potential fallout is catastrophic. If a connection, no matter how small, somehow developed inside the friable sandstone surrounding the concrete plugs, it could trigger a chain of events that would be impossible to control.

Driven by the hydrostatic pressure at the bottom of the reservoir—roughly 240 pounds per square inch—what started as a thin stream of water through the sandstone would rapidly widen, and as the breach expanded, the contents of the reservoir would begin rushing through that hole at the bottom. In the most extreme (and, it must be added, unlikely) scenario, the drain hole would be impossible to plug, and Lake Powell would basically perform an end run around the dam.

However it might happen, the prospect of some nine trillion gallons crashing through the Grand Canyon and racing toward Lake Mead was dreadful. Hoover itself would be fine. But after pouring over its face, the water would make a headlong rush for the Gulf of California, in the process taking out virtually every other dam, canal, and diversion structure along the lower stretch of the river. A portion of that surge would almost certainly drive toward the Salton Sea, wiping out most of the crops and infrastructure of the Imperial Valley, as well as the delivery system that supplied over half the water for the tens of millions of residents in greater Los Angeles, San Diego, Phoenix, Tucson, Las Vegas, and dozens of smaller communities across the Southwest.

Everyone was confident that this was unlikely. But as the runoff of 1983 continued to build and the surface of Lake Powell inched closer toward the tops of the plywood flashboards with each passing day, no one was willing to say with absolute certainty what the Colorado would or would not do.

~

All but one of the fourteen major reservoirs on the upper Colorado were now filled to overflowing, and the entire upper basin was a necklace of shimmering blue reservoirs linked by a swollen river. At Glen, the dam and its spillways were sending a combined discharge of 50,000 cfs into the Grand Canyon. Yet the surface of Lake Powell was still rising roughly five inches every twenty-four hours. At 6:00 a.m. on Monday, June 13, the surface of the water was well over halfway to the top of the plywood flashboards.

With even more snowmelt on its way, the Denver engineers faced an unpleasant dilemma. They had only two options for preventing the reservoir from overtopping the flashboards and tearing them away. Either the crippled east spillway would have to be returned to service or the minimal flows that were passing through the west spillway would have to be boosted dramatically. The question was how fast the cavitation damage inside both tunnels would accelerate as the amount of water increased—and the answer, which was contained in a series of calculations run by Henry Falvey, was unsettling.

If the concrete lining inside the west spillway was still intact, the tunnel would probably be able to continue passing water at its current level for another twenty-five days before the flow was impaired. But if the discharge was increased to 7,000 cfs, Falvey's calculations warned that catastrophic damage would begin in eight days. And at 12,000 cfs, the lining in the right tunnel—like its counterpart on the left—would start coming apart in less than thirty hours.

For Burgi, who had by now returned to Denver, those figures were doubly disturbing because the chances of an uncontrolled release were even greater inside the west tunnel. (Thanks to the configuration of the canyon walls, the elbow joint in the west tunnel was significantly closer to the wall of the dam than its eastern counterpart.) Based on this fact, Burgi and his team sat down and devised a somewhat counterintuitive strategy that would entail sending even *more* water through the crippled east tunnel. In effect, they were going to sacrifice one spillway in order to keep the other in reserve.

On Wednesday, June 15, while Burgi once again headed for the airport, Moyes telephoned Gamble and told him to prepare to take the discharge to 60,000 cfs. This marked a significant milestone: it was more water than the canyon had seen at any point since the dam's construction.

Burgi arrived at the dam at four o'clock and spent the next eight hours watching as the surge through the east tunnel sent chunks of debris flying over the flip bucket. The water inside the plume, however, remained a clear green.

The following morning, before leaving for Denver, Burgi warned Gamble that the booming noises would probably return and the water would once again turn orange. By Friday afternoon, however, Gamble was pleased to report that there was no sign of trouble. Both spillways had been running smoothly since Wednesday evening.

"A calm weekend is expected," Moyes informed the other members of the Denver engineering team at 4:30 p.m. before heading home. "See you Monday."

Once again, the river was about to prove them all wrong.

~

At fifteen minutes to midnight on Saturday, the phone rang at Bruce Moyes's home in Denver. Dick White, the manager of Glen's Control Room, was calling to let Moyes know that the discharge inside the east spillway seemed to be faltering. The plume of water, which the engineers now referred to as the sweep, was no longer blasting from the tunnel portal, shooting smoothly over the flip bucket, and forming the rooster tail over the river. Instead, White explained, violent surges were exploding from the tunnel's portal every ten seconds or so, and each surge was accompanied by a sharp blast of air that resounded along the walls of the canyon.

Moyes knew what had happened. Somewhere below the elbow of the spillway, a pile of shattered concrete and sandstone had built up and partially blocked the tunnel. As the jet of water sluiced through the upper section of the spillway and collided against this debris, the current rapidly decelerated, forming a standing wave whose crest reached almost all the way to the crown of the tunnel. This was the source of the short surges and the ominous "belching" sounds.

Although no one from Reclamation would have thought to draw such a comparison, the violence that was now being unleashed inside the spillway had an odd correspondence with the turbulence that a Grand Canyon boatman encountered when he collided against a standing wave on the downstream side of a keeper hole. In effect, a hydraulic jump had formed deep inside the tunnel—and the upshot was rather surreal. Somewhere between the elbow of the spillway and its mouth, a Class V hellbender was raging.

The next day was Father's Day, and the lake was coming up at an alarming rate. Moyes and Burgi left for the airport at 4:00 a.m. to catch a charter that would get them to the dam shortly after sunrise. During the three-hour flight, the surface of the reservoir rose another half inch.

By the time the two men arrived at the dam, the sweep in the east spillway was completely lost. After putting their heads together with Gamble, they decided that their only hope was to open the gates even farther, injecting a blast of water that might expel the debris from the spillway. In essence, they would try to restore the sweep by "pushing" the hydraulic jump out of the tunnel. The problem, however, was that the additional water falling upon the elbow would further the damage and generate even more debris. In other words, the very forces needed to neutralize this hydraulic jump would accelerate the formation of the next. Eventually, they knew, the damage would become so great that no amount of water would be able to restore the sweep and the tunnel would be lost.

With no other option, the gates were duly hoisted and the discharge was increased, first to 17,000 cfs and then, when that didn't work, to 20,000—at which point the belching subsided and the sweep returned. For the moment, the fix had worked.

~

By now, an odd ritual had arisen among the workers at the dam. Whenever anyone had a few minutes of free time as he was coming onto his shift or taking a break for lunch, he would walk out past the machine shop to the area where the jets from the two spillways roared over the flip buckets and arced into the Colorado from opposite sides of the canyon at 120 miles per hour. The spectacle was loud and thrilling—and thanks to the accelerating deterioration inside the tunnels, it was also like watching a disaster.

Once every hour or so, one or both spillway plumes would falter and belch, emitting a series of hollow booms. The concatenations resounded over the roar of the water, and their vibrations were severe enough to register on the US Geological Survey's seismic monitors in Pasadena, more than five hundred miles to the west. Then another load of debris—a scattering of shattered concrete or sandstone—would come coughing through the portal, blast over the flip bucket, and shoot sixty to eighty feet into the air before dropping into the river.

Watching the explosions of debris was dramatic enough, but even more chilling were the color shifts that accompanied these spasms. "The thing that affected me the most," a member of the maintenance crew, Richard Parsons, would recall many years later, "was watching the change in the spillways when it would go from clear to red, and wonder, 'What in the heck is going on here?'"

As the days wore on, as the violence increased, as one shift blended into the next, it seemed to Parsons and his coworkers as if the crisis were suspended in a surreal stasis, with no end in sight. "How much longer can the spillways take this?" they asked themselves. "Will this ever stop?"

Meanwhile, the reservoir kept rising. By Tuesday night, June 21, the surface of the lake was less than four inches from the tops of the flashboards. If the latest inflow figures from Gerry Williams's team at the River Forecast Center in

Salt Lake City were correct, the plywood would be under five inches of water by the end of the week unless the gates were raised and even more water was sent through both spillways.

With their options rapidly dwindling, the Denver engineers had no choice but to take the next step. The following morning, Moyes faxed a stark warning to his bosses in Salt Lake City:

"We strongly recommend that the discharges from Glen Canyon Dam be immediately raised to 70,000 cfs to protect the safety of the structure."

~

In the midst of this drama, the question of what impact the endlessly rising discharges could be having just downstream wasn't a priority for those who were grappling with the spillway crisis. There is no evidence to suggest that the water bosses in Salt Lake City, the engineers in Denver, or any member of Gamble's team at the dam knew anything at all about what was unfolding inside the Grand Canyon. They had no information about how many expeditions were on the river or what kind of danger those people might be confronting. Nor did they have the faintest idea that as the crisis worsened, Kenton Grua was mulling over plans, weighing the odds, and waiting for his opportunity.

PART VI
The Maelstrom

The black stream, catching on a sunken rock,
Flung backward on itself in one white wave,
And the white water rode the black forever.

—ROBERT FROST

A thirty-seven-foot motor rig is torn to pieces inside Crystal Rapid.

17

The Grand Confluence

Life is either a daring adventure or nothing at all.

—HELEN KELLER

WHEN a giant lowland river system experiences spring flooding, the water typically spills over the banks and spreads across the landscape like an invading army, inundating thousands of square miles and often carving entirely new channels for itself. In the spring of 1542, when an expedition led by the Spanish conquistador Hernando de Soto stumbled upon the Mississippi in flood stage, they discovered that the river had washed over the land for more than twenty leagues, almost sixty miles. Nearly four hundred years later, when the Mississippi overran its levees during the most destructive flood in American history in the spring of 1927, the river's width expanded to almost a hundred miles, forming an inland sea that stretched from Yazoo City, Mississippi, to Monroe, Louisiana.

This sort of dispersal is not an option for the Colorado inside the Grand Canyon. Yoked and trussed within its impossibly high rock walls, the runoff is forced to throttle through a narrow space. And as the volume and the speed of the water increase, so too does its ferocity.

When the river rises, rapids that are especially vicious at low water begin to wash out, and many choke points within the canyon's corridor are transformed into fast-water chutes that feature either smooth waves or none at all. As small- and medium-size rapids are eliminated, the Colorado achieves a kind of hydraulic sweet spot around 45,000 cfs—a level that P. T. Reilly, Martin Litton's old mentor, once described as "pure pleasure." But the moment the river rises beyond this point, the dynamics shift dramatically.

By June 19, Father's Day, the river corridor between Lee's Ferry and Lake Mead was all but overrun with boaters. There were eighteen big, motorized expeditions, most of which would complete their runs through the canyon in as few as five days. There were also seventeen oar-powered rafting trips, which were moving quite a bit slower. Slowest of all were three pods of dories run by Litton's company, plus another sixteen groups of private boaters who were piloting a colorful assortment of catamarans, paddleboats, kayaks, and small oar rafts. Finally, a special charter expedition was hauling a consignment of foreign ambassadors and diplomats from China, Peru, and other countries. As word of this venture spread downriver, it was swiftly dubbed the Dip Trip.

In all, roughly 213 boats were ferrying nearly thirteen hundred guides and passengers toward Lake Mead. Never before had the canyon been crowded with so many people on so many craft during such a high flow. And thanks to the additional water that Tom Gamble's team was now sending through the dam, every boatman on the river was being treated to a crash tutorial in the havoc that a flood tide can wreak deep in the canyon.

～

When the discharges shot past 60,000 cfs, the average velocity of the water accelerated from three miles per hour to six, and the current began to weave erratically back and forth from one side of the river to the other, banging against eddies and ricocheting off the sides of the cliffs. At first, the guides were thrilled by these changes, and the passengers, feeding off the excitement, were titillated to partake in an adventure that even their veteran hosts found novel and bracing. But as the current grew more confused, the danger seemed to build geometrically, ushering in a seriousness that everyone found urgent and disturbing.

Around June 22, the river entered a new and alien phase. In some areas, the stationary haystacks—the huge standing waves that normally define the topography of a rapid—suddenly began milling back and forth at random. To meet those monsters squarely on the bow of their boats—an absolute necessity for a dory or a small oar raft—the boatman had to react explosively, pivoting instantly before confronting the shifting waves. In other areas, rapids arose within some of the larger eddies, which meant that white water was actually moving *upstream*. Another oddity, for which no one had a name, was a foot-deep trough that would appear from out of nowhere and run swiftly across the river, perpendicular to the main current. But the strangest features, by far, were the whirlpools—gaping wells that would open up in the surface of the river, twenty-five feet in diameter, like miniature spiral galaxies.

The whirlpools tended to materialize along the upstream ends of the eddies, but once they had formed they spun off at random across the face of the river. A boat caught in the grip of such a vortex could be pulled five or six feet lower than the surface of the rest of the river. First the gunwales would disappear, then the torsos and shoulders of the boatman and the passengers. Eventually, all one could see were the tops of people's heads or their hats, spinning around like the second hand on a clockface. In those moments, no one on board said a word. Each person sat in rigid silence, eyes wide and white, like cattle on the brink of a stampede. Then, without warning, the whirlpool would mysteriously vanish and release the boat to the main current. The experience was eerie, and it left people deeply spooked.

Under such bizarre conditions, the key to safety lay in keeping together so that each expedition's boats could instantly render aid if one of their sisters got into trouble. Maintaining a tight formation was a simple enough goal. But the current was running so fast and the hydraulics were so powerful that the smaller oar boats found this almost impossible. Simply breaking through an eddy fence* and pulling to shore took Herculean effort, flawless timing, and a solid ration of luck. If six boats punched through the fence and the seventh was rebuffed, everyone had to pull back out, regroup, and make another attempt farther downriver.

The process was maddening, and with each boost in the discharge from the dam, the difficulties increased and the odds seemed to be stacked more heavily against the oarsmen. Every moment demanded absolute focus and ceaseless adjustments with their oars, and most of those adjustments required sharp, white-knuckle bursts of energy. This, they discovered, was perhaps the most brutal aspect of the flood tide—the manner in which it wiped them out physically. There were no respites, no intervals of tranquillity, none of the floating languor that typically forms some of the sweetest moments on the river. If they set their oars down for any reason—to snatch a gulp of water, to glance at their maps—and wound up missing a stroke, it might take fifteen or twenty desperate pulls to recover.

So it went, minute by minute, hour by hour, day after day. But even amid their exhaustion, they couldn't help but marvel at the changes unfolding along

---

*The seam of water that separates a river's downstream current from the upstream flow of an eddy is known as an eddy fence. When the line of crosscurrent is especially powerful, the fence may be several feet high, a dynamic barrier that can easily flip a kayak or a dory.

the bottom of the canyon. By now, most of their favorite beaches and their preferred pull-ins were underwater, and the banks of the river were lined with the tops of submerged tamarisk trees whose branches waved in unison with the current. One by one, familiar landmarks began to disappear. Ten-Mile Rock, a giant, midstream chunk of anvil-shaped sandstone that typically looms high above the surface of the river, slowly submerged. At Redwall Cavern, normally a huge expanse of sand that hosted games of volleyball and bocce, the boatmen drifted into the flooded chamber to permit the passengers to raise their arms and brush the tips of their fingers along the limestone ceiling of the cavern. As they approached House Rock, a big rapid at Mile 17, they listened for the roar, heard nothing, then shot through with their oar blades out of the water, looking left and right for the massive boat-eating hole. Nothing. Gone.

To the veterans, these things were extraordinary and wondrous, but the larger picture was deeply disturbing. As the speed and force of the current continued to build, with no end in sight, rumors began to fly up and down the river about what was happening upstream at the dam. Some guides informed their passengers that a catastrophic break was possible at any moment, and that if they heard anyone yell "High ground!" they were expected to start climbing the walls of the canyon as fast as possible to get clear of the tsunami that would be created by the release of Lake Powell. Others speculated that the reservoir might already be sluicing over the top of the dam.

Years later, engineers such as Tom Gamble and Bruce Moyes—men who understood the workings of the dam far better than any river guide—would scoff at the absurdity of those fears. But the rumors offered a glimpse into the confusion and anxiety of a group of boatmen who were cut off from reliable information, held the lives of others in the palms of their hands, and were confronting the most ferocious white water that most of them had ever seen.

~

No responsible commercial outfitter could afford to ignore such conditions, and as the first of these expeditions slowly trickled off the river with reports of what was taking place inside the canyon, companies responded in a variety of ways. Several outfitters began contacting their upcoming clients and offering them the option of canceling. Others gave people the chance to back out right there on the boat ramp at Lee's Ferry. The groups that were already on the river by mid-June, however, had no choice but to deal with the challenges as best they could, even as those events were beginning to undermine a quarter century of river-running wisdom.

For years, one of the guiding community's most widely held beliefs was that the most stable craft on the river were the big motor rigs—behemoths whose size and displacement enabled them to skate safely through the center of all but the worst stretches of white water. Toward the middle of June, to everyone's astonishment, those rigs started flipping over.

The first accident took place at President Harding, a minor rapid at Mile 44 that had never caused anyone much trouble. The flip triggered a full-scale rescue in which all of the passengers were thrown into the river and had to be evacuated by helicopter, alerting the Park Service that some sort of invisible threshold had been crossed. By the second flip, which took place on Saturday, June 18, the river rangers knew they had to find a way to broadcast the news each time the river rose.

In the absence of a reliable radio network or satellite phones—which would not arrive for another two decades—there was only one way to do this.* And so, late on the afternoon of Wednesday, June 22, a Park Service chopper lifted off from the heliport on the South Rim, made a beeline for Lee's Ferry, then headed down the canyon corridor on an unusual mission. On board were two rangers, one of whom crouched in the cargo bay filling small plastic baggies with sand from a cardboard box at his feet and tying off each bag with a long red streamer. The second ranger sat in the cockpit next to the pilot, peering through the curved glass and scanning the water and the shoreline for boats. The pilot was moving fast—they had more than 250 miles of river to cover before dusk. But whenever the ranger in the cockpit spotted a cluster of boats, the pilot banked toward the nearest sand beach. The ranger in the cargo bay then passed a plastic baggie to his colleague in front, who opened the window and dropped it out.

The presence of a Park Service chopper skimming through the canyon corridor was always noteworthy, but when the mysterious bags with their red streamers were released, a new ritual was added to the river pageant. In addition to its deposit of sand, each plastic bag contained a note that had been run through a mimeograph machine earlier that afternoon. Upon pulling to shore and retrieving the Ziploc, the guides huddled tightly while the trip leader opened the bag for the message:

DAM RELEASE UPDATE

BuRec releasing up to 70,000 cfs tonight.

CAMP HIGH—BE CAUTIOUS
National Park Service

---

*While most outfitters equipped their expeditions with VHF radios, the Park Service had not imposed a standard radio frequency; many river guides did not even know what channel to use to communicate with the helicopters.

This elicited low whistles and murmurs—not only from the guides on the river but from everyone who heard the news as word swiftly spread out of the canyon and through the boatyards of Flagstaff and Page, Hurricane and Marble Canyon.

In no one's mind, however, did this information register more keenly than in that of the diminutive doryman who was the captain of the *Emerald Mile.*

~

All spring, Kenton Grua had watched with growing fascination and excitement as the runoff raced out of the mountains and the reservoir rose behind the dam. With each successive boost of the discharge through the spillway tunnels, his thoughts were once again drawn to the unsolved problem that had been percolating in the back of his mind for three years. Was this the moment he had been waiting for? Was it finally time to think about another speed run?

In May, when an early-season commercial dory trip had given Grua his first glimpse of the burgeoning power of the Colorado, he was shocked by the water's fury—its violence, its complexity, and most of all its ruthlessness. As the face of the river changed and then changed again, his skills seemed increasingly inadequate to the task of simply keeping the *Emerald Mile* upright and intact. By June, with the force of the hydraulics seeming to expand with each passing day, the prospect of a nonstop sprint down the entire length of the canyon inched closer toward madness.

And yet, Grua could also see that something epic was unfolding. For years, every boatman in the Grand Canyon had heard the stories of what the unchained Colorado was capable of unleashing. Now, thanks to a freakish runoff and some rather appalling miscalculations by the bureaucrats, he and his colleagues were at last being given a chance to be part of it, and that prospect was absolutely intoxicating. Because no one who loved the river could fail to grasp the central truth that *this* water, *this* runoff, was the greatest display of the old Colorado in more than a generation, an event that would surely not come around again during their lifetimes, if ever. Anyone who was cursed and lucky enough to be on the river during the final week of June would not be witnessing history firsthand, he would actually be *running it.*

For Grua, however, the prospect of simply being on the river was not enough. The challenge, as he perceived it, was not merely to bear witness to the majesty of this reawakened Colorado, but to touch and participate in that majesty in the most direct and visceral way imaginable. And what could be more direct or visceral than using an ungovernable flood tide as a hydraulic slingshot for an unbreakable speed record?

The Factor was by no means alone in this assessment. Not only did Rudi Petschek feel precisely the same way, but the sentiment was emphatically echoed by nearly every doryman in Litton's operation. As the boatmen on those early-season trips had come staggering into the boathouse in Hurricane with ever more graphic tales of the river's rising intensity, the whispers about the possibility of another speed run had grown feverish. Everyone wanted to know if the *Emerald Mile* would be allowed to take another crack at the record. And if so, when did Grua and Petschek plan to launch? And now that Wally Rist was no longer around, how would they fill out their crew?

The debate raged for more than a fortnight until, finally, someone stepped forward with a proposition that cemented Grua's resolve.

~

Aside from Grua and Petschek, no one found the possibility of a high-water speed run more alluring than Steve Reynolds, the boatman known as Wren, who had wrecked and repaired the *Emerald Mile* seven years earlier up on the Snake River, then found himself forced to step back and watch in frustration as she was sent back to the Colorado. By now Wren himself had followed the path charted by the little dory, transferring down from Idaho and establishing a place for himself in Litton's Grand Canyon operation. There, amid the hell-benders and the hydraulics in the deepest part of the canyon, he had come into his own as a devotee of giant white water.

To say that Wren was an unusual character was the kind of statement that touched upon but failed to fully illuminate his complexities. His face, which was ovular, was dominated by a hook-boned nose, at the top of which floated a pair of deeply skeptical brown eyeballs. Thanks to that aquiline nose and his sharp Vandyke beard, he bore the look of one of those Spanish foot soldiers who had followed Coronado from the deserts of the Southwest to the plains of central Kansas in the early 1540s—a comparison that was doubly apt because, like that wandering company of conquistadores, Wren had, over the years, gotten himself profoundly lost.

Somewhere between Idaho and the Grand Canyon, he had embarked on a rather tempestuous affair with Jack Daniel's, an association that merged with his affection for wild times, both on the river and off. In addition to generating some rather serious friction between himself and Litton, those habits had concealed a range of subtler and far more appealing aspects of Wren's personality, chief among them the fact that he was a man who believed deeply in the practice of kindness—especially when it came to clients who found themselves intimidated by white water or immune to the harsh and brutal magic of the canyon. Whenever he spotted a passenger who was struggling or disoriented or crosswise with the world, Wren would take that person under his wing, speaking softly and gently, lavishing care and attention that seemed strangely at odds with his reputation as a reveler. And it was this compassion—his many quiet acts of empathy and tenderness—that had not only won him forgiveness and affection among his colleagues but also enabled them to celebrate his other great defining attribute: what he was capable of doing with a pair of oars.

Wren was the kind of boatman that the river folk sometimes refer to as a looker—an oarsman who pays special attention to reading water, and who takes an almost preternatural joy in being able to row a complex stretch of current without hitting a single thing. Plenty of other oarsmen were bigger and stronger and more aggressive than Wren, but few could match the ferocity of his focus. At the top of a rapid, he seemed to flip some kind of internal switch that brought a beam of intense concentration to bear on the task ahead. It was not unusual for him to rack up ten or fifteen golden trips in a row, acing every rapid, never so much as flirting with a rock, skating through the white water with a seamless perfection that made those who rowed with him shake their heads in admiration and envy.

He derived great pride from that ability, perhaps because it affirmed a level of command that had no cognate in any other part of his life. Among other consequences, his skills rendered him utterly reliable, a man on whom one could always depend. He was truly a great boatman—and a measure of that greatness achieved one of its purest expressions when, sometime in early June, he pulled Grua aside and said that if Grua and Petschek were considering another bid at a speed run, he wanted to throw his hat into the ring.

"If anything happens," he declared, "I'd love to be a part of it."

Wren's intensity and his rowing prowess would be obvious assets, but there may have been another element that carried even greater weight, and this was Grua's awareness—conscious or otherwise—that Wren's participation would complete a kind of circle in the story of the *Emerald Mile*.

These three boatmen spanned the whole of that little boat, all the way from the tip of her bowpost to the brass cleat on her stern—and their own stories were intimately entwined with her own. Could there be anything more fitting, more right, than the notion that they would set out to write her final chapter?

All right, Grua told Wren, they would do this thing together. But before that could happen, he added, they would first need to figure out a way to convince the Park Service to give them a permit.

A few days later, Grua found himself making the long drive from Hurricane to the South Rim, walking into the office of a ranger named Curt Sauer, who was the river boss of the Grand Canyon, and explaining that he wanted to apply for yet another permit—his second one in three years—to test evacuation procedures by taking a dory down the river in the shortest time possible.

Sauer, a reasonable man, replied that he would consider the request and that Grua should give him a call when he got off the river from his next commercial trip. With that assurance, Grua left for Lee's Ferry with high hopes of receiving a green light for a June 25 departure that, like the first speed run, would be timed to coincide with the full moon.

While he was gone, however, Sauer found himself questioning the wisdom of approving the application. Not only was Grua's proposal beginning to look patently unsafe amid the cascade of emergencies created by the ever-rising discharges, but Sauer had also received three separate complaints from other outfitters who had heard rumors that someone was planning to try to break the speed record under the guise of a "training trip"—a prospect that struck the outfitters as inappropriate and highly dangerous.

On June 17, Sauer telephoned Tuck Weills, Litton's operations manager in Hurricane, and informed him that Grua's request was denied. Five days later, after getting off the river and receiving the unwelcome news, Grua called Sauer to express his dismay.

When this had no effect, Grua declared that he would be forced to seek approval through other channels. Sauer told Grua that he was welcome to try, but the answer was still no.

With that, Grua hung up and dialed the number of the only person he knew who was even more stubborn and recalcitrant than himself.

∼

When Martin Litton answered the telephone at his home in California, he and Grua were entering the eleventh year of a relationship that was, in ways both large and small, as turbulent and mercurial as the Colorado itself.

For Grua, Litton presented both a role model and a father figure. "He's my hero," Grua once told a friend. "He basically raised me from a kid to where I am now, and I've got a lot of stuff to thank him for—he's just like a dad to me." In Grua's eyes, Litton's passion for the canyon, the river, and the dories were qualities to be admired and emulated. And in a more perfect story, those sentiments might well have laid a foundation for the type of bond that arises between fathers and sons. But in truth, Litton didn't actively reciprocate Grua's affections and often found his relentless young boatman rather annoying. Especially when it came to Grua's habit of calling up Litton and keeping him on the phone for forty-five minutes while he rattled on about his latest pet project—endless monologues in which Grua explained how something had been broken and then been fixed but hadn't been fixed in exactly the right way and so he, Kenton, was now taking it upon himself to start the project over and make things even better than they were before. Eventually, Litton realized that Grua was using these calls as a pretext to talk, to share ideas, to solicit approval, and, worst of all, to *emote*—which Litton found rather abhorrent.

One of Grua's most remarkable attributes was his titanic obliviousness to how enervating these exchanges were for Litton, who had adopted a policy of immediately saying yes to whatever Grua was proposing, not only because it was so much easier than saying no but because it was also the most efficient way of getting Grua off his back. In this instance, however, the scheme that Grua had in mind was so bizarre that Litton found himself asking *why*—always a tactical mistake, because it opened the door for another of Grua's relentless and impassioned arguments.

Kenton, you already *have* the record, Litton pointed out. Why in the world would you want to go and do the whole thing all over again?

With that, Grua launched into a soliloquy about what a unique juncture in time this was, a grand confluence in which the capricious dynamics of the river and the incompetence of the engineers who had tried to harness it had merged to create an opportunity that would never again be seen. This was one of those moments that a man either recognized and seized or sat back, allowed to pass him by, and then spent the rest of his life wondering why he had failed to act—because the river would never again rise to this level. A level that no more than a dozen oarsmen in the history of Grand Canyon boating had witnessed and rowed. A level that not even John Wesley Powell had ever seen. Against all odds, the river had somehow gotten the upper hand—and now, with the help of the *Emerald Mile*, Grua had the chance not only to test himself against the ancestral power of that river but also to offer up a symbolic gesture of defiance against the dam that Litton hated so deeply and had fought so fiercely against. Surely his boss could see the value of that?

Litton sighed and agreed that he did.

Well, continued Grua, the river had soared to 70,000 cfs the night before and the full moon would arrive the following night, so what he needed, *right now*, was for Litton to summon his eloquence, phone up Richard Marks, the superintendent of Grand Canyon National Park, and somehow find a way of turning a *no* into a *maybe*.

According to the legend that is told on the river, Litton shook his head and grudgingly conceded to the weight of the logic that was being laid before him. That may have been the case. But it is equally plausible, especially in light of the history between those two men, that what Litton wanted most in that moment was simply to get Grua off the damn phone.

In any event, the conversation ended when Litton said that he'd give the superintendent a ring and do his best to persuade him to sanction a speed run.

When Grua hung up, he knew he had done all he could and the matter now rested in Litton's hands. What he did not know—nor, for that matter, did anyone else—was that deep inside the canyon, far downstream from the dam and along the worst stretch of white water on the entire river, a monster had awakened and was preparing to emerge from its lair.

18

The White Demon

*Out there in the middle of the maelstrom the Eater awaits, heaving
and gulping, its mouth like a giant clam's . . . its mind a frenzy of
beige-colored rapid foam. A horrifying uproar, all things considered.
Imagine floating through that nonsense in a life jacket.*

—EDWARD ABBEY

ASIDE from the Grand Canyon helicopter squadron, perhaps the
most effective tool in the Park Service's disaster-prevention kit was
the River Unit, an unusual little pod within the ranger subculture
whose job was to patrol the bottom of the canyon in oar rafts to monitor the
camps, render assistance to anyone in trouble, and, when necessary, summon
evacuations. Unlike their starched-shirt, button-down counterparts who were
stationed on the rim, the river rangers were a backcountry squadron. Their
patrols could last up to a month, and those extended absences were reflected
in the way they carried themselves. Many wore their hair long and declined to
shave. All of them preferred baseball caps to Smokey the Bear hats. Most had a
deep antipathy to paperwork.

One of the most experienced boatmen in this unit was Terry Brian, and on
the morning of Thursday, June 23, Brian pulled into an eddy just above Mile 98
with a small platoon of rangers piloting two rafts and a pair of kayaks. Their aim
was to find out what was happening at Crystal Rapid.

After tying up their boats and ascending the one-hundred-foot cutbank that had been created by the flood of 1966, the rangers began climbing to the scouting terrace, which would give them a comprehensive view. They fully expected the latest discharges from the dam to have muted Crystal's savagery and essentially washed out the rapid. But when they reached the top, they discovered that something entirely different had taken place. Although none of the rangers was aware of it, they were witnessing a signature moment in white-water history—a unique hydraulic window that had opened less than two hours earlier.

During the seventeen years that had passed since the massive winter debris flow of 1966 had pinched off the river at the mouth of the Crystal Creek drainage, the Glen Canyon Dam had prevented a single spring flood from rushing through the canyon and expanding the rapid's constriction ratio. Nearly two decades after its formation, Crystal was still an "immature" rapid, and the giant boulders that were responsible for its massive hydraulics remained firmly in place. But as the dam's discharges increased throughout the middle part of June, the physics inside the choke point created by those obstacles had grown progressively more vicious. When the flows were boosted to 49,500 cfs on June 7, the speed of the water in the center of the rapid had increased to almost twenty miles an hour, and Crystal's standing wave rose from thirteen feet to twenty. Ten days later, when the engineers took the discharge up to 59,000 cfs, the standing wave had risen by another three feet. Finally, at roughly 8:45 a.m. on the morning of June 23, just a few minutes before Brian and his squadron arrived, the surge of 70,000 cfs that had been released from the spillway tunnels the previous night reached Mile 98, ushering in a new and unprecedented level of madness.

At the top of the terrace, the rangers were treated to a sweeping view of the river as it hurtled around the pink-and-orange boulders of the rapid's fan-shaped debris field in a long and seething arc of white water. The basic configuration remained the same as ever—the river funneling through the bottleneck between the debris field on the right side of the river and the cliffs of granite on the left; the Rock Garden looming just downstream, now partially submerged; and far below on the right, Thank God Eddy, which offered the only safe harbor. But the magnitude and the violence of the flood had reshaped the hydraulics to create an astonishing new feature that had never before been seen in the canyon.

At the narrowest point, the river was squeezed into a glassy tongue that bore the silken smoothness of a piece of polished jade. The tongue knifed through the bottleneck in the shape of an elongated V, and as the compressed water shot through this chute its velocity accelerated to almost thirty miles an hour until it collided—abruptly—against an impenetrable white wall known as an explosion wave. The trough-to-crest height of that wave approached thirty feet, and at the apex the water wrapped upstream and crashed back upon itself to form an unimaginably violent, endlessly recirculating keeper hole that spanned almost the entire width of the river channel, all the way from the right to the left bank.

The energy and the turbulence inside that hole, whose interior was invisible from shore, could be approximated by the sound emanating from its depths. Crystal's thunder was always stupendous, but this was something altogether different—an audible fury that seemed to slap the rangers across the face the moment they hit the top of the terrace. They were enveloped by the roar of a sustained explosion whose concussion seemed to reverberate up from the depths of the river, through the rock, and directly into the soles of the flip-flops on their feet.

One of Brian's kayakers, a ranger named Stan Steck, who had studied engineering in college, immediately understood that they were looking at an almost perfect hydraulic jump—and, intriguingly, part of the perfection resided in the fact that the jump had formed the sort of liquid pipeline that is normally visible only to big-wave surfers. By positioning himself in just the right spot on the terrace, Steck was able to peer through the pipeline's aperture and gaze along the inside of the wave all the way to the opposite side of the river. There, a small section of the pink-and-black granite cliff was framed within a smooth, emerald-green oval.

To Steck and the other rangers, this was the most magnificent and fearsome thing any of them had ever seen. Never in all their collective years on the Colorado had they encountered anything quite so marvelous or terrifying. And beneath the deafening roar, they discerned something else—a series of hollow, cannonlike booms that were detonating at irregular intervals every seven to ten seconds.

Deep below the surface, the boulders at the bottom of the river were shifting and colliding, cracking into one another like immense billiard balls as the current labored to shove them from its path. With a muscular assist from the dam's latest discharge, the Colorado was attempting to reestablish its proper constriction ratio, a process that had never before been witnessed. Exactly how long this would continue before the bottleneck expanded and the fury began to subside was anyone's guess. But the moment was singular—and as the rangers readily understood, it also created spectacular complications for anyone who needed to get a boat downstream.

Brian immediately saw that the solution to the problem rested with a massive lateral wave emanating from the right-hand shore at an oblique angle and extending toward the center of the river. That wave formed a barrier that blocked access to the only safe route past the chaos—a section of relatively calm and shallow water sluicing through a grove of submerged tamarisk trees along the edge of the debris field on the right shoreline. This was the safety zone, and any boatman who wanted to sneak past the rage in the center of Crystal would have to punch his bow or stern through the lateral with the perfect combination of angle, timing, and momentum. It would not be easy. But no one in his right mind would ever purposely try to take a boat into the face of that explosion wave.

As the rangers stood on the terrace, dumbstruck by the fury and reviewing the geometry of the rapid to confirm that there were no other options, Brian's attention was drawn upstream. An unusual contraption was rounding the corner—a convoluted arrangement of sausage-shaped bridge pontoons that he immediately recognized as the most infamous raft in the entire canyon.

Georgie White was about to make a run at Crystal, and she was heading straight for the center.

~

By the spring of 1983, White was entering the fourth decade of what would eventually qualify as the longest and most storied guiding career in the Grand Canyon. She had arrived on the Colorado back in the late 1940s and had built her business during an era when women were permitted to venture down the river only as passengers—and, even then, only with reluctance. Through a combination of audacity, stubbornness, and an incorrigible passion for white water, she had emerged as the first and only woman to captain a river-running outfit, as well as perhaps the single most colorful—and controversial—personality between Lee's Ferry and Lake Mead.

White was both wildly entertaining and gloriously disreputable. She survived mainly on canned tomatoes, wore a leopard-print bathing suit that featured its own tail, and spent her days roaring downstream with one hand on the tiller and the other clutching a can of Coors. Unlike her competitors, she declined to hire professional river guides, relying instead on a band of Los Angeles County firefighters who devoted their vacations to serving as her entourage and staff. They had nicknames like Rags and Smokey, Bing and Mule, and they spent much of their time on the river engaged in raucous practical jokes and pelting one another with fruit. Each night, White pulled into a camp, whipped up a batch of Kool-Aid laced with grain alcohol (a potent concoction known as Stupid), and spent the evening drinking and wrestling with her firemen, who called her Mother and did their best to keep these revels from getting too out of hand. (Once, White almost succeeded in biting someone's ear off.) But among her many distinctions, perhaps the most noteworthy was that she piloted the biggest raft in the entire canyon—an inflatable monstrosity consisting of three giant bridge pontoons whose dimensions exceeded the footprint of a double-wide mobile home and boasted an estimated gross displacement of thirty-nine tons.

Known as the *Queen Mary*, the barge was so enormous that when it was initially launched, there was some question in White's mind as to whether it would actually fit through the canyon's narrowest points. But the boat's genius—if that was the right word—resided in its sheer acreage, which smothered itself over the rapids like a wet neoprene blanket, thereby enabling White to take a unique approach to white water.

Aboard the *Queen Mary*, there was no need for White to cultivate or hone the subtler arts of reading water. She scorned the practice of scouting and she never cheated a single rapid, preferring to center-punch the biggest holes on the river while assuring her passengers that whatever went wrong would get sorted out in the tail waves.

Having relied on this technique for many years, White had no intention of modifying anything as she bore down on Crystal at the helm of her mammoth boat on the morning of June 23 and set herself up for a maneuver that Brian and his squad of river rangers could see was patently insane.

As the rangers watched, stupefied, White shut off her motor, levered the propeller out of the water, and allowed the current to carry her across the top of the rapid, a gambit known as dead-sticking. Without power, steerage, or any other form of control, the *Queen Mary* now boasted all the agility and responsiveness of a dead manatee. While her passengers—who had no idea what was about to occur—threw their arms into the air and screamed in excitement, White crouched in the bottom of her motor well and braced her feet against the rubber. Then the boat was seized by the accelerating current and hurled into the hole.

By dint of its prodigious mass, the *Queen Mary* was too large even for Crystal to flip upside-down. Instead, the boat danced indecisively inside the hole, first feinting downstream, then retreating upstream. In this violent game of cat and mouse, the pontoons were wrenched from side to side, pulsating like the bellows of an accordion as the current probed for a weak point.

In light of this punishment, the boat was faring remarkably well—the fact that it was still upright and intact probably qualified as some sort of milestone in the history of maritime design. Unfortunately, White's cargo and passengers were not so successful. Each time the raft buckled and sprang back, the rangers could see bodies and pieces of gear being ejected. "Not only were they catapulted *out*," Brian later told a friend named Scott Thybony, "they were also catapulted *through* the pontoons. It was just crazy."

The rangers onshore sprang into action. Realizing that more than thirty people were being flung into the middle of the meanest rapid in the canyon, they raced toward their boats, untied their bowlines, and hurled themselves downstream.

Unlike White, they speared through the lateral and rode the pocket of quiet water along the right shore. Once past the explosion wave, they started hauling swimmers from the water while visually assessing the people who had paddled into the shallows and were now clinging to the rocks. Some were suffering from shock or hypothermia. Others had swallowed water and were vomiting. One man was sitting in a position that made it look as if both of his legs had been broken.*

To the astonishment of the rangers, all of White's passengers had survived. After gathering everyone up and reuniting two young boys with their distraught fathers, both of whom were convinced that their sons had drowned, Brian pulled over to check on White, who was now standing in her motor well holding a can of Coors and surveying the damage.

Every item of gear and equipment on the *Queen Mary* had been stripped from the boat. Brian saw nothing left on board except for the motor, which was still strapped to its mount, and, remarkably, White herself.

"Georgie, what happened?" asked Brian.

She looked at him and winked. "I told 'em to hang on." She shrugged. "They don't make passengers like they used to."

White might have been a bit less smug if she had known that Crystal wasn't quite finished with her.

~

As it turned out, White had two other boats on the river, both of which were more than twenty miles upstream. They were piloted by two of her most trusted firefighters, one of whom, Chuck Mills, was running a thirty-five-foot raft with twenty-three passengers. Mills and his partner did not arrive at Mile 98 until many hours later, long after both White and the river rangers had departed. Instead of running Crystal at dusk, they opted to camp for the night.

When they set out to tackle the rapid the following morning, several other outfitters were poised to attempt the same run. Like those other boatmen, Mills had no interest in center-punching the main hole the way his boss had done the previous day. Nevertheless, his skills were no match for Crystal's hydraulics.

Mills's rig was flipped upside down in a heartbeat. Everyone on board was dumped into the river and flailed toward the surface—except for Mills himself

---

* He later turned out to be fine.

and a passenger named Alice Couts, both of whom became entangled in the rigging underneath the raft. Couts was trapped and unable to breathe. Mills was able to fight his way clear, swim to the surface, and catch a breath, but was immediately pulled back under by a rope that had wrapped around one of his ankles.

In the struggle to disentangle himself, a ligament gave way inside his knee. Somehow he managed to free himself, return to the surface, and pull his body onto the slippery bottom of the raft—at which point he caught sight of Couts's hand sticking out from underneath the boat. He grabbed hold and hauled her out.

As the upside-down boat raced downstream, Mills scanned the river for the rest of his passengers. Some were clinging to the sides of the raft. Others were in the water and struggling to keep their heads above water, catching a breath in the waves. Scurrying crabwise across the bottom of the boat, he raced to pull everyone in reach aboard.

While Mills scrambled to rescue as many people as possible, yet *another* accident was unfolding in the middle of Crystal, this one involving a cluster of motorized rafts from Cross Tours and Expeditions. The first Cross rig skated past the explosion wave without a hitch, but the second boat was trapped inside the hole when the third boat came flying through and was speared directly on top of it. The collision knocked both rafts out of the hole and through the main wave, but when they emerged at the bottom of the rapid, they looked as if they had been caught on the losing end of a vicious naval engagement. Their frames were mangled, their aluminum storage boxes had been blown to pieces, and the front and rear tubes of one of the rafts were deflated.

A total of thirty-three passengers had been dumped into the river, and as they were pulled from the water or retrieved from the rocks along the shore, they bore the shell-shocked look of refugees. The children were shivering and terrified. Several adults were grimacing in pain, and in the bow of the half-deflated boat was a woman whose head was covered with lacerations. One of her eyes was turning black, she had lost her glasses, and she was sobbing.

This accident was witnessed by several other expeditions, one of which was able to send out a Mayday by radio to the Park Service dispatch center on the South Rim. Within minutes, a helicopter was clattering over the river assessing the carnage. On board was a ranger named Kim Crumbo, a former SEAL, who was clutching a megaphone. While the pilot hovered above the stricken boats, Crumbo, who was perched on the skids, shouted orders.

An evacuation will be staged from Bass Camp, ten miles downstream, he announced repeatedly. *Proceed downriver and we will fly you out from there.*

By 10:00 a.m., Crumbo's chopper was airlifting people to the South Rim.

The injured went first, then the women and children. Chuck Mills and the people aboard his raft, which had been washed ashore two miles farther downstream, were evacuated by 1:00 p.m.

It was hard to believe that so much havoc had been wrought by a single rapid, but the destructiveness unfolding at Mile 98 was undeniable. Later that afternoon, a reporter walked into the Kiva Lounge at the Thunderbird Lodge, a motel on the South Rim where most of the passengers were spending the night. When the reporter asked what had happened, the reply was elegantly simple: "We got bit by Crystal."

~

Amid the scramble to manage this crisis, no one on the superintendent's staff, including Richard Marks himself, had given much thought to anything that wasn't directly connected with the matter at hand—including several phone calls from Martin Litton. Here, the final noteworthy event of the day unfolded, although the precise details of what transpired are obscured by the haze that often separates stories that are objectively true from stories that are told on the river.

Many years later, long after Marks was dead and Grua was no longer on the river and Litton had forgotten exactly who said what to whom, it was impossible to tease out the hard facts. But the legend goes something like this:

While Crystal was busy devouring those three motor rigs, Litton placed several phone calls to the office of the superintendent. He never managed to get through. Then, late in the evening, Litton dialed the superintendent's home number and got him on the line.

According to the story, Marks was in the middle of hosting a cocktail party—a scene that stretches credulity in light of the many problems the superintendent was dealing with. But what is eminently believable is that, borrowing a page from Grua's own handbook, Litton kept Marks on the phone forever with one of his speeches, rambling on about the transcendent importance of a speed run and the notion that what was now taking place inside the canyon called for the sort of grand and lyrical gesture that spoke to the iconic majesty of the river.

On and on Litton droned until, finally, the exasperated superintendent supposedly struck a dubious bargain by declaring that, although he was unwilling to change his mind about a speed-run permit, *if*—after reviewing the matter with his river rangers the following morning—the answer was *still* no, he would telephone Litton back and explain the reasons why.

There's probably a mixture of truth and exaggeration in all of that. But no one disputes what happened after the call was made.

Later that evening, Litton telephoned Grua at the boathouse in Hurricane and told him about his conversation with the superintendent.

"He says if the answer is no, he'll phone tomorrow," Litton explained. "Now if he *doesn't* call me, what do you suppose that will mean?"

Grua didn't need to answer the question.

Litton had done exactly what had been asked of him, which was to crack open the door of opportunity. All that Grua needed to do now was sit back for one more day and pray the phone didn't ring.

19

Ghost Boat

It was impossible not to think of the river as having a will and intent of her own . . . She seemed not only willful but demonic, bent on the simple act of drowning us.

—JOE KANE

ON Saturday, June 25, dawn arrived with the hot and crystalline transparency that rules the high desert in midsummer. By 7:00 a.m., the temperature was already in the low eighties and climbing rapidly toward one hundred. There was not a breath of wind anywhere along the North Rim, and the air was so clear that on the outskirts of Hurricane, visibility extended for twenty-four miles. Deep inside the canyon, however, the sun had still not yet topped the rim when a group of thirty-three passengers and guides roused themselves from their sleeping cots at a camp located four miles upstream from Crystal. Half an hour later, when they sat down to a breakfast of pancakes and orange juice, they were unaware that the events of the next several hours would mark each of them in profound and disturbing ways and would, for a select handful, change their lives forever.

Tour West was a mom-and-pop outfitter owned by a tight-knit family of Mormons who ran the river in motorized rafts equipped with a pair of inflatable side tubes that made each boat resemble a giant, floating hot-dog bun. This particular expedition, which had departed Lee's Ferry less than forty-eight hours earlier, was scheduled to last only five days, and the passengers, almost all of whom were seeing the canyon for the first time, came from all over the map. An attorney from Michigan named Walt Gallaher had booked the excursion for himself and five members of his family, including his wife, Nancy, his two sons, Matt and Scott, his daughter, Colleen, and her husband, Bob Paparelli. Four middle-aged women who had grown up together in Butte, Montana—Sally Lonner, Lin Sultzer, Marjie Hay, and Mary Ann McNammee—were on the river to celebrate the fact that all of them were turning fifty that year. In addition to fourteen other clients who hailed from as far away as Hawaii, there was also an elderly couple from Colorado, Bill and Ellen Wert, who had joined the trip because Bill was fascinated by geology and photography and wanted to capture as many images of the canyon as possible.

Like many outfitters, Tour West catered to its passengers' differing attitudes toward white water by designating one raft as the "adventure boat" and the other as the "sedate boat." Dave Stratton, the boss's son, was at the helm of the adventure boat, which carried most of the kitchen equipment and the camping gear. This raft, which included the Gallaher family, would seek out more thrilling action by going through the bigger waves. By contrast, the second boat—which was equipped with several extremely heavy ice chests filled with much of their perishable food—was supposed to confine itself to the calmer parts of the river and attempt to avoid the biggest features of the rapids.

This sedate raft, which included Bill Wert and his wife, together with the Butte Ladies and at least half a dozen others, was captained by Darrel Roberson, a garrulous guide who was leading the expedition and whose relaxed drawl and casual vibe put everyone at ease. Roberson was able to keep up a constant stream of instruction and banter over the sound of his motor because, although the boat was his responsibility, the helm was manned by a twenty-six-year-old rookie who was about to complete a crucial step along the path to becoming a full-fledged river guide.

Layne Parmenter had grown up in Idaho and had already guided nearly forty trips on the Salmon River. Before being allowed to handle the big water inside the Grand Canyon, however, he was required to complete three trips under the supervision of a senior guide, who would coach him through the rapids. This was Parmenter's third supervised canyon run, and if all went well, it would be his last trip as a trainee.

For two days, the rafts had raced downstream on the highest water any of the guides had ever seen, while the passengers gave themselves over to the simple seductions of moving through the canyon by day and sleeping out under the stars at night. Stratton's boat led the way as they shot through the Roaring Twenties, past Nankoweap, and down to the confluence with the Little Colorado at Mile 61.5, unaware of the dramatic wrecks that were piling up farther below at Mile 98.

There were no mishaps or close calls. But as they finished up their breakfast on Saturday morning, Roberson informed the group that they were about to tackle some of the largest rapids in the canyon, and that regardless of whether the passengers were in the adventure boat or the sedate boat, everyone should prepare to see some action at Crystal.

~

According to several of the most experienced guides in the canyon, by that morning Crystal was three times more dangerous than it had ever been, and the breakout move to avoid the hydraulic jump was an order of magnitude more difficult. That sort of math was subjective, of course, and impossible to verify, and perhaps it was the small details that most vividly conveyed the ferocity of what was unfolding inside the rapid.

Few of the guides who had spent the previous night camped above the rapid had been able to sleep because of the roar of the explosion wave, and several had taken the unusual precaution of duct-taping foam padding around their bottles of gin and tequila. One of the most surreal but emblematic moments actually occurred a few days later, when a boatman named Joe Sharber heard a splash while he was conducting his scout. He looked down to see that a beaver had climbed out of the water and was waddling through the rocks along the shore.

Oh, hell, thought Sharber, *even the beavers are portaging.*

When the Tour West group reached the glassy lake just above Crystal around 9:30 a.m., an eclectic assortment of rafts and kayaks was already moored inside the little cove along the right shore, just above the point where the water broke. Stratton, who was in the lead, pulled in first, and because space was so tight, Parmenter and Roberson were forced to tie off to his stern. As the passengers disembarked, Walt Gallaher stared quizzically up into the clear, cloudless sky and wondered why he was hearing the sound of thunder.

When everyone reached the top of the scouting ledge, they were met by a group of boatmen from half a dozen different oar-raft companies, all of whom were waiting for the opportunity to observe the motor rig make the run before taking a crack at the rapid themselves. Stratton and his team made a thorough job of the scout, spending almost forty-five minutes examining the rapid from at least three different angles, all the while discussing their strategy. As the guides shuffled from one spot to the next, they were shadowed by several passengers who were eager to get a sense of what the plan would be. Although it was hard to hear, two of those passengers discerned that a difference of opinion had arisen among the guides about how the rapid should be run.

Roberson and Parmenter, it seemed, were both advocating something unusual. They proposed initiating their run on the far left side of the river, then cranking their throttles and making a bold forty-five-degree cut across the current toward the right shore, which would build enough momentum and speed to carry them decisively over the lateral wave and into the safety zone. This idea was firmly opposed by Stratton, who was in no mood to take that kind of risk. As the son of the company's owner, Stratton's opinion carried decisive weight, so he pulled rank and politely explained to his colleagues they were all going to stay as close as possible to the right shoreline by executing a "turnaround run," a move that would slam the bows of their motor rigs into the shallows along the right shoreline just below the head of the rapid, then permit the current to swing their sterns around and pull them through backward. The maneuver was tricky and a bit crude, but done properly it was the perfect technique for hugging the shore and avoiding the chaos in the center of the river.

"See the tammies that are in the water? You've got to be running right over those," Stratton told Parmenter while pointing out the top of a tamarisk tree on the right side of the rapid. "Just stay out of the main current," he warned. "You get in there and it's over."

With the plan firmly set, they all walked back down to the boats. But as everyone was clambering aboard and preparing to launch, one of the passengers, Ellen Wert, remained on the shore, expressing second thoughts.

Ellen was concerned about her husband. Although Bill was in excellent shape for a sixty-two-year-old retiree—an avid outdoorsman who loved to hike, backpack, and ski—she knew that he was not a strong swimmer. Calling out to one of the guides, she announced that they preferred to walk around the rapid and be picked up downstream. By now, however, Bill was already aboard Parmenter's raft and was urgently motioning for his wife to climb aboard, assuring her that everything would be fine.

"What's the use of going on a river trip," he exclaimed, "if you walk around the rapids?"

Shaking her head, she complied.

Parmenter's rig then began easing out of the eddy. Stratton stayed put, intending to delay his own launch by several minutes to give Parmenter plenty of space and avoid the possibility of a collision.

From his mooring, Stratton watched as the sedate boat, with the trainee at the helm, lumbered out into the river, where it was swiftly seized by the current and snatched from view.

~

Inside Parmenter's raft, the Butte Ladies had taken up the first four positions in the bow. Mary Ann McNammee and Lin Sultzer were sitting in the front; Marjie Hay and Sally Lonner were directly behind them. Bill and Ellen Wert were positioned toward the back on the right side, and the rest of the passengers—half a dozen of them, including a couple with two children in their early teens—were spread out in the middle. Roberson was sitting in the stern, and Parmenter, who was wearing a blue-and-white baseball cap, was standing in the motor well with his hand on the stick.

During the initial moments as they pulled away from shore, the Butte Ladies felt as if they were at the start of a roller coaster as it clicked hollowly toward the top—a giddy sensation in which anticipation and fear braided together in a way that was scary but also thrilling. As the cliffs along the shore scrolled past, they could hear the dull roar growing louder. Up ahead, the dark green water rounded into a smooth hump before dropping off a lip. The rapid itself was still invisible, but they could see spray being hurled into the air, an indication of the violence and fury just below.

As the current picked up speed, everyone grew tense, and one of the Butte Ladies cried out, "Let 'er buck!" Then they were inside the smooth, V-shaped tongue and rapidly accelerating. Within seconds, they could feel the wind rushing past their faces. No one said a word, and each person faced forward, staring intently ahead.

Halfway down the tongue, Roberson yelled, "Down and in!" Everyone hunkered as low as possible on the aluminum decking, grabbing firmly onto the straps. In this position, it was difficult for the passengers to see much of anything over the huge side pontoons, and almost impossible to hear any communication above the encroaching roar of the white water.

They had no idea that neither of their guides had properly judged the velocity and power of the downstream current. The consequences of this, however, were about to be demonstrated to them in the most graphic manner imaginable.

~

Back onshore, an oar guide by the name of Jeffe Aronson had taken up a rather dramatic position from which to observe Parmenter's run. Together with a passenger named Richard Kocim, an electrical engineer from Chicago, Aronson had climbed down from the scouting terrace and positioned himself on a rounded boulder at shore level, almost directly across from the hydraulic jump.

This vantage was extremely noisy—the thunder of the explosion wave, less than fifty yards away, was so loud that they felt as if they were standing beneath the wing of a jumbo jet as the engines spooled up. To Kocim, it seemed an odd place to wait because they were completely cut off from the raft as it approached the entrance to the rapid. But Aronson knew that once Parmenter entered the tongue, they would have a perfect view of what unfolded.

The two men stood shoulder to shoulder for several long minutes. Then, silently and without warning, the silver-gray hulk of the raft made its appearance—at which point Aronson found himself doing a double take.

The raft wasn't at all where he expected it to be. Instead of hugging the right shore with its bow plowing through the tops of the tamarisk trees, the boat was coasting far out in the middle of the river and pointed straight downstream. This made no sense to Aronson, who knew that unless Parmenter initiated a hard turn to the right and gunned his throttle all the way, the raft was in danger of being speared directly into the hole.

One second ticked past. Then another.

Aronson stared helplessly, waiting for the boatman to make his move. Finally, he turned toward Kocim and cupped his hand around the man's ear.

Kocim, a keen amateur photographer, was carrying a Minolta SRT with a 200 mm lens.

"Do you have a fresh roll of film?" Aronson yelled.

Kocim nodded.

"See that pink dike off the wall?" shouted Aronson, pointing to a vein of Zoroaster granite running down the cliff on the far side of the river. "If they don't turn before they pass that, it's over."

As he completed this statement, the boat slid past the marker—and in that moment Aronson did something he had never before done, an act so instinctive and so involuntary that he was barely aware of his own performance.

He raised his arms high into the air, opened his mouth, and began to scream.

⁓

Although no one on the raft could hear Aronson, his scream marked the moment when Roberson reacted with explosiveness, pumping his right arm and pointing emphatically to the submerged tamarisk trees. The gestures had only one possible meaning.

Get right now!

It was too late. With Roberson continuing to gesticulate, the raft raced down the tongue. By now Parmenter had canted his bow slightly to the right, but it made little difference. The full force of the river was working decisively against him.

"Oh, God," Parmenter yelled at Roberson, "we're going to hit the hole!"

In the final seconds of their ride down the smooth surface of the tongue, they were moving so fast that the wind took the brim of Parmenter's blue-and-white baseball cap and flipped it back on him.

The second the cap flipped up, they were slammed directly into the hole and the white wall of water stopped them cold.

~

From the perspective of the passengers inside Parmenter's raft, things suddenly became terribly confusing.

Lin Sultzer, who was positioned at the front, abruptly felt herself being catapulted through the air.

Mary Ann McNammee, who was sitting opposite Sultzer, felt a sharp pain in her left leg.

Sally Lonner, who was directly behind Sultzer, reeled as something hard—she had no idea what it was—struck her squarely in the face. *We're going over*, thought Lonner as her glasses broke in two.

Amid this confusion, no one had a clear idea of what was happening to Bill and Ellen Wert. Several passengers later stated that instead of getting down as he was ordered, Bill had stood up just prior to the moment of impact to get a quick snapshot of the rapid with his camera. Others insisted that nothing of the sort had happened—or, alternatively, that Wert had failed to get down in the first place because he had been unable to hear Roberson's instructions.

In actual fact, no one in Parmenter's motor rig had the faintest idea what was taking place. Those details could only come from the shoreline, where Richard Kocim, who had the body of the Minolta glued to the front of his face and was shooting as fast as he could, was recording the most graphic series of stop-action white-water images ever captured on film—a step-by-step chronicle, in sixteen frames, of a four-ton raft being taken apart and consumed by the Colorado.

CLICK: *One of the first shots in Kocim's series catches the nose of the thirty-three-foot rig as it vanishes into the face of the twenty-five-foot-high standing wave. At this moment no one, including Bill Wert, is standing up.*

CLICK: *The sixth photo captures the rig as the wave rolls it sideways.*

CLICK: *In the ninth picture, the entire raft is standing vertically on its left side tube and is about to go over.*

CLICK: *The tenth shot shows the side tubes flailing wildly and the metal frame contorting as the rig is viciously window-shaded, an act of astonishing violence in which a boat becomes entrained in the turbulence at the bottom of the hole and is rolled over and over.*

But it is image number twelve that is perhaps the most remarkable.

CLICK: *As the rig is torn to pieces, something in the middle of the boat—something that looks vaguely like a piece of ribbon—appears to be flapping in the air. This is one of the main straps that are responsible for holding the entire boat together—a section of three-inch-wide nylon webbing whose breaking strength is rated at nearly fifteen thousand pounds.*

The instant that Kocim's finger triggers the shutter, Crystal has snapped the web-bing in two and is ripping the boat into pieces.

~

The sequence that Kocim recorded with his camera unfolded far too swiftly to register as discrete events in the mind of Jeffe Aronson, who was still standing with his arms upraised and his mouth open. In Aronson's eyes, it simply looked as if the raft had become a piece of prey that was being devoured by a ravenous monster. Amid its feeding, however, Aronson discerned something unusual.

Even over the roar of the rapid and the wail that was emanating from deep inside him, he detected a sharp and percussive sound, almost like a gunshot. Only later, when he had seen the flapping piece of ribbon in Kocim's twelfth photo, did Aronson realize that this was the moment the three-inch, fifteen-thousand-pound webbing had parted.

As Parmenter's rig was disemboweled, the boat disappeared beneath the surface of the river. While Kocim continued shooting, Aronson scanned the water for some sign of where it had gone.

For a moment, there was nothing. Then, just as abruptly as the raft had disappeared, a tangled mass of tubing was spat to the surface, churned around several more times, released from the hole, and cast contemptuously downstream.

And now Aronson noticed something else. All over the river, small black dots were popping to the surface, and each dot was surrounded by an orange-colored blob.

It took a moment for him to realize that these were the heads of the passengers and their life jackets. Some of those people appeared to be swimming hard for the shallows. The rest were simply fighting to stay afloat as they were hurtled downstream in the direction of the next rapid.

~

Back at the top of Crystal, Dave Stratton had no idea what had taken place. Having delayed his own departure by several minutes to allow Parmenter to make his run, Stratton was untying his lines when a sharp yell from shore pulled him up short.

"You just had a boat flip!" cried a raft guide named Suzanne Jordan, who was running toward him. "You've got to get down and get your people!"

Stratton immediately ordered his passengers off the raft. As everyone scrambled back onshore, Walt Gallaher's son Scott and his son-in-law, Bob Paparelli, turned to Stratton and said that they'd like to lend a hand. When Stratton asked if they were strong swimmers, both men nodded.

"Well, we may end up flipping too, possibly," replied Stratton. "No guarantees."

Both men nodded again. They were on board.

Accompanied by his two volunteers and a pair of swampers named Bob and Dave, Stratton backed his rig off the beach, eased the stern into the current, then pointed his nose toward the right shore and set up for his turn-around run.

The maneuver was flawless. As the boat neatly skirted the edge of the hole, a roar of elation rose above the thunder of the rapid as every single person on the scouting terrace, passengers and boatmen alike, cheered at the top of their lungs.

Stratton and his four-man rescue squadron were too preoccupied to notice the accolade. Long before they reached the tail waves at the bottom of the rapid, they were already spotting the survivors from Parmenter's boat.

The first person they keyed into was Sally Lonner, who had pulled herself onto some rocks at the side of the river and was sitting with her head in her hands, her face covered in blood.

Several yards downstream, Parmenter himself was clinging to the side of a boulder.

Just below him, two or three others crouched in the shallows, gasping for breath.

These people were clearly in distress, and one or two of them were waving for Stratton to pull over and render assistance, but he ignored them all and blew past, making a beeline for the middle of the river.

Suzanne Jordan, the guide who had delivered the news about the accident, had already promised that she and her crew would retrieve his stranded passengers. Stratton's only concern was thus the people who had failed to make their way to the shoreline—many of whom, he knew, were exhausted and fighting for their lives.

His job was to chase those people down and get them out of the water before they drowned.

~

By now, Lin Sultzer, who had been pulled down so deep that she didn't think she was coming back up, had popped to the surface and found herself in the middle of the river, racing downstream toward the next rapid.

As she fought to keep her head above the water, Sultzer noted that a plastic cooler in which most of their lunch supplies had been stored was drifting past. Bobbing in the water all around the cooler were dozens of oranges, and one of Sultzer's fellow passengers was treading water and frantically snatching them up. He tucked one beneath his chin, then seized another and offered it to her.

"What am I going to do with that?" she exclaimed.

"You might need something to eat," he replied.

Concluding that the man was in shock, Sultzer told him to forget about collecting fruit and focus on getting himself to shore.

As he paddled off, Sultzer spotted Mary Ann McNammee just a few feet away. Sultzer's relief at seeing that McNammee was alive vanished as she registered the expression on her friend's face.

"Are you okay?" Sultzer called out.

"Linny, I think my legs are broken!" cried McNammee.

"Well," replied Sultzer, doing her best to remain calm, "let's see if we can get you to shore."

The two women clasped hands so that Sultzer could begin pulling McNammee toward the rocks. But their wet skin was slippery and both women were being jostled violently. Amid the thrashing waves, they lost their grip and were separated.

As McNammee was torn from her grasp, Sultzer turned to see what lay ahead and spotted a large, misshapen silver-and-gray object drifting in the center of the river. This, she realized, was the middle section of their destroyed raft, floating upside down. Several passengers were clinging to the side of the boat, and Darrel Roberson, who had somehow climbed onto the bottom, was trying to haul them out of the water.

When Roberson spied Sultzer, he motioned for her to swim toward him, but she was too far away and, to her dismay, was carried downstream. As she was swept past the boat, she yelled out to Roberson, "Mary Ann's behind me. Try and get her—she's hurt!"

Then, to Sultzer's surprise, something even stranger than the oranges floated past. She realized that it was a box of cheap white wine—Chablis—merrily sailing downstream.

At that moment Sultzer, a recovering alcoholic, decided to make a deal with God. "If you get me out of this," she promised, "I will never take another drink for as long as I live."*

~

As Sultzer fought for her life, Dave Stratton was trying his best to save another one. He and his rescue team had by now been swept below Tuna Creek Rapid, which was a mile downstream from Crystal. Directly ahead, they could see that one of Parmenter's passengers was floating faceup in his life jacket, with his arms outstretched.

"He doesn't look very good," Stratton remarked to himself, an impression that was strengthened as the raft drew closer.

---

*Sultzer has kept her promise to this day.

When Stratton pulled alongside, one of his swampers tied a ring buoy onto the bowline and leaped into the water. With help from Scott Gallaher and Bob Paparelli, the swamper was able to hoist the passenger over the side tubes and onto the deck of the raft.

It was Bill Wert.

His skin looked slightly blue, he did not appear to be breathing, and when Gallaher turned him over onto his back and started searching for a pulse, there was none.

"Let's get him some CPR," barked Stratton from his position at the tiller.

As Gallaher and the second swamper removed Wert's life jacket and pulled up his shirt, they were shocked to see a massive bruise on the sixty-two-year-old man's chest. An ugly purple splotch, roughly the size of a fist, covered his sternum. During the flip, Wert had apparently sustained a blow from something heavy, most probably one of the metal storage boxes in the center of Parmenter's rig.

Now came an ugly moment. Whatever damage the blow had already inflicted was about to be exacerbated by the CPR treatment, which would have to be administered directly on top of the bruise.

Grimly, they set to work. Placing both fists on Wert's sternum, the swamper began counting out a series of five compressions, carefully spaced at two-second intervals. Then he paused while Gallaher, who was kneeling next to Wert's head, tilted the older man's chin upward and administered a pair of rescue breaths directly into his mouth.

On the second breath, Wert's chest convulsed and a surge of river water mixed with mucus came vomiting out of his throat and directly into Gallaher's mouth. Torn between the desire to revive Wert and his disgust at what had just happened, Gallaher turned his head to the side and spat.

While the two men continued their efforts, Stratton kept moving downstream, with Paparelli serving as a lookout, scanning the river for swimmers. The CPR continued for several minutes until the swamper paused, turned to Stratton, and said, "I just don't think this guy is going to make it. I don't think we can get him back around."

Stratton now faced the kind of decision that no river guide ever hopes to confront. Other survivors needed to be pulled from the water—and directly ahead were Roberson and a group of stricken passengers, including McNammee, who urgently needed help.

The choice was clear. Stratton ordered his team to leave Wert curled in the corner of the raft and turn to the work of getting those who were still alive on board.

~

At 10:36 a.m., an orange-and-white Park Service helicopter lifted off from the heliport on the South Rim. Minutes earlier, a rafting party on the river had sent out a Mayday, which was picked up by a sightseeing aircraft passing directly over the canyon, radioed to the control tower at Grand Canyon airport, then relayed to the park's emergency dispatch center. On board Helo 210 were a pilot named Mike Bertoldi and Curt Sauer, the river boss who had rejected Grua's speed-run permit application eight days earlier.

Less than ten minutes after takeoff, while they were still en route, Sauer received a more detailed report from his dispatchers. A motor rig had flipped in Crystal and twenty people were in the water. As they clattered upstream, Sauer caught sight of Parmenter's overturned raft with Roberson and several passengers huddled on the bottom. A short distance beyond the wreck, he spotted the second boat, with Stratton at the helm, snatching up survivors from the river. As Bertoldi continued flying upstream, Sauer counted five people clinging to the rocks at water level.

When Helo 210 reached Crystal, Bertoldi touched down briefly and Sauer climbed out to speak with a group of oar-raft guides, who described what had happened and assured the ranger that they would retrieve the passengers stranded on the rocks. Then Sauer strapped back in and told Bertoldi to head downstream. During their second pass over the scene, Sauer could see that at least two of the stranded passengers were suffering from head injuries.

By now it was evident that one helicopter would not be sufficient to cope with the multiple emergencies. Sauer radioed the South Rim to request that a second copter, Helo 210A, be mobilized with two rangers equipped with rescue-swimmer gear and a full emergency medical kit.

Then he noticed that one of the stranded passengers on the right side of the river had climbed halfway up a steep cliff and appeared to be stuck. Realizing that the man was now beyond the reach of a boat, Sauer sent out a request for a third chopper, Helo 210B, with a ranger and a length of climbing rope.

When the rescues were complete, Sauer told his dispatcher, the three helicopters would converge at Bass Camp, ten miles downstream from Crystal. All evacuations would take place from there.

~

Dave Stratton had now finally managed to catch up with Roberson's upside-down raft and transfer everyone to his own rig. As Scott Gallaher and Bob Paparelli pulled people aboard, they were shocked by some of the injuries.

There were many lacerations and several broken bones. Most of these people were also in shock, and some were exhibiting signs of hypothermia, having spent more than twenty minutes immersed in the fifty-degree water. One man, who had a deep cut on his leg, was shaking so violently that Stratton ordered one of the swampers to break into the duffels, pull out some sheets and blankets, and wrap him up. But the worst case, by far, was Mary Ann McNammee.

Contrary to what McNammee had thought when she was floating in the river, her legs were not broken. But the back of her left calf had been struck by a sharp piece of metal when her raft flipped, and as Stratton's team transferred her over from the wreckage of Parmenter's boat, they could see that her leg had been flayed all the way from the back of her knee to her Achilles tendon. The flap of skin, which was attached only by a narrow strip of tissue, was as white as the belly of a fish, and the muscles underneath her calf were fully exposed.

While his team tended to the injuries, Stratton chased downriver after Sultzer, who was among the last of the passengers still in the water. When the raft finally caught up to her, one of the men tossed out a rope and they heaved her out of the water and into the raft like a marlin.

As Sultzer struggled to her feet, she accidentally stumbled over Bill Wert's body. He was curled into a fetal position, and her first thought was that he had fallen asleep. But when one of the swampers gently covered him with a tarp, she realized he was dead.

With all of the swimmers now rescued, Stratton and his team turned to deal with McNammee.

Thanks to the chilly water and the adrenaline in her system, the blood vessels in her leg had contracted and her bleeding was not extensive. But both Stratton and Gallaher knew that this was about to change. If they didn't get McNammee bandaged immediately, she could bleed out right there on the deck. Unfortunately, the expedition's primary medical kit had been riding on Parmenter's boat and was stripped away with the rest of the gear during the wreck.

What the hell were they supposed to do?

It was then, in one of those bizarre coincidences that seemed in retrospect to stretch credulity, that Paparelli's eye was caught by a bright red object in the river, and he realized that the med kit was floating past them in the current, just a yard or two away. Gallaher and Paparelli were both about to leap into the river to retrieve the kit, but opted instead for a reach-and-grab. With Paparelli clinging to his ankles, Gallaher lunged all the way out of the boat, seized hold of the kit, and was pulled back in. Snatching a roll of tape, a wad of gauze, and an inflatable splint, they got to work on McNammee's leg.

Meanwhile, Stratton glanced up and spotted Curt Sauer's helicopter, directly overhead and flying downstream.

Assuming—correctly—that the rangers would be staging their evacuation at the first available spot with enough room to accommodate both the boats and the extra helicopters that were undoubtedly on their way, Stratton started motoring in earnest for Bass Camp, now less than five miles downstream.

~

When Stratton rammed his boat through the eddy fence at Bass and tied off, Sauer and his helicopter were waiting, and the cove was rapidly filling up as rafts of all sorts began to arrive, laden with the Tour West passengers who had been stranded upstream, as well as sundry pieces of gear that had been retrieved from the river.

All of this made for a bewildering scene, especially for the people who had been flung into the river. Most of them had lost all of their belongings—their extra clothing, their wallets, their personal gear, everything but the bathing suits they were wearing. Amid the confusion, Stratton found himself confronted by a disoriented and visibly anxious Ellen Wert, who had been retrieved from the side of the river and shuttled down to Bass in an oar raft.

The accident had taken place so quickly that she could not recall any details of what had happened, aside from, at some point, Bill's having called out to her. Now he appeared to be missing.

"I don't know where my husband's at!" she exclaimed.

"We don't have everybody accounted for right now," replied Stratton, who perhaps couldn't bring himself to break the awful news. "We still have people upriver."

Ellen Wert did not find this statement at all reassuring. "I know something's wrong," Stratton heard her say as she walked off in search of her husband.

Next, Stratton turned to confer with Sauer, who was demanding an update on whether everyone was accounted for and how many injuries there were. When Stratton informed the ranger that he had a body on board, Sauer radioed his dispatcher and asked them to notify the Coconino County sheriff's office.

When Helo 210A touched down, it deposited two of Sauer's colleagues, who began taking vital signs and preparing the injured for evacuation to the medical clinic on the South Rim. The third chopper, Helo 210B, was on its way, and when it arrived, the priority would be to get the most serious injuries into the air as quickly as possible. Mary Ann McNammee would be on the first flight out.*

For the next hour, the helicopters clattered back and forth between the

---

*McNammee's injuries were so severe that the doctors at the clinic on the South Rim refused to allow her to be sent to Las Vegas aboard a life flight, fearing her lower leg was likely to be amputated. Instead, they bundled her into an ambulance and rushed her eighty miles south to the Flagstaff Medical Center, where a team of surgeons saved her limb.

makeshift helipad at Bass Camp and the South Rim, shuttling all of the Tour West passengers out of the canyon. One of the return flights also brought down Deputy Sheriff Steve Luckeson and a ranger named Darrell Cook, who would supervise the removal of Bill Wert's body. It was Cook who took Ellen Wert aside and informed her that her husband was dead.

By 1:00 p.m., the Gallahers, the Butte Ladies, Ellen Wert, and the rest of the passengers had all been lifted to the South Rim. After Luckeson and Cook collected Wert's personal effects—his ring and his wristwatch—he was placed in a body bag and Luckeson accompanied the deceased man on the final leg of his river trip.

One of the last helicopter shuttles that afternoon included Roberson and Parmenter, whose wrecked boat had slid past the camp during the evacuation, disappeared downstream, and was now drifting into the depths of the canyon on its own.

~

TIME: EARLY EVENING
LOCATION: UPPER OWL CAMP,
38 MILES BELOW CRYSTAL RAPID

On the left side of the Colorado at Mile 136, along a scallop-shaped inlet that marked almost the exact midpoint of the Grand Canyon, Regan Dale stood staring out at the flood tide running past his camp and struggling to make sense of what was out there in the river.

Dale had been leading a squadron of Litton's dories down this torrent for the better part of a week—closer to two weeks, actually, now that he thought of it. Two days earlier, he and his crew had barely made it through Crystal, and the following morning they had stood by helplessly and watched in horror as one of Georgie White's upside-down rafts had rocketed past them with a group of terrified passengers clinging to the bottom and pleading for help.

But as disturbing as those events had been, nothing that he'd encountered so far was as surreal as the scene now unfolding before his eyes.

Dinner had just been served and everyone was sitting in canvas chairs with their plates in their laps when one of Dale's dorymen glanced upriver and exclaimed, "Hey—*lookit.*"

Something strange and sinister had emerged from the gloaming upstream and was now spectering past.

At the head of the procession was a string of soggy paper plates, dozens of them, floating out in the middle of the main current. Behind the plates came a cluster of torn life vests. These were followed by a collection of battered steel ammo cans, the watertight army-surplus boxes that the canyon folk used for storing their personal items.

Each piece of gear floated neatly behind the next, and together they formed a bobbing conga line that ran down the center of the river, offering up a mute testament to some terrible event that had taken place somewhere upriver—a disaster whose detritus was now bearing its news down-canyon.

As this trail of flotsam snaked past the boulder-lined beach, Dale ordered one of his guides to position a dory directly along the outside edge of the eddy and keep his eyes peeled for any swimmers.

Several tense minutes passed. When the wreckage finally petered out and disappeared, the dory returned to its mooring and the passengers got back to the business of trying to finish their dinner.

While the crew traded whispers about what might have happened, Dale kept his thoughts to himself and continued staring out at the river. He was fairly certain that the show wasn't over yet.

~

Sure enough, half an hour or so later, just on the far side of dusk, another object appeared.

It was the center section of a large motor rig, drifting upside down with its belly in the air. With shredded lines trailing in the water behind its bulbous, bloated body, the boat bore the look of an animal—some kind of river beast—that had died violently. Empty and silent. There wasn't a soul on board.

A ghost boat.

Dale shook his head and wondered whether anyone might be trapped underneath that wreck—perhaps the body of a passenger or a boatman who had become entangled in the rigging and run out of air before he could fight his way out.

The boat glided past without giving up an answer.

As it slipped into the gathering shadows, Dale tilted his head to read the upside-down logo, barely discernible in the last glimmer of twilight:

TOUR WEST

20

The Doing of the Thing

*We are now ready to start
on our way down the Great Unknown. . . .
We have an unknown distance yet to run;
an unknown river yet to explore.*

—John Wesley Powell

As Regan Dale pondered the mysteries of the ghost boat from the subbasement of the canyon, nearly five thousand vertical feet above him on the South Rim, Richard Marks found himself adding up the kind of numbers that every superintendent dreads. During the past thirty-six hours, a single pocket of white water had managed to destroy four motor rigs, flip as many as a dozen oar boats, and inflict serious injuries on fifteen passengers and guides. In the process, ninety-one people had been evacuated from the canyon using a trio of helicopters whose collective flight time of twenty-five hours and thirty minutes had cost $9,778. And in addition to all of that, now they had a fatality.

This last fact was especially noteworthy because, for all the havoc that white water had wrought over the years inside the canyon, death was actually quite rare. In more than a century of river running, the Colorado had managed to drown only nineteen boaters. Moreover, although the bulk of those tragedies had unfolded inside the fiercest rapids—House Rock and Sockdolager, Horn Creek and Upset and, of course, Lava Falls—not one of those accidents had taken place anywhere near Mile 98. Despite its savage hydraulics and notorious reputation, Crystal had never managed to kill a single person, until now.

In addition to setting a gruesome precedent, Bill Wert's death had significantly raised the profile of the Grand Canyon flood. Up at the Glen Canyon Dam, the spillway crisis was already drawing serious media attention from the *CBS Evening News*, and thanks to the wire services, newspapers from Los Angeles to Miami were covering the story. Now, calls were also pouring into the South Rim—from local television stations, from newspapers across Arizona, and one from a woman who worked for National Public Radio in Washington, DC. As the news spread, it was sure to provoke sharp queries about what was being done to prevent other fatalities inside the canyon.

The wheels in that process had already been set in motion. Even as Wert's body was being retrieved from the heliport and transported sixty miles south to the town of Williams for an autopsy, Marks had called together his river rangers, pilots, and communications team for a briefing to address the question that was uppermost in everyone's mind—what did they need to do to keep this situation from coming totally unglued?

Three options lay before them, the first simply being to shut down the river by prohibiting any more launches from Lee's Ferry until the crisis at the dam was brought under control and the flooding subsided. As everyone in the room understood, however, this would do nothing to solve the most pressing problem, which was the boats that were already on the water. Scattered along the river between Lee's Ferry and Mile 98 were fourteen separate river expeditions— twelve commercial trips and two groups of private boaters—all of which were headed straight for Crystal.

The second option, a mass evacuation of everyone on the river, raised a different set of concerns. Setting aside the daunting logistics and the obvious safety issues, scooping up every single passenger and chauffeuring them all out by helicopter would not only be expensive but would also trigger an uproar among the commercial outfitters—many of whom had the ear of their congressmen and senators, and all of whom would be outraged by the loss this would inflict on their businesses. No, something a bit more surgical was required. What Marks needed was a way to mitigate the risks where the danger was greatest, and the most effective way to do that was to figure out how to put up some kind of mandatory stop sign at Crystal.

If every expedition was required to pull over at the top of the rapid and discharge its clients, several things could happen at once. While the passengers clomped downstream along the shoreline, a ranger could deliver a pointed lecture to the boatmen about the critical importance of skirting along the tamarisk trees and staying out of the main wave train. Once the passengers had picked their way through the rounded boulders and reached the little beach at the bottom of the rapid, the boats could run the rapid empty except for the guides and the swampers, then pull into Thank God Eddy to pick everyone up before proceeding downriver. There was no guarantee that this would prevent another terrible accident, but it would virtually eliminate the potential for collateral damage. If Crystal did flip and dismember another motor rig, the only people who would be injured, maimed, or killed were the boatmen.

Such a thing had never before been tried inside the canyon, but once the decision was made, the process of applying the brakes started immediately. A few minutes after the meeting adjourned, Tom Workman, the ranger on duty at Lee's Ferry, was ordered to get down to the water and place a temporary halt on all launches. Until further notice, none of the expeditions that were poised on the boat ramp would be permitted to cast off. Meanwhile, Dave Buccello, Workman's counterpart at Phantom Ranch, eighty-eight miles below Lee's Ferry and ten miles upstream from Crystal, was told to position himself on the beach and start hailing boats and informing everyone on board that the river was closed until the following morning.

While Workman and Buccello shut down the river, Helo 210 was mobilized for its final mission of the day. Clattering upstream, the helicopter dropped another round of plastic baggies filled with sand and a mimeographed note. By sunset, every expedition on the river had received a message that read, in part:

> *The superintendent has closed Crystal Rapid to all passengers of both private and commercial trips. Passengers MUST walk around Crystal, with only boatmen and swampers to run Crystal. This closure is due to the extreme hazard of Crystal Rapid. . . . This closure is in effect until further notice.*

The final phase of the superintendent's plan, which would have to wait until the following morning, would be to get a ranger into a helicopter and drop him directly onto the scouting terrace at Crystal. There, he would organize the mandatory walk-around and do his best to prepare the boatmen for the ordeal of getting past the explosion wave.

Amid the scramble to put everything in motion, the furthest thing from the mind of anyone on the South Rim was a piece of unfinished business left hanging in the air—Martin Litton's phone conversation from the night before, and the superintendent's alleged promise that if he had not changed his mind about a speed run permit, he would call Litton back and explain the reasons why.

The records indicate that this subject was never discussed in any of the briefings that took place on the afternoon of June 25. Moreover, in light of the events that had already transpired, it's difficult to imagine that Marks considered himself under any obligation to telephone Litton and state the obvious. As anyone with half a brain could plainly see, approving a speed run to "test evacuation procedures" was patently ludicrous.

But that wasn't how Kenton Grua chose to interpret the matter.

~

At the Grand Canyon Dories boathouse in Hurricane, no one had the faintest idea what had been unfolding at Crystal. Throughout the long morning and afternoon, while the helicopters clattered up and down the river and the passengers swam for their lives, Grua and his two-man crew had piddled around, sweeping and polishing and performing whatever other odd jobs they could think of to pass the time—all the while keeping an ear peeled for the phone and hoping, fervently, that it would not ring. As the end of the day drew near without a single call coming through, they decided to start gearing up.

They began by hoisting the *Emerald Mile* onto Petschek's flatbed, a green metal trailer with hydraulic brakes and a floor fashioned from battered two-by-sixes. Once the boat was in position, it was time to begin loading. By now, Petschek had purchased a pair of Q-Beams, high-intensity halogen strobe lights encased in yellow plastic, which would be powered by a twelve-volt battery that they pulled from Grua's Scout. They connected the spotlights to the battery using some wire and alligator clips, tested the strobes to make sure they worked, then placed these items in the center footwell. Next they began gathering up miscellaneous pieces of gear—several sets of nylon cam straps, plenty of rope, a handful of pulleys, an extra set of oarlocks, and a metal anchor—and tossed all of that into the side hatches, the compartments that ran beneath the dory's port and starboard decking. Then it was time to prepare the rocket boxes.

These were narrow steel canisters originally designed to store antitank-grenade rockets for the US Army's M1A1 bazooka. Because the boxes were watertight and virtually indestructible, they were used on the river as storage containers for everything from food and charcoal to trash. On a normal trip a dory might carry half a dozen of these, but Grua had decreed that for this run they would need only three.

The first was stuffed with their heavy-duty repair kit: fifty pounds of hand tools, including saws, hammers, screwdrivers, wire cutters, screws, and drills, plus caulking, glue, and duct tape sufficient to patch a damaged boat just enough to float her out of the canyon. The second box held the medical supplies that would enable them to perform the same services for an injured boat-man. The third container, which was double-lined with heavy plastic garbage bags and included a roll of toilet paper and a toilet seat, would serve as their Porta Potti.*

When the trio of rocket boxes was placed in the cross-hatch, the locker located directly behind the boatman's seat, plenty of room was left for several jugs of drinking water, a bag stuffed with extra clothing for each member of the crew, and a small blue-and-white cooler that would hold their food. Two sets of oars, ten-foot-long Swansons made from straight-grained Pennsylvania ash, were lashed to the starboard deck. Then a strip of nylon webbing was threaded underneath the hull and affixed to the gunwales directly beneath the oarlocks. This would serve as their "flip line"—a device that would enable them to right the boat in midstream if they went over.

Finally, they tossed in two thermoses filled with coffee and clipped their life jackets to the gunwales with carabiners. With that, the job was essentially com-plete and the dory was ready to go—which forced each member of the team to pause and take stock of how empty the boat was.

The *Emerald Mile* was, for all practical purposes, stripped to the bone. Almost every piece of baggage and equipment that was deemed essential for a conventional three-week commercial dory trip—the silverware, the plates, the skillets and pots and pans, the lanterns, the coolers filled with dairy products and fresh vegetables and frozen meat, the cans of baked beans and fruit cock-tail and peas, the boxes of pasta, the crates of potatoes and onions and carrots, the rubber bags stuffed with tents, the six-burner stove and the aluminum propane canisters that fueled the stove, the folding chairs, the folding tables, the steel fire pan, the bags of charcoal, the cans of lighter fluid, the plastic buckets for hauling water, the rain tarp and its aluminum poles, the cast-iron Dutch ovens for frying bacon and baking pineapple upside-down cake, the huge coffee urn—almost every one of the hundred-odd items that normally went on board, the whole Grand Canyon kit and caboodle, was left behind. They were not even carrying a single bottle of gin or tequila—an omission that underscored the ruthless minimalism and extreme commitment of this enterprise.

With the preliminary loading complete, each man now headed into the pantry to build himself a couple of sandwiches and select a few pieces of fruit.

---

* Starting in 1976, in response to sanitation problems inside the canyon, Park Service regulations have required all river runners to "containerize" their human waste in rocket boxes and deposit the contents at a sewage-treatment facility at the end of their trip. The rule remains in effect to this day.

These items were duly deposited inside the cooler. Then, together, they rolled the trailer through the doors of the boathouse and into the parking lot, where they dropped the trailer's hitch over the towing ball on the rear end of the little van that served as Petschek's mobile home between river trips during the summer.

The vehicle's boxlike appearance—brown, windowless, and drab—suggested that it was nothing more than a retired delivery truck. But with the same care and patience that he lavished on everything else, Petschek had tricked out the interior with carpeting, a tiny sink and stove, a narrow bed with a Navajo rug for a quilt, and a set of brown-and-orange curtains. He called it Franklin, a name that admirably captured the vehicle's spirit of even-keeled sobriety and restraint.

~

Right around the time that they were locking down the ball hitch on the trailer and hooking up the brake lights, their driver and timekeeper showed up.

Cliff Taylor was a CPA from Las Vegas who moonlighted as a quasi-professional gambler and whose most memorable encounter with the canyon had taken place several years earlier when he and a friend attempted to conduct a misguided float down the river using truck-tire inner tubes. The highlight of this distinctly unpleasant experience was being passed by a dory trip—at which point Taylor, like Grua before him, had instantly fallen in love with the wooden boats and eventually pestered his way into a job with Litton. Unlike Grua, however, he had proved himself to be resoundingly devoid of any rowing talent and was an unmitigated disaster as a boatman. After several seasons in which he set and then broke some impressive records by racking up more wrecks than any other oarsman, the damage Taylor inflicted became so extensive and costly that Litton had no choice but to fire him—which had only heightened Taylor's ardor for the canyon. By the summer of 1983, he was willing to do almost anything that would allow him to retain his connection to the river, and when Grua had called to ask if Taylor would be willing to help out with the logistics of the speed run, he was only too happy to say yes.

Taylor's assistant was a young woman named Anne Marie Nicholson, who was about to start her second summer working as one of Litton's cooks. She hadn't been down the river yet this season, but all spring she had watched the shell-shocked dory crews stagger back to the boathouse and had seen how appalled and bewitched everyone was by the power of the river.

The plan was for Taylor and Nicholson to ride along during the long drive up to Lee's Ferry, where they would witness the launch and officially start the clock by noting down the start time. While the *Emerald Mile* embarked on her race down-canyon, Taylor and Nicholson would then drive Franklin and the trailer west back to Hurricane, where they would wait for twenty-four hours before making their way to the takeout at Pierce Ferry, where, if all went according to plan, they would meet the *Emerald Mile* sometime on Monday.

With the loading complete and the participants assembled, there was nothing left for them to do but stand around and wait until the clock struck 5:00 p.m., when the phone finally rang. It was Litton, calling to confirm that he had definitely *not* received a call from Richard Marks. This was the imaginary green light that Grua had been waiting for.

Time to hit the road, he announced, shooing everyone out the door before the phone could ring again.

In their haste, they held nothing in the way of a departure ceremony to mark the significance of the moment. Like Buzz Holmstrom's pioneering solo odyssey through the canyon forty-six years earlier, the reward of this venture, if there was one, would reside in the doing of the thing itself.

~

The first stage of the three-hour trip took them south across the Arizona state line, then east toward the base of the Grand Staircase, a staggered line of cliffs and terraces that extend like an immense ziggurat across the most remote section of the North Rim country. The evening was warm and clear, and Petschek drove with the windows down.

On the far side of the little Mormon town of Fredonia, they turned south again, and soon the road began to ascend the great dome of the Kaibab Plateau. Evening was drawing near, and the lengthening shadows began to soften the shaggy bark of the juniper trees lining the road and the cream-colored outcroppings of limestone.

Just east of Jacob Lake, they continued along Highway 89A, and as they descended the switchbacks on the far side of the Kaibab monocline, they were greeted by a vision unlike anything else in the West.

Up ahead, the Jurassic sandstones and shales of the Vermillion Cliffs were flaring with the last rays of the setting sun. Far off to the south, forty miles away along the edge of the Navajo reservation, the stratified layers of Triassic rock on the face of the Echo Cliffs were melting into viscous pinks and liquescent corals. Between those two sets of cliffs stretched a rock-strewn plain, and across its surface tidal currents of lavender light ebbed away before a surge of purple shadows that had been assembled by the gathering of night.

Somewhere deep within those shadows lay the upper end of the great canyon itself, running from the northeast to the southwest like an enormous serpent. Although none of them gave it much thought—for they had made this drive more times than they could remember—they were traversing the very same features toward which Cárdenas and his men had gazed from Desert View, their vantage on the South Rim, in the distant autumn of 1540.

By the time they pulled into the lodge at the tiny outpost of Marble Canyon, a favorite watering hole for river guides on pre-departure evenings, the heavens were sliding from violet to black. They lingered over their supper, and after they had finished they stepped out to see a sky salted with stars. Directly above, a vast wash of silver, the plume of the Milky Way, arched over a flawless midsummer's night in the high desert, a night polished by the soft shadows and the austere grace of the canyon country. And peeking over the cliffs like a Chinese lantern was a swollen, yellow globe that draped the folds of the surrounding plateau in moonbeams.

Then they started down the final leg of their drive, a six-mile stretch of road that took them past the water tower, beyond the ranger station, across an arroyo, and down to the place where all Grand Canyon river journeys begin.

～

As the Colorado completes the final stretch of its winding, fifteen-mile run from the base of the Glen Canyon Dam toward the break in the cliffs that marks Lee's Ferry, the river is normally gentle and calm. For these reasons, the boat ramp at the ferry is typically a place of repose for guides who gather there on the night before a trip to rig their boats and prepare for the buses and shuttles that will arrive with their passengers in the morning. Here the water seems to suspend its momentum and go languorous, as if pausing to inhale before embarking on the next and most tumultuous stage of its journey down from the distant Rockies to the no less distant Sea of Cortés.

At 10:30 p.m. on the night of June 25, however, the water was anything but peaceful. Out in the moonlight, the current seethed with dark energy, and the surface of the river was high enough that it had surged over the steel cable at the end of the ramp to which the boatmen typically tied off their bowlines. For this reason, the seven commercial oar rafts that had anchored for the night were all lashed to the frame of a large rig-truck parked at the water's edge. The boats were strung neatly in a row, and huddled on their aluminum decks, fast asleep, was a crew of weary river guides.

The leader of that expedition was a veteran boatman named Bruce Helin, and the senior guide was Michael Ghiglieri, whom everyone called the Doctor because he was one of the few boatmen with a PhD (awarded, in Ghiglieri's case, for the study of chimpanzees in Uganda). That very morning, the two men had reached Lake Mead with a different crew after an arduous two-week trip. Upon de-rigging their boats at Pierce Ferry, Helin and Ghiglieri had completed the long six-hour drive back to Lee's Ferry and re-rigged for their next trip, which was scheduled for the following morning. This kind of back-to-back schedule, which was known as a burn-around, did not allow the guides a single day off for rest or to do their laundry. When Helin's crew had arrived at the ferry a few hours earlier, however, they'd learned that they would be getting an unexpected break. Just as they'd started to unload, the ranger in charge had walked down to the ramp and announced that the river was temporarily closed.

Closed? Helin was confused. Such a thing had never happened before. The very idea seemed bizarre.

After offering a brief recap of the carnage that had taken place at Crystal, the ranger explained that the river might be reopened the following day, depending on what was decided up at the South Rim. But for the moment, all launches were suspended and no one was going anywhere.

A less exhausted crew might have received this news as an invitation to blow off some steam by heading up to the bar at the Marble Canyon Lodge or breaking out their guitars and treating the ferry's full-time residents—a flock of wigeons and a family of beavers—to an impromptu boatmen's concert. But Helin and Ghiglieri were interested in none of this. They were too drained to do anything more than unfurl their sleeping bags and bed down for the night. Thus, when Franklin finally rolled into the parking lot, the river's thrumming was mingled with the steady rumble of their snores.

Ghiglieri, who was on the last boat in line, was so worn-out that he slept straight through the flurry of activity that erupted when the truck arrived. He was undisturbed by the beam of headlights sweeping the rafts, and failed to register the crunch of tires on gravel as the trailer was backed into the river until the wheels were submerged. He even remained oblivious of the furious scrambling as the crew and their timekeepers loosened the buckles on the cam straps and heaved the boat off the back of the trailer. But when the dory's rockered bottom slapped the face of the river with a loud *ker-bloosh!* Ghiglieri's eyes popped open.

Who, he wondered, would be crazy enough to be raising such a ruckus in the middle of the night?

The furious whispers that emanated from a collection of shadowy figures next to the trailer provided no answer. But when he caught sight of the *Emerald Mile* bobbing in the shallows just a few yards away, the mystery resolved itself.

∼

Like every other guide on the river, Ghiglieri knew the story of the little green dory with the bright red gunwales—the horrific accident that had nearly consigned her to the flames several years earlier, her subsequent rescue and rehabilitation at the hands of the most fanatical boatman in the canyon, and the fact that if the speed record she had set in 1980 was ever to be broken, it would almost certainly have to take place during a runoff like the one they were witnessing now.

Ghiglieri shook his head with an amused and bleary-eyed indulgence. Although he did not appreciate being woken up, he harbored a grudging admiration for what was about to unfold. So along with Helin and the rest of the crew, who were by now also awake, he roused himself from his sleeping bag, grabbed his river sandals, and padded over to lend a hand.

Grua was determined to get on the water as quickly as possible before anyone who might have the power to stop them could arrive and put a halt to the venture. While the little crowd of onlookers stood in the shallows and steadied the dory, the three boatmen vaulted over the gunwales and scrambled into their places.

Grua, who was wearing a green life jacket and had a red bandana tied on his head, was the first aboard. After settling himself into the boatman's seat, he began threading the shafts of his oars through their locks. Wren, who was clad in a blue life vest and a dark blue splash jacket with rubber gaskets around the neck and the wrists, sent the dory wobbling from side to side as he scrambled across the deck toward the front footwell and took his place in the bow. Petschek, who was wearing a bright yellow vest and had neoprene booties on his feet, was the last aboard and took the seat in the stern.

Grua needed just a moment or two to complete a few last-minute tasks—knotting the cords to the leashes that would keep the oars tied to the boat if they tipped, shifting his weight sharply from side to side to confirm that the boat was properly trim, and extending his legs to place his feet against the two-inch dowel that served as a foot brace. Then, with tense deliberation, everyone sat and waited for Cliff Taylor to give them the signal that it was time to start.

When Taylor indicated that they were getting close, Grua took up the handles of his oars and gently swung the boat around so that the bow was facing the shore and the stern was pointed toward the river. Taylor counted down the seconds—and at precisely 11:00 p.m., Grua leaned back and hauled sharply on his oars.

The instant the hull penetrated the main current, the boat felt as if it had been shunted onto a set of rails and coupled to a runaway freight train. They shot downstream with a whoosh whose rush was magnified by the darkness and deepened even further by the knowledge that they were alone in that darkness, hurtling through the gateway to the canyon and everything that lay beyond.

"Wow," Wren murmured to himself. "This thing is *moving.*"

~

As the dory hurtled downstream, the guides and the timekeepers onshore found themselves lapped by successive waves of envy, resentment, and yearning. Amid these emotional undercurrents, none of them noticed that the dory's departure was being observed in a very different spirit by another group of boaters, a pod of noncommercial river runners from New Mexico led by Charles Zemach, a theoretical physicist who worked at the Los Alamos National Laboratory.

Having anchored their inflatable rafts at the ferry earlier that afternoon, Zemach and his group had driven up to Marble Canyon to grab a late dinner and arrived back at the ferry just as Grua was spearing the stern of the *Emerald Mile* into the main current. Zemach was neither amused by nor appreciative of what was taking place. In fact, he was rather offended.

Like all private boaters, Zemach and his companions had been obliged to place their names on a multiyear waiting list to secure a coveted permit for their trip. Now, a trio of yahoos had jumped the queue and were poaching a trip while the river was closed.

Zemach didn't know who these boatmen were or why they were launching under the cover of darkness on the near side of midnight. But what they were doing was evidently unlawful and potentially dangerous, and these were not things that he, Zemach, was prepared to overlook or ignore.

When morning arrived, he would find the ranger in charge at Lee's Ferry and let him know what had taken place.

~

Meanwhile, the little crowd of river guides continued staring into the darkness. For a few seconds the *Emerald Mile*'s crescent-shaped silhouette was etched perfectly by the moonbeams coruscating like hammered silver in the current.

The light held the dory for a moment.

And then, just like that, she was gone, swallowed up by the canyon.

When the rapids are mentioned, I forget everything else.
They cast a spell on me. Let's ride them all!

—Georgie White

Kenton Grua sets up to smash through the main wave in Crystal.

21

The Old Man Himself

And in the great wink of the moon
the river blazed more brightly than elves' gold.

—THOMAS WOLFE

DURING the early years of dory guiding, back when Martin Litton's crew was still struggling to unlock the secrets of the river, it wasn't unusual for one of the novice guides to commit a series of errors—flipping over and over again or hitting a long sequence of rocks—and find himself worrying that he might not have what it took to become a boatman. Under these circumstances, an older guide such as Kenton Grua or Regan Dale would often take the demoralized rookie aside and let him in on a little secret. If you truly want to learn to read white water, they would tell him, then study a rapid by moonlight. Moonbeams reverse the patterns of light and shadow, etching the surface and illuminating every facet and ripple in a way that daylight never can. Mysteries that are inscrutable at noon reveal themselves at midnight, enabling an oarsman not only to see the current but also to *understand* it—where it wanted to go, where it was actually headed, and why.

That was never more true than on a night like this, especially along the upper length of the canyon before the rims receded into the sky and the walls rose more than a mile above the surface of the river. In this initial stretch, as the Colorado began boring toward the great dome of the Kaibab Plateau, the white radiance lit up the surface of the water, burnishing the complex matrix of lines and waves, eddies and boils, with such clarity that even in those places where the river was blanketed by the deep pockets of shadow cast by the canyon walls—places where the moonbeams couldn't reach the water—Grua and his crew avoided switching on their searchlight, preferring instead to ride the luminous night.

Four miles downstream from the ferry, they shot beneath the twin spans of the Navajo Bridge, the last place a vehicle could cross the Colorado for four hundred miles. The bridge, which arced more than 450 feet above the river, marked the threshold where the industrialized world receded for good and was overtaken by the primeval world at the bottom of the canyon.

Their calculus was straightforward. At 70,000 cfs, the current was already moving at roughly 6 mph. To have a shot at breaking the record, however, the boatmen would need to achieve a total speed of somewhere between 9 and 10 mph through ceaseless, furious rowing. In addition to the enormous physical demands this would place on them, it would leave absolutely no margin for error. Any loss of time for any reason—extracting themselves from an eddy, righting the boat after a flip, repairing a broken oar—would have to be made up with even more speed. In addition, they would have to keep an eye open for river patrols and do their best to avoid the rangers. A helicopter would be a bad sign, signaling detainment and possible arrest, with whatever consequences might follow.

How those constraints might add up was impossible to predict. Their aim was simply to keep the dory's throttle wide open, especially during the daylight hours, when they would be surfing through the fastest segment in the Granite Gorge, which also contained most of the big white water. But first they would have to make it through this night—a challenge whose magnitude seemed to grow larger just beyond the bridge as the walls closed up and the cliffs began to ascend, bluntly foreclosing any possibility of retreat. From this point on, every stroke of their oars would usher them deeper into the earth, deeper into the past, and closer to the rapids that awaited them in the heart of the canyon.

~

As Grua pulled and recovered, pulled and recovered, he paused at the end of every third or fourth stroke to steal a glance over his shoulder and peer downstream for the telltale blur of whiteness that would signal a rapid. In the moonlit stretches, he could discern the glimmer of the wave tops. But in the long reaches where everything went black, he was forced to rely on what he could feel—the subtle tremors that the river sent up through the blades and shafts of the oars into his fingers and hands, and from there to those places where his knowledge of the river resided. As he felt his way downstream, the map of the canyon that he carried in his memory scrolled smoothly along the surface of his mind.

Meanwhile, Wren and Petschek were relying on a different set of sensory impressions to perform their job, the crucial task of high-siding. Drawing on their own innate feel for the river and its hydraulics, which they could sense by tuning their ears and by gripping the gunwales, they braced for each oncoming wave with a subtle lean of the shoulders here or there, and, when necessary, executing an explosive thrust of their torsos to maintain the boat's equilibrium. Each move was coordinated at bow and stern, performed at precisely the right moment, with just the right amount of force to counteract the current and keep the dory upright. This work unfolded in wordless harmony as all three members of the crew moved together, enabling boat and crew to merge with the current in a kind of dance, a ballet, that became an expression of the river itself.

Such teamwork was possible because, among the three of them, they boasted more than forty years of experience on the Colorado, years that had imparted the sort of understanding that could not be replicated by other means, and which now compensated for the advantages that they lacked: the unbridled energy and the fast-twitch muscle fibers of twenty-one-year-olds. Their wisdom and their ability to orient themselves in relation to the geometry of the river corridor—to calibrate their progress, to ration their resources, to brace for what lay ahead—were critical to the pacing of a marathon such as this. Without those assets, they wouldn't have stood a ghost of a chance. Yet, within the first hour, each man understood that although this storehouse of knowledge counted for quite a bit, it also amounted to nothing at all, because the river they were riding was something entirely new—a creature that did not resemble even the swollen torrent that they had encountered on their most recent trip, less than three weeks earlier. This was sobering and strange, but also deeply thrilling.

For more than twenty years, the boatmen of the Grand Canyon had lived and worked on a diminished Colorado, a river hobbled and constrained by a dam that most of them felt should never have been built. But now, with this flood, time had been reversed, and the past, for a brief and intoxicating moment, had switched places with the present. This was the Old Man himself, unbound, a thing of monstrous and terrible beauty. To be swept into its embrace, to race over its ancient bed of billion-year-old bedrock atop a watery crescendo that might never come down again, to contend with those challenges in the middle of the night while rowing faster than they ever had in their lives—that was a thing to marvel at, even more, perhaps, than the speed record itself.

In short, this was their only chance to meet the river that had flowed through the dreams of John Wesley Powell. Like Powell and his crew had done more than a hundred years earlier, they were now rocketing into the Great Unknown.

～

As they shot downstream in the darkness, what they noticed first was how much had simply disappeared. In this upper stretch, virtually every major feature—the keeper holes, the crashing laterals, the ribbons of current twisting upon themselves beneath the surface—had been washed out by the discharges from the dam. This liquid express lane that was whisking them downstream had neutralized obstacles that could have presented nightmare challenges in the dark. Thus, for a few delicious moments along that upper stretch, they found themselves toying with the possibility that their ordeal might be less arduous than they had initially feared.

Was this going to be a cinch? Grua wondered.

The answer arrived shortly after 1:00 a.m., as they entered a necklace of nine chain-linked rapids known as the Roaring Twenties and encountered the first of the bizarre hydraulics that would plague them for the rest of the trip. Here the eddy fences were massive, and the standing waves—which were supposed to be stationary—were milling on the surface of the river like a herd of coyote-spooked cattle, shifting position without warning, mindlessly colliding into one another or collapsing upon themselves with thunderous explosions. Trying to feel their way past these obstacles on the fly felt alien and surreal. It also scared the dickens out of them.

At 21 Mile Rapid, they had to dodge a series of whirlpools, huge and glistening in the dark. Then at 24.5, most of the current was flinging itself directly into the side of a limestone cliff on the right side of the river. Just to the left of that obstacle, the water formed three separate eddies, each adjacent to the next, a triple barrier between the main current and the shore.

The *Emerald Mile* didn't cut through these features with her normal grace. Instead, she was batted about like a cork, slammed from all sides. Each time she rose and fell to meet another swell, her bottom slapped down and a vicious crack reverberated through her chines and gunwales. The blows rattled not only the boat but also her white-knuckled crew, who were now wrestling in earnest with their biggest fear—the possibility that an exceptionally violent hit would fling one of them overboard and whisk him off in the dark.

The always-meticulous Petschek had foreseen this possibility and purchased Maglites for each of them to wear around his neck. But this would do little good in a stretch such as the Roaring Twenties, where the roar of the water would drown out a swimmer's cries as he was swept into the night. That notion would haunt them later, when they had time to think about it.

Around 2:15 a.m., they punched through the last of the Twenties and entered the Redwall, a limestone corridor whose landmarks, lost in darkness, flashed past almost faster than they could register. On the right at Mile 32, was Vasey's Paradise, where a waterfall burst from the side of a cliff and cascaded through a hanging garden of ferns and flowers. Two miles beyond that on the left lay Nautiloid Canyon, where the rocks were speckled with Paleozoic fossils. And several miles farther downstream, at Mile 40, was the site where the Bureau of Reclamation had drilled the test bores for the first of the two Grand Canyon dams.

These were some of the most interesting and provocative spots along the upper canyon, places where no dory trip would ever fail to stop.

The *Emerald Mile* blazed past them all.

~

They didn't talk much. The demands of reading the water were too intense for banter, and what little communication passed between them unfolded in clipped code: a warning about the current at Mile 36, where the water was racing beneath an overhanging rock; a quick word to keep an eye out for the President Harding Rapid at Mile 44, where the river was piling up against a midstream boulder. For the most part, each man kept silent and concentrated on his job until, once every fifteen or twenty minutes, whoever was in the cockpit would suddenly ship his oars and call out, "Okay, *go!*"

This was a key element of the plan. To prevent themselves from burning out, each oarsman rowed furiously for fifteen or twenty minutes until he neared exhaustion. Then he would call for a switch, and leap toward the stern or the bow while his replacement scrambled into the cockpit. The order of rowing—first Grua, then Petschek, then Wren—remained more or less the same, with each boatman circling the decks from cockpit to stern to bow as the dory raced downstream in the dark.

As the night wore on, the flat-out rowing and the ceaseless high-siding began to take a toll. By 4:10 a.m. as they passed Saddle Canyon, a tributary at Mile 47, the fatigue had begun showing up in the place that starts to hurt first, their hands. Now when it came time for each oarsman to give up his place in the cockpit, his fingers would refuse to uncurl, forcing him to slide his fist off the end of the oar. As he settled himself in the stern and peered downstream, he would straighten his fingers one by one, gently massaging them back to life.

In their oarsmanship, all three men were evenly matched. But as they penetrated deeper into the canyon, Petschek and Wren found themselves increasingly reliant on Grua to gauge what lay ahead. For years, he had been making careful notes, anticipating what the high water would do along each bend and curve, and now that homework began to pay off. As they shot downstream, he called off the invisible mile markers and features one by one with uncanny accuracy. "Astonishing man," Petschek would later remark, shaking his head at the memory. "He'd never run that water before, but Kenton had done it in his mind."

Around 4:45 a.m., Grua warned that they were nearing the top of Nankoweap, one of the longest rapids in the canyon, which now featured a series of heavy laterals—angular, rolling waves that built on a cycle of roughly ten seconds and crashed together at the center of the river. As the crew powered through this crosshatched section of current, they all sensed a subtle change in the night. Although the bottom of the canyon was still bathed in darkness, the narrow ribbon of sky framed by the walls had begun to lighten, shifting from black to violet, and the rimrock was clearly visible.

For the next hour they raced through the false dawn as the river, wide and broad in this reach, swung sinuously from side to side. At Mile 60, they entered a new layer of rock, the brown and coarse-grained Tapeats sandstone, and passed the confluence point where the turquoise waters of the Little Colorado River entered from the left. Then, just before 6:15 a.m., as they were approaching a rapid called Chuar at Mile 65.5, the first rays of sunlight angled over the rim and lit the upper bands on the eastward-facing cliffs like the inside of a cantaloupe.

"Ah, thank God," Wren said to himself. "We made it through the night."

Reaching into the bow hatch, Wren pulled out their green, stainless-steel thermos. Time for coffee. While unscrewing the cap, he failed to note that Chuar—normally no more than a riffle—was unusually active, filled with waves that were breaking from both the left and the right in an agitated herringbone pattern. One of these now slammed into the bow, almost flipping the boat and thoroughly drenching Wren. That wave was odd—it wielded a power, an alacrity, that Wren had never seen on this stretch before. It almost seemed as if the river had deliberately reached out and slapped him across the face, as if to say, *Wake up, dammit!*

Casting further thoughts of coffee aside, they shook off their fatigue and focused on the current with a renewed intensity, ignoring the dramatic vista that had just opened up as the walls widened to reveal one of the broadest views along the entire river corridor. If the crew of the *Emerald Mile* had bothered to look up at that moment, they would have spotted the section of the South Rim where García López de Cárdenas stood in the distant autumn of 1540, baffled and disoriented by his first encounter with the great chasm looming at his feet.

The Desert View Watchtower, a stone citadel now marking that location, was the only building on the rim that was visible from the bottom of the canyon. Under normal conditions, its slender silhouette seemed to underscore the remoteness of the world below the rims. At that moment, however, something was taking place up there that would, in just a few hours, bring these two realms colliding together.

~

A few minutes after sunrise at the little heliport on the South Rim, an orange-and-white chopper lifted off the tarmac, clattered above the main buildings at Grand Canyon Village, and passed over the corral for the Grand Canyon mule train. Seconds later, an ocean of air abruptly opened beneath the belly of the helicopter and the pilot initiated his descent into the night-chilled shadows below.

The ship angled along the steep, banded formations of rock until it reached the base of the first set of cliffs, then skimmed across the Esplanade, the flat, cactus-studded bench that extends north for nearly a mile. At the far edge of the bench, the pilot passed over another stomach-churning drop-off and plunged a thousand feet through another series of rock layers into the recesses of the Inner Gorge. There, more than a vertical mile into the earth, the helicopter caught the current of air suspended just above the river and raced downstream between the black walls of the Vishnu schist.

The flight took less than ten minutes, and by 6:30 a.m. the pilot had landed on the right side of the river at Mile 98 and deposited his passenger, a young man who zipped out of his flight suit to reveal the standard uniform of a river ranger—a short-sleeved khaki shirt and olive-green river shorts. His name was John Thomas, and on this particular morning his assignment was to prevent a repeat of the chaos that had unfolded the previous day by enforcing the "commercial closure" of Crystal.

When Thomas arrived, the bottom of the canyon seemed to be savoring the remaining minutes of coolness before the sun leered over the Powell Plateau, chasing away the shadows and turning the place into a furnace. For the moment, he had Crystal to himself and was thus able to take his time looking over the rapid.

Out in the main current, the immense standing wave was crashing upon itself and flinging spray high into the air. That wave looked as bad as ever, possibly even worse. But between the right shore and the shoulder of the big wave, Thomas could see that a lane of relatively smooth water was still sluicing through the tamarisk trees.

His orders were to stop every boat that came downstream, direct the passengers to walk around the rapid, and lecture the guides on the critical importance of tucking into those trees and avoiding the explosion wave. There would be no exceptions. With no sign of the boats that he knew were headed his way, Thomas gathered up his binoculars, his radio, and his clipboard and parked himself in a patch of shade to await their arrival.

~

Thirty-two miles above Crystal, the crew of the *Emerald Mile* were now able to spot things that had been invisible to them in the dark. As the early-morning light washed the bottom of the canyon, they could see that the eddies were full of flotsam, shattered tree branches and battered bits of driftwood. They also began to catch sight of other river expeditions, most still onshore with their boats tied up. The only people awake in those camps were the boatmen on kitchen duty, boiling water for coffee. As Grua and his team whipped past, the boatmen stared quizzically, wondering what a lone dory was doing on the river at this time of morning.

Around 7:20 a.m., the *Emerald Mile* reached Mile 76 and prepared to enter Hance, a jumbled stretch of standing waves studded with enormous boulders and ledges that offers one of the most complicated sections of white water in the canyon. Because the crew had no intention of stopping to scout, they had only a few seconds to take stock and register that the action ahead was violent enough to render a normal run down the center completely off-limits. Grua, who was at the oars, decided to go right and attempt to ride out a wave train that they normally sought to avoid. With flawlessly timed high-siding from Petschek and Wren, they flew over the rollers without a hitch, but the power of the waves left them stunned.

At the bottom of Hance, the walls on either side of the river closed up and the cheerful morning sunshine was abruptly cut off—a fitting marker for perhaps the most ominous of the canyon's transition points. Here, the Colorado narrowed dramatically and the river entered the Upper Granite Gorge, the canyon's subbasement. As the walls tilted toward dead vertical, it felt as if a set of massive stone gates had slammed shut behind them, a sensation that deepened as the river rose to a new level of fury.

Squeezed to less than half its width upstream, the current now began pushing against itself, and as the turbulence increased, so did its power. The water seethed and churned, folding back on itself and detonating with a ferocity that took the boatmen's breath away. Now brute force, plus several additional seconds, were required to execute pivots that had been performed upstream with little more than a deft flick of an oar blade. Even the smallest mistake—striking a wave at slightly the wrong angle, allowing the dory to brush against an eddy fence—would flip them over in a heartbeat. And added to the mix were a slew of new hydraulic features, particularly when it came to the big waves.

The size of some of those haystacks was shocking—almost twenty feet from trough to crest, dimensions normally found on the open ocean. But even more disconcerting was how squirrelly they were. The faces of the waves were rapidly changing direction, forcing the oarsman to make furious corrections to meet them squarely as they hit with staccato bursts from every direction:

> *Bam—a strike from the left—*
> *—wham—a blow from the right—*

—with two more ahead, no chance of correcting for both, and a third looming directly in the center just downstream—

> *—bam—*
> *—wham—*
> *—BAM!—*

The dory reeled—they were about to go sideways and broach; but Wren and Petschek hurled their weight from one side to the next, then back again. The waves were coming in every direction, drenching them in sheets of water that were heavy, green, shockingly cold.

Wren shook his head to clear his eyes—he had an ice-cream headache, he was *totally* soaked, the water was freezing—but they were *upright*, they were *intact*, and they were washing into the tail waves, which were bottlenecked between two massive eddies reaching toward the center from opposite sides of the river.

Grua rode the rooster tail of current between them, threading perfectly, keeping them from slipping off. But then a whirlpool loomed. It was moving in their direction. He corrected again—cranking sharply, pulling with his right oar while pushing on the left—*pushing hard, ramming the oar handle into the pit of his shoulder as he shoved with a twisting motion that came from his entire torso*, and the dory snapped around, spinning 180 degrees in half a second, and as the boat finished the turn, Grua leaned far forward, dug his blades into the water and *exploded*, pulling on both oars, spearing the boat down the center of the river, splitting the smooth water between the vortex and the eddy fence and— *whoosh*—they were through, bobbing in the heaves of the spent rapid. But now Petschek, who was in the stern, was shouting directions about what lay ahead.

Grua listened but didn't turn around. He could feel equal resistance with both oar blades, but now the right blade began to move easier. He was slipping toward the eddy so he took a second pull on the right, sending them back into the main current, and snatched a quick glance over his shoulder—the river was bending ahead, he'd need to correct for that.

—*Boil*, shouted Petschek. *On your right!*—

Another correction.

—*Whirlpool*, cried Petschek. *On your left!*—

Another correction.

And *another*.

And so it went. In this manner, they slammed through the washed-out bottlenecks along the upper part of the gorge. Into Sockdolager and Grapevine and 83 Mile. Then past Zoroaster and 85 Mile and into Pipe Creek and the Devil's Spittoon, a monstrous eddy along the outside end of a vicious series of S-curves. The rides were intense and brutal. But, by *God*, they were truly flying.

At Mile 90, they smashed through Horn Creek, and three miles downstream, they rammed past Granite, then started their approach toward Hermit, every boatman's favorite, because it featured some of the largest and smoothest waves in the canyon, each more exhilarating than the last. Here they had their first unpleasant brush with another expedition.

It was a commercial oar-raft trip on its fifth day on the water and led by a guide named Jimmy Hendrick. One of the wilder characters in the canyon, Hendrick enjoyed shocking his passengers by catching a scorpion, tearing off the tail, and popping the live creature into his mouth. He was leading his squadron out of the eddy at the top of Hermit, just as the *Emerald Mile* came tearing around the bend with Petschek at the oars. This meant that both boats would enter the tongue together, breaking the unwritten rule that forbade an upstream boatman from attempting to pass a downstream craft at the head of a rapid.

The offense was unintended, but Hendrick, who had no idea about the speed run and was baffled by the sudden intrusion of this rogue dory, was livid. As the rubber oar raft and the wooden dory rode side by side, Hendrick pulled off an impressively coordinated feat, cranking on his oars and squaring his bow to meet the face of each oncoming wave while simultaneously hurling an uninterrupted stream of verbal abuse at Petschek. Up the face of one wave, down into the trough of the next, Hendrick damned the doryman for his outrageous boatmanship, his flaming incompetence, and his unpardonable lack of river etiquette.

This confrontation was completely at odds with the culture of the river, the sort of incident that, under normal circumstances, would require a pause for an apology to smooth things over. But right then, Petschek didn't give a damn what Hendrick's problem was. Like Grua and Wren, he was focused intently on the next big obstacle, the one they'd been dreading all night, which was just downstream and coming up fast.

Crystal.

~

Just before 9:00 a.m., John Thomas, the ranger stationed at Mile 98, caught sight of the first of the big motor rigs rounding the bend upstream. Gathering up his things, he clomped down the footpath to the little cove just above the rapid that formed a parking inlet.

Using his clipboard as a semaphore, Thomas waved the rig and a second one that was following it into the cove and grabbed hold of the bowline. Leaving the swamper to tie the boat off to the trunk of a tamarisk, he clambered on board to have a conference with the trip leader and lay down the rules. Then, together, he and the guides started organizing the walk-around.

This was done stepwise. In the first stage, the passengers were helped off the boat and sent on their march downstream in the direction of Thank God Eddy. As the passengers winded their way through the boulders of the little delta, the guides and the swampers tramped in single file up to the scouting terrace to discuss how to cheat the explosion wave.

Several minutes later, another expedition appeared, then a third, and before long the Crystal Creek delta was a hubbub of color and activity. A flotilla of nearly a dozen brightly colored rigs of all shapes and sizes was now wedged in the inlet—all rubber, not a dory among them. A smaller cluster of rigs was also gathered at the pickup eddy below the rapid. Between those two points, nearly a hundred passengers, all of whom were still wearing their orange life jackets, were scattered along the shore, picking their way among the bushes or perched like herons atop the boulders to watch their guides make their runs.

The boatmen did their best to hug the right-hand shore as closely as possible, even if this meant bouncing over a few of the submerged rocks or getting raked by the branches of a tamarisk. One or two of the boats lost their angle and flirted with the shoulder of the standing wave. But none of them got clobbered. Below the rapid, a couple of oar rafts were unable to break out of the main current, failed to make the pull-in above Thank God Eddy, and were carried off downriver. But the motor rigs gunned their engines, rammed the eddy at full throttle, and gathered up the stranded passengers, with the aim of transferring them back to their rafts downriver.

Nobody flipped. Nobody got hurt. No one was thrown overboard. As the runs were successfully completed, John Thomas found himself nodding in satisfaction. Everything was proceeding smoothly, exactly as planned.

Within half an hour the congestion had already started to ease, and only a handful of rigs were in the parking inlet. Then around nine thirty, Thomas climbed aboard one of the last of the big boats—a giant, thirty-seven-foot motor rig. He was walking down the diamond-plated aluminum deck to talk to the guide when he glanced upriver and spotted something strange rounding the turn above the rapid.

It was a dory, a little Briggs boat, the first one of the day.

Her beryl-green hull and bright red gunnels seemed to shimmer in the morning air. She appeared to have a shallow draft—her hull was riding far too high in the water for her to be carrying much dunnage. And oddly, only three people were on board, all boatmen, judging by the colors of their life jackets.

Each man was staring rigidly downstream toward the entrance to the rapid, and Thomas could see that they were making no effort to pull in or slow down. Clearly, they had no intention of stopping.

Hell, they weren't even going through the motions of pretending.

22

Perfection in a Wave

Do or do not. There is no try.

—YODA

As the *Emerald Mile* neared the top of Crystal and its crew was preparing to parse out their approach to the rapid, their attention was drawn to a scene on the right-hand shore—the boats bobbing in the cove, the guides clustered along the terrace, the swarm of passengers dotting the hillside, the shoreline, and every point in between.

Then they took a closer look at the big motor rig in the cove. Standing on the deck, clearly visible and facing directly toward them, was a man in a ranger's uniform. He had a radio in one hand, a clipboard in the other, and he was shielding his eyes with the clipboard as he eyeballed the dory.

Wren, who was in the bow, spotted him first and snapped his head away immediately in order to break off any possible eye contact.

Eye contact was a bad idea.

Wren knew that if the ranger motioned for them to pull into the cove while they were looking directly at him, there would be no question that they had blatantly ignored the command, thereby compounding their sins. So, in the manner of a teenager hoping to coast past a policeman who has just watched him blaze through a stoplight, Wren kept his gaze pointed downstream and earnestly repeated to himself, *Don't look at the ranger. . . . Don't look at the ranger. . . . Don't look at the ranger. . . .*

All the while, of course, Wren was carefully examining the ranger out of the corner of his eye and asking himself, with equal earnestness, *What's he thinking? What's he doing with that clipboard? How much trouble are we in?*

Directly behind Wren, Petschek and Grua were conducting an abridged form of the same debate.

"What do you think we should do if he waves us in?" asked Grua, who was once again at the oars.

"Wave back?" replied Petschek.

That had a nice ring to it. Petschek's suggestion gave voice to the kind of brio that had launched this enterprise in the first place. Inside his heart, however, each boatman knew perfectly well that the rationalizations upon which their entire escapade had been based were bogus. No permission, formal or informal, stated or implied, had ever been given for this venture. They also knew that the responsibility of the ranger on the motor rig was to report what was about to unfold directly to the superintendent. And they understood that in the eyes of a man like Richard Marks, this stunt of theirs would be deemed offensive and wrong, a flagrant bid to thumb their noses at the rangers and ridicule the law.

And so, as Grua and his crew skimmed across the final few yards that separated them from the top of the rapid, the tiny pieces of hope to which each of them had been clinging, the little lies they'd been telling themselves all night long about how it might be possible to skate through the canyon without anybody's noticing and to keep this whole thing a secret—all of that blew away like the last leaves on the upper branches of a November cottonwood.

Yet delusion is a powerful thing. Which is why, there at the top of the rapid, in the moment of suspended composure before the river picked up speed and all hell started breaking loose, the three boatmen continued to fan the dying embers of their belief that, despite all evidence to the contrary, things might yet work out.

"We fantasized that it might be okay, but we kinda knew the truth too," Grua would later tell a friend. "We knew we had God on our side, though."

∼

As Grua and his companions maintained their rigid downstream stares, John Thomas found himself wrestling with an entirely different tangle of conflicting impulses.

When the *Emerald Mile* first appeared around the bend, Thomas knew nothing about the speed run. (Word of the *Emerald Mile*'s illicit departure had been reported to the ranger at Lee's Ferry, but by the time this news had reached the South Rim, Thomas was already aboard his chopper and headed for Crystal.) But in addition to being a ranger, Thomas was also a boatman who belonged to the River Unit—which meant that the instant he spotted Grua and his companions, a little train of dominoes swiftly tipped over in his mind.

"I knew *exactly* who it was and what they were doing," he would recall nearly thirty years later, chuckling at the memory.

He knew a few other things too, starting with how this stunt was going to put him into one hell of a fix. Which, in an unexpected twist, was now dovetailing with some rather complicated feelings that Thomas harbored about himself: who he was, what he did, and the place he occupied in the canyon.

Thomas's time on the river had straddled the golden age of guiding, the period in which visitation had skyrocketed from a handful of eccentrics such as Martin Litton and Georgie White to tens of thousands of river vacationers. Thus he was old enough to remember the freedom that had prevailed in the canyon country before the hordes of tourists had started pouring in, back when a man could launch a boat and disappear downriver without having to ask for permission or wait in line, devoid of any constraints other than those imposed by the water and the rocks, an adventure in the best sense of the word. And as those days receded ever further into the rearview mirror, there were moments— right now being one of them—when Thomas was forced to wonder about it all.

In truth, no one who had tasted those liberties could look back on that time with anything other than a deep sense of longing. Like everyone else who had known the river during that era of innocence, Thomas mourned its passing and privately grieved that it would never return. Which is why part of him sometimes rebelled at the very restrictions he sought to enforce, if only because rules—even rules that were universally accepted as necessary and good— seemed to cut so directly against the spirit that the river had once embodied. This sense of loss now prompted Thomas to ponder a notion that was not merely unorthodox but, when viewed from a certain angle, downright subversive.

Was it possible, he wondered, that a measure of what had been lost—the thing that had once defined the essence of this place, the thing that was now in the process of disappearing forever—was *that very thing* perhaps being offered a chance to express itself one more time, fleetingly, irresponsibly, nobly, right here before him? And in light of that possibility, Thomas wondered, where did his truest allegiances lie—with the duties that he was supposed to be performing as a uniformed employee of the Department of the Interior? Or to a sense of duty that had nothing whatsoever to do with the law?

Officially, of course, Thomas could in no way condone any of the nonsense that was about to take place, which was misguided on so many levels that he didn't even know where to begin. This piece of performance art that Grua was trying to pull off was not only dangerous and irresponsible but just plain wrong. In addition to undermining the authority of the Park Service, dishonoring the tragedy that had already taken place at Crystal, and setting an example that might be followed by others—which could lead to God only knew what kind of craziness—Grua's stunt was an insult to the people up at the Glen Canyon Dam, who were even now desperately trying to prevent Lake Powell from blowing its gasket.

But setting all that aside for a moment, what did the man *behind* the badge actually think?

Well, as he stood on the deck of the motor rig and watched the *Emerald Mile* complete its approach, Thomas had to acknowledge that tremors of admiration and envy were pulsating through his entire body. Yes, this was scandalous and deplorable and unforgivably dumb. But at the same time, there was no way to deny that a speed run under these conditions took ferocious courage, a shining sense of vision, and a hellacious set of balls. And for that reason, his most visceral response to the quest unfolding before his eyes was pure and absolute. It was fricking *glorious*. Like anyone who had ever slid the blade of an oar into that magnificent ribbon of water, the only objection he could possibly have raised resided in Grua's egregious failure to call him up and ask if he wanted to be part of the damn thing.

In light of those sentiments, Thomas had no interest in forcing the crew of the *Emerald Mile* to pull over. And thus his dilemma, rooted in the supremely inconvenient truth that his responsibilities and his feelings in this matter were irreconcilably opposed. What was called for, it seemed, was a miniature piece of Kabuki theater in which each party could adopt an attitude of imperious indifference and pretend to ignore the other. So what he did was this—

He simply walked away.

He turned his back on the river, stalked off the deck of the motor rig, and started climbing the hill in the direction of the scouting terrace to watch the run unfold.

~

As Thomas enacted this charade, Grua was focusing on another ritual of his own—a liturgy reserved for the tops of the biggest rapids, one whose components lay halfway between a pilot's preflight checklist and a Zen monk's meditation mantra. Every boatman had one, and although the details varied, the basic outline was more or less the same.

First, you cup your hand in the river and run the water over the back of your neck and face to reduce the shock of what's coming. Then you spit into your palms and twirl your oar blades a time or two to make sure they're rotating smoothly. Finally, you begin talking yourself into a special mental space where you prepare for the threshold moment—the point where the world drops away, the jitters subside, and a cold resolve seizes the tissues of the chest and belly.

Grua drew several deep breaths and rolled his shoulders. The muscles in his arms and legs were now poised on a hair trigger, and his ears were cocked, tuned to the sharpened sound of the rapid, a roar that was no longer dulled by distance. He cast a quick glance toward the shore to gauge his speed, then snapped his gaze back to the current line, bending his mind to the task ahead, allowing his concentration to narrow to a tiny aperture that encompassed a few square yards of river and a frozen instant in time.

Listen. Stare. Breathe.

Just beyond the bowpost, he could discern the line where the river dropped off. Beyond that line, erratic bursts of spray were being hurled into the air by the invisible waves. And now, he waited for it.

At the top of every rapid, a moment comes when the topography of the water reveals itself. This happens in an instant; there is no preamble. One second you are approaching a flat horizon line; the next second, the contours and mysteries of what lies beyond are visible in all their fury. That final flash comes like a slap in the face, one whose sting is amplified by the knowledge that the choices you have made up to this point—your angle, your timing, your speed— are now set.

As he approached this moment, Grua processed a few last-second details. A wide slice of calmer water was sluicing past the right-hand shoreline—he could see that now. But that water was also shallow, studded with half-submerged boulders, and laced with broken tree limbs that stuck out like punji sticks.

"Do you think I should cut right?" Grua shouted over his shoulder, seeking confirmation from Petschek.

"You don't have a chance of doing it," cried Petschek. "Keep her straight!"

Then all three boatmen braced as the current seized the hull and slung them toward the biggest mess of white water that any Grand Canyon boatman, living or dead, had ever seen.

~

Perched atop the scouting terrace, John Thomas had a full view of the scene, and as he watched it unfold, he was overcome by a growing sense of dread.

Instead of hugging the right-hand shoreline so closely that he was kissing the edge of the riverbank and swatting away the branches on the tamarisk trees, Grua was facing forward and coolly coasting along the shoulder of the lateral wave, a route that would bypass the escape lane and take them straight into the main hole.

The approach was so wrong, so misguided, so willfully self-destructive, that Thomas couldn't quite believe his eyes. "What the hell are you guys thinking?!" he wondered. "Why are you all the way out there?"

Then it hit him. Having sneaked onto the river without consulting anyone, Grua and his crew didn't have the faintest clue as to what had taken place at Crystal during the previous thirty-six hours—and thus had no idea of the horror show in store for anyone who failed to spear through the lateral into the safety zone.

As Thomas watched them slide toward the maelstrom, he groaned inwardly with the knowledge that he had contributed to their error. Thanks to his decision to walk away, no one had told those clowns to get themselves to the right.

Now he had no choice but to stand on the terrace and watch, all the while exclaiming to himself, *No, no, no, no!*

~

Petschek would never forget how it looked as they slid into Crystal's maw and he got his first glimpse of the thing that rose beyond the hole.

"I remember looking downstream over the front of the boat, and there it was, a wall of water, absolutely vertical, that extended almost clear across the river," he later recalled. "Between two and three stories high, I think. Just a white wall of boiling water. I remember it occurred to me that we were going to need an awful lot of luck to make it. . . . It was so much bigger than our little dory."

The bottom face of the wall featured the kind of water that rivermen call glass. Smooth and unblemished, it rose cleanly for almost thirty feet, and within its whiteness was an aspect of deep green.

The top, however, was not glass. It was enraged and seething—a churning fury created by the wave's breaking at its apex.

To the men inside the dory, it seemed as if the entire river were attempting to surge over that wall, then falling back upon itself to create an endless, recycling grinder. It looked like some kind of psychotic animal, a Leviathan trying to eat its own entrails.

There was no turning away from this monster, and as they slid into its lair, Grua found himself marveling at its terrifying splendor.

"It wasn't a regular hole," he would later declare. "It was perfection in a hole."

The very last bit of control that Grua still had in his hands was deciding precisely where and with what angle the *Emerald Mile* would strike.

Somewhere on that rampart of water, he was convinced, was a sweet spot, a keyhole no wider than the dory's bowpost. There was no time to analyze where it might be hiding. But if he somehow managed to hit it exactly right, he just might find the seam in the cosmos and blast through to the other side.

~

From the shore, Thomas watched the dory bulldoze into the trough, strike the palisade of water, and begin clawing toward its crest. He could see Grua leaning forward, arms extended, pushing on his oar handles for all he was worth in the hope of gaining a few extra degrees of traction. He could see the shafts of the oars cambering under the strain, while far out at the ends, twin streams of water curled off the tip of each blade. And he could see something odd too. Because in that moment the man in the front of the boat, who was clad in a blue life vest, appeared to be doing something illogical—an act that seemed to fly in the face of the most basic survival instincts.

With the dory now tilted almost directly toward the sky, and with the crown of the wave looming an entire boat length above the tip of the bowpost, it made no sense for the man in the front—Wren—to be making any attempt at high-siding. His best option (his only option) was to treat his front footwell, the space beneath his seat where his legs rested, as a kind of foxhole. If he ducked down and curled himself into a ball, he might be able to shield himself from the cannonade of water that was about to erupt over the bow.

But as Thomas watched in disbelief, Wren did the opposite.

He sprang from his seat, lunged forward, and seized the gunwales on either side of the bow, anchoring himself to the front hatch so that his torso and head extended far out over the bowpost. With his hooked nose and hawkish face, Wren was now sticking off the front of the *Emerald Mile* like a chrome-plated swan on the hood of a runaway tractor trailer.

Wren's primary hope was that the shift in his body weight might somehow help drive the boat through the top of the wall of water. But as Thomas could see, the forces arrayed against the dory—the height of the wave and the volume of water cascading off the top—were simply too powerful to counteract. What the ranger didn't know, however, was that Wren was also hoping to tap into some currents of energy that transcended ordinary physics. If the mass and the density of the molecules in his body weren't enough to do the job, then perhaps the cosmic scales could be tipped in the *Emerald Mile*'s favor by a *non*linear force—like, say, the terminal velocity of rectitude or the angular acceleration of dumb luck. Or maybe when the river gods saw him perched out there on the dashboard, they would fathom just how badly he *wanted* and *needed* the dory to get through.

What Wren was doing, in effect, was performing an act of supplication, a plea for hydraulic clemency, hoping the river might condescend to allow the *Emerald Mile* to surf through the chaos on the shining fortitude of her own righteousness.

No dice.

As the boat reached the top of the wave, she corkscrewed while simultaneously falling back on herself—an end-over-end flip with a twist. The maneuver was complex and double-barreled, the sort of performance one might expect if a strand of DNA were to go into a swoon. The kinetics struck Thomas, who now had a perfect view of the interior of the dory, with her three boatmen clinging like terror-stricken cats to the decking as she performed these dual rotations, as a kind of macabre ballet.

It was horrifying to witness, yet it possessed a mesmeric dimension of refinement and symmetry that Thomas would later describe as a kind of intricate gyre—a "pirouette." But for Grua and his companions, it was brutal, blunt, and utterly perfunctory, as if Crystal had simply bent back its thumb and flicked them away like the cap on a bottle of beer.

"The flip was instantaneous—there was nothing rhythmic or graceful or easy about it at all—it was just *boom*," recalled Petschek, who was instantly dumped into the river.

Grua was holding his oars as tightly as he could, determined not to let go because they were the only thing that tied him to the boat. As the dory snapped upside down, they flew from his hands and he followed Petschek into the current.

As harsh as this treatment was for Petschek and Grua, it bore no comparison with the special punishment reserved for Wren.

In effect, the river was now wielding the *Emerald Mile* like a seventeen-foot-long sledgehammer, and the force of the entire boat, all eleven hundred pounds of her, was now concentrated in the bowpost. As she tipped and spun, her bow shot out of the water with astonishing speed. The head of that hammer swung fast and hard. Too fast and too hard for Wren to turn away or even flinch.

The bowpost drove upward into his face, smashing directly into his glabella, the part of the skull that sits between the eyebrows just above the top of the nose.

Then, like Petschek and Grua, he too was gone.

～

Each man now found himself at the mercy of the same hydrodynamics—the savage turbulence and the wrenching crosscurrents—that had dismantled Tour West's four-ton motor rig twenty-four hours earlier. Grua got off the easiest. He felt himself pulled down hard and twirled like a baton, but the current swiftly spat him back to the surface. When he blinked the water from his eyes, he saw his upside-down boat, less than an arm's length away. He seized hold, then he turned his head toward the sound of some wet gurgles and spotted Petschek, bobbing just upstream about twenty feet away.

Petschek had been pulled a bit farther beneath the surface, where he underwent the classic experience of feeling himself tumbled around like a load of laundry. But as with Grua, the river had released its grip after just a few seconds, permitting him to flounder toward the surface. A few hard strokes were enough to put him within reach of Grua's extended foot and grab on.

Both men were now connected to the boat.

At that moment, their priority was to right the dory, get her oars into the water, and lever her into Thank God Eddy before the current swept them into Tuna, the next rapid below Crystal. There was no time for discussion, but none was needed—both men knew the drill.

Each grabbed a section of the chine and hauled himself onto the slippery bottom of the boat, where, together, they took hold of the flip line, the strip of one-inch nylon webbing that Grua had wrapped around the outside of the hull. One man loosened the buckles; the other gathered up the slack. Then they stood up side by side, bracing their feet against the chine, and started leaning backward, allowing their bodies to extend as far as possible out over the water.

For a long pause it seemed as if the hull would refuse to give. Then the suction released with a pop and the boat started its turn.

As the bottom angled into the air, Grua and Petschek leaned out farther and farther until their bodies were nearly horizontal. Their combined weight was barely sufficient, so the turn was agonizingly slow, but after a minute of grunting labor they were nearly there. They needed only another degree or two for the boat to pass beyond its tipping point and the job would be complete.

And then, without any warning—*snap*.

As both men were dropped into the river with a splash, the hull retraced its arc and slammed back to its upside-down stance with a hollow *ka-THUNK*.

Treading water for the second time, they stared at the ragged splice of nylon in their hands. Frayed by the edges of the chine, the flip line had broken in two. Once again, the *Emerald Mile* was surging downstream toward Tuna with its bottom facing the sky—and now the current was carrying them perilously close to the minefield of subsurface boulders along the right-hand shore.

Any second, both men knew, those rocks were going to start demolishing the interior of the boat. They simply *had* to get her righted—a task that would be fairly simple with Wren's assistance. In a moment such as this, his help was critical.

Where the hell *was* he?

~

By some miracle, the concussive blow that Wren received from the bowpost had fallen short of knocking him unconscious. That was exceedingly lucky. If the impact had laid him out cold, he would probably have suffered the same fate as poor Bill Wert. Instead, Wren was fully cognizant when he hit the water.

His first move was to run his hand across his forehead and hold it up in front of his face to see if there was any blood. "What a stupid thing to do!" he would mutter years later. "I'm three feet underwater and I'm wiping my head to see if it's bleeding. Of course I didn't see any blood. And then I just got sucked down deep."

"Going deep" is a horrifying ordeal, an involuntary trip to the nethermost recesses of the river, the absolute bottom of the canyon.

This, by its very nature, is a poorly understood place, where the topography and the hydraulics can vary so radically, even within the space of a few yards, that no two visits are ever the same. Those who have been pulled down and permitted to return have brought back conflicting testimony. Some say it is a watery version of being locked inside a sarcophagus. Others describe currents so vicious and feral that it feels like being caught in the belly of a cement mixer. Many insist it is completely silent, but others report hearing an eerie hissing sound, a sinister dirge that is apparently created by the suspended particles of sediment as they sluice downstream. If the canyon has a symphonic requiem, this is it.

Despite those differing accounts, almost everyone undergoes the same sequence of trials. First, pressure builds in the inner ears, similar to the pain that scuba divers suffer, which grows worse as one is pulled deeper. Next comes the cold, an icy grip that seems to grow more frigid the deeper one descends. But the most terrifying aspect of the trip is watching the light vanish. As one is sucked toward the bottom, the color of the water changes from foamy white to bright blue . . . then deep emerald . . . and, finally, absolute black.

Wren avoided this chromatic deliquescence because he had his eyes screwed shut as he was sucked deep. He could sense that the river meant business. It felt as if a gang of thugs had seized his body and were now ramming it toward the riverbed with the deliberate aim of drowning him. When he finally opened his eyes, it was pitch-black and he had no idea which way was up.

His plan was to follow accepted wisdom and curl himself into a ball while waiting for the current to release him. But after several long seconds he found himself running out of air, so he began a long and desperate crawl toward what he hoped was the surface.

At first, he was swimming in darkness, but as his strength ebbed he started to see signs of light—faint and tremulous and far above.

He kept swimming, despite how heavy his arms and legs had grown; he felt as if lead weights had been attached to his limbs. Finally, several seconds past the point where he thought he could not muster another stroke, his head broke the surface and he drew a ragged breath of air.

When he cleared his eyes and caught his bearings, he could see that he was in the middle of the river, racing downstream. Off to the right, he caught a glimpse of the dory, upside down, with Grua and Petschek clinging to the sides.

"Okay," Wren told himself, "get to the boat—*get to the boat.*"

Then something seized him from below and he disappeared again, pulled down for the second and what, he was absolutely certain, must be the final time.

～

With its flat bottom facing the sky, the *Emerald Mile* sped across the tops of the subsurface boulders. Petschek and Grua were now on opposite sides of the boat, and although neither man could see the rocks, their feet and shins were being dragged over them while the bowpost and stern of the dory took a series of brutal hits. Each impact registered as a muted concussion that reverberated through the hull of the dory.

"It was just *boom . . . boom . . . boom,*" said Petschek.

As the hammer blows continued, both men groped under the gunwales, fumbling for their spare line.

Retrieving the line, they flung it across the hull with a wet slap, then once more heaved their bodies onto the bottom for another attempt at righting the boat. And then came one of those odd moments of reprieve that the river sometimes grants those it seizes.

Like a giant opening his fist, the main current released its grip and a spin-off trail of water neatly shot them into the top of Thank God Eddy.

～

Wren's second dunking was neither as deep nor as prolonged as the first, but that hardly mattered. Savagely depleted and still reeling from the bowpost strike, he had only one aim when he flailed to the surface and caught his next breath.

"I just started swimming. I don't even know if I knew which direction I was going in. I just started swimming."

He seemed to be making no progress—he was barely able to go through the motions of dog-paddling, and his life jacket was impeding whatever gains he made. In this manner, he was swept past Thank God Eddy, and now the only remaining point of sanctuary was a tiny indent in the cliffs just below. Once beyond that, he would have to brace for the start of the next rapid.

Somehow he made it, mustering a supreme effort to paddle into the little pocket, where he wallowed through the shallows and draped himself over a boulder, convinced he would collapse and drown if he attempted to make the final steps to shore.

When he wiped the blood away from his eyes, he looked upstream to Thank God Eddy and saw his companions on the bottom of the dory, heaving on the lines and trying, without success, to turn her right side up.

"*Please* right the boat," he pleaded to himself. "*Please* right the boat. I don't want to get back in that water! *Please—please—please.*"

After several failed attempts, Grua and Petschek glanced downstream, caught sight of Wren, and glared at him. The meaning was unmistakable—

What the hell are you doing? Get out here!

With a groan, Wren slithered off the rock, slid back into the water, and started paddling. When he reached the dory, Grua and Petschek hauled him out, and together the three of them heaved on the lines until the bottom slowly rotated out of the water and the boat flipped over—once again dumping everyone into the river.

Clambering back aboard, they took a moment to collect themselves. Then they took stock of what had happened. Chunks of the bowpost and the stern were missing, one of the hatches was askew, and the top of their cooler had blown open, and as they cast their eyes around the surface of the water, they realized that the entire eddy was bestrewn with floating trash.

Some of that trash clearly belonged to the canyon—driftwood and twigs and little atolls of brown foam. But there were other objects too: soggy sandwiches, bobbing pieces of fruit, and a sodden lump that turned out to be Grua's wallet. After a moment of confusion they realized their front cross-hatch had blown open and most of their gear had been hurled overboard.

Now they enacted a kind of Keystone Kops routine, scooping wet items into the boat as fast as they could and stuffing everything into the hatches while simultaneously trying to dry off the battery and the spotlights. In the midst of this flurry, something hulking and huge emerged from the main current like a breaching whale.

It was a gray, thirty-seven-foot motor rig, plowing into the eddy so fast that it nearly smeared them against the rocks on the shoreline. In the stern was a guide with his hand on the throttle, and he was almost as surprised as they were.

"Wow, I'm glad I didn't hit you, man," shouted the boatman. "I'm sorry, but I have to make this eddy—and if I was you, I'd get outta here because in about two more seconds, another guy is pulling in right behind me, and he isn't *nearly* as good at this as I am."

With Wren still bailing and Grua continuing to snatch up pieces of fruit, Petschek scrambled into the cockpit, seized the oars, and pulled toward the eddy line. He snapped off a series of crisp strokes and had just broken through into the main current when something even worse than a runaway motor rig materialized.

Over the roar of the river, they heard a dull *thuk-thuk-thuk* and looked up to see that an orange-and-white helicopter was now hovering directly overhead.

The Park Service had arrived.

23

The Reckoning

*Is it wise to go on? . . . I almost conclude to leave the river. But for years
I have been contemplating this trip. To leave the exploration unfinished,
to say that there is a part of the canyon which I cannot explore, having
already almost accomplished it, is more than I am willing to acknowledge,
and I determine to go on.*

—JOHN WESLEY POWELL, *August 27, 1869,*
as three of his crew announced their intention
to abandon the expedition and hike out

WHEN the *Emerald Mile* performed its end-over-end flip in the explosion wave, John Thomas reached immediately for his two-way radio. The signal from his transmission was picked up by one of the repeaters on the South Rim, bounced to the dispatcher's office in the park's Emergency Services building, then relayed directly to Thomas's boss, Curt Sauer, who had reviewed and denied Grua's permit application for the speed run several weeks earlier. When Sauer heard that there had been an accident involving a lone dory, he knew it was Grua. Bracing himself for yet another airborne evacuation at Crystal, he ordered Thomas to summon Helo 210, which was now hovering just upstream over Phantom Ranch, barely five minutes away, to perform a sweep and find out if any of the boatmen were injured or dead.

When the chopper reached Thank God Eddy and hovered over the dory, Thomas spoke to the pilot by radio.

"You see the boat?"

"Yeah."

"Is it right side up? What's going on?"

"It's upright."

"How many people in it?"

"Three."

"Do they have oars in the water?"

"Yeah, they have oars in the water."

Thomas was relieved. The Park Service wasn't going to need to stage an evac. But the wheels of law enforcement had now been set in motion. At the moment, however, that was only one of several big problems besetting the crew of the *Emerald Mile*.

~

As Helo 210 rotored off, Petschek pulled the dory into a tiny pocket eddy just above the next set of rapids, and Grua tied them off to the rocks. They needed a time-out to collect themselves, attend to Wren's injury, and make some decisions.

While Grua applied a butterfly bandage to the gash on Wren's forehead and wrapped the wound in gauze, Petschek pulled a roll of duct tape from the repair kit and set about doctoring the dory. As they concentrated on their respective tasks, each boatman silently tallied up the cost of what had taken place.

Their situation was grim. Except for the fruit, most of their food was either lost or soaked, along with their spare clothing. The rangers obviously had a bead on where they were and what they were doing. Grua and Petschek were exhausted and almost as badly beaten up as the boat. Worst of all, their best oarsman had just been cut down.

As the youngest and strongest member of the crew, Wren was critical to the success of this venture. True, Grua and Petschek may have spent more time on the water, and in some ways they may have understood the river at a deeper level than Wren did, having weathered it under a wider range of its moods. But when it came to raw horsepower, Wren's youth gave him the upper hand. He was capable of summoning considerably greater strength and, when necessary, forcing significantly more speed from the dory than either of his companions. In short, he was the closest thing the *Emerald Mile* had to a turbocharger—and now he was dazed, concussed, and bleeding like a stuck pig.

The collective weight of those facts seemed daunting, especially given what lay ahead. They were barely a third of the way through the trip, with 179 miles still to go—a stretch that included the rest of the Inner Granite Gorge and another three dozen rapids, including Lava Falls. And in another ten hours they'd confront their second sleepless night of rowing in the dark.

The Colorado had delivered a roundhouse punch to the speed run, a blow that had restacked the odds and so scrambled the logic that the prospect of continuing the quest now seemed ludicrous.

"At that point, we were very demoralized—I mean, extremely so," Petschek later recalled. "We were so beat-up. I remember just wanting to get out of there—to not even *be* there."

Sitting in the boat, all three boatmen acknowledged that the river might actually have done them a favor by creating an altogether acceptable excuse for them to call it quits. Right now, the most prudent course of action—indeed, the only option that qualified as remotely sane—was to haul the *Emerald Mile* out of the water, anchor her to the shore, then climb out of the canyon, limp home, and swallow whatever punishment the Park Service was preparing to dish out.

In many ways, this scenario wouldn't be all that bad. Their dignity and their pride would still be intact. Their dory would still hold the speed record. No one in the river community would think any less of them for having been whipped by Crystal.

They looked at one another, each man seeking confirmation that his own instinct was shared by the others.

Screw *that*, they agreed—and scrambled back on board.

～

Just below Crystal lay an eleven-mile stretch of moderate rapids known collectively as the Jewels. Like the semiprecious stones for which they had been named, each was unique, and although none qualified as whoppers, every one of them could harbor nasty surprises at differing water levels.

With Petschek at the oars, the *Emerald Mile* cleared them all in just under an hour and fifteen minutes.

As they shot past Bass, the camp at Mile 108 that had served as a makeshift helipad for the air evacuations during the previous two days, they began seeing evidence of the havoc Crystal had wrought. On both sides of the river, the eddies were awash with gear of all sorts—life jackets and plastic coolers, fuel tanks and ammo cans, plastic sleeping pads and rotting fruit. Then they started seeing the wreckage of the abandoned motor rigs, moored among the rocks, limp and sagging like punctured balloons. At Mile 110 they passed Chuck

Mills's overturned boat. Canted at an angle and smashed almost beyond recognition, it looked as if a torpedo had hit it. Georgie White's upside-down logo was no longer readable. Farther downstream they passed two other rigs, equally destroyed. They surveyed each wreck in silence, shaking their heads in disbelief. Later, they would remember this as one of the most disturbing segments of the entire journey.

Adding to their disquiet was a burgeoning concern that the clock was now against them. By Petschek's reckoning, almost an hour had been lost during the flip and the recovery. The most effective way to make up that time would be through a series of hard sprints in which each man banged out furious, twenty-minute rowing intervals. But like the stricken baloney boats, the air had been let out of Wren. He did his best to spell his companions at the oars, but his chief assets—his focus and his fury—were gone. Wordlessly, Grua and Petschek began timing their switches to ensure that Wren's rowing stints coincided with the relatively calm and flat stretches. He would not row a big rapid again for the rest of the trip.

At half past noon, they whipped past Elves Chasm, a tributary just below Mile 116 that marked the end of the Upper Granite Gorge and the entrance to Stephen Aisle, a two-mile stretch of flat water. Under normal circumstances, Stephen's arrival provoked a sigh of relief. Guides who had just weathered the trials of the upper gorge could briefly relax as the river slowed down, winding sinuously from left to right and back again. But here the three boatmen once again detected the distinctive sound of rotors and looked up to spot the orange-and-white form of Helo 210. It was clattering toward them, flying low and keeping directly over the middle of the current.

They watched in dismay as the chopper passed overhead. Whoever was aboard would have to have been wearing blinders not to spot them.

As the helicopter reached the end of the aisle, it seemed to be descending even lower. The conclusion was obvious: the pilot was looking for a suitable sand beach on which to land. When the dory rounded the bend, a ranger would order them to shore and place them under arrest.

With no place to hide, they were busted.

~

Here, then, was the encounter they had been dreading, and its arrival made each man groan inwardly. The trials they had already endured had been difficult and demoralizing, but paled in comparison with what would happen if they were taken into custody, shuttled up to the South Rim, and hauled in front of the superintendent.

The possible repercussions of this confrontation extended far beyond Richard Marks's power to slap them with the kind of fine that could wipe out their earnings for an entire season. Their worst fears had nothing whatsoever to do with money, and everything to do with the small plastic card each man carried in his ammo can: his river-guide license. Because the Park Service controlled those licenses, the superintendent effectively held the car keys to the Grand Canyon. If he was angry enough, he could take the river away from them forever.

For men such as Grua, Petschek, and Wren, the stakes didn't get any higher. If there was ever a moment to take stock of whether the rewards of what they were trying to do justified the price they might be forced to pay, this was surely that moment—and its calculus was brutally stark.

Although they had not set out with the specific aim of humiliating the Park Service, theirs was undeniably a gesture of defiance. But having committed themselves so fully to this venture, what would it now mean if they permitted themselves to be stopped not by the forces of the river itself, but by a government agency that sought to control and regulate it?

When they thought about this—and each man did, separately, as the *Emerald Mile* cut through the flat water—they realized that submission was not an option. There could be no surrender, no moment of chastened humility in which they meekly pulled in to shore, hoping that the men with the badges would be gracious enough to consider cutting them a break and not ride them too hard.

If the rangers pulled out their weapons, maybe they'd have to reconsider. But short of gunplay, this train wasn't stopping. They didn't intend to be nasty about that—there would be no upraised fists, no curse words hurled across the water. They were even prepared to try to politely explain, in the few seconds the current would allow them, that they weren't *able* to stop because they answered to a higher authority than the federal government, which was the flaming righteousness of the Colorado and the memory of the crew that had come down the river with John Wesley Powell—men who had wagered more than they could afford to lose in order to master the game.

Whatever punishment the rangers might have in mind would have to wait until they were finished with the task at hand.

Through some mysterious alchemy, all three boatmen now caught a kind of second wind, a renewal of purpose. What the river had taken away from them at Crystal was now replaced and doubled down. And as they approached Blacktail Canyon, a hushed tributary at Mile 120 that was known for its profound acoustics, a place of holiness and silence, this made all the difference. Their fear of being banned from the river had been supplanted by something that had less heat and fire than bravado or defiance. Call it a skewed sort of curiosity. Whatever happened with that helicopter downstream would be interesting. But like detached witnesses watching a train wreck, it wasn't going to touch them, not where it truly mattered.

~

Grua was at the oars, pulling with his back facing downstream, and as they approached the final bend in the aisle, Petschek and Wren swept their gaze to the right, then to the left, scanning the shoreline. This stretch of the river usually featured wide sand beaches on both sides. But now the water was up to the cliffs. A few stretches of flat ground were still left, however, and if a pilot wanted to set a chopper down in this part of the canyon, it would be here.

As they rounded the bend, Helo 210 was nowhere to be seen.

Both sets of eyes now swung downstream to the next shelf. And the next. With the same result.

This they repeated for four miles—past the end of Stephen Aisle, then along the length of the even longer Conquistador Aisle, which followed.

The helicopter never showed.

By Mile 124, which marks the conclusion of Conquistador Aisle, they knew that whatever Helo 210 was pursuing, it didn't involve them. And for the first time, they began to consider the possibility that, despite the flagrancy of their transgression, perhaps the Park Service had more important things to worry about.

Once more, their thoughts returned to the business of making up lost time.

~

By midafternoon, the Vishnu schist had reappeared, rising vertically along both sides of the river as the *Emerald Mile* raced through the Middle Granite Gorge. Not only was the clock against them, but also the heat. The mercury had climbed well past one hundred degrees as the sun's rays, now directly overhead, essentially turned the corridor at the bottom of the canyon into an oversize convection oven. All three boatmen were sweating profusely and continuously refilling their water bottles from the river as they sought to replace the fluids that were being drained not only by the oppressive temperatures but also by the tremendous demands of pulling the dory downstream at top speed.

When done correctly, rowing looks elegant and effortless, but the toll it takes is enormous—in part because, unlike many other sports, the mechanics of moving a boat with a pair of oars recruits virtually every part of the upper and lower body, as well as its core. All four phases of a stroke—the catch, the drive, the finish, and the recovery—require explosive contributions from some combination of almost every major muscle group: the quadriceps, glutes, and hamstrings as the blade bites into the water and the legs drive forward; the rhomboids, trapeziums, biceps, deltoids, and latissimus dorsi as the arms and shoulders send the blades forward through the water toward the conclusion of one stroke, then planing backward for the next. And throughout this entire motion, the erector spinae, the back extensors, and the abdominals must all engage as the torso whips through its arc. Each separate stroke is formidable, but when multiplied over a period of just a few minutes during an intensive burst of speed, the cumulative toll is savagely depleting.

A single two-thousand-meter rowing race, which typically lasts between five and eight minutes, demands virtually everything the human body can deliver in terms of both aerobic and anaerobic performance. (This is the primary reason why rowing ranks at the very top of endurance sports, rivaled only by cross-country skiing and long-distance swimming and skating.) Although Grua and his crew weren't operating anywhere close to the cardiovascular level of Olympic-class rowers, the challenge they had laid before themselves was forcing each man to complete the equivalent of five back-to-back two-thousand-meter sprints each time he returned to the oars. As brutal as it may be to imagine one or two of these sequences, it is almost impossible to gauge the effect over many hours. Perhaps the most revealing metric is simply this: to reach the Grand Wash Cliffs within forty-eight hours and claim the record, all three oarsmen would need to execute, at top speed, a combined total of roughly fifty-four thousand individual oar strokes.

At 2:05 p.m., they rounded Bedrock, a nasty impasse at Mile 132 where the river is split into two channels by a garage-size chunk of granite. A mile farther downstream, they shot through Dubendorff, a long, sickle-shaped rapid that normally demands two precision moves to avoid a shallow table-rock in midstream. Now it was little more than a long train of fast water and huge standing waves.

Less than twenty minutes after clearing Dubie, they found themselves approaching Granite Narrows, a notorious bottleneck at Mile 135 where the river is forced through a gap that is only seventy-six feet wide, the narrowest point in the entire canyon. Here, as at Crystal, the hydraulics had created something for which they were unprepared.

As the river funneled through the constriction, the water rose almost forty feet above its normal levels, climbing the polished walls. Inside the chute, it was absolute chaos—as near as anyone could determine (and there would be much debate about this during the years that followed), the current actually corkscrewed, braiding back on itself in a kind of liquid helix. The surface of the river was undulating wildly, like a line of laundry snapping in a fierce wind, and the main body of current was slamming directly into the right-hand wall. Any boatman who wasn't fighting to keep off that wall would find himself scraped along the side of it for fifty yards. Evidence of this was already visible—dozens of boats had left banded stripes of white, blue, and orange paint that would remain there for the next decade.

Here, perhaps more than at any other place, the river took the measure of Grua's skills as a boatman. Assessing the situation and setting up the sequence of moves, he pivoted, entered the bottleneck and, pulling for all he was worth, inched the *Emerald Mile* along the cliff until she was finally free of the current's tractorlike pull. They were so close to the wall that Wren, who was in the bow, could have reached out and let his fingertips brush the rock.

After they passed through the Narrows, the walls opened up again and the turbulence subsided, and now Grua decided to start making some serious time. As he laid into his strokes, he dipped into his well of reserve energy, and they once again started flying.

At Mile 136, he shot them past Deer Creek Falls, a tributary canyon where a long waterfall dropped more than a hundred feet into the river. At Mile 139, he blazed through a rapid called Fishtail, which was so washed-out that they barely even registered passing through it. Then just before 3:30 p.m., as they were approaching Kanab, a huge tributary canyon that enters the river on the right at Mile 143, Grua turned the oars over to Wren and caught sight of something he'd been watching for.

Directly up ahead, dories were on the water.

~

There were five of them, tightly spaced and strung out in a line. Each boat carried a guide and four passengers, and the oarsmen were all facing forward, pushing downstream. At the tail end of the running order was a heavily loaded baggage raft, and all the way up at the front, leading his squadron in the *Dark Canyon*, was Grua's great friend and rival, Regan Dale.

Dale's crew were now into their eleventh day on the water, and even from behind, Grua could read the toll that those days had exacted. The strain of the relentless rowing and the constant vigilance was written in the corded sinews in the dorymen's forearms and the hunched tightness of their shoulders. Yet as the *Emerald Mile* flew past each boat, the worry and the weariness vanished as the crew turned in surprise, then called out greetings and encouragement to their comrades.

When Dale looked back to discover the cause of the commotion, he spotted the *Emerald Mile* bearing down on him like a bat out of hell. It was a memorable moment: the man who had almost consigned the dory to the flames of a

Viking funeral all those years ago, watching her sweep past the blade of his left oar as she gunned for a place in the history books.

They shot past so fast that there was no time for a colloquy. But Dale, who had taken in the most essential details in a single glance—the duct tape on the gunwales and stern, and Wren's blood-soaked bandages—knew exactly what to ask.

"How was Crystal?" he yelled.

"Flipped!" cried Petschek. "See you guys in a coupla days."

As Wren grunted past, sweat dripping from his bandages, unwilling to concede the loss of even a single oar-stroke, the ribbon of river between Dale's boat and the *Emerald Mile* rapidly unfurled.

In light of the history between them, Dale wasn't entirely sure whether he should be shaking his head in exasperation or pumping his fist and cheering. His only certainty was that this encounter deserved to be commemorated.

In the fleeting seconds before they were gone, he had just enough time to fumble with the latches of his hatch, whip out his camera, and snap off three shots, the last of which captured the dory's bow as she disappeared downstream, backlit against the glistening light of late afternoon and graced by a final salute from Petschek.

They would be the only photographs taken of the speed run.

⌢

During the next two hours they raced through the Muav Gorge, the limestone corridor where, six years earlier, Grua had completed the crux of his canyon through-hike by following the path shown to him by the bighorn sheep. Evening wasn't far now; the light off the water was beginning to take on a warm, pinkish haze as they passed some of the most gorgeous tributaries in the middle of the canyon—narrow and diminutive Matkatamiba at Mile 148, then Havasu, with its turquoise side stream and its travertine waterfalls, at Mile 156.

Thanks to the high water, the big commercial expeditions now had fewer and fewer places to camp along this stretch. National, a hulking side canyon on the left side of the river at Mile 166, was almost completely underwater. Ditto with Fern Glen, another popular pull-in spot about a mile and a half farther downstream. But a little after 6:30 p.m., as they approached the mouth of Mohawk, another big tributary that punched into the left side of the river just below Mile 171, they spotted a motor-rig camp consisting of two huge rafts and a party of about thirty people.

A guide named Jon Stoner was standing behind a metal table in the kitchen, facing the river and sipping on a beer while he prepared to get dinner started. Like Regan Dale, Stoner had spent the past two days monitoring a constant stream of detritus from the wrecks that had taken place at Crystal. That very afternoon he had discovered one of the side tubes of the Tour West rig on which Bill Wert had died, floating forlornly in an eddy all by itself. Now, here came something even stranger: a lone dory, patched with duct tape, sprinting downriver as if something were chasing it.

Stoner wasn't quite sure what to make of this, except to note that the dory had red gunwales and that it looked exquisite and fair, as all dories do, silhouetted against the peach-colored shallups of sunlight that were dappling the main current.

The boatman at the oars didn't even bother to look across the water and nod, but the figure in the bow snapped off a quick wave.

Stoner returned the greeting by raising his beer can—the universal boatman's salute. Then they were gone, lost in the early evening light.

~

Seventy-three miles upstream from the *Emerald Mile*'s position, that same low-angled light was telling John Thomas that it was time to start wrapping up his day at Crystal.

During the past nine hours, nearly two dozen commercial and private expeditions had navigated past the explosion wave, and although a few of the smaller oar boats had flipped, not a single one of the motor rigs had overturned. With the exception of Grua's crazy stunt, the operation had been a success. Now all that remained was for Thomas to summon Helo 210 and catch a ride up to the South Rim, where he was scheduled to attend a rangers' briefing with Richard Marks and discuss, among other matters, what should be done about the speed run. Before that briefing, however, Thomas decided that he needed to complete one last task.

All afternoon, Thomas had been worrying about Grua and his battered crew. In addition to Crystal, there was one other place on the river where the speed runners might get into serious trouble, and as his shuttle touched down, Thomas realized that several days had passed since anyone had provided any hard information on this spot.

"Let's go downriver," he said to the pilot as he clambered aboard the helicopter and put on his headphones. "We need to find out where that dory is, and then we need to take a look at Lava Falls."

First, they had to climb out of the canyon and stop at the fuel station on Hualapai Hilltop, a depot located along a remote stretch of the South Rim. By the time they had finished topping off their tanks, it was nearing 7:00 p.m. The light was beginning to soften across the uppermost bands of cliffs, and as they flew, Thomas could see that the shadows were already creeping down the walls and flooding the bottom. Dusk wasn't far behind.

To conserve fuel, the pilot kept the ship high, so Thomas was forced to scan the river corridor from a thousand feet above. They flew over National, Fern Glen, and Mohawk, but no boats were on the water. Then at Mile 174, where a small tributary called Cove Canyon enters the river from the left, he caught sight of his quarry.

In the evening, this stretch of the river turns gold and auburn, and as they flew down the corridor Thomas could see the little dory with its crew, far below, backlit against the river. They were about five miles above Lava Falls, and they must have been trying to make the most of the remaining daylight, because they were rowing for all they were worth.

As the helicopter rotored downstream, the pilot gradually descended so that by the time they reached Vulcan's Anvil, the tower of black basalt jutting straight up out of the middle of the river that signals the entrance to the lake above Lava, they were no more than five hundred feet off the deck.

They were moving fast, roaring straight toward the lip of the falls, and by Thomas's reckoning they had just enough time to find out how bad things looked and, if necessary, roar back upstream to warn the crew of the *Emerald Mile*.

As the chopper passed the point where the river ran over the ledge and exploded, Thomas leaned over and caught a good look at what Grua and his companions were racing into.

~

Nobody in his right mind plows straight into Lava Falls on water flowing at 70,000 cfs without stopping to scout. But this run was different. Far too much time had been lost at Crystal, the light would soon be gone, and as they tore past Vulcan's Anvil each man understood that, whatever Lava was about to dish out, they would have to absorb on the fly.

Years later, what Petschek would recall most clearly was Grua's confidence as he pulled them toward the top of the rapid. Unlike at Crystal, he didn't debate his options or ask what anyone thought. He was convinced that he had figured out what the river was doing and, by extension, knew exactly what he needed to do. And unlike at Crystal, he was absolutely right.

All the rocks were covered over and even the ledge hole was almost washed-out. There was no need to thread the Slot. The biggest worry was an enormous lateral that was coming off Black Rock on the right, where the *Emerald Mile* had been taken to pieces six years earlier. The aim would be to stay to the left, keep the bow square to the waves, and ride out whatever the river threw at them.

The standing waves were enormous, the biggest any of them had ever seen. But far from Crystal's savage hydraulics, these waves were rounded and smooth, and in the end, those haystacks would be what they remembered best about that run—the great dome-shaped mountains of water, green as emerald and smooth as glass, and the deep, curving valleys between them.

The dory sailed over each crest and throttled through each trough with the buoyancy of a bobbing apple. Up one and down the next, only to face another climb and another plunge that was as giddy as the last, until they had lost not only their count but also their fear and simply gave themselves over to the roaring joyousness of the motion, something so wild and free that it was worthy of Powell himself—a jubilant affirmation of the one-armed Major's words when he described how his own wooden boats, 114 years earlier, had gone soaring over the waves like "herds of startled deer bounding through forests beset with fallen timber."

This was the thing itself—the reason they ran white water.

Halfway down the rapid, Wren turned around and pumped his fist. "We're not through yet," barked Grua, torquing his oars to ensure that they hit the remaining haystacks on the point of the bow. But a few seconds later, they were bouncing merrily through the tail waves on the last of Lava's expended energy.

The ride was so silken and smooth, so much like a dream, that when he spoke of it years later, Grua had completely forgotten who was at the oars.

"Rudi was in the driver's seat," he would declare to a friend. "He had a really nice run!"

It was now just after 7:20 p.m. Between them and their goal lay another ninety-nine miles of river, and another night of moonbeam-dodging in the dark.

24

Beneath the River of Shooting Stars

*And forever, beyond the mysterious river's farthest shore, the great
earth waited in the darkness, and was still. It waited there with the
huge, attentive secrecy of night . . . and its wild, mysterious loveliness
was more delicate than magic.*

—THOMAS WOLFE, *Of Time and the River*

As Grua and the crew pressed on, the angled evening light was now
casting fantastic patterns across the honeycombed sections of the
columnar basalt—black, hexagonal expanses of Pleistocene lava that
were layered over the limestone on both sides of the river. The shadows were
growing by the minute while the sun played hide-and-seek, dipping beneath
a rise on the cliffs to the west, then reappearing briefly as the *Emerald Mile*
rounded another turn. A few miles downstream from Lava Falls, the setting
sun finally departed for good, and twilight closed in upon the river world.

The Colorado was trending west now and the canyon slowly widened and
grew straighter. Thick groves of tamarisk trees created a dense band of vegetation, a continuous layer of green along both banks. The mouths of the tributaries down here were bigger and more generous. In general, everything seemed
less constricted, less intense. And now there were camps on both sides of the
shore, lit in the hot darkness by the orange flare of a kitchen lantern here, the
blue glow of a gas stove there.

This was a special time to be on the water. The surface of the river was a faint and shimmering lavender, and as night swept down the walls, the shadows gathered in layers, each denser than the last, until the abyss was smothered in darkness and the only thing visible was the sky, which was plunging toward a soothing and bottomless indigo. With moonrise more than an hour away, the only point of light above was Saturn, a pink pinprick off to the west that hung like a beacon on the stern of a ship.

Then the first stars began to frost the heavens.

They emerged slowly, popping out one by one, and then they all came in a rush, spilling out of the ether until the narrow ribbon of sky above was no longer speckled with isolated motes but was a milky torrent, alive with eddies and whirlpools, a millrace of planets and stars whose combined translucence defined the ragged line of the canyon's twinned rims with such clarity, such crystalline precision, that anyone looking up could not help but gasp at what had been unveiled. Because there, six thousand feet above the dark and now invisible river, this torrent of winking lights in the heavens had formed a second river, a celestial estuary of starlight whose course and contour, each curve and camber, every bend and bowknot, perfectly mirrored the Colorado itself. A river so clear and transparent that the bright stones suspended within its currents could be seen with the naked eye, glittering with the traces of an incontestable radiance whose depth and distance and truth lay beyond the reaches of any terrestrial imagination.

The effect of this display might have been uplifting, perhaps even revelatory, if the crew of the *Emerald Mile* had not had far more pressing things to worry about, chief among them the fact that they could no longer see where they were going. Without the moon, it was too dark to make out any features on the water, and all but impossible to separate the rocks from the river.

Time to break out the Q-Beams. While Petschek rowed, Grua flipped open the side hatch, connected the wires to the car battery, and flicked the switches. Then, aiming the powerful lights downstream, he methodically swept the beams from left to right and back again, casting across the water, picking out the hazards, and calling out corrections over his shoulder.

In this manner they slid past Whitmore Wash at Mile 187 and, just before 9:30 p.m., found themselves bearing down on Parashant Wash, a massive tributary canyon that enters at Mile 198, where the river curves leftward. Unbeknownst to the crew of the *Emerald Mile*, a second group of dories had nestled into the Parashant eddy and were preparing to bed down. This expedition was another of Litton's commercial expeditions, currently spending its fifteenth night on the river.

The trip leader was one of the company's more cerebral guides, a professor named Roderick Nash, whose writings included *Wilderness and the American*

Mind, a seminal history of environmentalism. Like their dory brethren fifty miles upstream, Nash and his crew had spent most of the previous week fighting to keep their boats together and upright while trying to decipher the testimony of the wreckage they passed and the warning notes that were periodically dropped from the Park Service helicopters. Now, standing in the darkness, Nash peered out and tried to make sense of what he was seeing.

Acres of current were out there, sliding past in an invisible rush. To the weary guide, the river had never looked so immense, so alive. And there was a boat too—probably an oar raft or a dory, judging by the speed and the silence of it, racing downstream while someone played a pair of searchlights back and forth. Nash's first thought was that it was probably a ranger patrol searching for bodies or lost gear. But several members of his crew speculated that it could be Kenton Grua. When they'd left the boathouse in Hurricane two weeks earlier, there had been talk about the Factor's taking another crack at the speed record with Rudi and Wren. Could this be them?

The boat was too far away to call out, so no greetings were exchanged as the searchlights sluiced silently past, their beams planing across the surface of the water, then winked out and were gone. Whoever they were and whatever their purpose, mused Nash, it must have been important enough to run some serious risks, considering what lay just a couple of miles downstream.

~

Nash's caution was well placed. The rapids in the lower part of the canyon weren't nearly as big or as famous as those upstream, and for this reason, after Lava Falls, most river trips seemed to go flat in the eyes of the boatmen who love the big water. However, a couple of places between the bottom of Lava and Lake Mead presented genuine hazards, and one of the nastiest was at Mile 205, where the full force of the river banged into a promenade of hardened limestone on the right side. An alert oarsman could avoid the worst of this obstacle—which was known as Kolb Rapid—by pulling sharply to the left, but his timing had to be good, and over the years a number of boats had come to grief on that headwall. The consequences of a miss were serious enough that veteran trip leaders passed around a little warning, one of those special river axioms, whenever they sensed that their crews were getting too cocky or too complacent:

"Watch out for 205—it'll eat you alive."

Grua and his crew were well aware that attempting 205 in the dark was a lousy idea, especially in their current condition. They had been rowing for twenty-one hours without a break, not counting the forty-five minutes that had been lost at Crystal. With the exception of wolfing down a few pieces of fruit and some soggy sandwiches, they had eaten almost nothing, and they had barely slept—the turbulence and speed of the river having ruled out all but the briefest of catnaps in the bow or the stern. For whoever was in the cockpit, every stint at the oars seemed to last a little longer, and relief from it seemed to come a little later. The muscles in their shoulders and lower backs were cramped and twitching uncontrollably. Their thighs and forearms burned. Worst of all, their fingers never seemed to fully uncurl before the rotation came full circle and it was time to wrap their aching digits around the oar handles once more to resume rowing. All three boatmen had now burned through their reserves, yet with the return of darkness the need for constant, unstinting vigilance redoubled. Every second not spent pulling on the oars was devoted to intense concentration—peering, listening, muttering imprecations while trying to fathom what lay ahead, then high-siding explosively to restore the dory's balance when the waves appeared.

Shortly after 10:00 p.m., they spotted a little peapod-shaped inlet on the right and decided to tuck in, tie off, and pause for a breather. Their plan was to nap for a single hour—just enough time to allow the moonlight to reach the water and illuminate the entrance to 205. They didn't even bother to get out of the boat. Pulling out their wet sleeping bags, draping them over their bodies, they fell into a sleep as dense and dreamless as dolomite.

While they slept, the moonlight cascaded down the walls, splashed over the gunwales, and puddled on the decks of the dory. Luminous as a new pearl, it was bright enough to read a newspaper by, yet failed to wake them.

And so they slumbered on . . .

. . . past 11:00 p.m. . . . .

. . . then long past midnight, until—

Just before 1:00 a.m., Grua awoke with a start and sat up, staring at his watch in horror.

Jesus.

After everything they had endured—after the battles against the whirlpools and the haystacks on the first night, after the flip at Crystal, after their encounters with the helicopter and their desperate race to reach Lava—after all of that, a protracted boatmen's siesta had placed the entire enterprise in jeopardy.

How could they have been so feckless? So *stupid*?

Grua roused his companions. There was no possible way to recover the lost time, but they had to cast off immediately, punch into the current, and get back in the game.

At 1:02 a.m. they relaunched, groggy with the kind of ruinous, bone-battered fatigue that arises when extreme exertion is followed by inadequate recovery. Grua was at the oars. Wren, still suffering from his injuries, slumped in the bow. Petschek took the stern and scouted downstream.

When they heard the roar of 205, Grua swung his bow downstream and pushed toward the left to avoid being caught between the main current and the headwall. They barreled past without incident, then resumed trading off the rowing duties every fifteen or twenty minutes as they surged through the lower reaches of the canyon. Past Granite Park, a spectacularly open area at Mile 209 with the widest, most generous skies in the entire canyon. Past Mile 217, where the Vishnu schist returned for the final time and, as the river entered the last of the three granite gorges, the walls turned vertical. There, the moonlight was cut off, plunging them back into darkness and forcing them once again to resort to the Q-Beams.

Slightly less than four hours later—at precisely 4:59 a.m.—they reached Separation Canyon at Mile 239, a key benchmark on any river journey. This was the point where three members of Powell's crew had lost all hope and abandoned the expedition, hiking out of the canyon only to be taken prisoner and murdered. For the speed run too, Separation marked a kind of nadir, because it was here that the fire that had sustained them nearly went out.

By this point, Wren had shut down. For seventeen hours, he had been sleepwalking through his duties, dulled by the unending throbbing from the blow he had sustained, until he had finally slumped into a kind of stuporous coma.

Now Grua followed suit.

Unlike Wren, he succumbed to no specific insult or injury, but simply to the cumulative weight of the burdens he had voluntarily assumed and carried, at first cheerfully and then, later, with a kind of iron-willed stoicism, until finally, here at Separation, the neurons in his brain and the fibers in his muscle tissue surrendered, waving a tattered white flag in the face of his exhaustion and fatigue. Without a word, he passed the oars to Petschek, curled himself in the stern, and nodded off.

~

Now the fate of their venture rested in the hands of one of the most unusual men ever to run the Colorado, whose path to the river had drawn him from Nazi-occupied Europe through the lakes of Argentina and then to the laboratories of UC Berkeley before he had finally found his true home on the decks of a seventeen-foot wooden dory. At age forty-nine, Petschek was by far the oldest member of the crew and thus entirely unlikely to find within himself the endurance and the drive to carry them through when his younger and stronger companions could no longer continue. He had always talked with awe about Grua's remarkable stamina and steadiness, the astonishing manner in which the Factor was able to hold everything together because he never seemed to grow tired—or more accurately, that despite how weary he might be, Grua was somehow able to summon from within himself a source of energy that enabled him to persevere. Which was something that he, Petschek, could try to imitate but never truly reproduce. And yet that is exactly what he set out to do now, while his companions slumbered.

Taking up the oars, he settled himself in the cockpit, braced his feet, and launched a sequence of strokes whose pacing and rhythm were calibrated to pull them through the crux of the run. There was nothing flashy or dramatic about this. He didn't moan over the pain in his arms or lash the water with his oar blades. He simply snapped off one flawless stroke after another, quietly and without fanfare, declining to wake his friends when his twenty-minute stint was over and it was time to trade off, electing instead to continue pulling, without respite, without pause, until the night was over.

As he rowed, his thoughts turned back toward the first speed run, the shakedown to the main event, which had taken place three years earlier. On that voyage, somewhere in the lower part of the canyon, he had shared a conversation with Wally Rist that had always stayed with him. The flat stretches between the bottom of Lava Falls and the top of 205 had lent themselves to dialogue, and Rist, who at the time was in the midst of a divorce, had been talking about the nature of happiness. And Petschek had asked—because he was genuinely puzzled by this—why so many people, Americans especially, seemed to feel that happiness was an entitlement. By dint of his own experiences as a refugee and a wanderer, Petschek found the notion to be strangely naive and immature—especially here at the bottom of a chasm whose ramparts offered such irrefutable testimony not only to the smallness of human affairs but also to the universe's implacable indifference to those hopes and longings.

Yet right now, in a way that seemed to be crystallized by the task of shepherding his sleeping companions down this penultimate stretch, Petschek was forced to concede that he *had* found happiness. Not as a birthright or as an entitlement, but as something that had been bequeathed by the place itself, this river and this canyon, by virtue of its strangeness, its majesty, and above all by its peculiar ability to distill the essence of those who had been drawn into its orbit—their courage and insanity, their beliefs and their delusions—into something urgent and compelling. As the last of the night cupped the river in its hands, Petschek knew in his heart that it was simply impossible to come away from an extended encounter with the greatest canyon on earth without acknowledging that human life, despite its frailty and insignificance, represents a bestowal of grace for which one has done nothing whatsoever to deserve—and that for this reason, the river world vibrated with a harrowing beauty whose principal dividends were gratitude and joy.

In this manner, alone with his thoughts in the predawn darkness, Petschek took the *Emerald Mile* through the most forlorn phase of her odyssey. Past the end of the Lower Granite Gorge at Mile 259, where the black Archean schist arrowed deep into the earth and disappeared for the last time, replaced by tawny-colored layers of Tapeats sandstone and the green-and-purple Bright Angel shale. Past Spencer Canyon and Surprise Canyon and Clay Tank Canyon and Salt Creek and Jackson Canyon and Burnt Spring Canyon, and all the other half-forgotten little tributary drainages of the western end of the Grand Canyon until, somewhere in that stretch, he took them past the point where the mighty current that had borne them all the way from Lee's Ferry finally began to surrender its wondrous, unstoppable energy to the impounded slackwater of Lake Mead.

By now, his speed had slowed dramatically and the rowing had lost its burning fluency, drawing closer to something that resembled brute labor, the sort of duty one performs on a chain gang. But Petschek refused to quit.

He rowed them past the last of the stars. He rowed them clear of the night's embrace. He rowed them straight into and then beyond the break of day. And somewhere along that stretch of river, he also rowed them across an invisible fault line, a seam on the American continent that separates the terrain where the ephemeral events of everyday reality unfold from a more rarefied and singular realm, the place where mythic and permanent journeys of the imagination, such as those of John Wesley Powell, reside—the place of legends.

He did not stop rowing for three solid hours.

When Grua awoke and Petschek finally conceded to lay down his oars, it was just past 8:00 a.m. and they were passing an obscure little side canyon called Tincanebitts, seventeen miles from the end of the Grand Canyon.

~

Not far from the canyon's terminus, the cliffs on the left featured an enormous cavern that, more than eleven thousand years earlier, had served as a shelter for giant, three-toed Shasta ground sloths—prehistoric creatures that had shambled lethargically around the Southwest during the last Ice Age before slipping into extinction. The speed run was now about to devolve into a plodding bargepull that mirrored both the kinetics and the demeanor of the cavern's former inhabitants. Over the next two hours, as the speed of the current slowed further with each passing mile, the needle on the *Emerald Mile*'s speedometer ebbed inexorably lower, from eight miles an hour to seven, then six, then five.

Technically, this was still the Grand Canyon, but the behavior of the river suggested something else. The lurking presence of midstream sandbars, the near-total absence of current, and, most telling of all, the silence that descended as the swishes and purls that are the auditory signature of moving water faded and disappeared—all of these things indicated that the river was giving way to the uppermost tentacle of the reservoir created by Hoover Dam.

With the clock ticking against them, they would have to find some way of picking up the pace. So just before 10:00 a.m., Grua reached into his locker and broke out their second set of oarlocks while Petschek unlashed the spare oars. Now, instead of trading back and forth while Wren continued to sleep, both men would row in tandem.

Timing their strokes so that they pulled and recovered in unison, their speed improved somewhat, although the arrangement was exceedingly unpleasant— the boat had not really been designed to accommodate two oarsmen at once. But as they cranked out the final section, they reminded each other how lucky they were because the morning air was still and the upstream winds that often surge off the lake had not yet picked up.

They passed a large buoy with a sign announcing that farther upstream travel was off-limits to motorized boat traffic from the reservoir. They rowed past a limestone cave on the right that was occupied for thousands of years by a colony of Mexican free-tailed bats. Then, at about 11:15 a.m., the river bent sharply to the left and they rowed through a spectacular section of sandstone whose bedding had been tilted upward so sharply that the formation resembled a giant set of stone gates.

These were the Grand Wash Cliffs, and just beyond their portals the walls of the canyon fell away, replaced by the flat, flint-strewn desert along the shores of Lake Mead. As they passed through, they could see a road on the left side of the lake, snaking off into the distance. They could see the sky now too—truly see the sky—ampler and more extensive than inside the canyon, but also white and bleached, as if its vibrancy had been bled away by the removal of the canyon's walls.

By now, a small motor launch had puttered out across the reservoir to meet them. On board were their timekeepers, Cliff Taylor and Anne Marie Nicholson, who had made the long drive across the desert from Lee's Ferry and kept a vigil here on the shore of the lake.

The launch circled around and drew alongside the dory as Petschek and Grua's final strokes pulled them abreast of a rock on the left side of the reservoir that had been painted with the Lake Mead survey mark RS 273. Here, the Colorado underwent an odd change.

The current had now slowed to the point where the river could no longer hold sediment in suspension, and so the tiny particles of sand and dirt that the Colorado had been freighting all the way through the canyon began to drop out and settle toward the riverbed. As the sediment fell away, the reddish-brown color that was the river's hallmark abruptly disappeared and the water turned blue.

This exact spot delineated the border between the skirling dynamism of a living river and the torpor of a stagnating reservoir. It also marked the Grand Wash fault, the true end of the canyon.

Okay, wait . . . , ordered Grua.

Wait . . .

. . . not yet . . .

There was a long pause as the dory slid past the survey marker, then both men cried:

Now!

~

On a July morning three years earlier, when Grua, Petschek, and Wally Rist had completed their first speed run, Petschek had celebrated this same moment by seizing his conch shell, which boatmen use to call their passengers to dinner, and blowing a piercing blast that rang across the surface of the lake. Now there was no jubilation—no whistles, no yodeling, no cowboy whoops. As Taylor wrote down the time, Grua and Petschek simply removed their hands from the oars, slumped back, and permitted their blades to drop into the water.

Each blade left a little V-shaped wake that smoothed and disappeared as the dory slowly came to a stop. Then the boat floated there, motionless and still, suspended on the shimmering threshold between a world that refused to let them go and the world to which they were once again obliged to return.

It was 11:38 a.m., and their elapsed time was thirty-six hours, thirty-eight minutes, and twenty-nine seconds.

The *Emerald Mile* had not broken the speed record. She had smashed it to pieces by more than ten hours.

25

Tail Waves

The current that with gentle murmur glides
Thou knowest, being stopped, impatiently doth rage.

—WILLIAM SHAKESPEARE

PRECISELY seven minutes after the *Emerald Mile* arrived at the Grand Wash fault and Grua laid down his oars, the telephone rang in Tom Gamble's office, nearly three hundred miles upstream in the visitors' center high above the Glen Canyon Dam. The windows next to Gamble's desk looked out on the surface of Lake Powell, and as the dam's manager picked up the receiver, he could see the surface of the reservoir hovering just below the tops of the plywood flashboards on the spillway gates. The runaway torrent of snowmelt racing down the Colorado hadn't quite finished with the beleaguered team of engineers—and as Gamble was about to learn, things had just taken a turn for the worse.

On the other end of the line was Bruce Moyes in Denver, who had spent the better part of the past hour huddled with a group of colleagues staring disconsolately at the latest reports from the river forecast team in Salt Lake City. "Hydrographs look terrible," Phil Burgi had scribbled in his notebook, a reference to the fact that the runoff showed no sign of abating.

The purpose of Moyes's call was to inform Gamble that yet another surge was now heading toward Lake Powell. Despite the damage that had already been inflicted on the crippled spillways, they would have to send even more water through the tunnels and into the canyon.

While Gamble readied his team, the news was passed along to the Park Service. By the time the *Emerald Mile* was being towed back toward Hurricane—where Grua and his crew would crawl into their beds and sleep for two solid days—Helo 210 was making a beeline for Lee's Ferry to conduct another sweep of the canyon. Late that afternoon, every expedition between the ferry and Lake Mead received a plastic baggie that contained the following message:

DAM RELEASE UPDATE

BuRec will release 90,000 cfs from
Glen Canyon on June 27 after 5 p.m.
Flows will remain at 90K or above
for approximately two weeks.

CAMP HIGH—BE CAUTIOUS
National Park Service
6-27-83

Meanwhile, Burgi and Moyes caught a flight from Denver to Page to help Gamble boost the discharge in stages. At 7:00 p.m., all three men watched as the operators hoisted the cables on the spillway gates and sent more water crashing into the tunnels. At 9:00 the next morning, they raised the gates again. Then an hour later, they did so for a third time.

As the final phase of the operation unfolded, Burgi, who had walked out on the service deck above the east gates to peer into the top of the tunnel, leaned too far out over the railing and accidentally sent the white hard hat that he was wearing spinning into the spillway. The moment the hat struck the current of water rushing underneath the gate, it was snapped into the vortex and disappeared.

"Well, we're not gonna see that again," said one of the dam workers who stood next to him.

The amount of water now passing through or around the dam was stupendous. All but one of the penstocks were fully open and sending their streams into the turbines in the power plant. Ditto for the four river-outlet tubes, whose discharge was thundering through the jet valves at the base of the dam at 120 miles per hour. When combined with the two powerful plumes of water arcing over the flip buckets at the mouth of both spillway tunnels, the dam was feeding more water into the river than it had ever done: 92,000 cfs.

Reclamation had now cashed in its final insurance policy. Until the discharges were dialed back, the west spillway would be subjected to the same fury that had already ravaged its counterpart on the east side of the canyon, a situation that was fundamentally unsustainable. Everything now hinged on how much more snowmelt was still heading downstream and when that surge would reach its crest.

~

Meanwhile, the pulse of newly released water bored downstream from the toe of the dam at just under eight miles an hour, the pace of a trotting horse. A few minutes before noon, the head of the surge reached Lee's Ferry and started its journey through the canyon. It reached the bottom of the Roaring Twenties by 4:00 p.m., hit Nankoweap just before 7:00, passed through the entrance to the Upper Granite Gorge a few minutes before 10:00, and reached Phantom by 11:00. Then, at twenty-five minutes past midnight, it slammed into the explosion wave at Crystal, taking the rapid to the highest level ever witnessed—and triggering a series of changes that surprised everyone.

During the next thirty-six hours, as the engineers maintained their massive release through the spillway tunnels, the river got to work on the rocks that obstructed Crystal's thirty-five-foot-wide choke point, muscling aside boulders that the current had not been able to budge at the lower flows. Gradually, the channel widened—first by five, then ten, and finally fifteen feet—and as the gap opened up, the hydraulics weakened. As the height of the explosion wave decreased from thirty feet to ten, the ferocity began to subside, and a unique moment in the history of the river slammed shut. The white demon that had raged in the center of Crystal for six days—destroying four motorboats, killing Bill Wert, and nearly ending the speed run—retreated back into its lair, taking with it the seamless wall of water and the perfect pipeline curl.

They would never be seen again.*

Just as this process was completed, Gamble and his team at the dam finally caught a long-anticipated break. At 9:15 a.m. on Thursday, word arrived from far upstream at an earth-fill dam and reservoir on Big Sandy Creek, a tributary of the Green River in southwestern Wyoming. Big Sandy was one of the highest tributaries in the Upper Colorado Basin, which meant that it offered a telling barometer for the entire runoff. Early that morning, the engineers there had observed that the surface of the reservoir had dropped by almost a foot, which would enable them to cut back on the discharges they were releasing through the dam. A few minutes later, the engineers at Blue Mesa Reservoir, in Colorado, telephoned with news that their inflows were dropping as well. Soon, similar reports were trickling in from the reservoirs at Flaming Gorge

---

*Despite the diminished size of its hydraulic jump, Crystal would retain its status as the hardest and most savage rapid on the river for decades. During the years that followed the runoff of 1983, five more people perished at Mile 98. Although the fury subsided somewhat in the 1990s, Crystal remains a killer to this day. No other rapid in the canyon has claimed more lives.

and Morrow Point. In engineering parlance, they were now "on the back side of the hydrograph." The runoff had reached its peak.

At 1:30 p.m., Gamble ordered the gates on the left spillway to be lowered by two inches, the first in a series of reductions that would play out over the next several days. As this operation unfolded, the crest of Glen's highest discharge completed its surge through the Grand Canyon. It would take almost two more days before the tail end of this pulse finally reached the Grand Wash Cliffs and flattened itself out on the swollen surface of Lake Mead.

This meant that the handful of expeditions that were still on the river were able to witness and participate in something historic. For the rest of their careers, a few dozen river guides would be able to brag about having boated through the canyon at the apogee of a flood that had not been matched in two generations. Many of those guides would claim that they had rowed through Crystal or Lava during this unique and fleeting window. But as the speed run had already demonstrated, it didn't make a whit of difference who was where at the absolute peak. Everyone who was on the river during that magnificent and terrible time was changed by what he or she had seen and done. And in this sense, whether they liked it or not, the river folk and the engineers at the dam shared a bond that would tie them together for the rest of their lives.

The Grand Canyon had not seen a comparable injection of high water in at least a quarter century, but this was only part of the picture. For the first time in history, virtually every reservoir and flood-containment structure along the Colorado and its tributaries—an elaborate water-management system stretching from Wyoming to Mexico that had taken seven decades to build at a cost of many billions of dollars—was filled to the brim. In less than twenty weeks, a single load of snowmelt had pumped just under fourteen million acre-feet of water into that system, almost half the capacity of Lake Powell, a reservoir that had taken nearly two decades to fill. It had created the most damaging surges on the Colorado since the late 1920s, when Martin Litton was in grade school, making it the worst flood crisis in almost sixty years.

If the Bureau of Reclamation had any say-so in the matter, nothing like this would ever happen again. But first they had to see the crisis through to its conclusion.

~

For the better part of the following fortnight, the surface of Lake Powell continued rising as the balance of the runoff worked its way toward Glen. During that time, a team of sixteen specialized welders arrived at the dam, climbed onto the tops of the gates—which were still partially raised—and began replacing the plywood flashboards with a set of steel bulwarks that doubled the height of the barrier. When the job was through, everyone stood back and waited, until, around 1:00 p.m. on the afternoon of July 15, the surface of the reservoir finally crested at 3,708.34 feet above sea level. There it hovered, quivering, for almost twenty-four hours. Then, slowly and grudgingly, the waters began to recede. If the gates had been fully closed, the lake would have been almost four inches above the tops of the new flashboards.

A week later, the surface of the reservoir had ebbed to the point where Gamble was able to order the spillways closed. When the steel plates slammed shut at 8 a.m. on July 23, a platoon of about a dozen engineers and construction workers prepared to go into the tunnels. For the first time since Phil Burgi's descent aboard the "I Challenge U 2" cart back in early June, they were going to get a look at the carnage that had been wrought.

This time, instead of descending from above, they climbed over the flip buckets and walked into the mouths of the tunnels from the bottom. They started with the east spillway, which was partially filled with a column of cold, standing water, and they pulled behind them a rubber raft loaded with battery-powered floodlights, which illuminated the dark chamber.

They encountered massive destruction from the first step. The section of tunnel immediately beyond the flip bucket contained more than three hundred cubic yards of debris, mostly concrete rubble and broken chunks of sandstone, which they were forced to scramble through. Then a hush fell over them as they encountered their first surprise: a sandstone boulder, eighteen hundred cubic feet and easily the size of a delivery truck, sat directly in the middle of the tunnel. They christened it House Rock, unwittingly borrowing the name of the first major rapid in the Grand Canyon, seventeen miles downstream from Lee's Ferry. To remove the boulder, they realized, they would have to blast it to pieces with dynamite.

As they continued fumbling forward in the wet darkness, the spotlights revealed a scene that would not have been out of place in a building destroyed by an earthquake or a bomb. Along the walls, the three-foot-thick concrete lining was gone, stripped to the sandstone. Only the upper section of the roof was intact, and everywhere there were signs of rockfall. The most eerie elements of all, however, were the skeins of rebar, whose ends were still half embedded in the remaining concrete like the bones of a poached fish. The tangle of steel offered graphic testimony to the fury that had been unleashed inside the tunnel.

Now they reached the elbow joint, the most critical section, and even those who were braced for the worst were shocked by what awaited them.

The base of the elbow was submerged beneath a dark pool of water. The depth was impossible to gauge, so they decided to continue no further, but from this vantage they could see plenty. A column of light spilled down the steeply inclined tunnel section from the gate openings, more than five hundred feet above, illuminating the same series of cavitation holes that Burgi had observed during his descent almost two months earlier. The "Christmas tree," however, had been expanded so deeply that the tunnel was now bisected by a jagged gash, ten feet deep and twenty-five feet wide. Through this linked series of small ledges and basins, the discharge from the tunnel's weep holes cascaded merrily through the gash and into the plunge pool at the bottom, filling the chamber with the sound of falling water.

After recording the damage with their cameras and video equipment, they turned around and retraced their steps back toward the flip bucket. Then they crossed to the other side of the river to inspect the west spillway, where a similar scene awaited them.

The first order of business was to pump both spillways dry, which enabled them to address the biggest question on everyone's mind—how deep were the caverns that had been excavated at the base of the two elbows? The answer, when it was revealed, took their breath away.

Both holes were enormous, but the declivity in the east spillway, which had sustained the greatest damage, was slightly larger, so they called it the Big Hole. It was 134 feet long, 15 feet wide, and more than three stories deep. They would have to bring in a series of ladders just to get to the bottom. Even more astonishing than the extent of the damage, however, was that all of that destruction had been unleashed by a nodule of calcite no bigger than a walnut.

Later, while mapping out the contours of the Big Hole, a construction worker discovered a battered piece of white plastic that had gotten wedged into the rocks at the base.

It was Phil Burgi's missing hard hat.

~

Repairs on the spillways started in earnest in late August. With the dam's turbines and generators still running at full capacity and the four river-outlet jet valves continuing to channel their blasts of water into the river, the construction crews brought in a special drilling machine and bored through the canyon walls to access the tunnels from the powerhouse deck. This enabled them to drive a fleet of cement trucks, backhoes, and other pieces of heavy machinery directly into the tunnels. Then dozens of workers embarked on the task of removing the debris while preparing the walls for the latticework of rebar that would reinforce the new lining.

As this work proceeded, Dr. Henry Falvey, the bureau's cavitation specialist back at the Hydraulics Lab in Denver, applied the finishing touches to a simple but elegant pair of air slots that were designed to neutralize the effects of cavitation. Falvey's plan called for rings and troughs to be blasted four feet into the lining along the upper portions of both tunnels—an especially difficult job that was performed by the Loizeaux family, a group of explosives experts who would later handle much of the demolitions work at Ground Zero following the destruction of New York's World Trade Center during the 9/11 terrorist attacks. When the work on the tunnels was complete and the slots were finally tested, they introduced a cushion of air bubbles into the water racing through the spillways, virtually eliminating the possibility of cavitation damage in the future.

The cost of all these repairs came to more than $32 million, a rather shocking price tag. As Reclamation officials would hasten to point out to anyone who was willing to listen, those costs were offset by the additional hydropower generated by the excess water sent through the dam's power plant during the crisis. The sale of that electricity brought in $35 million. This calculation, however, did not account for the damage inflicted as the surge of high water passed through Hoover Dam—which was forced to open its own spillways—and into the lower Colorado, where flooding overwhelmed hundreds of homes and businesses, contaminated ground wells, and took out public irrigation systems (infrastructure, it must be added, that had been built directly inside the flood zone over the bureau's objections).

When those costs were added to the rest of the bill, the total came to more than $80 million, and on top of that, there were also several more fatalities. Six people drowned along the lower part of the Colorado as the remnants of the flood raced past the town of Yuma, into Mexico, and finally spilled into the Sea of Cortés, which received its largest infusion of freshwater in many years. But even the most adamant dam opponents had to concede that the destruction in 1983 was far less than what would have occurred if an unchained Colorado had run from the Rockies to the Pacific, as it had during the days of John Wesley Powell.

Nevertheless, in the court of public opinion anger over these events was vehement. Kim Crumbo, the Park Service ranger who had previously served as a SEAL in Vietnam, later put his finger on the question many people wanted answered. "The bureau knew damn well they had too much water in Lake Powell," he declared. "Why did they sit on so much water until it was too late?" The answer was forcefully articulated by Richard Bryan, the governor of Nevada, when he accused the bureau of losing control of the river through a "monumental miscalculation."

There was an element of truth to that charge; and as a result, Reclamation deserved to shoulder a hefty chunk of the blame. But amid the fury, some salient facts were ignored, beginning with the job that the engineers had pulled off. Years later, Tom Gamble, Phil Burgi, and Bruce Moyes, along with dozens of their colleagues, would look back on that summer as the most stressful but rewarding time of their careers. By preserving the spillway tunnels for as long as possible, they had contained a crisis that had no precedent in hydroelectric engineering. And at the height of that crisis, they had stopped a runaway river by turning to one of the humblest tools one could imagine. Their plywood flashboards had saved the day.

None of this, however, precludes acknowledging that the system itself was, and remains, profoundly flawed. Among the many disturbing issues that it exposes, the runoff of 1983 calls into question why the bureau manages its entire series of dams and reservoirs according to a set of imperatives—the need to store water, to generate power, and to control floods—that are fundamentally opposed to one another. And flowing from that is the question of whether the task of meeting these competing demands compromises public welfare—an issue that is underscored by the still-lingering question of whether the safety of one of the largest dams in the United States had been jeopardized.

Of the two views on this, the first is supported by virtually every engineer and scientist who was involved with the spillway crisis. The caverns that were excavated at the base of the elbows inside the spillway tunnels confirmed Henry Falvey's prediction that the worst of the cavitation-induced damage would drill downward, deep into the rock, and not backward toward the dam. As a result, the abutments remained intact and the safety of the dam was never compromised—an assessment that is supported by leading independent experts who have no direct affiliation with Reclamation. "I haven't seen anything that suggested the dam was in danger," says J. David Rogers, a professor of geological engineering at Missouri University of Science and Technology who is intimately familiar with Glen. "There are no serious questions about the integrity of the dam itself."

The second view, which is shared by many of these same people, is that the events that unfolded at Glen should never have been allowed to happen in the first place, and that the spillway crisis came far closer to disaster than should ever have been permitted—an idea that was perhaps voiced most chillingly by one of Reclamation's own.

In 1997, a pair of reporters from the *Sacramento Bee* who were completing a series of articles on the safety of America's dams interviewed John W. Keys, a civil and hydraulic engineer who had spent thirty-four years working for the bureau. Like his colleagues at Glen Canyon, Keys knew a thing or two about dams—at the time, he was completing a twelve-year stint as Reclamation's Pacific Northwest regional director, and would later spend another five years as commissioner, the highest post in Reclamation.

"How close did we come to losing Glen Canyon in 1983?" asked Keys. "We came a hell of a lot closer than many people know."

26

The Trial

I wish to speak a word for Nature,
for absolute freedom and wildness.

—HENRY DAVID THOREAU

As critics lashed out at the bureau and the repair work on the spillways went forward, there loomed the question of what, if anything, the Park Service intended to do about the stunt that Grua had pulled in the *Emerald Mile.*

All summer long, as the river guides rode the remnants of the high water, the only thing that Martin Litton's dorymen wanted to talk about was the speed run. Grua's feat was the hottest piece of news on the river, and the guides were now folding it into their frame of reference by doing what guides did best, which was to tell the story over and over to themselves and anyone else who would listen. Despite the fact that Grua clearly had no intention of publicizing or capitalizing on the achievement, they were fiercely proud that the record had been so decisively nailed by a dory. Late at night on the boats, early in the morning while they guzzled their coffee, they endlessly recounted what had taken place—how remarkable it was, how it could never be repeated, what a stellar achievement it represented.

Amid the backslapping and the bluster, however, were hints of something darker. The "eddy line"—the canyon's network of gossip that conveyed information up and down the river—was now transmitting some troubling rumors suggesting that the superintendent was on the warpath. Richard Marks was said to be livid and resolved to take drastic action. To ensure that nothing like this would ever happen again, he intended to make an example of Grua by hauling him into court, revoking his guide's license, and banning him from the river for the rest of his life.

Partly in an effort to control a mounting sense of panic, Grua, who was fully booked with a series of midsummer commercial river trips, grew indignant and angry. He castigated the Park Service for its pettiness and its overreach. He declared that Marks, who had never been a boatman and didn't know the first thing about the river, wasn't qualified to judge what the crew of the *Emerald Mile* had achieved. Meanwhile, however, Grua continued to fear the worst. When he got off the river in late July, he returned home to his trailer in Hurricane, opened up his mail, and saw his apprehensions confirmed in black and white.

The letter was addressed to Grua. Neither Petschek nor Wren was mentioned, and the wording was blunt:

"Enclosed is a citation for your participation in an illegal river trip. Your court date has been set for August 2 at 10:00 a.m."

~

Grua was scheduled to leave immediately on yet another trip, and thanks to his packed schedule for the rest of the guiding season, a series of continuances and delays followed. During this period, Litton got busy and started working the phones from California, launching a campaign of backdoor diplomacy, hoping that his entreaties would convince the aggrieved superintendent to drop the charges. None of it worked, and by the beginning of November, as the river season drew to a close, Grua was out of excuses. It was time to face the music.

On a blustery autumn afternoon, Litton took his plane from San Francisco down to the Orange County airport and picked up Mike Meade, a former river passenger who was also an attorney and who had agreed, at Litton's request, to represent Grua free of charge. The two men then flew east to Hurricane, where Litton touched down in a wind so strong they practically had to slip in sideways. When they opened the door for Grua, a gust of wind nearly tore the door off its hinges, forcing them to duct-tape it shut for the flight to the South Rim.

They arrived late in the day, skimming across a wintry canyon whose rims were dusted with snow and into which the cold, blue air had settled like smoke. They spent the night in a nearby motel, and the following morning they completed the short walk along Loop Road through the heart of Grand Canyon Village, the bustling little community where most tourists began and ended their encounter with the canyon.

Just down the street was El Tovar, the hotel perched on the rim where Litton and his wife had spent the first night of their honeymoon in the autumn of 1941. A few steps farther brought them to the former post office, a one-story lodge featuring a steeply gabled roof and log-cabin-style walls. Here, six mornings each week for many years, letters and packages had been dropped into a set of leather saddlebags and sent down the trail to Phantom Ranch, one of only two postal addresses in the United States where the mail was still delivered by mule. Although the mule train still ran, the post office had recently been moved, and now the little log building, whose front porch was supported by peeled trunks of ponderosa pines, served as the most picturesque and romantic outpost of the federal justice system.

Each national park has its own federal magistrate's courthouse, and in the autumn of 1983, presiding over the bench at Grand Canyon was Judge Thomas H. McKay, a former lawyer from Tucson whose face bore an expression of good-humored exasperation and weary decency that made him a dead ringer for the stand-up comedian Lewis Black. Over the years, McKay's court had witnessed more than its fair share of petty crimes. He had recently presided over a spate of cases involving hang-glider pilots who illegally plunged into the abyss, then folded up their gear and made a run for the rim before the rangers could catch them. Several arrests had also been made among a band of hippies who were tending marijuana gardens at some extremely remote corners of the canyon.

Regardless of how minor these and other crimes might be, each and every case that came before McKay bore unusual symbolic weight. Because the park fell within federal jurisdiction, the imprimatur of the language suggested that the proceedings demanded the attention of the entire country. Case Number 83-2079M was no exception:

UNITED STATES OF AMERICA, PLAINTIFF

VERSUS

KENTON GRUA, DEFENDANT

Like most of McKay's cases, this was a nonjury trial. Litton and Meade took their seats on the defense side of the room along with Grua, who had exchanged his river sandals and shorts for shoes, trousers, and a clean shirt, and was doing his best to look presentable. On the prosecution side, three other men also took their seats. The first was a ranger who was acting as the solicitor on behalf of the National Park Service. The second was John Thomas, the ranger who had witnessed the *Emerald Mile*'s run through Crystal. He looked decidedly uncomfortable about having been called to appear. Finally, arriving late and obviously pressed for time, was Richard Marks, the superintendent himself.

When McKay entered the room, everyone stood as he stepped onto the raised dais. Then the judge settled himself behind his desk, rapped his gavel, and inaugurated the final chapter of the speed run.

~

The Park Service solicitor began by explaining that Grua had violated Title 36, Section 7.4(h)(3) of the Code of Federal Regulations—a densely worded legal provision whose operative clause stated, "No person shall conduct, lead, or guide a river trip unless that person has a permit issued by the superintendent of Grand Canyon National Park." This offense fell under the category of a "moving violation," and the notice that Grua had received in the mail was, with unintended appropriateness, the same form that the rangers used for issuing speeding tickets to motorists inside the park. Having thus established the facts, the solicitor turned to his first witness and called his boss to the stand.

Contrary to what Grua had been led to believe, Marks didn't appear to be the least bit angry or upset. He settled into the witness box calmly, with a neutral expression on his face. But as he answered the questions put to him by the solicitor, the depositional layer of facts that Marks laid down brooked little in the way of alternative interpretation or wiggle room. Selecting his words carefully, the superintendent provided an efficient history of the permit application process and explained that Grua's efforts to obtain a special-use permit had been reviewed in the usual manner and nixed at every stage. In the absence of either written or verbal sanction, he therefore had no right whatsoever to conduct his river trip. And what's more, added Marks, Grua and his companions *knew* as much.

When the solicitor sat down, Meade, a savvy trial lawyer who had cut his teeth in the cutthroat world of divorce and real estate law in Newport Beach, was given the chance to see what he could do with all of this. He began by hitting Marks with a barrage of clever questions designed to get the superintendent to unwittingly admit the possibility that, in their own minds, Grua and his companions might have had some reason to believe that permission had been granted. True, Meade stipulated, the application had been turned down. But was anything said—or, more important, *not* said—that could have led the dorymen to conclude that the Park Service was tentatively or provisionally *considering* some kind of approval? Was it possible that something—*anything*—about the telephone conversation with Litton or the confusion surrounding all the other emergencies inside the canyon had somehow conveyed the shadow of an understanding that it was okay for them to launch?

Alas, Marks was having none of this.

Nope, he replied. Categorically impossible. They knew the answer was no. They went and did it anyhow. Period, full stop, end of story.

Having delivered up these facts, and with no further questions from Meade, Marks excused himself and went back to his office.

Next to take the stand was John Thomas, and the park solicitor's only aim was to establish before the judge that Thomas had witnessed the *Emerald Mile*'s illegal run and that he had recognized Grua at the oars. The solicitor's questions were perfunctory, and when he was finished, Meade declined to ask any questions of his own.

Meade now had only a single arrow in his quiver. At crucial times in the past—most notably before the Sierra Club board in May of 1963, Martin Litton's ability to stand up and deliver a stem-winder had saved the day. Perhaps by rekindling those fires, the old man could do the same here, thought Meade. If Litton's words had once helped to block a pair of giant hydroelectric dams and prevent the greatest river canyon on earth from being turned into a chain-linked series of bathtubs, how hard could it be to convince an aging magistrate that this effort to railroad the captain of the *Emerald Mile* was overzealous and wrong?

Litton gave it his best shot. The status of the permit, he declared, had been left open by the superintendent's failure to call him back, as Marks had said he would do. What's more, the run was entirely benign. It was not designed as a stunt—a bid for fame or notoriety—but had arisen instead from a genuine desire to add to the body of knowledge about what could be accomplished on the river. In fact, Litton added, his voice rising, the journey had been undertaken as a public service in the interest of expanding *river knowledge* and promoting *boater safety*. When viewed in that light, it was not only inappropriate but downright *offensive* to condemn Grua's run as a violation of the letter of the law when it was actually one of the best things that had ever happened on the river. The speed run partook of the same spirit that had inspired John Wesley Powell's own trip—an odyssey launched in the name of science and sustained by the noble purpose of unraveling the mysteries of the canyon. And what's more, it had worked, because now, after 114 years of rowing through the dark ages of ignorance, everyone on the river knew how long it would take to traverse the canyon by manpower alone. Not approximately how long, but precisely and without a shadow of a doubt:

Thirty-six hours, thirty-eight minutes, and twenty-nine seconds!

On and on Litton went, riding up the face of his own rhetoric, plunging forcefully into the trough of another argument, only to be catapulted by another surge of poetry and soar once more into the air. His oratory was eloquent and impressive and fabulously entertaining—and perhaps for those reasons, neither the judge nor the Park Service solicitor made the slightest effort to interrupt or contradict what he was saying. But unlike the great speeches of the past, in which his listeners had found themselves transfixed and wooed, his words fell flat and the audience was unmoved.

The reason for this was no great mystery. Unlike with the free-flowing rivers or the virgin stands of redwood or any of the other natural wonders on whose behalf Litton had spoken with such passion and such rage for so many years, his heart wasn't really in this. Yes, he found the Park Service meddlesome and irritating. No, he didn't like Richard Marks at all. But Litton also knew that the superintendent and his employees were the main reason why the inside of the Grand Canyon didn't look like the Jersey shore. And finally, Litton knew that the pretext under which Grua's venture had been launched was as ephemeral as a plume of virga, the delicate desert rain that is released from clouds above the canyon but evaporates and vanishes long before it ever has a ghost of a chance of reaching solid ground.

Everyone understood this, including Grua himself. Sitting there in court, he bore the look of a dark-horse candidate on election night who knows in his heart that he is about to lose.

～

The closing arguments were brief and devoid of hyperbole.

The Park Service solicitor stated that Grua had committed an unambiguous transgression. In response, Meade declared that there wasn't sufficient evidence to support that allegation and that in any case it was a victimless crime, which had harmed no one.

McKay didn't even pretend it was a hard call. After taking no more than a minute to deliberate, he seized his gavel and positioned his little wooden sound block in front of him.

"I do find the defendant guilty as charged," he declared, and brought the gavel down with a bang.

～

The punishment turned out to be rather benign. Truth be told, the whole thing was actually a bit of a joke—especially in light of the overheated rumors about Grua's being run out of the canyon and banned from the river.

If Marks had ever wanted to do those things, cooler thinking—including his own—had tempered the impulse and brought him back to the principle that the punishment should fit the crime. So McKay began by imposing a $500 fine, a sum that Meade immediately protested as larger than what any dirtbag river guide—a creature who, by definition, dwelled in permanent financial distress—could reasonably be asked to part with.

The matter was taken under advisement, and eventually, after further negotiations and verbal appeasements over the phone, it was agreed that Grua could work off his fine through some unspecified acts of community service. Which, depending on who was telling this part of the story in the years that followed (and how many beers had been consumed), Grua may not ever have bothered to perform. In other words, he pretty much got off scot-free.

This was deemed acceptable by the Park Service, however, because everyone, including the superintendent, was less concerned with making Grua pay for his crime than with upholding the idea that one was no longer allowed to do this sort of thing. The days when a trio of speed bandits could shove a dory into the river and go highballing through the canyon were now gone. For having defied this principle, Grua had been made to answer, and in the eyes of just about everyone involved, things had worked out more or less as they should. The Park Service pronounced itself vindicated and was now prepared to move on—thereby enabling the story to quietly subside and, with the passage of time and the erosion of human memory, eventually disappear.

There the matter should have been allowed to rest.

Except that it wasn't, because, simply put, too much had happened. Too much water had gone down the river. Too much drama had unfolded on its surface. And most important, too many people were unable to resist the irrational but wondrously seductive possibility that the *Emerald Mile* had cut a line of symbolic clarity that seemed to bring the river, the canyon, and, yes, even the dam itself into a new and irresistibly compelling focus. And so, unbeknownst to any of the players, including Grua himself, the wheels of the machine that would eventually turn this dubious exploit into a legend began to turn.

The process would take years to unfold, years that would usher profound changes into the lives of everyone involved. But the legend rested upon one simple truth, an idea that was perhaps most succinctly affirmed by the writer Philip Pullman, who has no connection to the canyon or the river, but whose words capture the essence of what Grua had brought to life:

> *"Thou shalt not" is soon forgotten,*
> *but "Once upon a time" lasts forever.*

EPILOGUE

~

Looking downstream from Nankoweap: perhaps the fairest stretch
of river in the canyon.

The Legend of the Emerald Mile

Brave boatmen come, they go, they die, the voyage flows on forever.
We are all canyoneers. We are all passengers on this little living mossy
ship, this delicate dory sailing round the sun that humans call the Earth.
Joy, shipmates, joy.

—EDWARD ABBEY

I F the speed run was an act of consummate recklessness, it also stands as one of the purest and most perfect journeys the Grand Canyon has ever seen, a voyage that embodied the essence of the river by moving through its corridor under conditions that were not only beset by immense physical challenges but, more important, were freighted with the extraordinary power of metaphor. Although at the time many people saw the trip—and continue to perceive it today—as irresponsible and self-indulgent, the story of what Grua and his companions pulled off eventually came to assume dimensions that neither they nor anyone else could have anticipated.

Over the next thirty years, the speed run would undergo an evolution in the minds of the boatmen of the canyon. A tradition that had originally arisen out of a survival necessity—a "race for a dinner" in the final days of Powell's journey—had already been transmogrified into a compelling quest by men looking to test themselves against the canyon. Yet, with time, the run came to be seen as something more: a statement of both commemoration and defiance—a celebration of the Colorado's ancestral majesty, as well as a symbolic act of protest against the manner in which the river had been so ruthlessly harnessed and sold. And then, finally, another idea arose, perhaps the most provocative of all, because its import extended so far beyond the boat or the men who piloted her, and, instead, spoke directly to the canyon itself.

The English novelist J. B. Priestley once said that if he were an American, he would make the final test of whatever men chose to do in art, business, or politics a comparison with the Grand Canyon. He believed that whatever was false and ephemeral would be exposed for what it was when set against that mass of geology and light. Priestley was British, but he had placed his finger on an abiding American truth: the notion that the canyon stands as one of our most important touchstones—a kind of roofless tabernacle whose significance is both natural *and* national. It is our cathedral in the desert, and the word *our* is key because although the canyon belongs to the entire world, we, as Americans, belong particularly to it.

As blasphemous as it may sound to those who love the river and the canyon most deeply, the speed run demonstrated that this space of worship and reflection includes not only the canyon but also the dam and the reservoir behind it. Like it or not, the Glen Canyon Dam and Lake Powell exemplify some of this nation's greatest achievements. They are bold affirmations of the science, the engineering, and the bureaucratic discipline that built the American century, and which, among many other things, enabled the country to harness the power of the atom and to peer into the most distant reaches of the universe.

The tempestuous stretch of river below that dam, however, represents something no less central to the national ethos: the fact that another aspect of our character as a people derives from an extended encounter with wilderness. That quality achieved its first expression in men such as Don García López de Cárdenas and John Wesley Powell. But it survives and flourishes to this day within the community of boatmen who have made the canyon their home. The subculture that they have created is cantankerous and incorrigibly headstrong—its members are irritatingly independent, impossible as cats to herd. But they have preserved an aspect of the American persona that is uniquely vital to the health of this republic. Among many other things, those dirtbag river runners uphold the virtue of disobedience: the principle that in a free society, defiance for its own sake sometimes carries value and meaning, if only because power in all of its forms—commercial, governmental, and moral—should not always and without question be handed what it demands.

What is illustrative and bewitching about the Grand Canyon, therefore, is not merely the world of the canyon itself but the juxtaposition of that world with its opposite: the dam and the drowned Arcadia that lies beneath its reservoir. Each feature without the other is important in its own way. But the collision of these elements is even more revealing. While those two worlds have always been perceived as separate and mutually opposed by their respective citizenry—the sober army of engineers above, and the fractious confederacy of river folk below—perhaps the most provocative aspect of the speed run was how it braided these narratives together in a way that had never before been done.

It may seem absurd to suggest that the canyon is somehow incomplete without the dam, but the speed run underscores the inescapable truth that every journey not only begins at the dam but is also enriched and challenged by it. And together the canyon and the dam offer a far more meaningful reflection of the society that claims them both: its triumphs and its failures; what it has been willing to sacrifice and what it has chosen to preserve; the things it celebrates and those it mourns; the price it has willingly paid for progress and modernity, as well as the lessons that have been levied by those transactions. Perhaps nothing else speaks so succinctly and with such eloquence to who we are as a people—where we have come from, what we have gained and lost on our journey, and what we must eventually embrace to make ourselves whole.

~

In this sense, the speed run did more than simply demonstrate the feats that a small, rigid-hulled boat was capable of pulling off. Yet, it is also important to acknowledge that her record has never been bested by anyone in a dory or a raft, nor even by a kayaker. This is partly because the water monster that batted the *Emerald Mile* through the canyon has gone into hibernation. The runoff of 1984 was huge, but since then the floods seem to have disappeared, and the Southwest is now in the grip of an extended drought that may eventually turn the Colorado into a trickle. Those facts have not stopped rival oarsmen and paddlers from making a run at the speed record—but so far, their best efforts have fallen short of the mark.

In the autumn of 2012, a talented young river guide named Harlan Taney, an independent-minded boatman not unlike Grua, wrangled a permit from the Park Service and gave it a go. He left Lee's Ferry at midnight, timing his launch to the first in a series of "high-flow" tests that was being conducted at the dam. He rode in a touring kayak, a craft that is difficult to maneuver, but which can achieve speeds that far exceed those of an oar boat. And after paddling all night through the upper stretch of the canyon, he tipped over in Grapevine, a nasty rapid at Mile 82, where he was slammed into the granite wall and injured his elbow.

The accident forced Taney to abandon his attempt and hike out of the canyon, but he demonstrated something noteworthy. Prior to reaching Grapevine, he was averaging almost eleven miles an hour, a pace that, had he been able to sustain it, would have shattered the *Emerald Mile*'s record by ten hours. This suggests that in time someone will succeed. When that person does, he or she will, oddly enough, have Kenton Grua to thank, in part, for the idea—because he dreamed of doing the same thing himself.

∽

Four years after the speed run, Grua retired the *Emerald Mile* and embarked on a series of experiments in boat design, building two additional dories, each more innovative and radical than the previous. All the while, he continued to think about a craft that would enable him to best his own record. The vessel he envisioned would be long and thin and able to track effortlessly, achieving speeds that no dory could ever hope to match. In many ways, it would resemble a touring kayak—although it would have oars instead of a double-bladed paddle, a kind of white-water rowing scull. And when it was finished, Grua intended to pull off something so astonishing that it would have made John Wesley Powell turn over in his grave: to race from Lee's Ferry to the Grand Wash Cliffs in under twenty-four hours.

Grua's friends greeted this plan, like so many of his other bold ideas from the past, with raised eyebrows, convinced that he was once again allowing wishful thinking to cloud reality. In addition to requiring the perfect water conditions, such a boat would demand that a single boatman perform the work of three. Nevertheless, he refused to give up on the idea, droning on endlessly about it even as he threw himself into yet *another* project—a venture that would, in the end, have far more lasting impact than anything else he had done.

In 1988, Grua surprised everybody all over again by pulling together a few friends and sitting down in front of a typewriter—one of the few hand tools with which he had almost no prior experience—and creating Grand Canyon River Guides, an organization that brought all of the canyon's boatmen and outfitters together under a single umbrella for the first time. His aim, which was directly inspired by the example that Litton had set, was for this to be an advocacy group, working to shield the canyon and the river from the depredations of dam operators, helicopter-tour companies, and anyone else bent on harming this world-class treasure. The organization has proved remarkably effective in this respect, but one of its most gratifying services has been for the divided river community.

At Grua's urging, the group inaugurated a series of annual boatmen's reunion parties, each of which culminated in a training trip through the canyon for young river guides—men and women alike—who would be mentored by veterans from every company, regardless of the kind of boat they piloted. As this new generation ran the river together, the ferocious clashes of the past—motors versus oars, rubber versus wood—fell away and were forgotten, and everyone became friends.

Meanwhile, Grua continued rowing his dories on a full roster of river trips each summer. His aim was to do so until he died inside the canyon, which would surely have been fitting. But along with the twenty-four-hour run, he was denied this wish. In the fall of 2002, while riding his mountain bike on a section of single track on the outskirts of Flagstaff, he suffered an aortic dissection, a tear in the inner layer of the large blood vessel branching off his heart, and passed away in the middle of the trail. He was fifty-two years old.

His memorial service was held in a mountain meadow just outside of town. Virtually the entire river community attended, and that night they built an enormous bonfire, a conflagration worthy of the Viking funeral that had once been planned for the *Emerald Mile*. Many people stood up and spoke about what a remarkable person he was. Many others wanted to speak, but found themselves unable to do so because they were crying too hard.

His absence left an immense void. Those who knew him, friends and enemies alike, say that it is almost as deep and as grand as the canyon he loved.

~

One of the few people who was unable to attend that memorial in the meadow was Steve Reynolds. In keeping with his character, he had shot off on a unique trajectory.

Shortly after the speed run, Wren finally bought a boat of his own. She was a thirty-seven-foot sailboat, a sweet little yawl that had been converted into a sloop. She had a rounded bilge and a hand-pounded steel hull with a three-quarter-ton keel, and in the autumn of 1984 he sailed her off into the South Pacific, chasing freedom in much the same way that Bernard Moitessier, the great single-handed yachtsman, had done fifteen years earlier.

First Wren went to Fiji and Vanuatu, and then headed down to New Caledonia and from there to Brisbane, where he waited for the typhoon season to pass before sailing up the coast of Australia to Townsville and setting off for New Guinea. From there, he headed for Guam, then across to the Carolines, where he met a man who knew how to navigate from the stars and the birds and the tides. There Wren's engine caught fire, which stalled him for several months, but when he had finished his repairs, he set a course for Tinian, where the planes had taken off to bomb Hiroshima and Nagasaki, and from there to Saipan and Pagan, where one morning an active volcano covered his decks with about an inch of soot. Then it was across to Okinawa, and from there up through the chain of little islands to Japan.

He ran out of money in Kyushu but found a job teaching English, and shortly after that, he met a Japanese woman named Noriko, whom he married. They started a little school, had two children, and lived in a town on the coast.

After several years had passed, Wren decided it was time to come back to the States and settle his family in Hawaii. So while Noriko and the children headed for the airport, he shipped his anchor and headed back across the Pacific. It was a difficult sail—a sixty-day crossing with poor winds and choppy seas, and although he saw plenty of dolphins and even some whales, he didn't catch a single fish. But one night, somewhere on the long, eleven-hundred-mile stretch of open ocean between Midway and Kauai, the full moon came up, fat and shining, just as it had done in June of 1983. The wind was steady and the seas were calm, so Wren made himself a bed in the cockpit and sailed sideways to the moon on one of the nicest nights ever. Out there along that silvery expanse of star-draped sea, he found a note of grace that reflected back something he had touched only once, and only briefly, deep inside the Grand Canyon.

When he finally reached Hawaii, he rejoined his family and lived happily, running charter tours to watch the humpbacks off the Na Pali coast, until 2010, when he was diagnosed with liver cancer and flew to California for a transplant that would never arrive. But in the final weeks of his life he came full circle and met with me in a motel room in Santa Rosa to reminisce over the speed run, an achievement that he had never bragged about to anyone, but had never forgotten either. As proof, he pointed to the T-shirt that Anne Marie Nicholson, one of their timekeepers, had made and presented to him, one of only three that were printed. Its only lettering was the elapsed time of the speed run—36:38:29. He had kept it close to him all these years.

He also talked a bit about what still stood out most in his mind, which was that terrible explosion wave in Crystal:

"We hit that wave dead-on in the best possible spot, as straight as could be—a *perfect* run. But our boat was seventeen feet long, and even when we were stood straight up, there was the wave above us."

Wren was dying when he made that remark. His skin had turned yellow, his hair was falling out, and his abdomen had swelled up with so much fluid that it looked as if he were carrying a bowling ball inside his belly. He was in terrible pain. But as he remembered what it felt like to slide down the tongue into that glittering maelstrom, the expression on his face softened and his lips curled into a smile.

"We just couldn't make it—it was that simple," he sighed. "We couldn't get over that wave, it was just such a huge thing. But it was a *beautiful* wave, a beautiful run."

He passed away six weeks later.

When he died, Rudi Petschek was by his side to hold his hand and say farewell.

~

Among the speed-run crew, this left only Petschek, the man who had pulled the *Emerald Mile* through her darkest and loneliest hour.

By the time of Wren's death, Petschek too had left the river, but only with reluctance. After the speed run, he had carried on for years, pulled back again and again by the flames of yearning that the canyon had ignited and sustained. At the end of every river season, on the first morning after he got back to California, he awakened to a sense of anticipation, looking toward the first run of the following spring.

As the years passed, however, the fire began to ebb. It took almost two decades, but with the flow of time, the anticipation of returning in the spring eventually stopped occurring the day after the last trip of the autumn. First it faded to a week. Then a month. When it finally receded to the better part of the winter, Petschek and the woman he had married—who was also one of Litton's dory guides—retired to their wooden house nestled among the dripping hemlocks in the foothills of the California Sierra. He's there now, and from his window he can look out on his own dory, the *Colorado*, which he and Kenton built together, and remember the desert and the way it smelled in the rain.

Along with his connection to the desert's austere enchantments, Petschek has never lost his sense of wonder at the complexity of the great canyon, both geologic and human. That a place so huge and so imposing could nurture, at its deepest center, a tiny community of misfits and outcasts and dreamers who are bound together by their addiction to its beauty. That a place that seems so cut off from the world can also seem so central to the world. And most of all, that a landscape so universally recognized and celebrated, a landscape that is said to lay bare the mysteries of nature and the forces of time, can be filled with so many hidden treasures, secrets known only to a select few—and that he, Rudi, a refugee from the city of Prague, can number himself among that company.

As for the speed run, yes, he still thinks about it, and quite often. Not as frequently as he once did, which for many years was almost every day. But the memory of that mad race atop the swollen floodwaters still rushes back in unexpected moments: the rapids that Kenton and Wren and he battled; the disasters they skirted; the skills and the courage that they called upon to get them through. Like the witchery of white water, it is a thing whose luster never seems to dim. But what abides utmost in his mind is his gratitude for and amazement at the unlikely journey that brought him to the river. He is astonished that he found his way home.

"It was like a perfect storm of luck," he says, chuckling at the improbable wonder of it all.

⌇

Perhaps the most improbable wonder of all, however, is the still-raging storm of Martin Litton.

After years of struggling to keep his sinking company afloat, Litton finally sold it in 1987—and promptly went off on a tear trying to save the sequoias of Northern California, his first love and the only rival to his affair with the canyon. That crusade, which continues to this day, still takes him to Sacramento and Washington, and he has emerged as something of an elder statesman of the environmental movement, respected and admired and loved.

As his hair has gotten whiter and his beard has grown longer, however, Litton has begun carrying a sadness whose weight is perhaps most visible in his eyes and in the tone of his voice. He is haunted by the past—a man who is tormented by the heartache of having seen too much of the country's beauty before it was taken away. So much has been lost, and only those like himself who knew the glory of it all before that loss can now take the measure of its magnitude.

His friends do their best to console him with assurances that somehow everything will be all right—that, like the rapids of the canyon, things have a way of working out for the best. But in light of what is now happening to the canyon, Litton's pessimism seems both appropriate and justified.

From every direction, the place is under assault—and unlike in the past, the adversary is not concentrated in a single force, such as the Bureau of Reclamation, but takes the form of separate outfits conducting smaller attacks that are, in many ways, far more insidious. From directly above, the air-tour industry has succeeded in scuttling all efforts to dial it back, most recently through the intervention of Arizona's senators, John Kyl and John McCain, and is continuing to destroy one of the canyon's greatest treasures, which is its silence. From the east has come a dramatic increase in uranium-mining claims, while the once remote and untrammeled country of the North Rim now suffers from an ever-growing influx of recreational ATVs. On the South Rim, an Italian real estate company recently secured approval for a massive development whose water demands are all but guaranteed to compromise many of the canyon's springs, along with the oases that they nourish. Worst of all, the Navajo tribe is currently planning to cooperate in constructing a monstrous tramway to the bottom of the canyon, complete with a restaurant and a resort, at the confluence of the Little Colorado and the Colorado, the very spot where John Wesley Powell made the famous entry in his report from the summer of 1869 about venturing "down the Great Unknown."

As vexing as all these things are, what Litton finds even more disheartening is the country's failure to rally to the canyon's defense—or for that matter, to the defense of its other imperiled natural wonders. The movement that he and David Brower helped build is not only in retreat but finds itself the target of bottomless contempt. On talk radio and cable TV, environmentalists are derided as "wackos" and "extremists." The country has swung decisively toward something smaller and more selfish than what it once was, and in addition to ushering in a disdain for the notion that wilderness might have a value that extends beyond the metrics of economics or business, much of the nation ignorantly embraces the benefits of engineering and technology while simultaneously rejecting basic science. This contradiction is underscored most blatantly, at least for Litton, by an incident that unfolded on the South Rim in 2003. Shortly after the superintendent tried to prevent a book that promoted a Creationist view of the canyon from being sold inside the park, he was pointedly overruled by his superiors in Washington. How can one sanction such attacks against science, Litton wonders, when more than a tenth of the population is already convinced that the entire world, including the Grand Canyon, was slapped together in the space of a single week less than seven thousand years ago?

In the midst of this bewilderment, however, Litton has retained his connection with the canyon. In 1997, he embarked on the first of what would prove to be a series of "farewell" river trips, each designed to serve as his final journey through the canyon—only to be rendered moot when Litton, with characteristic disobedience, tossed aside the script by refusing to compromise with old age and "failing to deteriorate at the rate I'm supposed to." Following each of these trips, he remained in good health and waited patiently until someone got around to issuing another invitation, then off he went again. On every one of these ventures, he has broken and reset his own record as the oldest person ever to row through the canyon.

In February 2013, he turned ninety-six. Although he has been forced to give up his pilot's license and sell off his Cessna, he is looking forward to his next trip through what he calls "America's greatest scenic treasure—the most satisfying, elevating experience you can have, an experience made-to-order in wonder—simply the best thing one can do."

In addition to his passion for the canyon, he retains his love for the dories, along with the eloquence that he can still summon on their behalf.

"In the end, the most remarkable properties of a dory are size, vulnerability, and beauty," he recently declared when asked to sum them up. "It is a thing that can be smashed to pieces if care and attention are not paid, which instills the virtues of attentiveness while removing you from the position of a passive observer who is simply there to be entertained. It is small in a large place, helping to keep you in perspective and in touch with truths that elude us in a world made by man: that we are, in relation to the forces that shape the universe, tiny and insignificant—and that we must therefore strive to live more humbly, and with humility. And it is a thing of grace, reflecting similar qualities in the rock, the water, and the light that are the essence of that place."

Many of the boats from Litton's old fleet still ply the canyon, and most are in the hands of his former boatmen. It should come as no surprise that his favorite remains the *Emerald Mile*—although a portion of her fate is another source of sadness and perplexity.

~

These days, if you pull off Interstate 40 at Flagstaff and follow Highway 180 north toward the Grand Canyon, the road will take you directly through town and then past a neighborhood zoned for light industrial businesses that feature a scattering of machine shops, a bottling distributor, and the boathouse for Grand Canyon Dories, now owned by an outfitter called OARS, which maintains the tradition of rowing dories on the Colorado.

If you pull into the parking lot and enter through the garage door, which is usually open during the day, the first thing you will note is that the interior of the boathouse is dominated by steel beams that run the length of the roof, and a cement floor strewn with the tools and detritus of the river-running trade. Your gaze, however, will swiftly be pulled toward the ceiling, which is festooned with large chunks of wooden boats—bows, sterns, transoms, hatch lids—that have been shattered almost beyond recognition. It will take a moment for you to realize that each piece has been salvaged because it bears the name of the wrecked dory to which it was once attached. Those names are sweet and evocative, and each was imparted by Litton in honor of a natural wonder that was destroyed by man: the *Flaming Gorge*, the *Vale of Rhondda*, the *Bright Angel*, the *Ticaboo*, and many others.

Then your eye will move toward the opposite wall, where more than a dozen river-ready dories are cradled in racks. They are painted in bold colors, and although many are double-enders, several feature flat transoms that are decorated with hand-drawn scenes from the canyon: a Swallowtail butterfly, a bighorn sheep, a cluster of verbena blossoms. What will strike you most, however, is that each boat is graced with the fairest lines you've ever seen. Their profiles are like nothing else—upturned prows that terminate in a sharp point, and hulls whose rockered bottoms curve like the blade of a scimitar.

Finally, you will spot a boat tucked off in the far corner that looks oddly neglected. Instead of nesting comfortably in a rack, she has been strung from the ceiling with blue nylon webbing, and her hull is suspended over a workbench piled with used cans of paint and battered power tools. This boat is covered in dust and is tilted at an angle that obscures her name. But you can see her colors plainly enough—a beryl-green hull and gunwales of bright red.

Unless you know her story, you will have no idea that you're looking at a legend of the Colorado. Nothing marks the achievements she pulled off. Nothing commemorates the man who rescued her from a bonfire and brought her back to life. She appears neglected, abandoned, forgotten—all of which may suggest that the voyage of the *Emerald Mile* ends in a sea of sadness. But that's not precisely the case.

According to some of the older dorymen, one of the things that made the twenty-seven wooden dories in Litton's original fleet so special was that when Jerry Briggs assembled them up in Oregon on the banks of the Rogue River, he put a little bit of magic in each of the hatches and even in a few of the footwells.

That may or may not be true. But if it is, it helps to explain the coda to her story.

~

More than a decade after the conclusion of the speed run, a doryman by the name of Lew Steiger decided to get an account of the *Emerald Mile*'s historic run down on paper. It was fortunate that he did because, among other things, he interviewed Grua extensively before he passed away. The thirty-five-page story that Steiger put together captured Grua's memories, in his own words, while also providing an account that had, until then, simply been part of the disordered oral history of the river—the tales boatmen tell one another at the end of the day when they are lounging around their decks drinking beer.

Steiger's story was included in a marvelous little book that features two dozen river stories written by the guides of the Grand Canyon, as well as their photographs, drawings, and paintings. The collection offers a moving testament to the guides' love for the river, and Steiger's story is a true gem in the collection, which is entitled "There's This River."

The book is not especially well known beyond the confines of the canyon. But it is beloved by many of the guides, who never fail to bring a copy with them on their river trips. It rides in their ammo cans or in their cross-hatches, and at night they pull out those dog-eared copies and read the tales inside to their passengers. This has created something of a perfect storm of luck for Grua's dory, because whenever the subject of the great runoff of 1983 comes up, as it invariably does on any river trip, one of the boatmen will retrieve the book, settle in front of the campfire, and share the story of the speed run.

And so the *Emerald Mile* has been granted a kind of reprieve, a gesture of redemption not unlike the fleeting hour of twilight that descends over the bottom of the canyon each evening. There, beneath the river of shooting stars, she endlessly retraces the same circle of wonder and madness that the man who brought her back to life once ran. And when her story is recited, people hang on the edge of their folding canvas chairs as the waves come at them from every direction, partaking once more of the chaos and the beauty of that legendary run, while attending to the dispatch the dory carries inside her.

The message she bears is a secret the dorymen already hold in the cross-hatches of their hearts: that the delicate class of watercraft to which they have devoted the best part of their lives is perhaps the finest of all metaphors for the canyon's inscrutable wonder—its seductiveness, its complexity, its symphonic merging of the evanescent and the eternal. As it turns out, nothing expresses those elements with greater eloquence or concision than a little wooden boat.

Those dory captains know one other thing, too.

They know that the canyon and her dories embody an elusive riddle. It is a paradox rooted in the dream that many of us share of immersing ourselves so deeply, so inextricably, into a pocket of landscape, or a stretch of river—anything that seems to embody the wildness we have lost—that we may somehow take possession of those places and make them ours. Yet the truth, like an eddy, runs in the opposite direction.

In the end, it is they that claim us. And we who belong to them.

ACKNOWLEDGMENTS

~

I N the spring of 2009, when Rudi Petschek first invited me into his home, saying that he had been waiting a long time for a writer to knock on his door who was prepared to tell the full story of the *Emerald Mile*, I had no idea how many debts of gratitude I would accumulate, but I knew that they would begin with the twelve-hour conversation that unfolded that day in Petschek's living room, which was amplified by a four-year correspondence. In addition to tapping the well of his own memories, Petschek provided an introduction to Steve Reynolds, the only other living member of the 1983 speed-run crew—although by the time Wren and I finally met, he had only six weeks to live. Hovering over both of those people was Martin Litton, the man with whom all stories about dories inside the Grand Canyon begin and end. Without the participation of these three individuals, this book would never have been possible.

John Blaustein, one of Litton's earliest dorymen, has opened doors and provided guidance, both on the river and off, since we initially met on my first river trip through the canyon. He has also been a valued friend. Lew Steiger has done more than anyone else to preserve the memory of Kenton Grua, not only by getting the story of the speed run down in writing for the first time, but also through his tireless efforts to interview and record the memories of dozens of Grand Canyon boatmen, whose thoughts and words are now preserved—and available to all—in the oral-history collection of Northern Arizona University's Cline Library in Flagstaff.

Beyond the oral histories, every member of the Grand Canyon river community owes a debt of gratitude to a handful of river historians, many of whom are also boatmen. I am deeply grateful to Michael Ghiglieri and Tom Myers, who have done extensive and painstaking research on fatalities inside the canyon; and to Brad Dimock, who has written wonderful books on Buzz Holmstrom and Glen and Bessie Hyde, and who probably knows more about wooden boats than anyone else in the canyon. I am also indebted to Richard Quartaroli, formerly of the Cline Library's Special Collections at NAU, and Jeff Ingram, who was one of the MIT trio who played a key role in blocking the Grand Canyon dams, and continues to push the cause of wilderness within the canyon.

In addition to Martin Litton and his astonishingly gracious wife, Esther, a number of Litton's former dorymen and staff were kind enough to share their memories with me. They include Wally Rist, who was both the inspiration and the driving force behind the *Emerald Mile*'s first speed run in 1980, as well as Curt Chang, Steve Dalton, Coby Jordan, Carol Starling, Jim Starling, Ellen Tibbets, Kenly Weills, Tuck Weills, and Jane Whalen. I am also grateful to Katie Lee, even though she prefers cataract boats to dories, because her voice and writing give shape and vitality to the lost world of Glen Canyon; and to Bob Rigg, who set the Grand Canyon's first oar-driven speed-run record with his late brother, Jim, in the summer of 1951.

Without the participation of several key eyewitnesses, it would have been impossible to piece together a number of important events that form the backbone of this narrative. The following people either observed or were caught inside the explosion wave in Crystal Rapid on the morning of June 25, 1983: Walt Gallaher, Bob and Colleen Paparelli, Gary and Elizabeth Ungricht, Dave Stratton, and the unsinkable Butte Ladies: Marjie Hay, Sally Rae Lonner, Mary Ann McNammee, and Lin Sultzer. Jeffe Aronson and Richard Kocim both witnessed the Tour West rig being torn to pieces in the center of the rapid, and Kocim's photographs (which he has generously shared) provide the most detailed evidence of what took place. Later that same night, Michael Ghiglieri, Bruce Helin, and Dr. Charles Zemach were present at the *Emerald Mile*'s launch from Lee's Ferry, along with Cliff Taylor and Anne Marie Nicholson, who were serving as the timekeepers. Dr. Roderick Nash witnessed the *Emerald Mile* during her second night on the river (and also provided me with valuable background on how the Grand Canyon fits into the history of American conservation); and Mike Meade, who defended Kenton Grua pro bono in court on the South Rim in the autumn of 1983, provided key details of the hearing. I am grateful to all of these people for being kind enough to speak with me—in many cases at great length.

Several members of the National Park Service who were either on or near the river in June 1983, all of whom are trained in search-and-rescue, were kind enough to come to my aid by sharing their memories with me. They include Kim Crumbo, Kim Johnson, Mark Law, Curt Sauer, Stan Steck, and Tom Workman.

I am especially appreciative of John Thomas, who walked me through a highly detailed account of his activities on June 25. I would like to thank Mathieu Brown and Kirstin Heins, Mike McGinnis, and Ken Philips, all of whom know the canyon deeply and were helpful to me in important ways. Leah McGinnis, chief of staff at Grand Canyon National Park, and Maurine Oltrogge in the park's public affairs office were both unstintingly helpful and kind. And I want to include a special note of appreciation to Kim Besom at the park's Museum Collection, who pulled off the astonishing feat of locating Case Incident Reports for June 24, 25, and 26; and to Dean Portman, who assembled the files.

One of the unexpected pleasures of this project was the opportunity to meet and learn from people affiliated with the Bureau of Reclamation. Foremost among this group are four individuals who helped to guide me to an understanding of the events that took place at the Glen Canyon Dam. Phil Burgi and Dr. Henry Falvey, both of whom worked in Reclamation's Hydraulics Lab in Denver, generously agreed to many hours of taped conversation over a period of months and walked me through some of the nuances of their discipline. Tom Gamble, who was in charge of the dam throughout the spillway crisis, generously invited me into his home for two days of interviewing, during which time he patiently guided me to a new perspective on both the canyon and the dam, for which I am grateful. Dick White went far beyond the call of duty in walking me through the details of the dam's operation while answering my incessant queries—and in the process, managed to pass along his passion for the colossal machine to which he devoted the better part of his career. In Page, Arizona, I am grateful to Richard Barton, Henry Dhieux, and Richard Parsons, who, among others, spoke to me about the dam. I particularly wish to thank the following members of the bureau's archives and public information team: Casey Snyder, Regina Magno-Judd, De Ann Brown, Brit Storey, Ginger Reese, Barry Wirth, Peter Soeth, and Ann-Marie Harvey—as well as Robert Einhellig, who was kind enough to give me a tour of the hydraulics lab in Denver.

It is always a pleasure to speak with members of the scientific and engineering community, people whose knowledge of the world, and whose clarity of thinking, so decisively surpass my own. The experts who assisted me include Don Laurine and David Westnedge, formerly of the Colorado Basin River Forecast Center; Lawrence Dunn with the National Weather Service; Christopher Vaccaro and Vernon Kousky at the National Oceanic and Atmospheric Administration; Nancy Hornewer at the US Geological Survey. I am also grateful to Doug Erwin, curator of Paleozoic invertebrates at the Smithsonian Institution National Museum of Natural History and chair of the faculty at the Santa Fe Institute, and to Susan Kieffer at the University of Illinois at Urbana-Champaign. Having conducted some marvelous research on the geomorphic evolution within the Grand Canyon by studying the hydraulic jump at Crystal Rapid in June 1983, Dr. Kieffer was not only kind enough to walk me through her conclusions but also sent me a set of the finest river maps that have ever been published on the rapids of the Grand Canyon, which she produced for the USGS in 1988. I would also like to thank Wayne Ranney of Flagstaff and Alan H. Cheetham of Santa Fe, both of whom (together with Doug Erwin) were instrumental in straightening out my hopelessly tangled attempts to understand the geology of the canyon, and J. David Rogers at Missouri University of Science and Technology.

I am grateful to the wonderful people at Lowell's Boat Shop in Amesbury, Massachusetts—George Odell, Pam Bates, Elizabeth Hartnell, and Graham McKay—where America's infatuation with dories began. Andrew Gulliford, Roger Fletcher, Michael Hiltzik, Byron Pearson, Judge Stephen Verkamp, and John Weisheit were all kind enough to speak with me about their respective areas of expertise. My thanks go out to each of them, as well as to Roger and Lena Trancik, in whose New Hampshire house many of the early chapters of the book were written, and to their daughter Jessika.

Whatever I may claim to know about the Colorado River as it runs through the Grand Canyon flows directly from the fact that a number of the people who understand the place best and consider it their home welcomed me into their world and shared their stories. I am grateful to those who taught me to row: Monte Tillinghast, Regan Dale, O. C. Dale, Bill Bruchak, Rondo Buechler, Ryan Howe, Bruce Keller, Elena Kirchner, Jeri Ledbetter, Curtis Newall, Billie Ray Prosser, and Nancy Redfern. My thanks as well to good friends on the river: Erika Andersson, Betsy Barker, Kate Belnap, the remaining members of the "Dale dynasty"—Ote, Roger, Duffy, and Kirsten—plus Chris Macintosh, Mike Martin, Andre Potochnik, Shana Watahomigie, Stephanie White, Sarah Kuhn, and Denise Napolitano at OARS. I am extremely grateful to George Wendt and his family, along with Steve Markle and the rest of the team at the OARS headquarters in California who, together with Regan Dale, have worked so diligently and with such passion to sustain Martin Litton's legacy of rowing commercial dories in the Grand Canyon. Special thanks also go to the amazing Lynn Hamilton at Grand Canyon River Guides in Flagstaff, and to Helen Ranney at the Grand Canyon Association, as well as to a pair of special passengers: Pat Koeppl and his late father, Jack—whose love of dories was a source of inspiration and delight to his family.

When this project ran up against the shoals of bureaucratic intransigence, several wonderful folks in the First Amendment community came to my aid. I am indebted to Mark Caramanica at the Reporters Committee for Freedom of the Press, who guided me through the intricacies of filing several FOIA requests, then later helped me put together a lengthy appeal that proved critical to securing records from the Glen Canyon Dam. In this respect, my thanks also go to Kirsten Mitchell at the Office of Government Information Services, who provided key assistance with my FOIA appeal, and to Barbara Petersen at the First Amendment Foundation, whose organization, among many other services, stands on the front lines of protecting the public's right of access to government information.

It has been my immense good fortune to be surrounded by a small circle of fellow writers and journalists in Santa Fe. Two colleagues in particular, both far better writers than I could ever hope to become, have steered various aspects of this book: Bob Shacochis and Hampton Sides. I am blessed to be able to count them as friends, along with several people at *Outside* magazine who have been unflinchingly helpful and decent to me over the years: Dave Cox, Kyle Dickman, Alex and Susan Heard, Nick Heil, Elizabeth Hightower, Chris Keyes, Hannah McCaughey, Sam Moulton, and Grayson Schaffer. Beyond New Mexico, I must also mention George Getschow, the man who created and runs the Mayborn Literary Nonfiction Conference at the University of North Texas, who has been a source of guidance and wisdom—as have Erik Calonius, Gregg Jones, and Dan Malone, all of whom I met through the Mayborn.

I would like to express my sincere appreciation to the terrific publishing and editorial staff at Scribner, the sort of place where every writer hopes to be lucky enough to work, and where I am indebted to Susan Moldow, Nan Graham, Roz Lippel, Kelsey Smith, Jason Heuer, Tal Goretsky, Katie Rizzo, Ellen Sasahara, Steven Boldt, Kara Watson, Brian Belfiglio, and Kate Lloyd. The entire team at Scribner has been a marvel, but I want to make special mention of my editor, the incomparable Colin Harrison. Like the canyon itself, he is a force of nature. Without his wisdom and guidance, this book would never have emerged.

In addition to Colin, there is only one other person who has been with this project from the very beginning—and whose determination and vision have often exceeded my own. It is impossible for me to express how truly grateful I am to Jennifer Joel, except to say that she is simply the finest literary agent any author could ever wish for. My gratitude also extends to her colleagues at ICM: Sloan Harris, Liz Farrell, and Clay Ezell.

My deepest thanks are reserved for my family: my parents in Pittsburgh, to whom this book is dedicated; my brother, Aaron, and his wife and children in Maine; and the members of our extended circle of kinship and affection in Rochester and throughout northwestern Pennsylvania. Together, they are the constellation that tells me where home is.

Whatever merits this book may possess derive directly from the people mentioned above. Any mistakes or errors that may be contained herein, however, belong entirely to me.

NOTES ON SOURCES

~

THIS is a work of nonfiction. Anything between quotation marks was said directly to the author, is part of the transcript of an oral-history interview, or was expressed to another source whose attribution is included in the notes section of this book. Similarly, any notation of a time and a date derives from primary documents—most of which were obtained through either the Bureau of Reclamation or the National Park Service—or were notations taken by eyewitnesses to the event in question.

Much of the initial work to assemble this story required piecing together a complex "time puzzle" that involved braiding together three separate narratives: events unfolding at the Glen Canyon Dam; actions being taken by National Park Service search-and-rescue personnel both inside the Grand Canyon and along the South Rim; and events affecting the lives of several dozen people who were at various locations along the Colorado River, all of whom were traveling downstream on a fast-moving river according to different schedules.

The pieces of that puzzle were assembled from a variety of sources, the most important being the accounts of eyewitnesses and participants who were either at the dam or inside the canyon during the final weeks of June 1983. Whenever possible, those accounts were corroborated with memos, transcripts, telephone logs, faxograms, Case Incident Records, and handwritten notes stored within the archives of the Bureau of Reclamation and the National Park Service. These materials were obtained by filing multiple Freedom of Information Act (FOIA) requests. The FOIA staff at Grand Canyon National Park was unflinchingly helpful in this respect, making every effort to track down obscure documents that had never before been requested or accessed. The employees at the Bureau of Reclamation's headquarters in Denver were also enormously kind in providing information from Reclamation's Denver archives.

∽

The subjects of the Grand Canyon and the Colorado River are enriched by many colorful layers of scholarship and writing. In the process of mining this information, I benefited enormously from the tremendous work done by other authors. I have listed these, as well as other important sources, in the bibliography while also doing my best to cite specific instances where I am indebted to their work in the notes and in the main text. There are, however, a number of works that merit particular mention.

Any understanding of John Wesley Powell begins with Wallace Stegner's classic work *Beyond the Hundredth Meridian*, which includes one of the finest treatments of the Major's pioneering voyage through the canyon in the summer of 1869. The companion pieces to that work are *A River Running West* by Powell's other great biographer, Donald Worster, and Edward Dolnick's *Down the Great Unknown*, which is a delightful piece of writing and research, as well as an excellent primer on the mechanics of white water. Powell is a contentious subject, however, and discussions of his character and behavior are rife with differing interpretations. While parsing through those nuances lay far beyond the scope of this book, a useful place to turn for a differing point of view is *First Through the Grand Canyon* by Michael Ghiglieri, a writer who, among other services, has painstakingly compiled the diaries and journals of Powell's crew and laid them out chronologically in a single volume. All of these works were indispensable to the narrative herein.

Anyone who attempts to tackle the subject of the Grand Canyon swiftly discovers and comes to rely upon Earle Spamer's thorough and exhaustive *Bibliography of the Grand Canyon and the Lower Colorado River*, which remains the definitive source for almost everything that has ever been written about the canyon and the river (and which is available, for free, in an updated and searchable version on the Internet, at www.grandcanyonbiblio.org). For a clear and helpful treatment of the canyon's geology, Wayne Ranney's *Carving Grand Canyon* is excellent. It is bookended by two provocative works whose scope includes geology but also embraces the complex history of human interaction within the chasm: *Grand Canyon: Solving the Earth's Grandest Puzzle* by James Lawrence Powell and Stephen Pyne's magnificent *How the Canyon Became Grand*. Perhaps the loveliest treatment of all, however, is John Blaustein's *The Hidden Canyon*, a book that is noteworthy not only for its beautiful dory photographs but also because the main text was written by Edward Abbey, while Martin Litton penned the introduction.

The history of white-water boating within the Grand Canyon has received one of its most comprehensive treatments in David Lavender's *River Runners of the Grand Canyon*, whose historical photographs are especially revealing. For specific history on dories, the two most important contributions are John Gardner's classic, *The Dory Book*, and Roger Fletcher's *Drift Boats and River Dories*. For white-water boating, one of the most eloquent of all treatments can be found in David Quammen's *Wild Thoughts from Wild Places*, although this is supplemented admirably by William Nealy's *Kayak: The New Frontier*. Within the Grand Canyon, the two standard guidebooks for the river corridor are the classic *Belknap's Waterproof Grand Canyon River Guide* and Larry Stevens's *The Colorado River in Grand Canyon: A Comprehensive Guide to Its Natural and Human History*. Most river guides carry both inside their ammo cans; on the river, they are as indispensable as duct tape.

To hear the stories that are told on the Colorado River, the best thing one can do is to take a river trip through the canyon and listen to the boatmen at night around the campfire. Short of that, Christa Sadler's anthology, *There's This River*, is the place to start. Many of the anecdotes in this narrative, however, have been assembled from Northern Arizona University's massive river runners' oral-history database. The histories are cataloged in the Special Collections at NAU's Cline Library, and most are available, both in recorded form and in transcript, online. Here you will be able to find the three long interviews that Lew Steiger conducted with Kenton Grua, which include many details of Grua's early life, as well as of the first speed run and his pioneering through-hike of the canyon.

Anyone who writes about the politics of rivers and dams of the American West owes a specific note of thanks to Marc Reisner for *Cadillac Desert* and Donald Worster for *Rivers of Empire*, as well as, more generally, to Steven Solomon for his more comprehensive historical overview, *Water*. For the story of the dams that were built on the Colorado itself, I drew heavily on Philip Fradkin's *A River No More*, Michael Hiltzik's *Colossus*, John McPhee's *Encounters with the Archdruid*, and Byron Pearson's well-researched and cogently argued *Still the Wild River Runs*. *The History of Large Federal Dams*, edited by David Billington and his colleagues, is also extremely useful.

On the lost world of Glen Canyon, Edward Abbey's various writings—most specifically *Desert Solitaire*—offer perhaps the most beautiful and evocative sense of what Glen once was, although Abbey's words are admirably supplemented by Eleanor Inskip's *The Colorado River Through Glen Canyon: Before Lake Powell* and Jared Farmer's *Glen Canyon Dammed*.

As for the Glen Canyon Dam itself, probably the single best work is Russell Martin's *A Story That Stands Like a Dam*, although anyone who wants to truly understand the inner workings of the dam must, sooner or later, obtain a copy of *Glen Canyon Dam and Powerplant: Technical Record of Design and Construction*, which includes many of Glen's schematics. For the history of dams, I drew on a number of sources, the two most important being Norman Smith's *History of Dams* and Nicholas Schnitter's *History of Dams: The Useful Pyramids*, plus Resse Palley's *Concrete: A Seven-Thousand-Year History*. On turbulence and hydraulic jumps, I have leaned heavily on Luna Leopold's *Fluvial Processes in Geomorphology*, and R. J. Garde's *History of Fluvial Hydraulics*.

Finally, there is *Cavitation in Chutes and Spillways: Engineering Monograph No. 42*. The theme is an esoteric one, to be sure. But no one can deny that Henry Falvey has supplied the first and last word on the complex subject of cavitation.

NOTES

~

Epigraphs

vii   "If there is magic": Eiseley, *The Immense Journey*, 15.

Launch: June 25, 1983

2   the hunched shoulders of Shinarump shale: The Shinarump is a conglomerate that includes both siltstones and sandstones that are part of the Chinle Formation.

3   they scratched their heads in confusion: Author interviews with Bruce Helin and Michael Ghiglieri, both of whom were present at the ferry that night, assisted in putting the *Emerald Mile* into the water, and witnessed the launch.

3   She hit with a sharp slap: Author interview with Ghiglieri.

3   and waited calmly for his two companions: Author interviews with Rudi Petschek and Steve Reynolds.

3   the driver cried, "*Go!*": Ibid.

4   a family that had driven all the way: Author interview with Dr. Charles Zemach.

4   an incident that they planned on reporting: Ibid.

4   What in the world were those clowns up to: Ibid.

Leviathan

7   a distance of some fifteen miles: Stevens, *Colorado River in Grand Canyon*, 61.

7   who had started assembling its frame in 1960: Martin, *Story That Stands Like a Dam*.

8   more than twice the height of the Statue of Liberty: The Statue of Liberty is 305 feet high. See http://www.nps.gov/stli/faqs.htm (accessed 12/15/2012).

8   its length exceeded that of the *Seawise Giant*: The *Seawise Giant* was 1,504 feet long. See "Maritime Connector," http://maritime-connector.com/worlds=largest=ships (accessed 12/15/2012).

8   Staffed by a team of ten technicians: Author interview with Richard White, manager of the Glen Canyon Dam Control Room in 1983. Also see *Operating Log*, Glen Canyon Dam.

8   who worked on three eight-hour shifts: Author interview with White.

8   At night, however, there were usually no more than two: Ibid.

8   a large steel desk equipped with three telephones and a two-way radio: Ibid.

8   has long been particular about disclosing the names: The Bureau of Reclamation was uncooperative about releasing Control Room records from 1983 at the Glen Canyon Dam, initially denying a Freedom of Information Act (FOIA) request. Partially redacted records were released only after a lengthy appeal was filed with assistance from Mark Caramanica at the Reporters Committee for Freedom of the Press.

9   a bank of panels studded with so many lights: Author interview with White. Also see *Glen Canyon Dam and Powerplant*, 305–16.

9   a body of water that extended 186 miles: National Park Service, Glen Canyon National Recreation Area; see http://www.nps.gov/glca/faqs.htm (accessed on 12/15/2012). Also see Martin, *Story That Stands Like a Dam*.

10   there was something almost as gratifying: Author interview with White.

10   when a call arrived from the Western Area Power Administration dispatcher: Ibid.

10   the moment when most of the twenty million people: Carothers and Brown, *Colorado River Through Grand Canyon*, 178–81.

10   this would register as a low whine: Author interview with White.

10   a generator that housed a six-hundred-ton rotor: Author interview with Tom Gamble. Also see *Glen Canyon Dam and Powerplant*.

11   a massive El Niño event: Although the El Niño of 1982–83 was the largest on record up to that point, it was surpassed by subsequent El Niños. For additional information on sourcing for the weather events of 1983, please turn to the notes for chapter 13, "Deluge."

11   the runoff from 108,000 square miles: Colorado River Water Users Association. See http://www.crwua.org/ColoradoRiver/RiverUses/Reclamation.aspx (accessed on 12/15/2012).

11   the size of Poland: While the drainage basin for the entire Colorado River is about 243,000 square miles, which is roughly the size of Somalia, the river's upper basin—which includes most, but not all, of the water that drains into Lake Powell—is significantly smaller, only about 108,000 square miles. Also note that, for comparison purposes, Poland is somewhat larger, at 117,000 square miles.

11   had been bored through 675 feet of Navajo sandstone: *Glen Canyon Dam and Powerplant*.

11   were capable of inhaling a combined flow of more than 200,000 cfs: Ibid.

12   shock waves had scoured away: Extensive sourcing and documentation on the cavitation-induced damage to the dam's spillway tunnels can be found in the notes for chapters 13, 14, and 15. For a quick reference to the details laid out here, see Burgi, "Operations of Glen Canyon Dam Spillways—Summer 1983," 260–64.

12   chunks of concrete, pieces of rebar, and boulders: Author interviews with Richard White, Tom Gamble, and Philip Burgi, head of the Hydraulics Lab at the Bureau of Reclamation's Engineering and Research Center in Denver in 1983. Also see Burgi, "Operations of Glen Canyon Dam Spillways—Summer 1983," 260–64.

12   the goal of every person who worked at the dam: Author interviews with White, Gamble, and Burgi.

12   at 120 miles per hour: Author interviews with White and Burgi. Also see *Glen Canyon Dam and Powerplant*.

12   You could hear the thunder of the discharge: Author interview with White.

12   the water would overwhelm the steel gates that guarded: Moyes and Burgi, *Glen Canyon Dam Chronology of Events*. Also see Burgi, "Operations of Glen Canyon Dam Spillways—Summer 1983," 260–64.

13   If luck was running: Sourcing and documentation for worst-case scenarios can be found in the notes for chapters 15, 16, and 17. For a quick reference to the details laid out here, see Moyes and Burgi, *Glen Canyon Dam Chronology of Events*. Also see Wolf, "How Lake Powell Almost Broke Free of Glen Canyon Dam."

13   and over the lip of Hoover Dam: Most experts are confident that Hoover would have withstood the impact of an uncontrolled release coming downstream from Lake Powell. See Latham, *Dam Failure Inundation Study*.

13   much of that water would probably wind up taking out: Author interview with J. David Rogers, Karl F. Hasselmann Chair in Geological Engineering, Department of Geological Sciences & Engineering, Missouri University of Science & Technology.

13   had dismissed the terminal scenario as absurd: Moyes and Burgi, *Glen Canyon Dam Chronology of Events*.

13   more than two hundred boats and nearly thirteen hundred people: Grand Canyon National Park river permits records, obtained via author's FOIA request.

13   downstream in fifty-degree water: *William R. Wert Fatality, Case #83-1592,* June 25, 1983. "Water temperature was estimated at 45–50 degrees . . ." Patricia Baker, Summary, Supplementary Case/Incident Record, Case/Incident Number 831592, 8/1/1983.

14   a borderline that seemed: John McPhee expresses this same idea on page 191 of *Encounters with the Archdruid*.

14   a living and breathing thing: Author interview with Dr. Henry Falvey, who was the Bureau of Reclamation's cavitation expert at the Hydraulics Lab, part of the Engineering and Research Center in Denver.

14   the dam was an offense against nature: This idea is echoed by many people within the Grand Canyon river-guiding community. Most specifically for this book, see Martin Litton, oral-history interviews.

Part I
The World Beneath the Rims

16 By far the most sublime of all earthly spectacles: Dutton, *Tertiary History of the Grand Canyon*, 142–43.

1: First Contact

19 "It is a lovely and terrible wilderness": Stegner, "Wilderness Letter," December 3, 1960, in Stegner, *Sound of Mountain Water*, 153.

19 "the most brilliant company ever collected": DeVoto, *Course of Empire*, 34.

20 were encrusted with emeralds: Flint and Flint, eds., *Coronado Expedition*, 34. Cited by Hiltzik, *Colossus*, 5.

20 the doors were studded with sapphires: Waters, *Colorado*, 138.

20 tiny bells of hammered silver . . . and fine cotton shawls to a depth of nine feet: DeVoto, *Course of Empire*, 38.

20 nineteen crossbows, seventeen harquebuses: Ibid., 35.

22 a stronghold of religious orthodoxy: I am indebted to Stephen Pyne, who developed many of these ideas about Spain in connection with the Grand Canyon. See Pyne, *How the Canyon Became Grand*, 7–9.

23 Spain was the seedbed of the technologies: See Smith, *History of Dams*, 129. Also see Schnitter, *History of Dams*, 107.

23 no one now knows precisely where: Pyne, *How the Canyon Became Grand*, 6.

25 the Kaibab actually predated not only the continent: When the Kaibab was first laid down more than 240 million years ago, it was part of the primordial landmass known as Pangea, whose breakup created the continents and the oceans as we know them today. See Bjornerud, *Reading the Rocks*, 139–40.

25 *before* the step above and *after* the step below: Geologists now recognize that molten rock may force itself between older layers of rock, creating an exception to Steno's law. Tilting, folding, and faulting may also complicate the stratigraphic sequence. Nevertheless, the basic principle remains valid: sedimentary rocks are *originally* deposited in a time sequence, with the oldest on the bottom and the youngest at the top. See Winchester, *Map That Changed the World*, 37–39.

25 This is not a revolutionary idea to us: Ibid., 38.

28 the first meetings with the tribes of the Great Plains, and the first buffalo: DeVoto, *Course of Empire*, 44–45.

2: The Grand Old Man

29 "I do not know much": Eliot, "The Dry Salvages," 36.

29 Just before two o'clock: Union Pacific Railroad Passenger Schedule, May 1869. Available online at "Railroad and American Politics," http://voteview.com/rtopic1_ucsd_3.htm (accessed 12/15/2012).

29 walnut-paneled Pullman Palace: For details of the interior of a Pullman Palace saloon carriage, see White, *The American Railroad Passenger Car*.

30 attempting to drain the entire liquor supply: Stegner, *Beyond the Hundredth Meridian*, 47.

30 "much blowing off of gas": Sumner, "Lost Journal of John Colton Summer." Cited by Worster, *River Running West*, 161.

30 "a stick of beef jerky adorned with whiskers": This marvelous image belongs to Dolnick, *Down the Great Unknown*, 2.

31 sheltering mud-spattered miners: Dasmann, *Destruction of California*, 176.

31 now boasted ostentatious Victorian mansions: Ibid., 178.

32 descended in part from the herd: It is important to acknowledge that the provenance of the Comanches' original horse herd is unclear, and that some historians dispute the notion that these animals were descendants of Coronado's fifteen hundred horses and mules. See Gwynne, *Empire of the Summer Moon*, 29.

32 to retreat more than a hundred miles to the east: Ibid., 3–4.

32 another Franciscan priest had poked along: Worster, *River Running West*, 128.

33 After chugging nearly three hundred miles: Ibid., 129–31. Also see Ives, *Report upon the Colorado River*.

33 "Ours has been the first": Ives, *Report upon the Colorado River*, 70. Cited by Worster, *River Running West*, 130–31.

33 the last truly uncharted territory: Billington, *History of Large Federal Dams*, 136–37. Also see Stegner, *Beyond the Hundredth Meridian*.
33 emblazoned in the middle: Worster, *River Running West*, 127–28.
34 what he rather poetically called "the Great Unknown": Although John Wesley Powell did not coin this phrase, he is most closely associated with these words in the context of the Grand Canyon.
34 river pilot named Samuel Clemens: The speculation that Powell may have passed Twain is noted on page 16 of Stegner's classic *Beyond the Hundredth Meridian* and on page 77 of Worster, *River Running West*.
35 entered his wrist and plowed toward the elbow: Worster, *River Running West*, 93.
35 sawed off two inches below the elbow: Ibid., 94.
35 supplies of salt, gunpowder, lead: Zwinger, *Run, River, Run*, 81. Also see DeVoto, *Across the Wide Missouri*, 103.
36 the only major mountain range in the United States: The Uintas, a subrange of the Rockies, are located roughly 100 miles east of Salt Lake City and run approximately 160 miles from east to west.
36 flaming-red quartzite and shale: Zwinger, *Run, River, Run*, 137.
36 the actual details of most of that journey: In the fall of 1867, an itinerant prospector named James White claimed to have pulled off the first descent of the Colorado through the Grand Canyon by flinging himself into the river to escape marauding Indians and floating downstream on a make-shift log raft while subsisting on raw lizards, his leather knife scabbard, and the rancid hindquarters of a dog. Although White may have descended a portion of the canyon, the possibility that he made his way down the entire stretch of river from what is now Lee's Ferry to the Grand Wash Cliffs is disputed by most (although not all) experts. See Worster, *River Running West*, 133–34.
37 The grade is unequaled by any major waterway: Martin, *Story That Stands Like a Dam*, 32.
37 The Nile, in contrast, falls: Ibid., 32.
37 spectacular bursts of change: Reisner, *Cadillac Desert*, 122.
37 In the space of a week: Ibid., 121.
38 the river annually removes nearly sixty: Martin, *Story That Stands Like a Dam*, 32.
38 the compulsive intensity with which it cuts away: Hiltzik, *Colossus*, 3.
38 an average of nearly half a million tons: Martin, *Story That Stands Like a Dam*, 32.
38 seventeen times more silt-laden than: Ibid.
38 dust could be seen blowing off the water's surface: Hiltzik, *Colossus*, 36.
38 psychotic in its surges: Reisner, *Cadillac Desert*, 122.
39 seventeen major canyons: 1. Flaming Gorge; 2. Kingfisher; 3. Horseshoe; 4. Hidden; 5. Red; 6. Swallow; 7. Lodore; 8. Whirlpool; 9. Split Mountain; 10. Desolation; 11. Gray; 12. Labyrinth; 13. Stillwater; 14. Cataract; 15. Glen; 16. Marble; 17. Grand Canyon. See Zwinger, *Run, River, Run*; Martin, *Story That Stands Like a Dam*.

3: Into the Great Unknown

40 "Wherever we look there is but a wilderness of rocks": Powell, *Diary*, July 19, 1869, 79.
40 a remarkably ragged bunch: For details on Powell's crew, see Dolnick, *Down the Great Unknown*, 9–19. Also see Stegner, *Beyond the Hundredth Meridian*; and Worster, *River Running West*.
40 earning his keep as a trapper: Powell, *Diary*, 42.
40 the acknowledged leader of the group: Worster, *River Running West*, 158.
40 a hazel-eyed sergeant: Stegner, *Beyond the Hundredth Meridian*, 46.
40 wounded at Fredericksburg: Ghiglieri, *First Through the Grand Canyon*, 12.
40 who knew anything about boats: Ghiglieri, "George Young Bradley," 137–44.
41 his established trade as a printer and editor: Powell, *Diary*, 31.
41 a quiet and pensive young man: Ibid.
41 who had fought at Gettysburg: Ghiglieri, *First Through the Grand Canyon*, 23–26.
41 the cheerful eighteen-year-old: Powell, *Diary*, 31.
41 almost twice as high as Niagara: Niagara Falls is 167 feet high.
41 knew the first thing about white water: Powell's trips on the wide, placid rivers of the Midwest and Bradley's experiences in the New England cod fishery bore no comparison to the violent and wrenching hydraulics of the Colorado.
42 a sleek design that had originated: Ghiglieri, *First Through the Grand Canyon*, 51.
42 gangs of thieves who plundered: Dolnick, *Down the Great Unknown*, 26.
42 all but impossible to pivot: Ghiglieri, *First Through the Grand Canyon*, 52.
42 the trio of "freight boats": General details and analysis of Powell's boats come from Stegner, *Beyond the Hundredth Meridian*, 46–47; Worster, *River Running West*, 157; Dolnick, *Down the Great Unknown*, 26–29; Lavender, *River Runners of the Grand Canyon*, 13; Ghiglieri, *First Through the Grand Canyon*, 51–66.

42   running up against sandbars: Powell, *Diary*, 32.
42   late on the afternoon of June 17: O. G. Howland, cited by Ghiglieri, *First Through the Grand Canyon*, 126.
43   at 4:45 p.m. on the afternoon of: Sumner, cited by Ghiglieri, *First Through the Grand Canyon*, 173.
44   "I had a pair of buckskin breeches": Stanton, *Colorado River Controversies*, 26.
44   "If I had a dog that would lie where": Bradley, cited by Ghiglieri, "George Young Bradley," 137.
44   *"dumb luck*, not good judgment": Bradley, cited by Ghiglieri, *First Through the Grand Canyon*, 121.
45   they arrived at a turquoise-colored stream: Ibid., 198. Also see Dolnick, *Down the Great Unknown*, 234.
45   "We are three quarters of a mile": Powell, *Diary*, 107.
46   "The boats are entirely unmanageable": Ibid., 116.
46   On August 15, Hawkins broke: Bradley, cited by Ghiglieri, *First Through the Grand Canyon*, 209.
46   their location and their proximity to the end of the canyon: It is perhaps worth noting that the Powell expedition's precise position was largely a matter of conjecture, even when the barometers were functioning properly.
46   "If it keeps on this way": Ibid., 218.
47   "Starvation stared us in the face": Sumner, cited in Stanton, *Colorado River Controversies*, 193. Also cited by Dolnick, *Down the Great Unknown*, 254.
47   "a race for a dinner": Powell, *Diary*, 128.
47   as a "perfect hell of foam": Sumner, cited by Ghiglieri, *First Through the Grand Canyon*, 226.
48   "The last thing we saw of them": Sumner, cited in Stanton, *Colorado River Controversies*, 205. Also cited by Dolnick, *Down the Great Unknown*, 254.
48   "now become a race for life": Journals of George Bradley, cited by Ghiglieri, *First Through the Grand Canyon*, 229.
50   his obituary in the *Washington Post*: *Washington Post*, September 25, 1902. Cited by Dolnick, *Down the Great Unknown*, 292.

Part II

America's Pyramids

51   "I have climbed the Great Wall of China": Author interview with Dr. Henry Falvey.

4: The Kingdom of Water

53   "The more a man can achieve, the more he may be certain": Mailer, *Presidential Papers*, preface.
54   twice the size of Rhode Island: Solomon, *Water*, 332.
54   a prolific confederation of wild creatures: For an evocative description of the delta and its denizens, see Leopold, *Sand County Almanac*, 150–58.
54   Hall and Sumner became the first men: Sumner, cited by Ghiglieri, *First Through the Grand Canyon*, 292.
54   "burned to a cinder": Ibid., 232.
54   "I find myself penniless": Ibid.
55   headless brown serpent: *Colorado River: A Natural Menace*, 138. Also see Reisner, *Cadillac Desert*, 122.
55   repeated at regular intervals: Studies of the ancient shoreline suggest that between 1824 and 1904, the sink had filled no fewer than eight times. Hiltzik, *Colossus*, 10.
55   This treeless inferno: Ibid, 9.
55   the Palm of the Hand of God: Nadeau, *Water Seekers*, 142.
55   which amounted to roughly 2.4 inches: Reisner, *Cadillac Desert*, 122.
56   he could crush an apple in one palm: David O. Woodbury, *The Colorado Conquest* (New York: Dodd, Mead, 1941), 45. Cited by Hiltzik, *Colossus*, 20–21.
56   Rockwood made his way to the Southwest: Hiltzik, *Colossus*, 21.
56   population had jumped from exactly zero whites: Nadeau, *Water Seekers*, 143.
57   "Water Is King," the *Imperial Press* proclaimed: Ibid., 144.
57   most of the river hurtled toward the Sink: Waters, *Colorado*, 293.
57   took several weeks to assemble and cost $60,000: Ibid., 294.
57   one of the railroad's most competent construction engineers: Hiltzik, *Colossus*, 44.
58   virtually the entire Colorado was now diverting north: Ibid., 43.
58   sediment-saturated water as thick and dark: Waters, *Colorado*, 295.
58   the drop of the waterfall grew to eighty feet: Hiltzik, *Colossus*, 45.
58   widening the channel to half a mile: Nadeau, *Water Seekers*, 152.
58   a brick hotel, the railroad station: Ibid., 153.
58   geysers of water shooting forty feet into the air: Hiltzik, *Colossus*, 47.
58   "Damn the expense," came the reply: According to Nadeau, this comment was uttered by Epes Randolph, president of the California Development Company, which was taken over by the

Southern Pacific Railroad when Charles Rockwood ran out of funds. Randolph was the lieutenant of Edward H. Harriman, president of the Southern Pacific, who held final decision-making power in the campaign to control the flooding. See Nadeau, *Water Seekers*, 149.

59   the only men willing to work: Ibid., 156.

59   a makeshift dam began to rise above the brown surface: Ibid., 160–62.

59   Six work trains were now lumbering: Ibid., 162–64.

59   was now the largest lake in California: Hiltzik, *Colossus*, 49–50.

60   Congress had created the Reclamation Service: There were actually two forces behind the creation of the Reclamation Service. In addition to the vision of irrigating land for farming, the other impetus was the Johnstown flood (covered in chapter 16). That disaster contributed directly to the notion that the private sector had no business building dams, and that in future major flood-control and irrigation structures needed to be constructed under the aegis of the federal government. See Reisner, "Age of Dams and Its Legacy," 16. Reisner credits Wallace Stegner with this theory, although other historians, most notably David McCullough, echo it as well.

60   who was appointed Reclamation's chief engineer in 1903: US Bureau of Reclamation profile. See http://www.usbr.gov/history/CommissBios/davis.html (accessed 5/25/2012).

61   a diminutive plant in the tiny town of Appleton: Billington, *History of Large Federal Dams*, 458.

61   scaled up at Niagara Falls: Solomon, *Water*, 286.

61   dividing up the water rights among the seven states: In 1922, in a compact negotiated by Herbert Hoover, the river was split into upper and lower basins with the dividing line just downstream from Lee's Ferry. Half the water was claimed by the "upper basin" mountain states—Wyoming, Utah, Colorado, and New Mexico—where most of the rain and snow fell; half was claimed by the "lower basin" desert states—California, Arizona, and Nevada—where most of the farms and cities would be.

61   came together during the final weeks of 1928: Solomon, *Water*, 333–35.

61   The site where Davis proposed: Hiltzik, *Colossus*, 61.

61   At the point where the southern shard of Nevada stabs: *Colorado River: A Natural Menace*, 11.

62   Fifteen hours later, the Colorado sluggishly turned: Nadeau, *Water Seekers*, 214.

63   sixteen tons per minute: Ibid.

63   220 cubic yards an hour: Reisner, *Cadillac Desert*, 130.

63   It soared 726 feet and five inches: Ibid.

63   double the height of any other dam on earth: Solomon, *Water*, 330.

63   capable of holding more than twenty-six million acre-feet: Ibid.

63   enough water to flood the entire state of Connecticut: Franklin D. Roosevelt, speech given at the dedication of Boulder Dam, September 30, 1935, cited in Nixon, *Franklin D. Roosevelt and Conservation*, 438–41.

63   buckle roadbeds between Boulder City: Hiltzik, *Colossus*, 386–87.

64   cut the cooling time from 125 years: Nadeau, *Water Seekers*, 216.

64   "This is a first glimpse of what chemistry": Priestley, "Arizona Desert," 365. Although the writer Barry Lopez originally directed me to Priestley's article, I'm also indebted to Michael Hiltzik, who cites this quote in *Colossus*, xii.

65   embodied in the bureau's motto: Farmer, *Glen Canyon Dammed*, xv.

65   to harness and exploit virtually every drop: Barcott, *Last Flight of the Scarlet Macaw*, 82.

65   under construction along the rivers of the western United States: Solomon, *Water*, 228.

65   whose mass outstripped that of Hoover and Shasta: Reisner, *Cadillac Desert*, 158–59.

65   exceed the volume of the Great Pyramid of Cheops: Barcott, *Last Flight of the Scarlet Macaw*, 82.

65   generating half as much electricity as the rest of: Solomon, *Water*, 340.

65   the plutonium-239 that fueled the atomic bomb: Ibid.

65   every major river in the United States had been dammed except: Barcott, *Last Flight of the Scarlet Macaw*, 82–83.

65   thirty-six on the Columbia: Solomon, *Water*, 339.

65   forty-two on the Tennessee: Ibid., 343.

65   nothing compares to what we did to the Colorado: Reisner, *Cadillac Desert*, 130.

66   The work of harnessing the rest of the river had just begun: The process had started quite a bit earlier. For nearly four decades, dating back to the days of Arthur Powell Davis, the bureau had assiduously been conducting the surveys, geologic testing, and a host of other fieldwork necessary to determine what it would take to achieve complete mastery of the river by constructing a series of dams and reservoirs along the entire length of the Colorado and its major tributaries.

66   Nicknamed the Blue Book: Martin, *Story That Stands Like a Dam*, 48.

66   would exceed the Colorado's flow by 25 percent: *Colorado River: A Natural Menace*, 11.

66   "Only a nation of free people have the vision": Ibid., 25.

67   thanks to a series of massive congressional appropriations: Hiltzik, *Colossus*, 396.

67   No river in the world was the subject of fiercer litigation: Ibid., 397. Also see Fradkin, *River No More*, 15.

67   reused seventeen times before reaching the sea: Solomon, *Water*, 349.
67   a single drop ever reached the Sea of Cortés: Fradkin, *River No More*, 16.
67   "a small but measurable change in the wobble of the earth": Peter H. Gleick, "Making Every Drop Count," *Scientific American*, February 2001, 42. Cited in Solomon, *Water*, 361.

5: Flooding the Cathedral

69   "Something will have gone out of us as a people": Stegner, *Sound of Mountain Water*, 146–47.
69   Litton's father, a migrant from Tennessee: The details of Litton's life come from extensive author interviews.
71   Known as flying coffins: It should be acknowledged that the Glider Corps' losses were relatively light when compared with those suffered by the bomber crews. Also, the phrase *flying coffin* derived not from the number of crashes but instead reflected that many of the early machines were manufactured in coffin factories.
71   "the most uninhibited individualists in the army": Leonard and Arthur Northwood, Jr., *Rendezvous with Destiny: A History of the 101st Airborne Division*, cited by Devlin, *Silent Wings*, frontispiece.
71   delivering troopers into northern France: Litton was not part of the glider armada on D-day; he flew a day later as a copilot in a C-47 transport plane. He was not subject to enemy fire during this flight, and thus, unlike Market Garden and Bastogne, he does not consider his D-day flight a combat mission.
73   "When it comes to saving wilderness, we cannot be extreme *enough*": Author interview with Litton.
73   the budget was so tiny that the handful of rangers didn't even have money: Farmer, *Glen Canyon Dammed*, 140.
73   The reservoirs of these dams: The Echo Park dam would have created a reservoir that would reach sixty-four miles up the Green River and forty-four miles up the Yampa.
73   "unimpaired for the enjoyment of future generations": National Park Service Organic Act, 16 U.S.C.1.
73   when Reclamation formally unveiled: Aka 1950. See Pearson, *Still the Wild River Runs*, 18.
73   the construction of six major dams and twelve irrigation projects: Martin, *Story That Stands Like a Dam*, 54.
74   Litton was amused: Author interview with Litton.
74   The decisive part of the fight took place in Washington, DC: Martin, *Story That Stands Like a Dam*, 59.
75   "the abominable nature-lovers": Martin, *Story That Stands Like a Dam*, 61.
75   Brower was a rookie: Veteran wilderness advocates included Howard Zahniser of the Wilderness Society and Fred Packard of the National Parks Association. See Pearson, *Still the Wild River Runs*, 20–21.
75   subtract the Echo Park reservoirs' evaporative loss: Martin, *Story That Stands Like a Dam*, 61–62.
75   "cannot add, subtract, multiply, and divide": Reisner, *Cadillac Desert*, 284.
75   when combined with the negative publicity generated: Fox, *American Conservation Movement*, 285.
75   the dam's leading proponents were starting to reconsider: Ibid.
75   only 53 of which expressed: Martin, *Story That Stands Like a Dam*, 67.
75   as one cabinet official had derisively dubbed the conservationists: Fox, *American Conservation Movement*, 284.
76   the biggest and most important feature of the package: In his remarks, Brower had urged that the height of the dam at Glen Canyon be raised even farther to provide additional storage that would compensate for the loss of the two reservoirs at Dinosaur.
76   would inundate a little-known river corridor: Billington, *History of Large Federal Dams*, 183. Also see Pearson, *Still the Wild River Runs*, 21–24.
76   Watkins rammed the plunger down: Martin, *Story That Stands Like a Dam*, 86–87.
76   crews were drilling into the cliff at the portal: Ibid., 88.
76   the Swiss finished a pair of even higher dams: Ibid., 190. This is backed up by a list of the highest dams in the world and the dates of their construction (see Infoplease, "World's Highest Dams").
77   Grand Canyon is geology's Götterdämmerung: For this idea, I am indebted to the writer Bob Shacochis, who expressed this far more eloquently than I could have in *Between Heaven and Hell*, 32.
78   "the equivalent of several Dinosaur National Monuments": Brower, *Environmental Activist, Publicist, and Prophet*, 131.
79   he could see Brower scowling in the back of the room: Brower, *Environmental Activist, Publicist, and Prophet*.

79 guillotine-shaped gates: Martin, *Story That Stands Like a Dam*, 208.

79 Brower's sense of contrition was his resolve: Ibid.

79 That struggle would be waged without negotiation: Ibid.

80 The club's old guard: Litton, *Sierra Club Director*. Also see McPhee, *Encounters with the Archdruid*, 206–20.

80 One of the most powerful proponents of this approach: Litton, *Sierra Club Director*. Also, author interview with Litton.

80 it was unwise to declare war: Sierra Club minutes of the Annual Organization Meeting of the Board of Directors, May 4, 1963.

80 whether Brower would be given license to deploy: Ibid.

81 He and Esther signed on: Author interviews with Litton.

81 an odd duck called the *Gem*: Martin, *Big Water, Little Boats*, 103–19. Also, author interviews with Litton.

81 "major order of experience": Balzar, "Old Man and the River."

82 he found himself in Oregon: Author interviews with Litton.

82 double-ended cockleshells with open decks: Ibid.

82 Litton was smitten: Ibid. Also see Martin, *Big Water, Little Boats*, 192–93.

82 Reilly pronounced his dory the finest thing: Author interviews with Litton. Also see Martin, *Big Water, Little Boats*, 194.

82 had become inextricably entwined with the boats: Author interviews with Litton.

83 The meeting convened at 10:14 a.m. on May 4: Sierra Club minutes of the Annual Organization Meeting of the Board of Directors, May 4, 1963.

83 The club's smartest move, Robinson: Brower, *Environmental Activist, Publicist, and Prophet*, 143.

83 that a set of elevators be built: Litton, *River Runners Oral History*, October 10, 1992. Also, Litton, author interview, and Pearson, *Still the Wild River Runs*, 45.

83 nevertheless sent him into a fit of rage: Litton, *River Runners Oral History*, October 10, 1992. Also, author interviews with Litton.

83 "In the Grand Canyon, Arizona has a natural wonder": Roosevelt, *Presidential Addresses and State Papers*, 370.

83 it didn't make a hoot of difference: "Directors Launch Campaign for Expanded Grand Canyon Protection," *Sierra Club Bulletin*, 6–7. Also see Brower, *Environmental Activist, Publicist, and Prophet*, and author interviews with Litton.

84 It's *our* canyon. It's *our* national park: Litton, *River Runners Oral History*, October 10, 1992.

84 a man or woman steps up to the plate and takes: Author interview with Byron Pearson.

84 "Martin doesn't have to prime for a speech": This quote is taken from two separate interviews that Brower later gave. In his oral history for the Sierra Club, which was conducted in 1980, Brower said that Litton "got up and so devastated Bestor Robinson's arguments that there was applause from the audience, and the board voted to oppose the Grand Canyon dams." In a separate oral-history interview that Brower gave to Lew Steiger for Northern Arizona University's Cline Library in 1997, Brower stated, "Martin poured it on—what a ridiculous thing this would be to do, and the audience applauded, and Bestor subsided, and we voted no." See Brower, *Environmental Activist, Publicist, and Prophet*, 143; and David Brower, *Boatman's Quarterly Review* 10, no. 3 (Summer 1997): 33.

85 "Oh?" Litton retorted. "I wouldn't say that": Author interview with Litton.

85 at Brower's urging, Litton commissioned another dory from Oregon: Author interviews with Litton. Also see Lavender, *River Runners of the Grand Canyon*, 130.

85 they passed by a line of bright red fire hydrants: Leydet, *Time and the River Flowing*, 38.

85 Here, a series of test tunnels had been drilled: Ibid., 52.

85 similar test bores had been drilled at the second site: Ibid., 128.

85 helping to develop a traveling photo exhibit: Pearson, *Still the Wild River Runs*, 77.

86 a trio of young graduates from MIT: Martin, *Story That Stands Like a Dam*, 270–71. Also see Pearson, *Still the Wild River Runs*, 144–45.

86 banker from Tucson named Morris Udall: Martin, *Story That Stands Like a Dam*, 266.

86 its donors should be made aware that their contributions: Ibid., 271–72.

87 "an assault on the right of private citizens to protest": Ibid., 272.

87 Morris Udall described it as a "deluge": Pearson, *Still the Wild River Runs*, 147.

87 "I never saw anything like it": Reisner, *Cadillac Desert*, 286.

87 "Mailbags were coming in by the hundreds": Ibid., 288.

87 was heralded by *Life* as "his country's number-one working conservationist": Martin, *Story That Stands Like a Dam*, 291.

88 "Some people get the kudos and others, out of inequity, don't": Litton, *Sierra Club Director*; see introduction, written by Brower.

Part III
The Sweet Lines of Desire

89   "If rightly made, a boat would be": *A Week on the Concord and Merrimack Rivers* (1849), in *The Writings of Henry David Thoreau* (Boston: Houghton Mifflin, 1906), 1:13.

6: Dories

91   "The glory of the dories is their lightness": P. T. Reilly, cited by Welch, "In Praise of Port Orford Cedar."

91   had emerged as the classic American wilderness experience: Nash, *Big Drops*, 168–69.

92   Grand Canyon Dories was officially launched: Although Litton's commercial trips started in earnest during the summer of 1969, his company was not formally incorporated until 1971.

93   part of a tradition that reached back to medieval Europe: Gardner, *Dory Book*, 1–39.

94   "There must be something about dories that intrigues people": Ibid., vii–viii.

94   "to remind us of places we've destroyed without any necessity": Author interviews with Litton.

94   the Sierra Club had lost a bitter battle in 1968: Cohen, *History of the Sierra Club*, 403–4.

94   one of the many gemlike features inside Glen Canyon that now lay: Inskip, *Colorado River Through Glen Canyon Before Lake Powell.*

95   scratching makeshift blueprints in the sand next to Briggs's driveway: Author interviews with Litton.

95   He also straightened out the chine: Fletcher, *Drift Boats and River Dories*, 272.

96   What he wanted now were copies: Ibid.

96   an entire mountainside mantled in some of the tallest virgin trees: Litton, *Sierra Club Director*, 39–41.

97   those first twenty-seven dories that emerged from Briggs's shop: There is some discrepancy over how many dories Briggs produced. According to Roger Fletcher, Briggs built thirty-three, including the *Emerald Mile*. However, Brad Dimock, a respected Grand Canyon boating historian, puts the number at thirty-six. I have elected to stick with the twenty-seven dories whose names can be verified, all of which are listed in an article published in the 1994 edition of the *Hibernacle News*, "The Dories—Whence and Whither?," 14–15.

99   he was charging the same for a no-frills trip: *Grand Canyon Dories Catalogue*, 1972.

99   Diane Sawyer, James Taylor, Bruce Babbitt, Richard Holbrooke, and Bill Moyers: Author interviews with Litton and John Blaustein.

100   a vintage tail-dragger with a radial engine and a propeller: John Litton, *The Life and Times of Martin Litton*, an unfinished film by Don Briggs, available on Vimeo. Also, author interviews with Litton.

100   In river hydrology, a phenomenon known as headwater capture: This idea has been explained by many writers, perhaps the most eloquent of whom is Gretel Ehrlich. See http://test.ourhome ground.com/entries/definition/river_capture.

7: The Golden Age of Guiding

102   "Believe me, my young friend, there is nothing": Grahame, *Wind in the Willows*, 8.

102   no one had the faintest clue how to run: Norm Nevills, the founder of Nevills Expedition, had used hard-hulled boats inside the canyon during the thirties and forties, but Nevills completed only seven trips through the canyon in his entire career. By the early seventies, some members of Litton's crew were running that many trips in a single season.

103   looking for a dry space to stow his cigar: Jeri Ledbetter, *The Life and Times of Martin Litton*, an unfinished film by Don Briggs, available on Vimeo.

105   a whirlpool laid on its side with its axis of rotation perpendicular: Quammen, *Wild Thoughts from Wild Places*, 48–49.

106   "The face of the water, in time, became a wonderful book": Powers, *Mark Twain*, 76.

106   composed of Arabic numerals ranging from 1 to 10 and spread across four different levels: See *Belknap's Waterproof Grand Canyon River Guide.*

108   an awful lot of luck was involved: Many boatmen speak about this quality of luck. For a good example, see Mitch Dion's untitled article on pages 6 and 7 of the 1996 *Hibernacle News.*

111   anyone in a motor rig or a rubber raft: It is perhaps important to acknowledge that not every guide in the Grand Canyon envied the dorymen or dreamed of rowing their boats. Even today, many motor- and oar-raft guides take great pleasure in their craft—which, when viewed from a strictly utilitarian point of view, are unquestionably superior to the delicate and highly finicky dories. It is also worth noting that most of these guides will readily concede that they would

never turn down the opportunity to get behind the oars of a dory for at least one trip through the canyon.

111   "Lord knows what can happen aboard those contraptions": Author interview with Litton.

8: Crystal Genesis

113   "In the rock record, the tranquillity of time": McPhee, *Annals of the Former World*, 171–72.
114   the rain fell steadily for twenty hours on Saturday, paused briefly: Cooley et al., "Effects of the Catastrophic Flood," 4. Note: the rain did stop for a three-hour break between Sunday and Wednesday.
114   adding to the magnitude of what unfolded: Carothers and Brown, *Colorado River Through Grand Canyon*, 41.
114   is commensurate with the kind of rainfall that the jungles: See McCullough, *The Path Between the Seas*.
115   unconsolidated silt, fine sand, and a heterogeneous blend of chert: Cooley et al., "Effects of the Catastrophic Food," 34.
115   clays and minerals that can act as crude lubricants: Childs, *Secret Knowledge of Water*, 190.
115   This type of flash flood is known inside the Grand Canyon: Zwinger, *Downcanyon*, 143.
116   "As the rain increased, I heard some rock tumbling down": This quote comes from Dolnick (*Down the Great Unknown*, 231), who is apparently quoting from Stanton (*Down the Colorado*). The wording, however, is different from a similar quote cited by Webb (*Grand Canyon*, 125–26), who is apparently citing Dwight L. Smith's *The Colorado River Survey: Robert B. Stanton and the Denver, Colorado Canyon & Pacific Railroad*, 88. Moreover, wording of both quotes are different from a similar quote that Lavender uses on pages 6 and 25 of *River Runners of the Grand Canyon*, for which Lavender provides no citation.
117   "he was running as wildly as any human being could": Ghiglieri and Myers, *Over the Edge*, 100. All details of the Clubb tragedy come from Ghiglieri and Myers.
118   the gradualists had not only won this long-running debate: There are many excellent accounts of this debate. The texts from which I have drawn include McPhee, *Annals of the Former World*, 171–72; Bjornerud, *Reading the Rocks*, 26–29; and Bryson, *Short History of Nearly Everything*, 69–75.
118   assumed that this landscape was shaped slowly: I am indebted to Ghiglieri and Myers, who lay out this notion quite nicely in chapter 3 of *Over the Edge*.
118   objects that none but the largest floods could ever dislodge: Webb, *Grand Canyon*, 143.
118   nearly a hundred separate debris flows were touched off: Cooley et al., "Effects of the Catastrophic Food," 42.
119   The amphitheater consists of two main drainage streams: Steck, *Hiking Grand Canyon Loops*, 53.
119   a group of six scientists with the US Geological Survey: See Cooley et al., "Effects of the Catastrophic Flood"; Webb et al., "Debris Flows from Tributaries"; and Webb, *Grand Canyon*.
119   it generated so much centrifugal force that the surface actually tilted: For several details in this section, I am indebted to Jeremy Schmidt's clear and eloquent treatment in *A Natural History Guide*, 55–56.
120   The debris flow obliterated it: Cooley et al., "Effects of the Catastrophic Flood," 16.
120   it was now sixty feet wide: Carothers and Brown, *Colorado River Through Grand Canyon*, 42. Also see Zwinger, *Downcanyon*, 141.
120   almost thirty dump-truck loads of material: Author calculation. There are 18 cubic yards, or 486 cubic feet, in a dump-truck load.
120   rushing past each second: Webb et al., "Debris Flows from Tributaries," 1–39.
120   When the debris flow burst from the mouth of the Crystal Creek: Quite a bit of hyperbole surrounds the details of what took place. According to one account, the debris flow was moving at fifty miles per hour and at nearly 30,000 cfs—triple the flow of the river itself. Another version claimed that giant boulders skipped across the surface of the river and bounced off the cliffs on the opposite side of the canyon. A third account claims that the event went on for several hours and the entire river was temporarily blocked. In recent years, those assertions have been tempered by the patient research of Robert H. Webb and several other scientists with the USGS. Thanks to their work, we now know that some of the most colorful elements of the story are simply not true. The peak discharge lasted for minutes, not hours. The boulders that were dumped into the Colorado probably did not dam up the entire river, even temporarily. Nevertheless, what actually happened was impressive enough. By the time the debris flow reached the bottom of the drainage, it had reached about 10,000 cfs, roughly the same flow levels as the river itself.
120   the heaviest of them being nearly fifty tons: Carothers and Brown, *Colorado River Through Grand Canyon*, 42.
121   Seconds later, it was constricted to a channel of about 55 feet: Webb and Magirl, "The Changing Rapids of Grand Canyon," 42–44.

121 it has since been contested by at least one scientist: See Webb, *Grand Canyon*; and Cooley et al., "Effects of the Catastrophic Flood."

121 On February 24, 1967, Ken Sleight: Sleight, "Letter to members of the Western River Guides Association, Inc., February 24, 1967."

121 Cross had spoken to the same helicopter pilot: Sleight, "Letter to members of the Western River Guides Association, Inc., March 23, 1967."

122 "that a boat trying to break out of the current and get around the right side": Ibid.

123 "Any way you look at it, Crystal has become one of the worst rapids": Ibid.

123 the rapid's topographic and hydraulic contours would remain firmly in place: A handful of floods, the most noteworthy of which occurred on the Little Colorado in 1972, created brief pulses of higher water that shifted things around but failed to expand the bottleneck or reestablish the constriction ratio.

123 The river no longer had the muscle to move them aside: According to Susan Kieffer's findings, almost all of the work to establish the constriction ratio took place during floods, when the runoff burgeoned to 100,000 cfs and the river had the power to perform this kind of work.

9: The Death of the *Emerald Mile*

124 "And the river was there": Conrad, *Heart of Darkness*, 5.

125 dubbed Nixon Rock: Among the Grand Canyon boating community there is some good-natured disagreement about where Nixon Rock is located. While some argue that it is in Tuna Rapid, others are convinced that it is a mile downstream of Waltenberg Rapid and was originally named "Tricky Dicky."

127 "We're not going to carry these boats around": Donald Litton, *The Life and Times of Martin Litton*, an unfinished film by Bill Briggs, available on Vimeo.

128 "We really could do without it": Author interview with Martin Litton. Note: Litton deemed the post-1966 Crystal "unnatural" because the Glen Canyon Dam held back high spring runoffs that otherwise would have significantly altered the rapid.

128 Regan Dale, who had signed on with a motor company: Dale, *Oral History*, NAU.

129 Rist set out to master these nuances: Author interview with Wally Rist.

130 *Golden Trip!* on the inside cover: Author interview with John Blaustein.

130 "We'd hear his approach and it'd be like": Author interview with Andre Potochnik.

130 "They'd come up to me with these big cow-eyes": Author interview with Litton.

131 In the years to come, a number of these women would demolish: See Teal, *Breaking into the Current*.

131 "Oh, if we get ten trips out of her, I'd be happy": Author interviews with Litton and Petschek.

131 Wren hailed from a logging burg: Author interview with Steve Reynolds.

132 Late in the summer of 1977: Author interviews with Regan Dale and O. C. Dale.

134 one afternoon in the summer of 1971, Wally Rist: Author interview with Rist.

134 In the spring of 1995, another flood would race down Prospect Canyon: March 6, 1995. http://wwwpaztcn.wr.usgs.gov/fscc/stanton-repeat-photography/repeat-photos.php?mode=stake&StakeID=431 (accessed 12/16/2012).

135 Dalton was just a few feet to the right: Details of Dalton's accident at Lava come from author interviews with Regan Dale and Rudi Petschek, both of whom were eyewitnesses.

137 to haul her off to the town garbage dump and give her a "Viking funeral": Author interviews with Regan Dale, Petschek, and Tuck Weills, manager of Grand Canyon Dories in 1983.

Part IV

The Master of the *Emerald Mile*

139 "If a man is to be obsessed by something, I suppose a boat": White, *E. B. White Reader*, 188.

10: The Factor

141 "And you really live by the river?": Grahame, *Wind in the Willows*, 10.

141 an eccentric and contrarian boatman: Details of Grua's childhood and his early years on the river come from his four oral-history interviews that are cataloged at NAU's Cline Library, plus author interviews with Petschek, Litton, Blaustein, Tom Myers, Regan Dale, Kenly Weills, and Rist, among others.

144 "Let's wait for the little man": Author interview with Rist.

144 "an instant flash picture": Author interview with Petschek.

145 "It just seems like it's going to go on forever and then—*boom*": Grua, oral histories, NAU.

146 "He's the most considerate person I know": Author interview with Rist.

146 "Christ, he could be impossible": Author interview with a colleague of Grua's who wishes to remain anonymous.

148 there was not a single route: See Tom Myers, "Down the Gorge with Uncle George: Hiking the Length of the Grand Canyon" in *Grand Canyon History Symposium*. "While it is possible that over the millennia a collective line of foot travel by Native Americans would connect one end of the Canyon to the other, no conclusive evidence of this exists."

148 Harvey Butchart, a mathematician from Flagstaff: See Butler and Myers, *Grand Obsession*.

148 was published by Colin Fletcher: See Fletcher, *Man Who Walked Through Time*.

148 "the first man ever to have walked through the entire length": Ibid., jacket copy.

149 "Somebody else needs to do it and do it right": Author interview with Petschek. Also see Grua, oral histories, NAU.

150 Grua started scoping out his route during his first season: Details of Grua's Grand Canyon transect come primarily from his oral histories, NAU, and from the definitive research on canyon thruhikes that Tom Myers has laid out in his article, "Down the Gorge with Uncle George."

150 He departed on the twenty-ninth of February: It is important to note that although Grua was by himself for nearly two-thirds of his hike, he did have two companions during two separate segments of the journey. He was accompanied by Bart Henderson from Jackass to Tanner, and by Ellen Tibbetts from Hermit to Havasu. It is also worth noting that although Grua's feat has since been reproduced by sixteen other hikers, several of whom have conducted their traverses on the north side of the canyon, Grua's total elapsed time of thirty-seven days remained for many years the fastest of all the recorded thru-hikes (see Myers). Grua continued to hold the speed record not only for rowing the length of the Grand Canyon but also for hiking it until 2013.

11: Speed

155 "And so in time": Bode, *First You Have to Row a Little Boat*.

157 "You could do this until you died": Grua, oral histories, NAU.

157 "You could do it straight through the year": Ibid.

157 "the best drug in the world": Ibid.

157 the only boatman on the Colorado: It is important to note that although Grua's obsessions and his personality may have placed him in a class of his own, virtually all of Martin Litton's early guides harbored a similar level of passion for the dories and the canyon.

158 he and a handful of his colleagues: Grua was not the first dory boatman to run through the Big Hole in the middle of Crystal. That distinction belongs to Steve Gantner, who nailed the run in 1972.

158 a sequence of ferocious arguments: Author interview with Regan Dale.

158 Kenton, these people aren't our guinea pigs: Ibid.

159 How could he have been so *selfish*?: Ibid.

161 he broke out his tools and applied himself: Author interviews with Petschek, Rist, and Tuck Weills.

162 the advent of the water-jet engine: Lavender, *River Runners of the Grand Canyon*, 108.

162 modeled along the lines of a Higgins landing craft: Ibid. Also see the website of the Grand Canyon River Heritage Coalition, http://www.gcrivermuseum.org (accessed 7/27/2012).

162 Propelled by a seventy-five-horsepower inboard engine: Lavender, *River Runners of the Grand Canyon*, 117. Also see Brune, "Historic River Running."

163 had stampeded and strewn fuel: Lavender, *River Runners of the Grand Canyon*, 118.

163 Jim Rigg, the older of the pair: Rigg, *USGS Old-Timers' Collection*, September 10, 1994, NAU.

164 "Man, we got rocks on the oars": Ibid.

164 "We're going the right way!": Ibid.

164 a brand-new speed record of fifty-two hours and forty-one minutes: Martin, *Big Water, Little Boats*, 68.

164 the most impressive feats of boatmanship: Author interview with Petschek.

166 that stretched the principle of slow-boating to its outer limits: Author interviews with Bego Gerhart, Ote Dale, O. C. Dale, and Petschek.

167 The participants of the Hundred Days Trip included: O. C. Dale, Bego Gerhart, Roberta Pedan, Nels Niemi, Sharon Tanberg, and Sue (Ote) Tesch.

167 Bernard Moitessier, the great French yachtsman: See Moitessier, *Long Way*.

167 an Oregon gas-station attendant named Buzz Holmstrom: Welch, Conley, and Dimock, *Doing of the Thing*, 121–23.

167 become the first person to row every rapid on both rivers: Holmstrom skipped a few rapids—including Lava Falls—by lining them during his 1937 trip; the following year, he returned and rowed them all.

168   "I had once thought—once past here—my reward will begin": Ibid.
168   At the center of the book is a scene in which Hemming: Salter, *Solo Faces*, 63–64.
168   "There are routes the boldness and logic of which are overwhelming": Ibid.
169   another speed run formed a major topic of discussion: Author interviews with Rist and Petschek.
169   The river level that had borne: In fact, the stories were not true. Although the Rigg brothers were under the impression that the river level exceeded 60,000 cfs during their run—an impression that Bob Rigg still holds to this day—the USGS gauging station records indicate that the river was actually flowing at 41,300 cfs and dropping when they started their run.

12: Thunder on the Water

171   "Once it was a boat, quite wooden": Sexton, "The Kiss," from *Love Poems* by Anne Sexton. Copyright © 1967, 1968, 1969 by Anne Sexton. Reprinted by permission of Houghton Mifflin Harcourt Publishing Company. All rights reserved.
171   Wayne Aspinall, traveled to Page: Rusho, "Bumpy Road for Glen Canyon Dam."
172   a good time to conduct a partial test-drive of the spillways: Ibid.
172   lower the gates and crimp the flow: Ibid.
172   driven primarily by Wally Rist: Author interview with Rist.
173   Petschek had been born into a family of: Author interview with Petschek.
174   "test evacuation procedures": Ibid.
174   They launched at just after 4:00 p.m.: Details of the 1980 speed run come from author interviews with Rist and Petschek, as well as Petschek's handwritten notes of the run, which record their progress through the canyon.
175   They had beaten the Rigg brothers by almost six hours: There is an important difference between the Rigg brothers' speed run and the 1980 Rist/Grua/Petschek run that must be taken into account, even though it does not affect the outcome. While the Rigg brothers timed their run to the Grand Wash Cliffs, Rist and his companions timed theirs to Pierce Ferry, roughly one hour farther downstream, depending on wind conditions. Therefore, the difference between these two speed runs was, technically, a matter of nearly five hours, not six. As a further complication, the 1983 speed run would be timed to the Grand Wash Cliffs, not to Pierce Ferry.
177   "Well, did you do it?": Author interview with Petschek.

Part V
The Gathering Storm

179   "And farther off, where darkness met it": Wolfe, *Of Time and the River*.

13: Deluge

181   "Even this may be the eventful year": Thoreau, *Walden & Other Writings*, 296.
183   were showing up outside the entrance to San Francisco Bay: Lindsey, "California Journal," 22. Also see Lea and Miller, "Shark Attacks," 136–50.
183   The first of the '83 El Niño superstorms: "El Niño Storms Make Weather Top Topic."
183   sending semiliquid avalanches slumping: Cott, "Calmer County Keeps Mopping Out."
184   the queen of England was forced: "Queen Elizabeth Braces Stormy U.S. Weather." Also see "Storm Halts Queen's Sail to 'Frisco."
184   The eighteen-foot seas and the fifty-mile-an-hour: Thomas, "Royalty of Hollywood and England Get Together."
184   *restarting* the Pony Express: Lindsay, "Pony Express Rides Again." Also see Youngblood, "Resurrected Real Pony Express Service."
184   much of the Great Basin, an arid hardpan: The runoff roared down Ophir Creek into the Washoe Valley, between Carson City and Reno, destroying homes and vehicles. "Mud Smothers 3 Mountain Towns." See Reisner, *Cadillac Desert*.
184   Pacific's railroad bed to keep: "Floodwaters Start to Recede."
184   Crested Butte in the Elk Mountains: Stoner, "Oral History Interview," 37.
184   an even bigger storm dumped another two feet: "Snowpack Buries Colorado; California Braces for Rain."
185   "All that we can hope and pray for": "Floodwaters Start to Recede."
185   seven hydrologists ran the Colorado Basin River Forecast Center: Accounts of events at the Colorado Basin River Forecast Center in Salt Lake City come primarily from author interviews with Don Laurine and David Westnedge, both of whom were meteorologists working at the CBRFC during the runoff of 1983.

186   the information that was streaming into his office: Cox, "Raging River Scuttles Forecasts."

186   the snowpack in January had burgeoned to 14 percent above normal: Paltrow, "Who, If Anybody, Is to Blame for Floods?"

186   Then on Saturday, May 28: Ibid.

186   no precedent in the thirty years: Cox, "Raging River Scuttles Forecasts."

186   Never before had it melted off with: Ibid.

187   the government simply had not placed enough snow-telemetry: Mathews, "Huge Surge of Mountain Water."

187   far less water had been lost to evaporation and infiltration: "Summary of 1983 River Operations," 4, US Bureau of Reclamation Archives. Corroborated by author interview with Westnedge.

187   "Our models are among the best in the world": Cox, "Raging River Scuttles Forecasts."

187   "You can't go in and completely model": Ibid.

187   almost no resemblance to what the river was actually doing: Normally, most of the snowpack is gone by June 1. Indeed, snow data on the first of June was so limited that typically it was not even used in adjusting the forecasts—there simply was not enough of a historical record on which to build a comparison.

188   freighting the runoff of a region whose landmass: The Upper Basin of the Colorado amounts to nearly 108,000 square miles. Source: Colorado River Water Users Association, http://www.crwua .org/ColoradoRiver/RiverUsers/Reclamation.aspx.

188   approached the size of Poland: The drainage basin for the entire river is 243,000 miles, roughly the size of Somalia, but the Upper Basin is considerably smaller (see previous note). Also note that Poland, at 117,000 square miles, is slightly larger than the Upper Basin.

188   In the summer of 1921, for example: Martin, *Big Water, Little Boats*, 146.

188   the flooding may have surpassed 240,000: Ibid.

188   a cat trapped in an apple tree: Ibid. Also see Webb, *Grand Canyon*.

188   On more than a dozen: Fifteen, to be exact.

189   Among the sixty-four Reclamation employees who worked at Glen: Author interview with Tom Gamble.

14: Into the Bedrock

190   "Rivers, rivers, we can never": Abbey, *Down the River*, 3.

190   Tom Gamble was a trim: All details about Gamble—his childhood, early career, ideas about engineering and environmentalism, and his time at Glen Canyon—come from a series of author interviews conducted at Gamble's home in California.

191   Shasta stood as one of the Bureau of Reclamation's jewels: Rogers, "Lecture on Dam Safety."

194   five members of a newly formed environmental organization: Lee, *Earth First!*, 45–46.

194   back in the late 1950s: See Abbey, *Desert Solitaire*.

195   "No man-made structure in modern American history": Lee, *Earth First!*, 45–46.

195   Oregon to urinate off the parapet: Farmer, *Glen Canyon Dammed*, 171.

196   a group of misguided people who couldn't bring themselves: In some respects, this characterization of the environmentalists' opposition to the dam is unfair. The Bureau of Reclamation knows perfectly well that the dam is burdened by a number of glaring liabilities that argue against—or at least question—the wisdom of having authorized its construction. One especially compelling issue is the fact that Lake Powell currently loses some 700,000 acre feet of water each year to evaporation. This represents more than 5 percent of the Colorado River's annual flow—almost enough to supply the entire city of Los Angeles, and worth nearly $200 million at current rates. During the prevailing era of increasing drought and diminished river levels due to climate change, the value and impact of this evaporative loss will only grow with time.

197   Each winter, these conflicting demands: See Carothers and Brown, *Colorado River Through Grand Canyon*.

197   From the beginning of March through the first week of April: US Bureau of Reclamation, Upper Colorado River Region Reservoir Operations, Lake Powell. See http://www.usbr.gov/uc/crsp/ GetSiteInfo.

197   in charge of the river gathered in Boulder City: Dozier, "Summary of Communications and Actions," 3, Bureau of Reclamation Archives.

197   Glen was equipped with two such tunnels: See *Glen Canyon Dam and Powerplant*.

198   At 1:00 p.m. on the afternoon of Thursday: Rusho, "Bumpy Road for Glen Canyon Dam."

198   At first, everything proceeded smoothly: Ibid.

198   They planned to hold it there over the weekend: Moyes and Burgi, *Glen Canyon Dam Chronology*, "Spillway Discharge Tables," 13–15, Bureau of Reclamation Archives.

198   When the pair of operators: Ibid. Also, author interview with Richard White, manager of the Control Room at the Glen Canyon Dam.

199   This was the assistant operator's task: Most details of what happened inside the Control Room on June 5 through 7 come from the author's interview with Richard White.

201   "Did you see that?!": Author interviews with Gamble and White.

201   *It's into the bedrock:* Author interview with White.

15: The Mouth of the Dragon

202   Bureau of Reclamation's Engineering and Research Center: Details of the E&R Center and the Hydraulics Lab derive from the author's tour of the facility in the summer of 2011 and interviews conducted on-site.

202   When Gamble got through to the E&R Center: Author interview with Gamble.

203   he barked into the receiver, "Concrete dams!": Wolf, "How Lake Powell Almost Broke Free."

204   the three men conducted a quick huddle: Details of Burgi's meetings at the E&R Center, his background, his first trip to Page, and his descent into the east spillway come from the author's interview with Burgi and from Burgi's own notes.

206   "that He may have an answer to the first question": Ibid.

206   The east spillway tunnel intake: For specs on the spillway gates and tunnels, see *Glen Canyon Dam and Powerplant.*

208   *If this gate fails:* Author interview with Burgi.

210   When work on the dam began in 1956: For details on the reasons behind the spillway design, see Martin, *Story That Stands Like a Dam.*

210   "Jiminy Christmas": Author interview with Burgi.

211   This force, called cavitation: Henry Falvey, Burgi's colleague at the Hydraulics Lab, wrote a definitive monograph on cavitation: *Cavitation in Chutes and Spillways.* Also, author interviews with Falvey.

212   this repair at Glen Canyon had been scheduled to start on June 1: Rogers, "Hoover Dam," 195, 212. Also see Moyes and Burgi, *Glen Canyon Dam Chronology of Events,* Bureau of Reclamation Archives.

212   Burgi discovered a total of six holes: Author interview with Burgi. Also see Moyes and Burgi, *Glen Canyon Dam Chronology of Events,* Bureau of Reclamation Archives.

213   Christmas tree: Author interviews with Burgi and Falvey. Note: Burgi estimated at this point that fifty cubic yards of concrete had already been excavated from the tunnel invert.

16: Raising the Castle Walls

214   "The distant lightning glowed": McCarthy, *All the Pretty Horses,* 67.

215   Gamble and his team had something in mind: Although the author was unable to unearth any written records that point to where the decision to erect the flashboards originated, it is highly unlikely—indeed, it is virtually impossible—that Tom Gamble and his team at the dam would have been permitted to undertake this project unilaterally. During the spillway crisis, Jim Brown, the Bureau's chief engineer in Denver, met daily with Bruce Moyes and Henry Falvey to review all proposed engineering recommendations before passing these along, by telephone, to Cliff Barrett, the Bureau's Upper Colorado regional director in Salt Lake City. After discussing these recommendations with his staff, Barrett would then telephone Gamble and provide direction on what should be done next. In light of the fact that Gamble was not authorized to act independently, the idea of erecting flashboards on the spillway gates almost certainly originated in Denver and was sanctioned in Salt Lake City before being delivered to Gamble in Page. For the record: Burgi, Falvey, and Gamble have no specific recollection of who first voiced the flashboards proposal.

215   the dam's maintenance department summoned his crew: Details of the actions taken by the dam's maintenance crew come from the author's interview with Richard Parsons, a member of the crew, who was present at the dam throughout the spillway crisis in 1983.

215   "I want most of you guys to get up to the warehouse": Author interview with Parsons.

216   Henry Dhieux, the foreman of the mechanics crew: Details of the actions taken by the welders come from the author's interview with Henry Dhieux, foreman, who was present at the dam throughout the spillway crisis in 1983.

216   "Let's grab our gear": Author interview with Dhieux.

217   Within hours the outlets' expansion joints were leaking: Moyes and Burgi, *Glen Canyon Dam Chronology of Events,* Bureau of Reclamation Archives.

217   manhole covers in the parking lot next: Schultz, "Design Features of the Glen Canyon Dam."

217   heaved upward and began to tilt: Moyes and Burgi, *Glen Canyon Dam Chronology of Events,* Bureau of Reclamation Archives.

217   the discharge they were sending through the dam would decrease: "Report of Telephone Call,"

from Bruce Moyes to Tom Gamble, Water and Power Resources Service, Division of Design, June 8, 1983, Bureau of Reclamation Archives in Denver.

218   *something* was being rattled: Author interview with Parsons.

218   Those vibrations were especially noticeable in the lunchroom: Ibid.

218   something about a dam break that seems: For details about the history of dams and dam breaks, see Smith, *History of Dams* and Barcott, *Last Flight of the Scarlet Macaw.*

218   the oldest structure for which evidence remains: For insights on Sadd el-Kafara, I am indebted to Barcott, *Last Flight of the Scarlet Macaw,* 78–79.

219   "then shall he in whose dam the break occurred be sold for money": For insights on Hammurabi's laws, I am similarly indebted to Barcott, *Last Flight of the Scarlet Macaw,* 78–79.

219   cascading through the Conemaugh Valley toward Johnstown: For the definitive account of the Johnstown dam break, see McCullough, *Johnstown Flood.*

220   The exact number of victims is still unknown: The only disaster that has taken a greater toll of life in California's history is the San Francisco earthquake of 1906. The dam collapse was the worst civil-engineering disaster in the United States in the twentieth century. See Reisner, *Cadillac Desert.*

220   By eight o'clock that night, the Teton reservoir: For details on the Teton Dam break, see Reisner, *Cadillac Desert.*

221   ninety-four times bigger than the volume of Johnstown: The little lake surrounded by the hunting and fishing retreat above Johnstown, which was one of the largest man-made reservoirs on earth at the time, contained 15,000 acre-feet. The St. Francis reservoir held 38,000 acre-feet, and Teton contained more than 234,000. See McCullough, *Johnstown Flood,* and Reisner, *Cadillac Desert.*

221   The initial dam-break wave, traveling about twenty miles an hour: For details and calculations on the effect of a dam-break wave traveling through the Grand Canyon, see Latham, *Dam Failure Inundation Study: Glen Canyon Dam, Arizona,* 7–9.

221   "would have to climb the equivalent of a 40-story building": Ibid.

221   Glen's chief designer was an engineer: For details on Louis Puls and the design decisions that he made at Glen Canyon, see Martin, *Story That Stands Like a Dam,* 187.

222   As a result, Glen was spectacularly strong: For this analysis of Puls's design, I am indebted to Martin, *Story That Stands Like a Dam,* 188–89.

222   The first—overtopping the dam: In Burgi's view, the eleven feet of additional storage in the reservoir made the overtopping of the dam's parapet extremely unlikely, especially given that flows would also be passing over the tops of the radial gates. In essence, Burgi did not think the runoff was sufficient to overwhelm the parapet.

222   a number of the Denver engineers did harbor concerns: Author interview with Burgi. Also see Moyes and Burgi, *Glen Canyon Dam Chronology of Events,* Bureau of Reclamation Archives.

223   Each plug was 150 feet long and notched into: See Martin, *Story That Stands Like a Dam,* 209. Also see *Glen Canyon Dam and Powerplant: Technical Record of Design and Construction*; and author interview with J. David Rogers.

223   the Denver engineers had weighed this possibility: Moyes and Burgi, *Glen Canyon Dam Chronology of Events,* Bureau of Reclamation Archives, 19. Also, author interview with Burgi.

224   "The inherent stability of the dam and its ability to bridge": Moyes and Burgi, *Glen Canyon Dam Chronology of Events,* Bureau of Reclamation Archives, 18–19.

224   "a lateral progression of any damage pattern": Ibid.

224   Hoover itself would be fine: Author interview with Rogers.

224   Everyone was confident that this was unlikely: Author interview with Burgi.

225   All but one of the fourteen major reservoirs: Roy D. Gear, faxogram; To: Commissioner, LBR, Washington, DC; From: Regional Director, LBR, Boulder City, Nevada; Subject: Increased Flows in the Colorado River from Hoover Dam to Mexico, June 20, 1983. Memo states that "all upstream reservoirs on the upper Colorado are now 'essentially full'" and that "remaining storage space has been calculated to fill before the complete volume of the snowmelt runoff is completed."

225   shimmering blue reservoirs linked by: Udall, "Floods Reveal Water Policy Chaos."

225   was still rising roughly five inches every twenty-four hours: During the previous week, the reservoir had risen 5.76 inches on Tuesday, 3.48 inches on Wednesday, and 4.56 inches on Thursday. On Friday it increased another 4.08, on Saturday an additional 5.52, and another 4.68 on Sunday. Glen Canyon Dam data tables, Bureau of Reclamation Archives in Denver.

225   And at 12,000 cfs, the lining in the right tunnel: "Report of Telephone Call" from Wayne Cook to Wes Hirschi, Jim Brown, Tom Gamble, Jim Wedge, and Bruce Moyes, Water and Power Resources Service, Division of Design, June 13, 1983, Bureau of Reclamation Archives in Denver.

225   For Burgi, who had by now returned to Denver: Author interview with Burgi.

225   Burgi and his team sat down and devised: Moyes and Burgi, *Glen Canyon Dam Chronology of Events,* Bureau of Reclamation Archives, 20.

225   Moyes telephoned Gamble and told him: Ibid., 2. Also see "Report of Telephone Call" from Bruce

Moyes to Tom Gamble, Water and Power Resources Service, Division of Design, June 15, 1983, Bureau of Reclamation Archives in Denver.

226   Burgi warned Gamble that the booming: "Report of Telephone Call" from Bruce Moyes to Tom Gamble, Water and Power Resources Service, Division of Design, June 16, 1983, Bureau of Reclamation Archives in Denver.

226   Gamble was pleased to report: Moyes and Burgi, *Glen Canyon Dam Chronology of Events*, Bureau of Reclamation Archives.

226   "A calm weekend is expected": Bruce Moyes, personal notes, June 18 and June 19, 1983, Bureau of Reclamation Archives in Denver.

226   the ominous "belching": Bruce Moyes, "Proposed Operation Plan for Discharge of Flows at Glen Canyon Dam," June 21, 1983, Bureau of Reclamation Archives, Denver.

226   Moyes and Burgi left for the airport at 4:00 a.m.: Moyes, personal notes, June 18 and June 19, 1983, Bureau of Reclamation Archives, Denver.

226   During the three-hour flight: Ibid.

226   By the time the two men arrived at the dam: Moyes and Burgi, *Glen Canyon Dam Chronology of Events*, Bureau of Reclamation Archives.

227   the discharge was increased, first to 17,000 cfs: Ibid.

227   "The thing that affected me the most": Author interview with Parsons.

227   "Will this ever stop?": Author interview with Gamble.

228   "discharges from Glen Canyon Dam be immediately raised to 70,000": Faxogram, June 23; To: Regional Director, LBR, Salt Lake City, Utah, and Boulder City, Nevada; From: Assistant Commissioner, Engineering and Research, LBR, E&R Center, Denver, Colorado; Subject: Glen Canyon and Hoover Dam Operations, Colorado River Storage Project, Arizona and Boulder Canyon Project, Nevada and Arizona, Bureau of Reclamation Archives, Denver. Also see Moyes and Burgi, *Glen Canyon Dam Chronology of Events*, Bureau of Reclamation Archives.

Part VI

The Maelstrom

229   "The black stream, catching on a sunken rock": Frost, *West-Running Brook*, in Lathem, ed., *The Poetry of Robert Frost*.

17: The Grand Confluence

231   "Life is either a daring": Keller, *The Open Door.*

231   Hernando de Soto stumbled upon: Garcilaso de la Vega, *The Florida of the Incas*, quoted in H. C. Frankenfield, "The Floods of 1927 in the Mississippi Basin," *Monthly Weather Review*, suppl. 29 (Washington, DC, 1927), 10; cited in Barry, *Rising Tide*, 173.

231   in the spring of 1927, the river's width: Barry, *Rising Tide*, 170–71.

231   an inland sea that stretched from Yazoo City: Veronica Devore, "As Mississippi Rises, Historian Discusses 'Great Flood' of 1927," PBS *Newshour*, http://www.pbs.org/newshour/rundown/2011/05/as-mississippi-rises-flood-historian-discusses-great-flood-of-1927.html (accessed 11/16/12).

232   hydraulic sweet spot around 45,000: Reilly, "My High Water Experience," 3. "In my opinion, our 1962 trip provided the best flow for river running that I ever encountered; from June 25 through July 14 we averaged 45,500 cfs per day. This level was pure pleasure."

232   213 boats were ferrying nearly thirteen hundred guides and passengers: According to the Park Service's river permit records, between 94 and 150 commercial passengers launched from Lee's Ferry on twenty-six out of thirty days in June 1983. Twenty-one of those days also saw at least one launch of a private boating expedition that included up to twelve members.

232   accelerated from three miles per hour to six: Graf, *Colorado River in Grand Canyon*, 2.

232   white water was actually moving *upstream*: Reilly, "My High Water Experience," 3.

234   if they heard anyone yell "High ground!": Author interview with Dick Kocim.

235   which took place on Saturday, June 18: Quiroz, *Case Incident Record No. 831466*, US Department of the Interior, National Park Service.

235   While most outfitters equipped their expeditions with VHF: *William R. Wert Fatality, Case No. 831592*, Grand Canyon National Park Archives.

235   opened the bag for the message: Ibid.

237   a rather tempestuous affair: Author interview with Steve Reynolds.

238   Whenever he spotted a passenger who was struggling: Author interview with Petschek.

238   river folk sometimes refer to as a looker: Ibid.

238   "If anything happens": Author interview with Reynolds.

238 they would do this thing together: Ibid.
239 Sauer, a reasonable man: Details of Sauer's and Grua's interaction are documented in *Case Incident Record No. 831941*, Grand Canyon National Park Archives.
239 "He basically raised me from a kid to where I am now": Grua, oral histories, NAU.
240 which Litton found rather abhorrent: Author interview with Martin Litton.
240 Kenton, you already *have* the record: Ibid.
240 Grua launched into a soliloquy: Ibid.
240 Litton sighed and agreed that he did: Ibid.
240 According to the legend that is told on the river: Steiger, "Speed."
240 was simply to get Grua off the damn phone: Author interview with Litton.

18: The White Demon

242 "Out there in the middle of the maelstrom": Blaustein, *Hidden Canyon*, 64.
242 on the morning of Thursday, June 23, Brian pulled into: Thybony, "Crystal Rapid, 1983," 17. Also, author interview with Stan Steck.
243 had grown progressively more vicious: Kieffer, "The 1983 Hydraulic Jump in Crystal Rapid," 394.
243 when the engineers took the discharge up to 59,000 cfs: USGS surface-water statistics for the Bright Angel gauging station.
243 spillway tunnels the previous night reached Mile 98: USGS surface-water statistics for the Bright Angel gauging station indicate that the 70,000 cfs hit Phantom Ranch at 6:45 a.m. If the current was traveling at 6 mph, this surge would have taken approximately another two hours to reach Crystal.
244 directly into the soles of the flip-flops: Aronson, "High Water of 1983," 36.
244 they were looking at an almost perfect hydraulic jump: Author interview with Steck.
244 a series of hollow, cannonlike booms: See Zwinger, *Downcanyon*, 142; and Kieffer, "Hydraulics and Geomorphology of the Colorado River," 375.
244 the boulders at the bottom of the river were shifting: Kieffer, "The 1983 Hydraulic Jump in Crystal Rapid," 394.
245 Brian's attention was drawn upstream: Thybony, "Crystal Rapid, 1983," 17.
245 By the spring of 1983, White: For details on Georgie White, see Westwood, *Woman of the River*, and Sayre, "Georgie's Roaring River."
246 an estimated gross displacement of thirty-nine tons: See Sayre, "Georgie's Roaring River."
246 Known as the *Queen Mary*: Ibid.
246 As the rangers watched, stupefied: Thybony, "Crystal Rapid, 1983," 17. Also, author interview with Steck.
246 "Not only were they catapulted *out*": Thybony, "Crystal Rapid, 1983," 17. Note: It is possible that Brian, who loved to embroider his river anecdotes (he often declared that there was "no reason to ruin a good story with too much truth"), may have been exaggerating somewhat with respect to the passengers being spit through the pontoons. Source: author correspondence with Nancy Brian.
247 Others had swallowed water and were vomiting: Author interview with Steck.
247 "Georgie, what happened?": Thybony, "Crystal Rapid, 1983," 17.
247 "They don't make passengers like they used to": For this marvelous quote, which is a staple of most river stories about Georgie White, I am indebted to Scott Thybony, ibid.
247 was running a thirty-five-foot raft with twenty-three passengers: See *Case Incident Record No. 831574*, Grand Canyon National Park Archives.
247 Mills's rig was flipped upside down: Gorospe, "Crystal @ 72,000," 44–45. Also see Westwood, *Woman of the River*, 221–22.
248 catching a breath in the waves: Gorospe, "Crystal @ 72,000," 44–45. Also see Westwood, *Woman of the River*, 221–22.
248 yet *another* accident was unfolding: Cross Expeditions. Ironically, John Cross, Jr., the son of the owner of this company, had been the first boatman to successfully run the rapid after the debris flow of 1966. See *Case Incident Record No. 831574*, Grand Canyon National Park Archives.
248 Thirty-three passengers had been dumped into the river: Ibid.
248 *An evacuation will be staged from Bass Camp:* Ibid. Also, author interview with Kim Crumbo.
248 By 10:00 a.m., Crumbo's chopper was airlifting people: *Case Incident Record No. 831574*, Grand Canyon National Park Archives.
249 a reporter walked into the Kiva Lounge: "Passengers on Capsized Boats Rescued."
249 "We got bit by Crystal": Ibid.
249 Litton placed several phone calls to: Steiger, "Speed," and author interviews with Litton.
249 Marks was in the middle: Steiger, "Speed."
250 "He says if the answer is no, he'll phone tomorrow": Ibid., 161.
250 "Now if he *doesn't* call me, what do you suppose": Ibid.

19: Ghost Boat

The details of this day are drawn from a variety of sources. The author has conducted interviews with a number of passengers who were eyewitnesses, including Walt Gallaher, Bob and Colleen Paparelli, Sally Lonner, Lin Sultzer, Mary Ann McNammee, Elizabeth and Gary Ungricht, Jeffe Aronson, and Richard Kocim. Extensive details are drawn from *William R. Wert Fatality, Case No. 831592* and *Case Incident Record No. 831941*, as well as from Dave Stratton's *Oral History* and Ghiglieri and Myers, *Over the Edge: Death in Grand Canyon*.

251   "It was impossible not to think": Kane, *Running the Amazon*, 114.
251   the temperature was already in the low eighties: *Old Farmer's Almanac*, June 25, 1983.
251   the air was so clear that: Ibid.
252   Bill was fascinated by geology and photography and wanted: The details about Wert's curiosity come from the author's interview with Lonner and are corroborated by interviews with Sultzer and McNammee.
252   Layne Parmenter had grown up in: Most of the details about Parmenter come from *William R. Wert Fatality, Case No. 831592*.
253   Crystal was three times more dangerous: Ghiglieri, *Canyon*, 5. Also see author interviews with Petschek and Aronson.
253   duct-taping foam padding around their bottles: Aronson, "High Water of 1983," 38.
253   Joe Sharber heard a splash: Sharber and Ranney, "Memories of the 'Way Too Fast Trip,'" 20.
253   *even the beavers are portaging:* Ibid.
253   spending almost forty-five minutes examining: See *William R. Wert Fatality, Case No. 831592*.
254   explained to his colleagues they were all going: Stratton, *Oral History*, NAU. Corroborated by author interviews with Walt Gallaher and Gary Ungricht.
254   "See the tammies that are in the water?": Stratton, *Oral History*, NAU.
254   "You get in there and it's over": Ibid.
254   Ellen was concerned: "Interview with Ellen May Wert," Supplementary Case Incident Record, *William R. Wert Fatality, Case No. 831592*.
254   "What's the use of going on a river trip": Ibid.
255   one of the Butte Ladies cried out: Author interview with Sultzer.
255   Roberson yelled, "Down and in!": Ibid.
255   they felt as if they were standing: Author interviews with Aronson and Kocim.
256   "Do you have a fresh roll of film?": Aronson, "High Water of 1983," 38.
256   "See that pink dike off the wall?": Ibid.
256   The gestures had only one possible meaning: Ghiglieri and Myers, *Over the Edge*.
256   "we're going to hit the hole!": *William R. Wert Fatality, Case No. 831592*.
257   *We're going over:* Author interview with Lonner.
257   Bill had stood up just prior to the moment: This detail comes from Sultzer, who says that this story later circulated among the group. It is echoed by Elizabeth and Gary Ungricht.
257   Those details could only come: These details are illustrated by Kocim's photographs and corroborated by Kocim and Aronson, but I am indebted to Ghiglieri and Myers (*Over the Edge*), who have parsed out what took place with exceptional clarity.
259   "You've got to get down and get your people": Stratton, *Oral History*, NAU.
259   "Well, we may end up flipping too": Ibid.
260   His job was to chase those people down: Ibid.
260   "What am I going to do with that?": Author interview with Sultzer.
260   "You might need something to eat": Ibid.
261   "Are you okay?": Ibid.
261   "I think my legs are broken!": Author interview with McNammee.
261   "let's see if we can get you to shore": Author interview with Sultzer.
261   "Mary Ann's behind me": Ibid.
261   "I will never take another drink for as long as I live": Ibid.
261   "He doesn't look very good": Stratton, *Oral History*, NAU.
262   "Let's get him some CPR": Ibid.
262   Gallaher turned his head to the side and spat: Author interview with Bob Paparelli.
262   "I just don't think this guy is going to make it": Stratton, *Oral History*, NAU.
263   At 10:36 a.m., an orange-and-white Park Service helicopter: *William R. Wert Fatality, Case No. 831592*.
263   On board Helo 210 were a pilot named Mike Bertoldi and Curt Sauer: "Pilot Interview/Debriefings," *William R. Wert Fatality, Case No. 831592*.

263   Less than ten minutes after takeoff: Ibid.
263   Sauer radioed the South Rim: Ibid.
264   immersed in the fifty-degree water: "Water temperature was estimated at 45–50 degrees." Patricia Baker, Summary, Supplementary Case/Incident Record, *William R. Wert Fatality, Case No. 831592.*
265   "I don't know where my husband's at": Stratton, *Oral History,* NAU.
265   "We don't have everybody accounted for right now": Ibid.
265   "I know something's wrong": Ibid.
265   McNammee's injuries were so severe: Author interview with McNammee.
266   It was Cook who took: "Darrell Cook Interview," *William R. Wert Fatality, Case No. 831592.*
266   Dale had been leading a squadron: Author interview with Regan Dale. Also see Dale, *Oral History,* NAU.
266   "Hey—*lookit*": Dale, *Oral History,* NAU.
267   Dale kept his thoughts: Author interview with Dale.
267   The boat glided past without giving up an answer: Ibid.

20: The Doing of the Thing

268   "We are now ready to start": Powell, *Diary,* 107–10.
268   Ninety-one people had been evacuated: "Evacuations on 06/24 and 06/25/83," *William R. Wert Fatality, Case No. 831592.*
268   had cost $9,778: "Helicopter Costs," *William R. Wert Fatality, Case No. 831592.*
268   the Colorado had managed to drown only nineteen boaters: Twenty people had died while attempting to cross the river at places such as Lee's Ferry, twelve while swimming, and six by falling into the river and drowning—three of whom were drunk. See Ghiglieri and Myers, *Over the Edge,* 215–25.
268   not one of those accidents had taken place anywhere near Mile 98: Ibid.
269   drawing serious media attention from the *CBS Evening News*: "At the beginning of the CBS National News in late June, Dan Rather announces that the Grand Canyon is flooding." Steve Nicholson, "The Three Day Grand Trip of 1983," *Boatman's Quarterly Review* 21, no. 1 (Spring 2008), 24.
269   his river rangers, pilots, and communications team for a briefing to address: Thomas and Lawton were both debriefed on the South Rim at 7:29 p.m. that night. The Overhead Meeting was scheduled for 8:30 p.m. Source: "Crumbo/Goodrich on South Rim," *William R. Wert Fatality, Case No. 831592.*
269   Three options lay before them: "14:00 Meeting in Albright," *William R. Wert Fatality, Case No. 831592.*
270   Dave Buccello, Workman's counterpart: "David Buccello, Supplementary Case/Incident Record," *William R. Wert Fatality, Case No. 831592.*
270   "The superintendent has closed Crystal Rapid": Jennifer Lawton, "Crystal Rapid to Lee's Ferry: Message Drops," *William R. Wert Fatality, Case No. 831592.*
270   The records indicate that this subject was never discussed: *William R. Wert Fatality, Case No. 831592.*
271   they decided to start gearing up: Details for the speed-run preparation and drive to Lee's Ferry come from the author's interviews with Petschek and Reynolds.
272   This would serve as their "flip line": Although Grua is often given credit for pioneering the use of flip lines on Grand Canyon dories, kudos for this innovation go to one of his colleagues, a dory guide named Charlie Stern, who drew inspiration from his experience with small sailboats.
275   At 10:30 p.m. on the night of June 25, however: Author interviews with Bruce Helin and Michael Ghiglieri, two of the OARS guides who were sleeping aboard their rafts that night at the ferry.
276   Who, he wondered, would be crazy enough: Author interview with Ghiglieri.
277   Ghiglieri shook his head with an amused and bleary-eyed indulgence: Ibid.
278   "Wow," Wren murmured to himself: Author interview with Reynolds.
278   led by Charles Zemach, a theoretical physicist: Author interview with Charles Zemach.
278   Zemach was neither amused by nor: Ibid.
278   obliged to place their names on a multiyear waiting list: Perhaps a note of clarification is appropriate in light of the possibility that the reader may be tempted to conclude that Zemach was behaving in a manner that was nasty and overzealous. Until quite recently, the business of securing a private Grand Canyon river permit could be extremely arduous. Although Zemach himself was generally quite supportive of the manner in which the Park Service administered the river, the permit allocation process was—in the opinion of many—an unjust and imbalanced system that was heavily weighted in favor of commercial river outfitters while forcing private boaters to wait as

long as a decade (and sometimes longer) for a chance to run the river. Thus, reporting a rogue dory that was launching illegally from Lee's Ferry in the middle of the night was not an unreasonable response, especially when a concern for the dory boatmen's safety is added to the mix. Indeed, this may well have been the most responsible thing that Zemach could have done.

278   Zemach didn't know: Ibid.

Part VII
The Speed Run

279   "When the rapids are mentioned, I forget everything else": See Westwood, *Woman of the River.*

21: The Old Man Himself

Note: All scheduling times come from Petschek.

281   "And in the great wink of the moon": Wolfe, *Of Time and the River*, 514.
284   Was this going to be a cinch? Grua wondered: Steiger, "Speed," 148.
284   Roaring Twenties and encountered the first of: The Roaring Twenties are designated not by names but by their mile-marker numbers, an artifact of the Birdseye Expedition, the government's first official survey of the canyon, conducted in 1923. See Lavender, *River Runners of the Grand Canyon.*
284   It also scared the dickens out of them: Author interviews with Petschek.
284   in earnest with their biggest fear: Ibid.
285   and call out, "Okay, *go!*": Ibid. Confirmed by Reynolds.
285   Petschek and Wren found themselves increasingly reliant on Grua: Author interviews with Petschek and Reynolds.
286   "He'd never run that water before, but": Author interview with Petschek.
286   angular, rolling waves that built on a cycle of roughly ten seconds: Details of the hydraulics of Nankoweap come from P. T. Reilly, who ran the rapid at a somewhat higher level in the late 1950s. See Reilly, "My High Water Experience."
286   "We made it through the night": Author interview with Reynolds.
286   as if to say, *Wake up, dammit!*: Ibid.
287   the only man-made structure that was visible from the bottom of the canyon: Many years later, the Hualapai tribe built a "skywalk" at the edge of a tributary canyon much farther downstream, which is now visible from the bottom of the canyon.
287   clattered above the main buildings: Details of John Thomas's experiences on June 25 come from an author interview with Thomas. However, many of these elements are also elaborated on and confirmed in the Park Service's *Case Incident Record No. 831941.*
289   The size of some of those haystacks was shocking: Details of what it felt like to handle the hydraulics come from author interviews with Petschek and Reynolds.
290   Hendrick pulled off an impressively coordinated feat: Details of the speed run's encounter with Hendrick come primarily from an author interview with Petschek. Also see Hendrick, *Oral History*, NAU, and *Case Incident Record No. 831941.*

22: Perfection in a Wave

I am indebted here to Lew Steiger, whose work is further described in the final chapter of this book. As noted below, several quotations have been taken from Steiger's superlative 1994 story, "Speed," which was published in the anthology *There's This River: Grand Canyon Boatman Stories.*

293   "Do or do not": Yoda, *The Empire Strikes Back.*
294   *Don't look at the ranger:* Author interview with Reynolds.
294   "What do you think we should do if he": Author interview with Petschek. Also see Steiger, "Speed," 165.
294   "Wave back?" replied Petschek: Author interview with Petschek. Also see Steiger, "Speed," 165.
294   Inside his heart, however, each boatman knew perfectly: Author interviews with Petschek and Reynolds. Also see Grua, oral histories, NAU.
294   "We fantasized that it might be okay": Steiger, "Speed," 165.
294   with an entirely different tangle of conflicting impulses: All details about John Thomas's state of mind come from an author interview with Thomas.
295   "I knew *exactly* who it was": Ibid.
295   Thomas wondered, where did his truest allegiances: Ibid.

296 Grua was focusing on another ritual: Author interview with Petschek.
297 "Do you think I should cut right?": Ibid.
297 "You don't have a chance of doing it": Ibid.
298 "What the hell are you guys thinking?!": Author interview with Thomas.
298 exclaiming to himself, *No, no*: Ibid.
298 "I remember looking downstream over the front": Steiger, "Speed," 167.
298 "It was perfection in a hole": Ibid., 169. Also see Grua, "Oral History," *Boatman's Quarterly Review*, Winter 1997–98.
300 "The flip was instantaneous—there was nothing": Steiger, "Speed," 167.
300 determined not to let go because they were the: Ibid., 168.
302 "What a stupid thing to do!": Author interview with Reynolds.
302 "I'm three feet underwater and I'm wiping my head": Ibid.
303 "get to the boat—*get to the boat*": Ibid.
303 "It was just *boom . . . boom*": Author interview with Petschek.
303 "I don't even know if I knew in which direction": Author interview with Reynolds.
304 "I don't want to get back in that": Ibid.
304 *What the hell are you doing?:* Ibid.
305 "Wow, I'm glad I didn't hit you, man": Steiger, "Speed," 171. Later recounted by both Petschek and Reynolds in author interviews.

23: The Reckoning

306 "Is it wise to go on?": Powell, *Diary*, 137–39.
306 John Thomas reached immediately for his two-way radio: All details of John Thomas's actions come from an author interview with Thomas and from *Case Incident Record No. 831941.*
306 When Sauer heard that there: See *Case Incident Record No. 831941.*
307 "You see the boat?": The dialogue between Thomas and the pilot of Helo 210 is according to Thomas's recollection in an author interview with Thomas.
308 "At that point, we were very demoralized": Steiger, "Speed," 172.
308 They looked at one another, each man seeking confirmation: Author interviews with Petschek and Reynolds.
309 shaking their heads in disbelief: Author interview with Petschek.
310 When they thought about this—and each man did, separately: Ibid.
310 They were even prepared to try to politely explain: Ibid.
310 all three boatmen now caught a kind of second wind: Ibid.
314 "How was Crystal?" he yelled: Ibid.
314 Dale wasn't entirely sure whether he should be: Author interview with Regan Dale.
314 Stoner had spent the past two days monitoring a constant stream of detritus: Stoner, "Oral History Interview." Also see Steiger, "Speed."
314 Stoner returned the greeting by: Stoner, "Oral History Interview." Also see Steiger, "Speed," 172–73; and author interview with Petschek.
315 "We need to find out where that dory is": Author interview with Thomas.
317 "herds of startled deer bounding through": Powell, *Exploration*, June 1, 16; cited by Dolnick, *Down the Great Unknown*, 41.
317 "We're not through yet," barked Grua: Author interview with Reynolds.
317 "Rudi was in the driver's seat": This quote is from Petschek's recollection in an author interview with Petschek, who insists to this day that Grua's memory was faulty and that he, Petschek, did not row Lava Falls. Also see Steiger, "Speed," 173.

24: Beneath the River of Shooting Stars

318 "And forever, beyond the mysterious river's farthest shore": Wolfe, *Of Time and the River*, 514.
319 chief among them the fact that they could no longer see where they were going: Author interview with Petschek.
319 The trip leader was one of the company's: Author interview with Roderick Nash.
320 several members of his crew speculated: Ibid.
320 and whatever their purpose, mused Nash: Ibid.
320 "Watch out for 205—it'll eat you alive": Author interview with Litton.
321 Grua awoke with a start and: Author interview with Petschek.
321 How could they have been so feckless?: Ibid.
322 Wren had shut down: Ibid.
322 Without a word, he passed the oars: Ibid.

323   he had shared a conversation with Wally Rist: Ibid.
323   Petschek was forced to concede: Ibid.
325   Grua reached into his locker and: Ibid.
326   *Okay, wait . . .* , ordered Grua: Ibid.
326   seizing his conch shell, which boatmen: Ibid.

25: Tail Waves

327   "The current that with gentle murmur": Shakespeare, *Two Gentlemen of Verona*, 56.
327   the telephone rang in Tom Gamble's office: Moyes and Burgi, *Glen Canyon Dam Chronology of Events*, Bureau of Reclamation Archives. Also, author interview with Burgi and Burgi's notes.
327   On the other end of the line: Moyes and Burgi, *Glen Canyon Dam Chronology of Events*, Bureau of Reclamation Archives.
327   "Hydrographs look terrible": Burgi's notes and author interview with Burgi.
327   send even more water: Moyes, "Cavitation Damage to Glen Canyon Dam Spillways," 17. Also see "Spillway Discharge Tables," Denver E&R Center. Also see Burgi et al., "Operations of Glen Canyon Dam Spillways," 261.
327   into their beds and sleep for two solid days: Author interviews with Petschek and Reynolds.
328   Helo 210 was making a beeline: Ghiglieri, unpublished manuscript, "Chapter Six: High Water in the Great Unknown."
328   "BuRec will release 90,000": Ibid.
328   At 7:00 p.m., all three men watched as the mechanics: First they raised the east gate 9.3 inches and sent 25,000 cfs racing into the east tunnel. An hour later, the gate cables on the opposite side of the canyon were *lowered* 2.1 inches, reducing the flow through the west tunnel from 15,000 to 10,000. The combination of raising and lowering, when combined with the discharge from the power plant and the river outlets, added up to 80,000 cfs. See "Spillway Discharge Tables," Denver E&R Center.
328   Burgi, who had walked out on the service deck: Author interview with Burgi.
328   "Well, we're not gonna see that again": Ibid.
328   All but one of the penstocks were fully open: During the runoff of 1983, the Glen Canyon Dam was able to use only seven of its generators because one of the units was out of service. The pole pieces on this unit were being replaced and the generator was being "up-rated"—part of a four-year project that involved augmenting the rating of two generators per year until all eight were complete.
329   Despite the diminished size: Author correspondence with Michael Ghiglieri. Also see Ghiglieri and Myers, *Over the Edge: Death in Grand Canyon.*
329   than it had ever done: 92,000 cfs: Burgi et al., "Operations of Glen Canyon Dam Spillways," 261. Also see Moyes and Burgi, *Glen Canyon Dam Chronology of Events*, Bureau of Reclamation Archives; and Moyes, "Cavitation Damage to Glen Canyon Dam Spillways," 17.
329   During the next thirty-six hours, as the engineers: Burgi et al., "Operations of Glen Canyon Dam Spillways," 261. Also see "Spillway Discharge Tables," Denver E&R Center. Also see Burgi notes; author interview with Burgi.
329   the hydraulics dramatically weakened: Kieffer, "Hydraulics and Geomorphology of the Colorado River," in Beus and Morales, *Grand Canyon Geology*, 365.
329   As the height of the explosion wave decreased: Ibid., 375.
329   At 9:15 a.m. on Thursday: Exact date: June 30, 1983.
329   word arrived from far upstream: "Report of Telephone Call," Bureau of Reclamation Division of Design, to Peter Grey, Sup. Civil Engineer, Concrete Dams, Spillways and Outlets, E&R Center, Denver; from Bud Bay, Salt Lake City, Utah, June 30, 1983.
329   the engineers at Blue Mesa Reservoir: "Report of Telephone Call," Bureau of Reclamation Division of Design, to Peter Grey, Sup. Civil Engineer, Concrete Dams, Spillways and Outlets, E&R Center, Denver; from Larry Anderson, Chief, CRSP Power Operations, Curecanti Field Division, Montrose, Colorado, 11:40 a.m., June 30, 1983.
329   Soon, similar reports were trickling in: Burgi notes; author interview with Burgi.
329   "on the back side of the hydrograph": "Report of Telephone Call," Bureau of Reclamation Division of Design, to Peter Grey, Sup. Civil Engineer, Concrete Dams, Spillways and Outlets, E&R Center, Denver; from Lee Morrison, UC-430, Regional Office, Salt Lake City, Utah, 9:15 a.m., June 29, 1983.
329   At 1:30 p.m., Gamble ordered the gates: Faxogram to Regional Director, LBR, Boulder City, Nevada, and Salt Lake City, Utah; from Assistant Commissioner, Engineering and Research, LBR, E&R Center, Denver, Colorado; subject: Conference Call of June 29, 1983, Monitoring and Status of the Colorado River. Also see Moyes and Burgi, *Glen Canyon Dam Chronology of Events*, Bureau of Reclamation Archives, 7.

330   billions of dollars—was filled to the brim: Cox, "Raging River Scuttles Forecasts."

330   most damaging surges on the Colorado: It is important to acknowledge that a dozen runoff crests greater than 92,000 cfs overtook the Grand Canyon following the 1920s, including 1957 and 1958. The magnitude of the '83 runoff, however, is not reflected in the peak flow through the canyon, but in the sustained inflows into Lake Powell, which crested at 122,739 cfs on July 1. That figure—*not* the 92,000 cfs that was metered through the Glen Canyon Dam—captures the true size of the '83 runoff.

330   everyone stood back and waited until, around 1:00 p.m.: Faxogram from Robert Towles, Regional Director, LBR, Boulder City, Nevada, and Salt Lake City, Utah; to Assistant Commissioner, Engineering and Research, LBR, E&R Center, Denver, Colorado; subject: Conference Call of July 15, 1983. Also see Bureau of Reclamation Lake Powell Reservoir Tables. Also see Moyes and Burgi, *Glen Canyon Dam Chronology of Events*, Bureau of Reclamation Archives, 11.

330   the surface of the reservoir finally crested: Summary of 1983 River Operations, Bureau of Reclamation Archives, 6. Also see Burgi et al., "Operations of Glen Canyon Dam Spillways," 262.

330   quivering, for almost twenty-four: Moyes and Burgi, *Glen Canyon Dam Chronology of Events*, Bureau of Reclamation Archives, 22.

331   the waters began to recede: Ibid.

331   When the steel plates slammed shut: Wolf, "How Lake Powell Almost Broke Free." Also see Moyes and Burgi, *Glen Canyon Dam Chronology of Events*, Bureau of Reclamation Archives.

331   workers prepared to go into the tunnels: Moyes and Burgi, *Glen Canyon Dam Chronology of Events*, Bureau of Reclamation Archives, 12.

331   a rubber raft loaded with battery-powered: Rusho, "Bumpy Road for Glen Canyon Dam."

331   encountered their first big surprise: a sandstone: The dimensions of the boulder were eight feet by fifteen feet by fifteen feet. See Burgi et al., "Operations of Glen Canyon Dam Spillways," 262.

331   sat directly in the middle: Keys, "The 1983 Flood," 30.

331   They christened it House Rock: Rusho, "Bumpy Road for Glen Canyon Dam."

331   were the skeins of rebar: Ibid.

331   like the bones of a poached fish: For this image, I'm indebted to Steven Hannon, "The 1983 Flood at Glen Canyon," 2003, http://www.glencanyon.org.

331   The base of the elbow: Rusho, "Bumpy Road for Glen Canyon Dam."

332   retraced their steps back: Moyes, "Cavitation Damage to Glen Canyon Dam Spillways," 18.

332   so they called it the Big Hole: Keys, "The 1983 Flood," 30.

332   It was 134 feet long, 15 feet: Burgi et al., "Operations of Glen Canyon Dam Spillways," 262.

332   Phil Burgi's missing hard hat: Author interviews with Burgi, Dick White, and Henry Falvey. Note: There is some confusion over this story. While White distinctly remembers retrieving the battered hat from the base of the spillway, Falvey recalls engraving Burgi's name on the front of a used hard hat and, as a joke, presenting it to Burgi either during one of their morning coffee breaks in 1983 or several years later at his boss's retirement ceremony. It is possible that both versions of this story may be true.

332   the latticework of rebar: Rusho, "Bumpy Road for Glen Canyon Dam."

332   performed by the Loizeaux: Author interview with Falvey; confirmed by documentation in Reclamation Archives, Denver.

333   and the slots were finally tested: Rusho, "Bumpy Road for Glen Canyon Dam."

333   virtually eliminating the possibility of cavitation damage: The rings, which were four feet wide, four feet deep, and twenty-nine feet long, were the largest ever designed by the bureau. "BuRec Blasts Tunnel Repairs," *Engineering News-Record*, December 8, 1983, 11. This technology was first used at Yellowtail Dam in 1967. During the 1980s, the same technology was also placed in each of Reclamation's tunnel spillways on the Colorado River Basin, Hoover Dam, Blue Mesa Dam, and Flaming Gorge Dam.

333   As Gamble would hasten to point out: Author interview with Gamble.

333   The sale of that electricity: Keys, "The 1983 Flood," 31.

333   flooding overwhelmed hundreds of homes: Schmidt, "Floods Along Colorado River."

333   over the bureau's objections: Ibid.

333   more than $80 million: There was more than $12 million in property damage, the worst of which occurred in an area known as the Parker Strip, a sixteen-mile stretch of the river south of Needles that was lined with restaurants, casino resorts, and marinas. US General Accounting Office, Washington, DC, "Statement of Robert S. Procaccini, Senior Group Director, Resources, Community, and Economic Development Division, Department of the Interior, before the House Subcommittee on Investigations and Oversight, Committee on Science and Technology, on the 1983 Flooding of the Lower Colorado River," 3.

333   as the remnants of the flood raced past: South of Yuma, 25,000 cfs flowed into Mexico, a rate

that was roughly four hundred times normal. See "Colorado Flooding Peaks," *Engineering News-Record*, July 7, 1983, 13.

333   received its largest infusion: Ibid.
333   "The bureau knew damn well": Udall, "Floods Reveal Water Policy Chaos."
333   "monumental miscalculation": Cox, "Raging River Scuttles Forecasts."
334   "I haven't seen anything that suggested": Author interview with J. David Rogers.
334   "How close did we come to losing Glen": Knudson and Vogel, "Aging Dams, Already Under Siege."

26: The Trial

Details of the events that took place at the US magistrate's court on the South Rim come from interviews with Martin Litton, John Thomas, and Mike Meade, all three of whom were present for the hearing, and from Meade's case file and notes.

335   "I wish to speak": Thoreau, *Walking*, 7.
335   they endlessly recounted what had taken place: Author interview with Petschek. Also, author interview with Mike Meade, who was on a commercial river trip with Grua immediately following the speed run.
336   grew indignant and angry: Author interview with Petschek.
336   "Enclosed is a citation for your participation": US Park Service Violation Notice. Original copy in author's possession.
336   Litton got busy and started working the phones: Author interview with Litton.
337   one of only two postal addresses: Sente, "No Fries 'Til Mail," 10.
337   a spate of cases involving hang-glider pilots: Verkamp, *Story of the U.S. Magistrate Court in Northern Arizona*, 11–12.
337   a band of hippies who were tending: Ibid.
337   Case Number 83-2079M was no exception: Author interview with Meade, who was reading from the original complaint and citation as well as from the Code of Federal Regulations.
338   by explaining that Grua had violated: Ibid.
338   Marks didn't appear to be the least bit angry: Author interviews with Litton, Meade, and Thomas.
338   True, Meade stipulated: Author interview with Meade.
339   They knew the answer was no: Ibid.
339   Litton gave it his best shot: There is no transcript of what Litton said. The gist of the speech is reconstructed from interviews with Litton and Meade.
340   Everyone understood this, including Grua: Author interview with Meade.
340   "I do find the defendant guilty as charged": Ibid.
340   McKay began by imposing a $500: Author interviews with Litton and Meade.
341   Grua may not ever have bothered: Author interviews with Litton, Meade, and Petschek.
341   the idea that one was no longer allowed to do: Author interviews with John Thomas and Kim Crumbo.
341   The Park Service pronounced itself vindicated: Ibid.

Epilogue: The Legend of the *Emerald Mile*

343   "Brave boatmen come, they go": Blaustein, *Hidden Canyon*, 115.
344   The English novelist J. B. Priestley: This quote comes from Priestley, *Midnight on the Desert*. However, the entire idea, including the manner in which the thought itself is framed and worded, comes from the writer Barry Lopez, to whom I am wholly indebted for having both conceived of it in the first place and then expressed it far more eloquently than I could have. The passage can be found on page 175 of Lopez's marvelous book *Crossing Open Ground*.
345   her record has never been bested by any other oarsman: In the summer of 1993, three boatmen from Moab—John Weisheit, John Williams, and Clyde Deal—piloted a rigid inflatable sport boat with a 50-horsepower motor on a speed run through the Grand Canyon. They damaged their motor in Bedrock Rapid, but were able to perform repairs farther downstream when they unexpectedly ran into Kenton Grua, who helped them complete the fix. After spending the night on shore, Weisheit and his companions polished off the remainder of their run the following morning and, according to Weisheit's journal, passed through the Grand Wash Cliffs approximately fifty-five minutes faster than the *Emerald Mile*'s time. The motorized speed record now rests in the hands of Weisheit, Williams, and Deal.
346   Four years after the speed run: Details of Grua's various projects after the speed run come from author interviews with Litton, Petschek, and Reynolds, among others. Also see Steiger, "Speed," 176–77.

346   Grua's friends greeted this plan: Author interview with Petschek.
347   His memorial service was held: Ibid.
347   Wren finally bought a boat: All details of Reynolds's life after the speed run come from an author interview with Reynolds that was conducted six weeks before he passed away.
348   "We hit that wave dead-on in the best": Ibid.
348   "it was just such a huge thing": Ibid.
348   Rudi Petschek was by his side: Author interview with Petschek.
349   Petschek too had left the river: All details of Petschek's life after the speed run come from author interview and e-mail correspondence with Petschek.
349   "a perfect storm of luck": Ibid.
350   the still-raging storm of Martin Litton: All details of Litton's life after the speed run come from author interviews with Litton.
351   How can you defend against such things: Ibid.
351   "America's greatest scenic treasure": Ibid. Also see "Faith-Based Parks?" by Leon Jaroff, *Time*, November 17, 2004; and "Renewed Concern About Creationism of Grand Canyon National Park," by Glenn Branch, *Reports of the National Center for Science Education* 27, issue 3–4 (May–August 2007).
351   "In the end, the most remarkable properties": Ibid.
352   If you pull into the parking lot: Description of the *Emerald Mile* at the Grand Canyon Dories boathouse in Flagstaff comes from the author, who worked for the company as a baggage boatman for seven summers.
352   The thirty-five-page story: See Steiger, "Speed."

SELECTED BIBLIOGRAPHY

~

Books and Articles

Abbey, Edward. *Desert Solitaire*. New York: Touchstone, 1968.
———. *Down the River*. New York: Plume, 1991.
———. *The Journey Home: Some Words in Defense of the American West*. New York: Plume, 1991.
———. *The Monkey Wrench Gang*. New York: Harper Perennial, 1975.
Anderson, Michael F. *A Gathering of Grand Canyon Historians: Ideas, Arguments, and First-Person Accounts—Proceedings of the Inaugural Grand Canyon History Symposium, January 2002*. Grand Canyon, AZ: Grand Canyon Association, 2005.
———. *Polishing the Jewel: An Administrative History of Grand Canyon National Park*. Grand Canyon, AZ: Grand Canyon Association, 2000.
Annerino, John. *Canyoneering*. Mechanicsburg, PA: Stackpole Books, 1999.
Aronson, Jeffe. "High Water of 1983." *Boatman's Quarterly Review* 21, no. 1 (Spring 2008).
Baars, Donald L. *The Colorado Plateau: A Geological History*. Albuquerque: University of New Mexico Press, 2000.
Bagley, Mark B. *The G Stands for Guts: A Glider Pilot Remembers WWII*. Ashland, OR: Hellgate, 2008.
Balzar, John. "The Old Man and the River." *Los Angeles Times*, May 11, 1997.
Bangs, Richard, and Christian Kallen. *Rivergods: Exploring the World's Great Wild Rivers*. San Francisco: Sierra Club Books, 1985.
Banks, Leo W., and Craig Childs. *Grand Canyon Stories: Then & Now*. Phoenix: Arizona Highways Books, 1999.
Barcott, Bruce. *The Last Flight of the Scarlet Macaw: One Woman's Fight to Save the World's Most Beautiful Bird*. New York: Random House, 2008.
Barnes, F. A. *Canyon Country Geology*. Salt Lake City: Wasatch Publishers, 1993.
Barry, John M. *Rising Tide: The Great Mississippi Flood of 1927 and How It Changed America*. New York: Simon & Schuster, 1997.
Beer, Bill. *We Swam the Grand Canyon: The True Story of a Cheap Vacation That Got a Little out of Hand*. Seattle: Mountaineers, 1988.
Belknap, Buzz, and Loie Belknap Evans. *Belknap's Waterproof Grand Canyon River Guide*. Evergreen, CO: Westwater Books, 1969.
Berger, Todd R. *It Happened at Grand Canyon: From the Coronado Expedition to the Return of the California Condor, Thirty Episodes That Shaped the History of the Grand Canyon*. Guilford, CT: Twodot, 2007.
———. *Reflections of Grand Canyon Historians: Ideas, Arguments, and First-Person Accounts*. Grand Canyon, AZ: Grand Canyon Association, 2008.

Beus, Stanley S., and Michael Morales, eds. *Grand Canyon Geology.* New York: Museum of Northern Arizona Press, 1990.

Billington, David P., Donald C. Jackson, and Martin V. Melosi. *The History of Large Federal Dams: Planning, Design, and Construction in the Era of Big Dams.* Denver: Bureau of Reclamation, US Department of the Interior, 2005.

Bjornerud, Marcia. *Reading the Rocks: The Autobiography of the Earth.* Cambridge, MA: Westview Press, 2005.

Blakey, Ron, and Wayne Ranney. *Ancient Landscapes of the Colorado Plateau.* Grand Canyon, AZ: Grand Canyon Association, 2008.

Blaustein, John, with a journal written by Edward Abbey. *The Hidden Canyon: A River Journey.* New York: Penguin, 1977.

Bode, Richard. *First You Have to Row a Little Boat.* New York: Warner Books, 1993.

Bolger, Philip C. *Boats with an Open Mind.* Camden, ME: International Marine, 1994.

Bowden, Charles. *Blue Desert.* Tucson: University of Arizona Press, 1986.

Bradley, Harold. "Testimony in Support of Dinosaur House Subcommittee on Irrigation." Washington, DC: Distributed by the Sierra Club, document located in Martin Litton personal papers, March 28, 1955.

Brinkley, Douglas. *The Wilderness Warrior: Theodore Roosevelt and the Crusade for America.* New York: HarperPerennial, 2009.

Brower, David. *Work in Progress.* Salt Lake City: Peregrine Smith Books, 1991.

Brower, Kenneth. *The Starship and the Canoe.* New York: Bantam, 1978.

Brune, Bonnie. "Historic River Running." In *A Gathering of Grand Canyon Historians: Ideas, Arguments, and First-Person Accounts—Proceedings of the Inaugural Grand Canyon History Symposium, January 2002,* compiled and edited by Michael F. Anderson.

Bryson, Bill. *A Short History of Nearly Everything.* New York: Broadway Books, 2003.

Buchanan, Eugene. *Brothers on the Bashkaus: A Siberian Paddling Adventure.* Golden, CO: Fulcrum Publishing, 2007.

Burgi, Philip H., Bruce M. Moyes, and Thomas W. Gamble. "Operations of Glen Canyon Dam Spillways—Summer 1983." Reprinted from *Proceedings of the Conference "Water for Resource Development."* HY Div., ASCE, Coeur d'Alene, ID, August 14–17, 1984.

Burgi, Philip H., and M. S. Eckley. "Repairs at Glen Canyon Dam." *Concrete International* 9, no. 3 (March 1987), 24–31.

Butler, Elias, and Tom Myers. *Grand Obsession: Harvey Butchart and the Exploration of Grand Canyon.* Flagstaff, AZ: Puma Press, 2007.

Calvin, William H. *The River That Flows Uphill: A Journey from the Big Bang to the Big Brain.* San Francisco: Sierra Club Books, 1986.

Carothers, Steven W., and Bryan T. Brown. *The Colorado River Through Grand Canyon: Natural History and Human Change.* Tucson: University of Arizona Press, 1991.

Casey, Susan. *The Wave: In Pursuit of the Rogues, Freaks, and Giants of the Ocean.* New York: Doubleday, 2010.

Chapelle, Howard I. *American Small Sailing Craft: Their Design, Development, and Construction.* New York: W. W. Norton, 1951.

———. *Boatbuilding: A Complete History of Wooden Boat Construction.* New York: W. W. Norton, 1941.

Childs, Craig. *The Secret Knowledge of Water: Discovering the Essence of the American Desert.* Boston: Little, Brown, 2000.

Clark, Georgie White, and Duane Newcomb. *Georgie Clark.* San Francisco: Chronicle Books, 1977.

Coder, Christopher M. *An Introduction to Grand Canyon Prehistory.* Grand Canyon, AZ: Grand Canyon Association, 2000.

Cohen, Michael P. *The History of the Sierra Club, 1892–1970.* San Francisco: Sierra Club Books, 1988.

The Colorado River: A Natural Menace Becomes a National Resource. Washington, DC: US Department of the Interior, March 1946.

Cooley, M. E., B. N. Aldridge, and R. C. Euler. "Effects of the Catastrophic Flood of December 1966, North Rim Area, Eastern Grand Canyon, Arizona." *Geological Survey Professional Paper 980.* Washington, DC: US Government Printing Office, 1977.

Conrad, Joseph. *Heart of Darkness*. Mineola, NY: Dover Publications, 1990.

———. *Lord Jim*. New York: McClure, Phillips, 1899.

Cott, Harris. "Calmer County Keeps Mopping Out; More Storms Keep Coming." *Los Angeles Times*, March 5, 1983.

Cox, Jack. "Raging River Scuttles Forecasts." *Denver Post*, July 17, 1983.

Crumbo, Kim. *A River Runner's Guide to the History of the Grand Canyon*. Foreword by Edward Abbey. Boulder, CO: Johnson Books, 1981.

Cunningham, O. Edward. *Shiloh and the Western Campaign of 1862*. New York: Savas Beatie, 2007.

Dank, Milton. *The Glider Gang: An Eyewitness History of World War II Glider Combat*. Philadelphia: J. B. Lippincott, 1977.

Dasman, Raymond F. *The Destruction of California*. New York: Collier, 1966.

Davis, Wade. *Grand Canyon: River at Risk*. San Rafael, CA: Earth Aware Editions, 2008.

Devlin, Gerard M. *Silent Wings: The Saga of the U.S. Army and Marine Combat Glider Pilots During World War II*. New York: St. Martin's Press, 1985.

DeVoto, Bernard. *Across the Wide Missouri*. New York: Mariner, 1947.

———. *The Course of Empire*. New York: Mariner, 1952.

Dimock, Brad. *Sunk Without a Sound: The Tragic Colorado River Honeymoon of Glen and Bessie Hyde*. Flagstaff, AZ: Fretwater Press, 2001.

———. *The Very Hard Way: Bert Loper and the Colorado River*. Flagstaff, AZ: Fretwater Press, 2007.

"Directors Launch Campaign for Expanded Grand Canyon Protection." *Sierra Club Bulletin*, June 1963, 6–7.

Dolnick, Edward. *Down the Great Unknown: John Wesley Powell's 1869 Journey of Discovery and Tragedy Through the Grand Canyon*. New York: Perennial, 2001.

"The Dories: Whence and Whither?" *Hibernacle*, 1994, 14–15.

Dutton, Clarence E. *Tertiary History of the Grand Canyon District*. Tucson: University of Arizona Press, 2001.

Eisely, Loren. *The Immense Journey*. New York: Vintage Books, 1946.

Eliot, T. S. "The Dry Salvages," from *Four Quartets*. New York: Mariner Books, 1968.

"El Niño Storms Make Weather Top Topic." *Press Courier* (Oxnard, CA), December 25, 1983.

Englehard, Michael, ed. *Hell's Half Mile: River Runners' Tales of Hilarity and Misadventure*. Halcottsville, NY: Breakaway Books, 2004.

Erwin, Douglas H. *Extinction: How Life on Earth Nearly Ended 250 Million Years Ago*. Princeton, NJ: Princeton University Press, 2006.

Falvey, Henry T. *Cavitation in Chutes and Spillways: Engineering Monograph No. 42*. US Department of the Interior, Bureau of Reclamation, April 1990.

Faragher, John Mack. *Rereading Frederick Jackson Turner: "The Significance of the Frontier in History" and Other Essays*. New Haven, CT: Yale University Press, 1994.

Farmer, Jared. *Glen Canyon Dammed: Inventing Lake Powell and the Canyon Country*. Tucson: University of Arizona Press, 1999.

Fletcher, Colin. *The Man Who Walked Through Time*. New York: Vintage Books, 1967.

———. *River: One Man's Journey Down the Colorado, Source to Sea*. New York: Vintage Books, 1998.

Fletcher, Roger L. *Drift Boats and River Dories*. Mechanicsburg, PA: Stackpole Books, 2007.

Flint and Flint, eds. *The Coronado Expedition from the Distance of 460 Years*. Albuquerque: University of New Mexico Press, 2012.

"Floodwaters Start to Recede." Associated Press, *Victoria Advocate*, May 24, 1983.

Fortey, Richard. *Fossils: The Key to the Past*. New York: Van Nostrand Reinhold, 1982.

———. *Trilobite! Eyewitness to Evolution*. New York: Alfred A. Knopf, 2000.

Fowler, Don D. *The Glen Canyon Country: A Personal Memoir*. Salt Lake City: University of Utah Press, 2011.

Fox, Stephen. *The American Conservation Movement: John Muir and His Legacy*. Madison: University of Wisconsin Press, 1981.

Fradkin, Philip L. *A River No More: The Colorado River and the West*. New York: Alfred A. Knopf, 1981.

Frémont, John Charles. *Memoirs of My Life: Including Three Journeys of Western Exploration During the Years 1842, 1843–1844, 1845–1847.* New York: Cooper Square Press, 1886.

Frost, Kent. *My Canyonlands.* London: Canyon Country Publications, 1997.

Garde, R. J. *History of Fluvial Hydraulics.* New Delhi: New Age International, 1995.

Gardner, John. *The Dory Book.* Camden, ME: International Marine Publishers, 1978.

Garland, Joseph E. *Lone Voyager: The Extraordinary Adventures of Howard Blackburn, Hero Fisherman of Gloucester.* New York: Simon & Schuster, 1963.

Gerr, David. *The Nature of Boats.* Camden, ME: International Marine, 1995.

Ghiglieri, Michael P. *Canyon: The Ultimate Book on Whitewater Rafting in the Grand Canyon.* Tucson: University of Arizona Press, 1992.

———. *First Through the Grand Canyon: The Secret Journals and Letters of the 1869 Crew Who Explored the Green and Colorado Rivers.* Flagstaff, AZ: Puma Press, 2003.

———. "George Young Bradley: Chronicler of the 1869 John Wesley Powell Expedition Down the Green and Colorado Rivers." In *A Gathering of Grand Canyon Historians: Ideas, Arguments, and First-Person Accounts—Proceedings of the Inaugural Grand Canyon History Symposium, January 2002,* compiled and edited by Michael F. Anderson.

Ghiglieri, Michael P., and Thomas M. Myers. *Over the Edge: Death in Grand Canyon—Gripping Accounts of All Known Fatal Mishaps in the Most Famous of the World's Seven Natural Wonders.* Flagstaff, AZ: Puma Press, 2001.

Gleick, James. *Chaos: Making a New Science.* New York: Penguin, 1987.

Glen Canyon Dam and Powerplant: Technical Record of Design and Construction. Denver: US Department of the Interior, Bureau of Reclamation, December 1970.

Glynn, Peter. "El Niño–Southern Oscillation, 1982–1983: Nearshore Population, Community, and Ecosystem Responses." *Annual Review of Ecology and Systematics* 19 (1988): 309–45.

Gordon, J. E. *Structures: Or Why Things Don't Fall Down.* Cambridge, MA: Pereus, 1978.

Gorospe, Raymond. "Crystal @ 72,000." *Boatman's Quarterly Review,* Spring 2011.

Graf, Julia B. *The Colorado River in Grand Canyon: How Fast Does It Flow?* Grand Canyon Monitoring and Research Program, US Department of the Interior, US Geological Survey, December 1997.

Grahame, Kenneth. *The Wind in the Willows.* New York: HarperCollins, 1907.

Grim, Norman J. *To Fly the Gentle Giants.* Bloomington, IN: AuthorHouse, 2009.

Grua, Kenton. "Oral History," *Boatman's Quarterly Review,* Winter 1997–98.

Gwynne, S. C. *Empire of the Summer Moon.* New York: Scribner, 2010.

Hamblin, Kenneth W. *Anatomy of the Grand Canyon.* Grand Canyon, AZ: Grand Canyon Association, 2007.

Hamblin, Kenneth W., and J. Keith Rigby. *Guidebook to the Colorado River, Part I: Lee's Ferry to Phantom Ranch in Grand Canyon National Park.* Provo, UT: Department of Geology, Brigham Young University, 1968.

———. *Guidebook to the Colorado River, Part II: Phantom Ranch in Grand Canyon National Park to Lake Mead, Arizona-Nevada.* Provo, UT: Department of Geology, Brigham Young University, 1969.

Hannon, Steven. *Glen Canyon.* Denver: Kokopelli Books, 1997.

Harvey, Mark W. T. *A Symbol of Wilderness: Echo Park and the American Conservation Movement.* Seattle: University of Washington Press, March 2000.

Heller, Peter. *Hell or High Water: Surviving Tibet's Tsangpo River.* New York: Plume, 2005.

Heyerdahl, Thor. *The Kon-Tiki Expedition.* London: Flamingo, 1996.

"Highway Opened Linking Valley and Malibu." *Los Angeles Times,* July 3, 1952.

Hiltzik, Michael. *Colossus: Hoover Dam and the Making of the American Century.* New York: Free Press, 2010.

Holmes, Joseph. *Canyons of the Colorado.* San Francisco: Chronicle Books, 1996.

Horwitz, Tony. *Confederates in the Attic: Dispatches from the Unfinished Civil War.* New York: Vintage, 1999.

Houk, Rose. *An Introduction to Grand Canyon Ecology.* Grand Canyon, AZ: Grand Canyon Association, 1996.

Huisinga, Kristin, Lorie Makarick, and Kate Waters. *River and Desert Plants of the Grand Canyon.* Missoula, MT: Mountain Press Publishing, 2006.

Ingram, Jeff. *Hijacking a River: A Political History of the Colorado River in the Grand Canyon*. Flagstaff, AZ: Vishnu Temple Press, 2003.

Ingrisano, Michael N. *Valor Without Arms: A History of the 316th Troop Carrier Group, 1942–1945*. Bennington, VT: Marriam Press, 2009.

Inskip, Eleanor. *The Colorado River Through Glen Canyon: Before Lake Powell: Historic Photo Journal, 1872 to 1964*. Moab, UT: Inskip Ink, 1995.

Ison, Yvette D. " 'Dinosaur Rush' Created Excitement in Uinta Basin." *History Blazer*, March 1995.

Ives, J. C., and John Strong Newberry. *Report upon the Colorado River of the West, Explored in 1857 and 1858 by Joseph C. Ives*. Washington, DC: Government Printing Office, US Army Corps of Engineers, 1861.

Junger, Sebastian. *The Perfect Storm: A True Story of Men Against the Sea*. New York: HarperPerennial, 1997.

Kane, Joe. *Running the Amazon*. New York: Vintage Departures, 1990.

Kelland, Otto. *Dories and Dorymen: The Story of a Spry Little Boat and Those Who Knew Her Best*. St. John's, Newfoundland: RB Books, 1984.

Keller, Helen. *The Open Door*. New York: Doubleday, 1957.

Keys, John. "The 1983 Flood: How the Glen Canyon Dam Held up Under the Impact of Cavitation." *Canyon Legacy: Journal of the Dan O'Laurie Museum of Moab* 59 (Spring 2007).

Kieffer, Susan Werner. "Hydraulics and Geomorphology of the Colorado River in the Grand Canyon," in *Grand Canyon Geology*, S. S. Beus and M. Morales, eds. New York: Oxford University Press, 2002, 333–84.

———. "The 1983 Hydraulic Jump in Crystal Rapid: Implications for River-Running and Geomorphic Evolution in the Grand Canyon." *Journal of Geology* 93, no. 4 (July 1985).

Kline, Benjamin. *First Along the River: A Brief History of the U.S. Environmental Movement*. Lanham, MD: Acada, 2000.

Knudson, Tom, and Nancy Vogel. "Aging Dams, Already Under Siege, Face New Pressures." *Sacramento Bee*, November 25, 1997.

Krutch, Joseph Wood. *The Desert Year*. Tucson: University of Arizona Press, 1951.

———. *Grand Canyon: Today and All Its Yesterdays*. New York: Morrow Quill Paperbacks, 1957.

Kurlansky, Mark. *Cod: A Biography of the Fish That Changed the World*. New York: Penguin, 1998.

Lambert, David, and the Diagram Group. *The Field Guide to Geology*. New York: Facts on File, 2007.

Lankford, Andrea. *Ranger Confidential: Living, Working, and Dying in the National Parks*. Guilford, CT: Falcon Guides, 2010.

Latham, Stephen E. *Dam Failure Inundation Study: Glen Canyon Dam, Arizona*. Denver: Sedimentation & River Hydraulics Group, US Department of the Interior, Bureau of Reclamation, July 1998.

Lathem, Edward Connery, ed. *The Poetry of Robert Frost*. New York: Holt, 1969.

Lavender, David. *River Runners of the Grand Canyon*. Grand Canyon, AZ: Grand Canyon Natural History Association, 1985.

Lawton, Rebecca. *Reading Water: Lessons from the River*. Dulles, VA: Capital Books, 2002.

Lea, Robert, and Daniel J. Miller. "Shark Attacks off the California and Oregon Coasts: An Update, 1980–84." *Memoirs of the Southern California Academy of Sciences* 19 (1985): 136–50.

Lee, Katie. *All My Rivers Are Gone: A Journey of Discovery Through Glen Canyon*. Boulder, CO: Johnson Books, 1998.

Lee, Martha F. *Earth First! Environmental Apocalypse*. Syracuse, NY: Syracuse University Press, 1995.

Leopold, Aldo. *A Sand County Almanac: With Essays on Conservation from Round River*. New York: Ballantine Books, 1966.

Leopold, Luna B., M. Gordon Wolman, and John P. Miller. *Fluvial Processes in Geomorphology*. New York: Dover Publications, 1964.

Leveson, David. *A Sense of the Earth*. Garden City, NY: Doubleday, 1971.

Leydet, François. *The Last Redwoods and the Parklands of Redwood Creek*. San Francisco: Ballantine Books, 1969.

———. *Time and the River Flowing*. San Francisco: Sierra Club Books, 1964.

Lindsay, Leon. "The Pony Express Rides Again: California Towns Cut Off by a Landslide Still Get Letters." *Christian Science Monitor*, April 20, 1983.

Lindsey, Robert. "California Journal; New Pacific Mysteries: Red Beaches and Return of Sardines." *New York Times*, June 12, 1983, 22.

Litton, Martin. "Dinosaurs' Home May Become Lake." *Los Angeles Times*, December 16, 1951, 6.

———. "What the Bureaucrats Conspire to Destroy." *Los Angeles Times*, December 30, 1953, A5.

"Local Man Dies on Rafting Trip." *Valley Journal* (Carbondale, CO), June 30, 1980.

Lopez, Barry. *Crossing Open Ground.* New York: Vintage Books, 1989.

———. *The Rediscovery of North America.* New York: Vintage Books, 1990.

Lowell, Robert. *Collected Poems.* New York: Farrar, Straus and Giroux, 2007.

Mailer, Norman. *The Presidential Papers of Norman Mailer.* London: Panther Books, 1964.

"Malibu Canyon Road to Sea Opens Tomorrow." *Los Angeles Times*, July 1, 1952.

Martin, Russell. *A Story That Stands Like a Dam: Glen Canyon and the Struggle for the Soul of the American West.* Salt Lake City: University of Utah Press, 1989.

Martin, Tom. *Big Water, Little Boats: Moulty Fulmer and the First Grand Canyon Dory on the Last of the Wild Colorado River.* Flagstaff, AZ: Vishnu Temple Press, 2012.

Masters, Charles J. *Glidermen of Neptune: The American D-Day Glider Attack.* Carbondale: Southern Illinois University Press, 1995.

Mathews, Jay. "Huge Surge of Mountain Water Bearing Down on Hoover Dam." *Washington Post*, June 29, 1983.

Matthiessen, Peter. *Wildlife in America.* New York: Penguin, 1959.

McCarthy, Cormac. *All the Pretty Horses.* New York: Vintage, 1993.

McCourt, Tom. *White Canyon: Remembering the Little Town at the Bottom of Lake Powell.* Price, UT: Southpaw Publications, 2003.

McCullough, David. *The Johnstown Flood.* New York: Simon & Schuster, 1968.

———. *The Path Between the Seas.* New York: Simon & Schuster, 1977.

McCully, Patrick. *Silenced Rivers: The Ecology and Politics of Large Dams.* London: Zed Books, 2001.

McDonough, James Lee. *Shiloh: In Hell Before Night.* Knoxville: University of Tennessee Press, 1977.

McMillin, T. S. *The Meaning of Rivers: Flow and Reflection in American Literature.* Iowa City: University of Iowa Press, 2011.

McNamee, Gregory. *Grand Canyon Place Names.* Boulder, CO: Johnson Books, 1997.

McNeil, J. R. *Something New Under the Sun: An Environmental History of the Twentieth-Century World.* New York: W. W. Norton, 2001.

McPhee, John. *Annals of the Former World.* New York: Farrar, Straus and Giroux, 1981.

———. *Encounters with the Archdruid.* New York: Farrar, Straus and Giroux, 1971.

Melloy, Ellen. *Raven's Exile: A Season on the Green River.* New York: Henry Holt, 1994.

Miller, Char, ed. *Water in the West: A High Country News Reader.* Corvallis: Oregon State University Press, 2000.

Miller, Steve. *The Grand: The Colorado River in the Grand Canyon.* Grand Canyon, AZ: Grand Canyon Association, 2005.

Moitessier, Bernard. *The Long Way.* New York: Sheridan House, 1995.

"Mud Smothers 3 Mountain Towns." *Milwaukee Journal*, May 31, 1983.

Murakami, Haruki. *Kafka on the Shore.* New York: Vintage, 2006.

Murray, John A. *The Colorado Plateau: A Complete Guide to the National Parks and Monuments of Southern Utah, Northern Arizona, Western Colorado, and Northwestern New Mexico.* Flagstaff, AZ: Northland Publishing, 1998.

Myers, Tom. "Down the Gorge with Uncle George: Hiking the Length of the Grand Canyon," proceedings of the Grand Canyon History Symposium, Grand Canyon Village, Grand Canyon National Park, January 26–29, 2012.

Nadeau, Remi A. *The Water Seekers.* Bishop, CA: Chalfant Press, 1950.

Nash, Roderick. *The Big Drops: Ten Legendary Rapids of the American West.* Boulder, CO: Johnson Books. 1989.

———, ed. *Grand Canyon of the Living Colorado.* San Francisco: Ballantine Books, 1970.

———. *Wilderness & the American Mind.* New Haven, CT: Yale University Press, 1967.

National Park Service Organic Act, 16 U.S.C.I.

Nealy, William. *Kayak: The New Frontier—The Animated Manual of Intermediate and Advanced Whitewater Technique.* Birmingham, AL: Menasha Ridge Press, 1986.

Nelson, Nancy. *Any Time, Any Place, Any River: The Nevills of Mexican Hat.* Flagstaff, AZ: Red Lake Books, 1991.

Neuman, Mark. *On the Rim: Looking for the Grand Canyon.* Minneapolis: University of Minnesota Press, 1999.

Nixon, Edgar B., ed. *Franklin D. Roosevelt and Conservation, 1911–1945.* 2 vols. New York: Ayer, 1957.

Outwater, Alice. *Water: A Natural History.* New York: HarperCollins, 1996.

Palley, Reese. *Concrete: A Seven-Thousand-Year History.* New York: Quantuck Lane Press, 2010.

Palmer, Tim. *Endangered Rivers and the Conservation Movement.* Berkeley: University of California Press, 1986.

———. *The Wild and Scenic Rivers of America.* Washington, DC: Island Press, 1993.

Paltrow, Scot J. "Who, If Anybody, Is to Blame for Floods Along the Colorado?" *Wall Street Journal,* July 12, 1983.

"Passengers on Capsized Boats Rescued." *Grand Canyon News–Visitor Information* 94, no. 26 (June 30, 1983).

Pearson, Byron E. *Still the Wild River Runs: Congress, the Sierra Club, and the Fight to Save Grand Canyon.* Tucson: University of Arizona Press, 2002.

Pike, Robert E. *Tall Trees, Tough Men: An Anecdotal and Pictorial History of Logging and Log-Driving in New England.* New York: W. W. Norton, 1984.

Porter, Eliot. *Glen Canyon on the Colorado.* Salt Lake City: Gibbs Smith Publisher, 1963.

Powell, James Lawrence. *Dead Pool: Lake Powell, Global Warming, and the Future of Water in the West.* Berkeley: University of California Press, 2008.

———. *Grand Canyon: Solving Earth's Grandest Puzzle.* New York: Plume, 2006.

Powell, J. W. *Diary of the First Trip Through the Grand Canyon.* In *Down the Colorado.* New York: E. P. Dutton, 1969.

———. *Exploration of the Colorado River of the West and Its Tributaries. Explored in 1869, 1870, 1871, and 1872, Under the Direction of the Secretary of the Smithsonian Institution.* Washington, DC: Government Printing Office, 1875. Reprinted in revised form as *The Exploration of the Colorado River and Its Canyons,* 1895.

Powers, Ron. *Mark Twain: A Life.* New York: Free Press, 2005.

Preston, Doug. *Talking to the Ground: One Family's Journey on Horseback Across the Sacred Land of the Navajo.* Albuquerque: University of New Mexico Press, 1995.

Priestley, J. B. "Arizona Desert." *Harper's,* March 1937, 358–67.

———. *Midnight on the Desert: Being an Excursion into Autobiography During a Winter in America.* New York: Harper & Brothers, 1937.

Pugh, C. A. "Modeling Aeration Devices for Glen Canyon Dam, Proceedings of the Conference on Water for Resource Development," ASCE Hydraulic Division Conference, Coeur d'Alene, Idaho, August 14–17, 1984.

Pyne, Stephen J. *Fire on the Rim: A Firefighter's Season at the Grand Canyon.* New York: Ballantine, 1989.

———. *How the Canyon Became Grand: A Short History.* New York: Penguin, 1998.

Quammen, David. *Wild Thoughts from Wild Places.* New York: Scribner, 1998.

"Queen Elizabeth Braces Stormy U.S. Weather." Associated Press, *Phoenix,* March 2, 1983, 17.

Ranney, Wayne. *Carving Grand Canyon: Evidence, Theories, and Mystery.* Grand Canyon, AZ: Grand Canyon Association, 2012.

Reilly, P. T. "My High Water Experience in Marble and Grand Canyons." *Boatman's Quarterly Review,* Spring 1997.

Reisner, Marc. "The Age of Dams and Its Legacy." Lecture, published in *Colorado Water,* December 1999.

———. *Cadillac Desert: The American West and Its Disappearing Water.* New York: Penguin, 1986.

Reynolds, Terry. *Stronger Than a Hundred Men: A History of the Vertical Water Wheel.* Baltimore: Johns Hopkins University Press, 1983.

Rogers, J. David. "Hoover Dam: Operational Milestones, Lessons Learned, and Strategic Import." *Hoover Dam 75th Anniversary History Symposium 2010, ASCE*, 195, 212.

———. "Lecture on Dam Safety at the California Colloquium on Water." University of California at Berkeley, November 12, 2002.

Roosevelt, Theodore. *Presidential Addresses and State Papers, February 19, 1902, to May 13, 1903.* Vol. 1. New York: Review of Reviews Company.

Rusho, W. L. "Bumpy Road for Glen Canyon Dam." Paper presented at the Symposium on the History of the Bureau of Reclamation, University of Nevada at Las Vegas, 2002.

———. *Lee's Ferry: Desert River Crossings.* Salt Lake City and St. George, UT: Tower Productions, 1998.

Russell, Jerry, and Renny Russell. *On the Loose.* San Francisco: Ballantine, 1967.

Russell, Renny. *Rock Me on the Water: A Life on the Loose.* Questa, NM: Animist Press, 2007.

Sadler, Christa. *Life in Stone: Fossils of the Colorado Plateau.* Grand Canyon, AZ: Grand Canyon Association, 2005.

———, ed. *There's This River: Grand Canyon Boatman Stories.* Flagstaff, AZ: Red Lake Books, 1994.

Salter, James. *Solo Faces.* New York: Farrar, Straus and Giroux, 1979.

Sandlin, Lee. *Wicked River: The Mississippi When It Last Ran Wild.* New York: Vintage Books, 2010.

Savoy, Lauret E., Eldridge M. Moores, and Judith E. Moores, eds. *Bedrock: Writers on the Wonders of Geology.* San Antonio, TX: Trinity University Press, 2006.

Sayre, Joel. "Georgie's Roaring River," *Sports Illustrated*, June 23, 1958, 69–71.

Schmidt, Jeremy. *A Natural History Guide: Grand Canyon National Park.* Boston: Houghton Mifflin, 1993.

Schmidt, William. "Floods Along Colorado River Set Off a Debate Over Blame." *New York Times*, July 17, 1983.

Schnitter, Nicholas J. *A History of Dams: The Useful Pyramids.* Rotterdam: A. A. Balkeman, 1994.

Schrepfer, Susan R. *The Fight to Save the Redwoods: A History of Environmental Reform, 1917–1978.* Madison: University of Wisconsin Press, 1983.

Schullery, Paul, ed. *The Grand Canyon: Early Impressions.* Boulder: Colorado Associated University Press, 1981.

Schultheis, Rob. *Bone Games.* New York: Breakaway Books, 1996.

———. *The Hidden West.* New York: Lyons & Burford, 1969.

Schultz, Ernest R. "Design Features of the Glen Canyon Dam." Paper for presentation at ASCE Convention, Construction Division, Phoenix, AZ, April 1961.

Schwenk, Theodor. *Sensitive Chaos: The Creation of Flowing Forms in Water and Air.* London: Rudolf Steiner Press, 1969.

Seelye, John. *Prophetic Waters: The River in Early American Life and Literature.* New York: Oxford University Press, 1977.

Sente, Majory L. "No Fries 'Til Mail: How Tourists Brought Mail Service to the Grand Canyon." Paper presented at the National Postal Museum conference "How Commerce and Industry Shaped the Mails," September 16, 2011.

Sexton, Anne. *Love Poems.* New York: Houghton Mifflin Harcourt, 1967.

Shabecoff, Philip. *A Fierce Green Fire: The American Environmental Movement.* New York: Hill and Wang, 1993.

Shacochis, Bob. *Kingdoms in the Air.* San Francisco: Byliner, 2012.

Shakespeare, William. *Two Gentlemen of Verona.* Edited, with notes, by William J. Rolfe. New York: American Book Company, 1905.

Sharber, Joe, and Wayne Ranney. "Memories of the 'Way Too Fast Trip.'" *Boatman's Quarterly Review* 21, no. 1 (Spring 2008).

Smith, Norman. *A History of Dams.* Secaucus, NJ: Citadel Press, 1972.

"Snowpack Buries Colorado; California Braces for Rain." Associated Press, *Palm Beach Post*, March 16, 1983.

Snyder, James E. *The Squirt Book: The Manual of Squirt Kayaking Technique.* Birmingham, AL: Menasha Ridge Press, 1987.

Solomon, Steven. *Water: The Epic Struggle for Wealth, Power, and Civilization.* New York: HarperPerennial, 2010.

Stanton, Robert Brewster. *Colorado River Controversies*. Evergreen, CO: Westwater Books, 1984.
———. *Down the Colorado*. Edited and with an introduction by Dwight L. Smith. Norman: University of Oklahoma Press, 1965.
Staveley, Gaylord. *Broken Waters Sing: Rediscovering Two Great Rivers of the West*. Boston: Little, Brown, 1971.
Steck, George. *Hiking Grand Canyon Loops: Adventures in the Backcountry*. Guilford, CT: Globe Pequot Press, 2002.
Stegner, Page. *Adios Amigos: Tales of Sustenance and Purification in the American West*. Berkeley: Counterpoint, 2008.
Stegner, Wallace. *Beyond the Hundredth Meridian: John Wesley Powell and the Second Opening of the West*. New York: Penguin, 1953.
———. *Mormon Country*. Lincoln and London: University of Nebraska Press, 1942.
———. *The Sound of Mountain Water—The Changing American West*. New York: Penguin, 1969.
———. "Water Warnings, Water Future." *Plateau* 53, no. 3 (1981): 2–3.
Steiger, Lew. "Speed." In *There's This River: Grand Canyon Boatman Stories*, edited by Christa Sadler. Flagstaff, AZ: Red Lake Books, 1994.
Stevens, Larry. *The Colorado River in Grand Canyon: A Comprehensive Guide to Its Natural and Human History*. Flagstaff, AZ: Red Lake Books, 1983.
Stoner, Jon. "Oral History Interview." *Boatman's Quarterly Review* 23, no. 4 (Winter 2010–11).
"Storm Halts Queen's Sail to 'Frisco." *Philadelphia Daily News*, March 2, 1983, 16.
Sumner, Jack. "The Lost Journal of John Colton Sumner." *Utah Historical Quarterly* 15 (1969): 173–89.
Suran, William C. *The Kolb Brothers of Grand Canyon*. Grand Canyon, AZ: Grand Canyon Natural History Association, 1991.
Teal, Louise. *Breaking into the Current: Boatwomen of the Grand Canyon*. Tucson: University of Arizona Press, 1994.
Thomas, Bob. "The Royalty of Hollywood and England Get Together." *Times-News*, February 28, 1983, 1.
Thoreau, Henry David. *Walden & Other Writings of Henry David Thoreau*. Edited by Brooks Atkinson. New York: Modern Library, 1937.
———. *Walking*. Rockville, MD: Arc Manor, 2007.
Thybony, Scott. "Crystal Rapid, 1983: Georgie Goes for the Big One." *Boatman's Quarterly Review* 21 no. 1 (Spring 2008).
———. *The Incredible Grand Canyon: Cliffhangers and Curiosities from America's Greatest Canyon*. Grand Canyon, AZ: Grand Canyon Association, 2007.
Trimble, Stephen. *Lasting Light: 125 Years of Grand Canyon Photography*. Flagstaff, AZ: Northland Publishing, 2006.
Turner, Jack. *The Abstract Wild*. Tucson: University of Arizona Press, 1996.
Twain, Mark. *Life on the Mississippi*. New York: Bantam, 1896.
Udall, James R. "Floods Reveal Water Policy Chaos." *High Country News*, October 3, 1983.
Udall, Stewart L. *Majestic Journey: Coronado's Inland Empire*. Santa Fe: Museum of New Mexico Press, 1987.
Van Dyke, John C. *The Grand Canyon of the Colorado: Recurrent Studies in Impression and Appearances*. Salt Lake City: University of Utah Press, 1920.
Verkamp, Stephen L. *The Story of the U.S. Magistrate Court in Northern Arizona*. Flagstaff, AZ: Aspen Printing, July 2004.
Wallace, David Rains. *The Klamath Knot: Explorations of Myth and Evolution*. San Francisco: Sierra Club Books, 1983.
Waters, Frank. *The Colorado*. Athens, OH: Swallow Press, 1946.
Watkins, T. H., and contributors. *The Grand Colorado: The Story of a River and Its Canyons*. American West Publishing Company, 1969.
Webb, R. H., P. T. Pringle, and G. R. Rink. "Debris Flows from Tributaries of the Colorado River, Grand Canyon National Park, Arizona." US Geological Survey, 1989.
Webb, Robert H. *Grand Canyon, a Century of Change: Re-photography of the 1889–1890 Stanton Expedition*. Tucson: University of Arizona Press, 1996.
Webb, Robert H., and Chris Magirl. "The Changing Rapids of Grand Canyon—Crystal Rapid." *Boatman's Quarterly Review* 15, no. 2 (Summer 2002): 42–44.

Webb, Roy. *If We Had a Boat: Green River Explorers, Adventures, and Runners.* Salt Lake City: University of Utah Press, 1986.

Welch, Vince. "In Praise of Port Orford Cedar." *Boatman's Quarterly Review,* Winter 2005–6.

Welch, Vince, Cort Conley, and Brad Dimock. *The Doing of the Thing: The Brief Brilliant Whitewater Career of Buzz Holmstrom.* Flagstaff, AZ: Fretwater Press, 1998.

Westwood, Richard E. *Woman of the River: Georgie White Clark, Whitewater Pioneer.* Logan: Utah State University Press, 1997.

White, E. B. *An E. B. White Reader.* Edited by William W. Watt and Robert W. Bradford. New York: Harper & Row, 1966.

White, John H., Jr. *The American Railroad Passenger Car.* 2 vols. Baltimore, MD: Johns Hopkins University Press, 1996.

Wilkinson, Charles F. *Crossing the Next Meridian: Land, Water, and the Future of the West.* Washington, DC: Island Press, 1992.

Winchester, Simon. *The Map That Changed the World: William Smith and the Birth of Modern Geology.* New York: Perennial, 2001.

Wolf, T. J. "How Lake Powell Almost Broke Free of Glen Canyon Dam." *High Country News* 15, no. 22 (December 12, 1983).

Wolfe, Thomas. *Of Time and the River.* New York: Scribner, 1999.

Worster, Donald. *A River Running West: The Life Story of John Wesley Powell.* Oxford: Oxford University Press, 2001.

———. *Rivers of Empire: Water, Aridity, and the Growth of the American West.* New York: Oxford University Press, 1985.

Wyrick, Traci. "Life at River Mile Zero." *The Ol' Pioneer: The Quarterly Magazine of the Grand Canyon Historical Society* 18, no. 1 (January/February/March 2007).

Youngblood, Wayne. "Resurrected Real Pony Express Service." *American Philatelist,* September 2008.

Zwinger, Ann. *Downcanyon: A Naturalist Explores the Colorado River Through the Grand Canyon.* Tucson: University of Arizona Press, 1995.

———. *Run, River, Run: A Naturalist's Journey Down One of the Great Rivers of the American West.* Tucson: University of Arizona Press, 1975.

Bureau of Reclamation Archives

Dozier, Larry, Regional Supervisor of Water and Land Operations, Lower Colorado Region. "Summary of Communications and Actions Concerning 1983 Flood Control Operations on the Lower Colorado River." July 28, 1983.

Moyes, Bruce M., and Philip H. Burgi. *Glen Canyon Dam Chronology of Events: 1983 Spill—June 2, 1983, Through July 23, 1983.* August 15, 1983.

Operating Log, Glen Canyon Dam, Monday, June 6, 1983, to Sunday, June 26, 1983. Obtained through author's Freedom of Information Act request and subsequent appeal when original request was denied; partially redacted by the US Bureau of Reclamation.

"Report of Telephone Call" from Bruce Moyes to Tom Gamble. Water and Power Resources Service, Division of Design, June 8, 1983.

Grand Canyon National Park Archives

Case Incident Record No. 831574. US Department of Interior, National Park Service, Grand Canyon National Park, June 24, 1983.

Case Incident Record No. 831592. US Department of Interior, National Park Service, Grand Canyon National Park, June 25, 1983.

Case Incident Record No. 831941. US Department of Interior, National Park Service, Grand Canyon National Park, June 26, 1983.

William R. Wert Fatality, Case No. 831592. US Department of Interior, National Park Service, Grand Canyon National Park, June 25, 1983.

Oral Histories, Cline Library, Northern Arizona University

NAU's Cline Library archives hosts online access to a special collection of more than a hundred oral-history interviews with members of the Grand Canyon river community (www.nau.edu/library/speccoll).

Dale, Regan. *River Runners Oral History Project.*

Grua, Kenton. *Runners Oral History Project: Interview number 53.23A.* Interview conducted by Lew Steiger, 1990.

———. *Runners Oral History Project: Interview number 53.23B.* Interview conducted by Lew Steiger, December 2, 1997.

———. *Runners Oral History Project: Interview number 53.23C.* Interview conducted by Lew Steiger, December 30, 1997.

———. *Runners Oral History Project: Interview number 1994.100.42.* Interview conducted by Lew Steiger, September 19, 1994.

Hendrick, Jimmy. *River Runners Oral History Project.*

Litton, Martin. *River Runners Oral History Project: Legends Trip.* Interview conducted by Lew Steiger and Karen Underhill, September 18, 1994.

———. *River Runners Oral History Project: Grand Canyon Dories Boathouse.* Interview conducted by Lew Steiger, October 10, 1992.

———. *River Runners Oral History Project: Litton Home.* Interview conducted by Kenton Grua, June 2, 1992.

Litton, Martin, and David Brower. *River Runners Oral History Project.* Interview conducted by Lew Steiger, March 31, 1997.

Rigg, Bob. *USGS Old-Timers' Collection: Interview number 1994.100.9–10.* September 10, 1994.

Stratton, Dave. *Oral History Interview.* March 27, 1994.

Special Collections, Cline Library

Sleight, Ken. "Letter to Members of the Western River Guides Association, Inc., February 24, 1967." Old Timers' River Trip Archives.

———. "Letter to Members of the Western River Guides Association, Inc., March 23, 1967." Old Timers' River Trip Archives.

Oral Histories, Bancroft Library, University of California, Berkeley

Brower, David. *David R. Brower: Environmental Activist, Publicist, and Prophet—Sierra Club Oral History.* Regional Oral History Office, 1980.

Litton, Martin. *Martin Litton: Sierra Club Director and Uncompromising Preservationist, 1950s–1970s, with an Introduction by David Brower, an Interview Conducted by Ann Lage, 1980–1981.* Regional Oral History Office, 1982.

Sierra Club Minutes of the Annual Organization Meeting of the Board of Directors. BANC FILM 2945. May 4, 1963.

PHOTOGRAPH CREDITS

~

Text

Pages ii–iii: John Blaustein

Pages 16–17: Courtesy of the US Geological Survey

Page 51: Courtesy of the US Bureau of Reclamation

Page 139: Courtesy of Rudi Petschek

Page 179: Luke Parsons

Page 229: Courtesy of Richard Kocim

Page 258: Courtesy of Richard Kocim

Page 279: John Blaustein

Page 342: Courtesy of Grand Canyon National Park Archives

Insert

1. US Geological Survey
2. US Geological Survey
3. US Geological Survey
4. Photo by Kurt Markus
5. Bureau of Reclamation
6. Drawing by Paul Conrad, courtesy of the Conrad Estate
7. Bureau of Reclamation
8. Bureau of Reclamation
9. Bureau of Reclamation
10. Bureau of Reclamation
11. Bureau of Reclamation
12. Bureau of Reclamation
13. Bureau of Reclamation
14. Photo by Rudi Petschek
15. Photo by Rudi Petschek
16. Drawing by Roger Fletcher, courtesy of *Drift Boats and River Dories*
17. Photo by Rudi Petschek
18. Photo by Rudi Petschek
19. Photo by Rudi Petschek
20. Photo by Rudi Petschek
21. Photo by Rudi Petschek
22. Photo by Rudi Petschek
23. Photo by Kenly Weills
24. Bureau of Reclamation
25. Bureau of Reclamation
26. Bureau of Reclamation
27. Bureau of Reclamation

INDEX

❧

Page numbers in *italics* refer to illustrations.
Page numbers beginning with 364 refer to notes.

A CONVERSATION WITH KEVIN FEDARKO

~

What originally drew you to the dories of the Grand Canyon?

The first time I laid eyes on a white-water dory was during a road trip through the Southwest when I dropped by the offices of a river outfitter in Flagstaff that runs commercial expeditions through the Grand Canyon. It was March 2003, and a spring blizzard had roared into town the previous night, so it took a moment to kick the snow off my boots before stepping inside the boathouse. There I found myself staring at a navy of a dozen diminutive rowboats that were unlike any kind of watercraft I had ever seen.

Most were painted in bright colors, and several of them featured squared-off transoms in the stern that had been adorned with hand-drawn scenes from the desert rivers of the Southwest: a bighorn sheep, a cluster of scarlet monkey flowers, a peeping frog. What struck me most forcefully, though, was that the profile of each boat boasted the simplest and loveliest set of lines that I had ever seen.

At the time, I had no idea that those boats are legends on the Colorado, renowned not only for their dexterity and grace but also for the skills required to pilot them through the river's seething cauldrons of white water without smashing to pieces. Perhaps the only thing I did know was that I was entranced. My jaw just hit the floor. And in an impulse that defied both logic and common sense, I decided—right there—that I was going to have to follow those little boats into the hidden world of white water at the bottom of the Grand Canyon by signing on as an apprentice river guide.

So you sought work on the Colorado River. Doing what, exactly?

A commercial rowing trip in the canyon usually involves sixteen passengers who ride in four boats and are served by a crew of six. If it's an expedition run by Grand Canyon Dories, which is the outfitter I worked for, each guide captains a seventeen-foot dory christened in memory of a natural wonder that was heedlessly destroyed by the hand of man—haunting names that include the *Ticaboo*, the *Music Temple*, and *The Vale of Rhondda*. Each trip is also supported by a pair of large inflatable rafts that boast absolutely none of the dories' seductiveness or charm. The first raft, the kitchen boat, hauls a tangled assortment of tables, food coolers, propane tanks, rescue gear, and watertight bags containing the clients' clothing. That boat bears the name not of a vanished ecological treasure but of a barnyard animal: either the *Mule*, the *Ox*, or the *Clydesdale*.

The other raft, which was my boat, was called the *Jackass*.

And what did your boat do?

This is somewhat embarrassing, but there's no way of getting around it. Every river trip is required by the National Park Service to containerize all human waste, so one of those baggage boats is responsible for carrying the toilet, plus all of the sewage and the trash generated during the course of the expedition. It's called the poop-boat, and that's the role that the *Jackass* performed when I rowed her. I once calculated that in the course of my fourteen trips through the canyon, I transported more than 7,800 pounds of excrement over a total distance of 3,800 river miles. That's roughly equivalent to rowing a septic tank from Tijuana, Mexico, to Point Barrow, Alaska. During that entire time, my paramount goal—which was the aim of every young baggage-raft pilot—was to move out of the gear-boat pool and into the driver's seat of a dory.

Did you succeed?

No. In fact, I failed quite spectacularly. Very early on, I managed to demonstrate such a colossal level of incompetence when it came to rowing white water that it was immediately obvious to everyone—including me—that I had no business holding the lives of passengers in the palms of my hands. During the six summers that I spent in the canyon, I was never permitted to row a dory.

So you pursued a dream of rowing a dory and wound up doing something quite a bit more humiliating. Was that a disappointment?

Oddly, no. The *Jackass* opened doors for me that I may never have been able to unlock otherwise—doorways that were key to enabling me to understand and come to terms with a place that is not only beautiful but also harsh and filled with mystery. In many ways, that world is as much a cerebral wilderness as a physical one—a place whose boundaries extend far beyond the borders of the familiar and thereby reshape the sensibilities of those who bind themselves to it. One of the many lessons the canyon imparts, for example, is the humility that flows from immersion in an environment framed by towering walls of unimaginably ancient rock in which human beings—indeed, all of human civilization—is largely irrelevant. Among many other insights, I came to realize that it is categorically impossible to be anything other than humble when you're rowing through the heart of the most sublime natural wonder on the face of the planet while piloting a floating outhouse laden with other people's poop.

There was another lesson, too—one that I began to appreciate only when I sat down to write about those experiences. The *Jackass* afforded me a perspective that was, in some ways, essential for a writer, which is to be close to one's subject but also removed at some distance from it. Although I never got to pilot a dory, by dint of my position at the tail end of the flotilla (the *Jackass* was almost always the last boat in our running order), I had the chance to do something almost as marvelous. I was able to study and ponder them like no one else. I watched those boats at all hours of the day, along every stretch of river, across each season and in every kind of weather. If you do that sort of thing long enough, you arrive at a place that is provocative and rather unique.

How did those experiences inform your writing?

The answer is, simply: in every way one could imagine. During all those weeks and months of rowing behind the dories, I came to learn the "world below the rim" from the bottom up: the layers of stone that surge toward the sky in terraced, pastel-hued bands; the light that drops into the abyss each morning and smoothly claws its way back out at night; the moods and cadences of the river as it pushes through the canyon. The descriptions of the river corridor in my writing—the rock, the light, the colors, the weather, the birds and animals, the feel of the place, and above all and always, the magic and the brutality of white water—arose directly from my experiences as the captain of the *Jackass*. Best of all, perhaps, I was also allowed to join the dorymen each night on the decks of their boats and listen to them do what they do even better than tackling rapids, which involves entertaining one another by telling river stories.

So what made you decide to craft this particular river story into a book?

Well, first and most obviously, it's a tremendously exciting adventure narrative—one of the few such tales inside the canyon that, at least in my view, rivals that of the greatest river story of all, which is John Wesley Powell's pioneering expedition down the Colorado River in the summer of 1869. But I also came to understand that the legend of the *Emerald Mile* was more than a turbocharged anecdote about a speed run. In addition to being that, it embraces the larger story of the canyon itself: its discovery and its exploration, as well as the complex and fascinating narrative of the Glen Canyon Dam. All of those elements came together—quite violently, as it turned out—during the spring of 1983, when the runoff on the Colorado achieved a size and a level of savagery that had not been witnessed in generations. The speed run braids those elements together in a manner that I find irresistibly compelling. I don't know of another Grand Canyon river story that encapsulates everything about that unique and special place as succinctly and as powerfully as what Kenton Grua and his companions set out to achieve aboard the *Emerald Mile*.

But it's also true, is it not, that the idea of a speed run was both ill-advised and illegal? In that sense, was the *Emerald Mile*'s sprint into the record books noble or absurd?

Well, it was both—and therein, I think, lies the essence of its appeal. On one level, racing down the river as fast as humanly possible cuts directly against the manner in which most people strive to experience the canyon. Those who truly understand that place almost invariably strive to take as long as possible, to linger and prolong their odyssey until the moment when they are forced to return to the world above the rim. By that standard, the speed run was anathema to the ethos of the river world. But in a paradoxical way that is explored in the book—and that was also very much a part of Kenton Grua's personality—the speed run enabled its participants to forge a visceral and direct connection to the Colorado by navigating through its deepest and most splendid canyon under some of the most extreme conditions imaginable. Not only was the white water unspeakable—especially in one particular spot that created a terrible tragedy—but there was also the looming specter of the crisis unfolding far upstream at the Glen Canyon Dam.

There is, surprisingly, a great deal of science and engineering in this book, and you write a lot about dams. This is unusual for an adventure story. Why did you devote so much time and energy to these elements?

The great hydroelectric dams of the West represent a phase of this country's development that touches upon some central aspects of who we are as Americans—especially our relationship with the land itself. Those dams stand as some of our greatest technological achievements, the instruments through which we sought to master and control nature by harnessing a force that is synonymous with unfettered wildness—a free-flowing river—and turning that energy to the benefit of human beings. But those same dams also embody a level of hubris that we are only now fully beginning to confront and grapple with. These enormously impressive machines that we thought represented the best of who we were—after all, they helped to pull us out of the Great Depression and they supplied much of the energy required to win the battles of World War II—turned out to have a dark side. That journey of awareness, which we are still traveling, started with the Hoover Dam, and it is tentatively approaching its conclusion with the Glen Canyon Dam. At its essence, this book explores the tension between the glorious myths of those dams and the complex reality of their legacy inside the Grand Canyon.

Are the dam engineers the villains of this story?

No—although I suppose I thought they were at first. Anyone who works on the river is encouraged to think of the Glen Canyon Dam as evil and the people who are associated with it as misguided and wrong. But that's just not true—or to frame the idea with slightly more nuance, it's not *entirely* true—and this was something I needed to discover. Another discovery was that the battle that the engineers fought to save the dam is so compelling as a story, in terms of sheer drama, that it almost threatens to overshadow the speed run itself.

In the end, perhaps the theme that resonates most deeply for me is that the collision of ideas between the two worlds at the center of this story— the values of science represented by the Glen Canyon Dam and the values of nature represented by the unruly citizens of the river—was crystallized and underscored by the flood of 1983 in a way that had never been done before. You have these two separate subcultures that don't even speak the same language and which, in many ways, truly hate one another—and yet they were united, unwittingly, by an event that challenged them both. And flowing forth from that collision is the notion that that the canyon itself—the insights it contains, the lessons and discoveries it offers up—embraces both subcultures, and that each without the other is somehow incomplete.

How did you investigate those two subcultures?

Although they are fundamentally opposed in terms of their beliefs and character, both are close-knit societies that can be rather distrustful of outsiders. Within the corps of river guides, I literally worked my way into the matrix by living and laboring alongside of them. I was never really considered an insider, but with time, the men and women who row the dories came to accept my presence and took me under their wing—mainly because they are decent and generous people; but also in part, perhaps, because I was rowing their sewage down the river. As for the engineers, the challenge was a bit different because I could never even pretend to do what they do. I was quite forthright, however, about my ignorance, and I asked them to teach me what I didn't know. It's sometimes surprising how people can open up when you demonstrate a willingness to listen to their stories with attentiveness and respect.

Tell us about some of the research you did for this book.

The research was rather complicated and time-consuming. For the speed-run narrative, most of the work involved tracking down old dorymen, as well as park rangers and passengers who were present in the canyon during the massive flood in June 1983, and then piecing together their impressions and memories. I also was able to unearth a series of highly detailed Case Incident Reports filed by the rangers that chronicled a number of horrific accidents that unfolded on the river as the speed run was taking place. These documents were essential in enabling me to assemble the river chronicle.

As for the events that took place at the Glen Canyon Dam—the "spill-way crisis" that is braided into the story of the speed run—much of that research would be familiar to a professional historian: rifling through cardboard boxes at the Bureau of Reclamation's archives in Denver, combing through a wealth of primary materials (memos, faxograms, telephone logs, diary entries, handwritten notes), and slowly building an account of exactly what took place at the dam: how the team of engineers and managers who were responsible for confronting the crisis ultimately solved that challenge.

Those documents also yielded the names of Reclamation employees, all of whom are now retired, thereby enabling me to track down and interview many of them to mine their memories.

How long did it take to put everything together, and what was the biggest challenge for you?

The whole process, from start to finish, took almost ten years. The hardest part was assembling the treasure trove of information into a coherent narrative, and then deciding what to leave out. In a sense, building a book-length narrative is sort of like running a Class V rapid in a wooden dory. More than anything else, threading one's way through the chaos and steering clear of the rocks hinges on finding a clean line.

ABOUT THE AUTHOR

~

Kevin Fedarko was a staff writer at *Time* magazine from 1991 to 1998, where his work helped garner an Overseas Press Club Award. His freelance writing has appeared in *Esquire*, *Outside*, and other publications and has been anthologized in *The Best American Travel Writing*. He attended Columbia and Oxford, where he was a Marshall Scholar. He lives in Santa Fe, New Mexico, and works as a part-time river guide in Grand Canyon National Park. This is his first book.